IT DIDN'T HAVE TO BE THIS WAY

Also available in the CULTURE OF ENTERPRISE series

Human Goods, Economic Evils:
A Moral Approach to the Dismal Science
Edward Hadas

Third Ways:
How Bulgarian Greens, Swedish Housewives, and
Beer-Swilling Englishmen Created Family-Centered Economies—
and Why They Disappeared
Allan C. Carlson

A Path of Our Own:
An Andean Village and Tomorrow's Economy of Values
Adam K. Webb

Econoclasts:
The Rebels Who Sparked the Supply-Side Revolution
and Restored American Prosperity
Brian Domitrovic

Toward a Truly Free Market:
A Distributist Perspective on the Role of Government, Taxes, Health Care,
Deficits, and More
John C. Médaille

Redeeming Economics:
*Rediscovering the Missing Elemen*t
John D. Mueller

Back on the Road to Serfdom:
The Resurgence of Statism
Edited by Thomas E. Woods Jr.

IT DIDN'T HAVE TO BE THIS WAY

Why Boom and Bust Is Unnecessary— and How the Austrian School of Economics Breaks the Cycle

HARRY C. VERYSER

ISI
BOOKS

Wilmington, Delaware

The Culture of Enterprise series is supported by a grant from the John Templeton Foundation. The Intercollegiate Studies Institute gratefully acknowledges this support.

Library of Congress Cataloging-in-Publication Data

Veryser, Harry C.
  It didn't have to be this way : why boom and bust is unnecessary—and how the Austrian school of economics breaks the cycle / Harry C. Veryser.
     pages cm. — (Culture of enterprise)
  Includes bibliographical references and index.
  ISBN 978-1-935191-07-0
  1. Austrian school of economics—History. 2. Economics—History. 3. Economic history. 4. Financial crises—History. I. Title.
  HB98.V47 2013
  330.15'7—dc23
                              2013005867

Published in the United States by:

ISI Books
Intercollegiate Studies Institute
3901 Centerville Road
Wilmington, Delaware 19807-1938
www.isibooks.org

Manufactured in the United States of America

For my parents,
Harry and Loraine Veryser,
heroes in war and in peace

Contents

Introduction   It Didn't Have to Be This Way   1

Part I   Warnings Ignored
Chapter 1   A Science of Human Action   9
Chapter 2   Looking at Today and Dreading Tomorrow   21
Chapter 3   A Short History of the Austrian School   33

Part II   How We Got Here
Chapter 4   The Age of Classical Liberalism   63
Chapter 5   Chaos: The Legacies of World War I   79
Chapter 6   The Age of Bretton Woods   105
Chapter 7   Nixon's Folly   115
Chapter 8   Reagan's Rally   131

Part III   A Reconstruction of Economics
Chapter 9   The Division of Labor   147
Chapter 10   The Prerequisites of Prosperity   165
Chapter 11   The Nature of Human Action   191
Chapter 12   Inflation and Deflation   205
Chapter 13   Faustian Bargain: The Trade Cycle   225

Conclusion   The Austrian Moment   257

Notes   261
Bibliography   279
Acknowledgments   295
Index   299

Introduction

It Didn't Have to Be This Way

This book is an effort to tell the story of the modern economic condition, which began about 150 years ago. Like most good stories, it will be almost completely new to most readers. It has fascinating plots and subplots, heroes and antiheroes, bizarre and unforeseen crises, wars, poverty and prosperity, virtue and vice, ideas and expectations.

As the story rolls on, there are amazing turning points—often unforeseen and apparent only in retrospect—that present opportunities for new thoughts and theories that open new vistas, new policies, new life (or death) for many. New leaders arrive on the scene and change the course of events. Sometimes their contributions are remembered for generations; sometimes, despite their awesome power, they are not even historical footnotes. Does anyone know who came up with the formula that determined how many soybeans millions of American farmers were allowed to plant, for decades, with far-reaching consequences for the hungry in far-distant lands? Or who came up with the idea that it was best *not* to give federal money to poor families when the father lived in the same home as his wife and children?

Political upheaval and revolution are part of the drama, as ideologies too often replace religion, resulting, like adoration of false gods, in tremendous distress. As the story unfolds, we see that the differing perspectives of a socialist or a free-market political leader can shape the lives of tens of millions of people for decades.

1

The global economic meltdown that began in 2007 has brought suffering to countless millions. We have all witnessed—and in many cases experienced—the devastation: The bursting of the housing bubble. Fore-closures. The collapse of whole industries. The worst unemployment in a quarter century. Life savings wiped out as mutual funds, pension funds, and 401(k)s plummeted in value. The litany of woes goes on and on.

But it didn't have to be this way. This kind of financial devastation has been predicted again and again—decade after decade—by propo-nents of the Austrian School of economics. Ludwig von Mises, one of the most prominent Austrian economists, summed up the perennial cri-sis in the title of one of his many books, *Planned Chaos* (1947). Mises, especially in *The Theory of Money and Credit* (1912) and *Human Action* (1949), maintained that the boom-and-bust cycle that has afflicted mod-ern economies is both unnatural and unnecessary. It worsens living conditions for just about everyone. Since the publication of his books, abundant scholarly studies have validated the Austrian view. Yet few people—even among those teaching economics in colleges and universi-ties worldwide—know or understand the Austrian School. This book is an effort to solve that problem.

If there is a bright spot in the recent economic crisis, it is this: people everywhere are giving much more serious thought to foundational ques-tions about the economy. What caused our woes, and more important, how can we prevent future calamities?

To answer those questions, we need to understand the Austrian School of economics. I have intended to write this book, or something like it, for well over twenty years. I feel particularly able to tell the story because, in my forty years as both a professional economist and business-man, I have been fortunate to have a front-row seat to watch the develop-ment of modern American economics, banking, and business. For me, economics is not an abstraction or the "dismal science," as it is so often dismissed. Rather, it is a vibrant and fascinating process of unleashing human potential and thereby liberating whole nations from misery, pov-erty, and war, and ushering them into prosperity and peace.

My earliest exposure to economics came when I was a young child. My father lived through the Great Depression, served three years in the U.S. Navy during World War II, and participated in the invasions of North Africa, Sicily, Anzio, and Normandy, winning three Bronze Stars for bravery. He then founded a tool and die shop in suburban Detroit that supplied the auto industry for a half century. I worked in that shop in my youth, watching it become a direct supplier for General Motors. Eventually, in 1978, my brothers and I took over the business. At the company's height we had nearly sixty employees and two locations, one in Texas and one near Detroit, and we embarked on a joint venture with a German firm.

In addition to teaching me how to run a manufacturing facility, my father taught me much more. For decades at family gatherings, the men would gather around and talk about the Great Depression. Some of them suffered the worst of it as child laborers, while their parents were unable to find work. My father believed he was caught in a maelstrom that he did not understand, and none of them had a sophisticated understanding of what happened. These conversations sparked my intellectual curiosity. I wondered how the international economic order could fall apart so badly that even in a land as great as the United States, children were forced to work while their parents were destitute.

My curiosity about the Great Depression, the Great War, and the interplay between financial affairs and international relations led me to major in economics as an undergraduate at the University of Detroit in the 1960s. There I came under the influence of a much-learned professor, H. Theodore Hoffman, who introduced me to the Austrian School. For the past three decades I have had a richly rewarding career teaching economics—first at Northwood University (then Institute); then Walsh College, where I was chairman of the Economics and Finance Department for two decades; and now at the University of Detroit Mercy.

From these two vantage points—as a businessman and as an academic—I have had the unique opportunity both to see how economics operates in the real world and to study its theory and practice from the ivory tower. Over the course of my career it became clear that my father was not alone in failing to understand the forces that cause economic crisis. In fact, much of the economics establishment badly misreads the situation.

The crisis that began in 2007 should be seen not as an isolated incident but as part of a continuing drama that has its origins in U.S. government manipulation of markets and currency. It is merely part of the cycle that has been the scourge of the West since 1913—which gets us back to the story of our modern condition.

The two major and intertwining plots in the story are (1) the development of economic theory and (2) the events that shaped global history, especially in the early twentieth century. Economic theory has always had a tremendous influence on government action and policy. Before World War I, governments based public policy on so-called classical economic theories about money and trade. Almost all economic theory was committed to free markets and private property. Governments did not exert much energy in regulating commerce. The U.S. Constitution, for instance, includes provisions establishing free markets and specie-based money systems. Needless to say, things changed following World War I, as monarchies and traditions were smashed and new theories came into play. The troubles of the 1920s and 1930s encouraged economists to rework the classical theory to explain why things happened as they did and what should be done as a result. These new theories—however well meaning—have had profound and often devastating consequences around the world.

Economics is *not*—or does not have to be—a mysterious science. Quite simply, it is the study of reconciling the unlimited wants of man with limited resources. Distilled further, it is the study of human action. In this book, I aim to demonstrate that economics involves certain immutable laws of human behavior. Further, I hope to show that the Austrian School has most clearly and effectively discovered those laws. The world has needlessly suffered unspeakable misery as a result of theories and policies that ignore these principles.

It didn't have to be this way—not in the recent economic crisis, or in the crushing stagflation of the 1970s and early 1980s, or in the Depression of the 1930s that plagued my father's generation. More important, it doesn't have to be this way in the future. The world's economies *can* get back on track and return to prosperity, which can lead to more peaceful relations among nations.

To be more precise, the Austrians were right all along. In the early 1930s, two professors in England looked at the worldwide economic catastrophe and came up with very different solutions. John Maynard Keynes at the University of Cambridge created the notion of spending one's way out of recession, while Friedrich A. Hayek of the London School of Economics took the classical stance, calling for sound money and the traditional virtues of saving, prudent investing, and balanced budgets.

Keynesianism became the byword of the developed world and has profoundly influenced the response of governments in the most recent crisis. Meanwhile, governments largely ignored Hayek, one of the great Austrian economists. We have all paid the price since.

One of the greatest failings of mainstream economic thinking, seen clearly in the lead-up to the financial crisis, has been to view economics as a science on the order of physics, one that can be reduced to numbers, quantities, and mathematical formulas. The Austrian School, understanding economics as a science of individual human action, makes a crucial contribution with its distrust of mathematical modeling or "financial engineering" of the type that helped cause the subprime mortgage collapse. It is a warning that must be heeded today.

Of the many contributions the Austrian School has made to economic thought, the other most relevant to our situation today is the explanation of the insidious effects of expanding the money supply. The modern Federal Reserve, which seems intent on pumping new money into the system, clearly violates this Austrian tenet.

In recent times a number of internationally acclaimed experts in economics who are *not* part of the Austrian School have validated Austrian tenets. Two causes of the economic crisis, many scholars and practitioners now recognize, were the Fed's artificial lowering of interest rates and the use of mathematical equations in a futile attempt to lessen risk. These people are coming to conclusions that the Austrians reached decades ago.

For years now, we have endured a barrage of bad news: businesses going belly-up, people losing their jobs and homes, government debt soaring. *It didn't have to be this way.* The Austrian School presents the most coherent explication of the economic relations among men and—more so than any other system today—lays out economic guidelines that offer real prospects for prosperity worldwide.

Part I

Warnings Ignored

1

A Science of Human Action

An economist is someone who sees something happen in practice
and wonders if it would work in theory.
—*Ronald Reagan*

D oes economics have any real value?
That blunt question has been voiced with greater frequency
in recent years. After all, mainstream economics, with its cherished theories and complex mathematical models, failed to predict or to
prescribe adequate remedies for the economic meltdown that began in
2007. These failures led liberal columnist Paul Krugman, the 2008 winner of the Nobel Prize in Economics, to call the previous thirty years of
macroeconomics "spectacularly useless at best, and positively harmful
at worst." Similarly, Willem Buiter of the London School of Economics
described the past three decades of macroeconomics training at American and British universities as a "costly waste of time."[1]

It's not just macroeconomics that has been called into question.
Financial economics was another key culprit in the crisis. *The Economist*
observed: "Convenience, not conviction, often dictates the choices economists make. Convenience, however, is addictive. Economists can become
seduced by their models, fooling themselves that what the model leaves
out does not matter." Wall Street fell in love with "the quants," the math
whizzes who devised new investment technologies to slice, dice, and

repackage all sorts of different asset classes.[2] Wedded to its mathematical models, *The Economist* continued, mainstream economics became "a poor guide to the origins of the financial crisis, and left its followers unprepared for the symptoms."[3]

Investment wizard Warren Buffett put it succinctly: "Beware of geeks bearing formulas."[4]

Claes Ryn, a professor of politics at the Catholic University of America, explains how the embrace of models and formulas led to a decline in morality: "In finance, rationalism and mathematicization inspired trends towards ever-more abstract, amoral operations. It assisted the progressive fiscalization of the economy. Not only equities but also the creation of intricate new fiscal instruments, such as derivatives and, most recently, 'credit default swaps,' created opportunities for shifting assets and control to financiers far removed from the people actually running the business or lending money."[5]

But the practitioners of strictly mathematical economics had the utmost faith in the wisdom of their approach. Several years ago a dean at one of the schools at which I taught economics and finance criticized our department for its lack of "rigor." He advocated a heavily mathematical approach (he used phrases such as "mezzanine financing" and "subordinated debt") and challenged us to teach something called financial engineering. Asked what financial engineering was, he said that it gave one the ability to transform what might be called dodgy debt into AAA bonds by the use of sophisticated statistical tools. When I replied that I thought this method would simply cheat a lot of little old ladies out of their money, he became incensed and told me that he had letters from companies who would not hire our graduates because they were not sufficiently trained in this alchemy.

That was 2005. Today many of those companies are gone, and they left a lot of empty retirement funds. The ladies were cheated out of their money as the world economy suffered a multitrillion-dollar meltdown.

Although the technologies that allowed the proliferation of mathematical models were new, the attitude underlying them was anything but. For centuries, economists have tried to imitate methods from the physical sciences. More important, they have tried to put economics on par with the hard sciences, to afford themselves the lofty status of scientists. F. A. Hayek, one of the leading members of the Austrian School, explained how this process played out in the first half of the nineteenth century:

> The term "science" came more and more to be confined to the physical and biological disciplines which at the same time began to claim for themselves a special rigorousness and certainty which distinguished them from all others. Their success was such that they soon began to exercise an extraordinary fascination on those working in other fields, who rapidly began to imitate their teaching and vocabulary. Thus the tyranny commenced which the methods and techniques of the Sciences in the narrow sense of the term have ever since exercised over the other subjects. These became increasingly concerned to vindicate their equal status by showing that their methods were the same as those of their brilliantly successful sisters rather than adapting their methods more and more to their own particular problems.[6]

Therein lies the flaw that has led so many commentators to question the value of economics. The problem lies not in economics per se but rather in a distorted understanding of its role and ambitions. Economics is *not* like physics or chemistry. One of the fundamental contributions of Austrian economics is to remind us that economics is a science of *human action*. As Hayek put it, the vigorous attempts to mimic the methods of the physical sciences have "contributed scarcely anything to our understanding of social phenomena."[7] The failure to predict or solve the economic crisis is only the latest and most dramatic example of the lack of understanding that the modern economic approach yields. Mainstream economics has adopted the wrong ambitions and the wrong methods.

To get the economy back on the right path requires a proper understanding of the role of economics.

Economics as a Science: Two Paths

When Hayek refers to "the Sciences in the narrow sense of the term," he reminds us that the sciences have traditionally been understood more broadly than they are today.

Writing more than two thousand years ago, Aristotle divided the sciences into three categories: speculative, practical, and productive. Speculative science is pure or theoretical science that seeks truth for truth's sake, such as mathematics, physics, chemistry, biology, and astronomy. Practical science seeks general principles to obtain the goals—and understand the actions—of human beings; ethics, politics, and economics are the most important of the practical sciences. Productive science explores how things are to be made; architecture, for example, is a productive science.[8]

In modern times, we generally distinguish between the physical sciences and the social sciences. Both types share certain characteristics that qualify them as scientific: they deal with universal principles; they are logically organized; and they are tested against the real so as to have a degree of predictability.

Universal principles are essential. When a medical student examines a body in anatomy class, he is studying not just that particular body but the general principles that apply to every human body. The same holds for social sciences as well as physical sciences. When Aristotle presents his case for the achievement of human happiness in *Nicomachean Ethics*, for instance, he is laying out principles that apply to every human person. Likewise, certain general principles of economic action apply to every person, as Carl Menger, the founder of the Austrian School, demonstrated.

Every science must be logical as well. That is, it must tell a straight story about some aspect of reality. When facts appear that contradict the accepted explanation, the theory must be reworked to explain the new facts in a consistent way. Consider physics: Einstein and other scientists were faced with facts that Newtonian physics seemingly could not explain; they had to adjust the theory to account for these facts. In economics, the classical school had to confront inconsistencies in its explanation of value—namely, how could the prices of goods in the marketplace be so much more or so much less than the cost of the labor needed to produce those goods? A consistent explanation of value requires close observation of actual market participants.

Finally, because the value of any science lies in its ability to describe or explain an aspect of reality, it should be able to predict certain outcomes. For example, an engineer constructing a bridge must be able to predict accurately the load that the building materials will be able to carry once assembled. Such predictions rely on knowledge of the nature of physical things.

In the modern understanding of science, this element of predictive ability has become enormously important. Note the distinction between the following definitions of science, the first reflecting a traditional view and the second reflecting a modern view. *The Dictionary of Scholastic Philosophy* defines a science as "the certain intellectual knowledge of something in its causes; universal, demonstrated, organized knowledge of facts and truths and the reasons or causes of these." *The New Merriam-Webster Dictionary* explains that science is "knowledge covering general truths or the operation of general laws especially as obtained and tested through the scientific method."[9] The latter's emphasis on the scientific method—precise experimentation to test hypotheses and measure exact physical outcomes, usually using statistical methods to assemble data—reflects the narrowing of which Hayek wrote. In *The Philosophy of Science*, Fulton J. Sheen sums up the matter well when he writes that in "the traditional view . . . science meant knowledge," but "it means experiment and observation for the modern mind."[10]

Economics has taken to emphasizing the testing of hypotheses to try to ensure its predictive ability. In a famous essay entitled "The Methodology of Positive Economics" (1953), the eminent twentieth-century economist Milton Friedman lays out a framework for economics as science. By itself, the essay's title suggests the scientific rigor Friedman is aiming at. The "methodology" he attempts to establish borrows from the scientific method of the hard sciences. Meanwhile, he uses the term *positive economics* to explain how economics can be an objective science. In the essay he notes that positive economics explains "what is" and is thus distinct from *normative economics*, which concerns itself with judgments about "what ought to be."

Friedman makes his goal explicit when he writes, "In short, positive economics is, or can be, an 'objective' science, in precisely the same sense as any of the physical sciences."

How can economics claim the mantle of the hard sciences? By taking an empirical approach that makes prediction the central test of its worthiness. The performance of positive economics, Friedman explains, "is to be judged by the precision, scope, and conformity with experience of the predictions it yields." He expands on this point with a broader statement about the role of theory in the sciences:

> Viewed as a body of substantive hypotheses, theory is to be judged by its predictive power for the class of phenomena which it is intended to "explain." Only factual evidence can show whether it is "right" or "wrong" or, better, tentatively "accepted" as valid or "rejected." . . . The only relevant test of the *validity* of a hypothesis is comparison of its predictions with experience. The hypothesis is rejected if its predictions are contradicted ("frequently" or more often than predictions from an alternative hypothesis); it is accepted if its predictions are not contradicted; great confidence is attached to it if it has survived many opportunities for contradiction.[11]

Friedman was one of the most influential economists of the twentieth century. Not surprisingly, then, these arguments have had a lasting impact. As Cambridge University Press noted in a 2009 book dedicated to assessing "the impact and contemporary significance of Friedman's seminal work," the 1953 essay "has shaped the image of economics as a scientific discipline, both within and outside of the academy."[12] Those who took up Friedman's charge tried to match the hard sciences in methodological rigor. That meant establishing mathematical rigor, and it was a major reason we have seen the headlong push toward strictly mathematical economics. Friedman himself was not a proponent of some of the complex mathematical systems that became so prevalent. As Johan Van Overtveldt writes in his study of the Chicago School of economics, of which Friedman was a leading member, Friedman was "suspicious of econometric forecasts based on multiple regressions and statistical mathematical economic models."[13] But many who followed Friedman took his call to put economics on par with the physical sciences as a mandate for precisely the sorts of models and formulas of which he was suspicious.

Milton Friedman was not alone in casting economics in the mold of physical sciences. Another proponent, at least early on, was Joseph Schumpeter. As a student at the University of Vienna and later a distinguished economist teaching at Harvard University, Schumpeter argued that by using mathematics and the physical sciences as a model, economics could claim objectivity. He later reconsidered the accuracy of this approach, but not before the line of thought helped lay the foundation for so many present-day problems.

Those problems resulted despite—or more precisely because of—the widespread conviction that the economy could be carefully planned and that mathematics could be used as a reliable guide to government and private-sector policy. The U.S. Federal Reserve System, the American central bank, thought it could use sophisticated mathematical models to influence the economy through monetary policy. The private sector thought that it could minimize or even eliminate risk doing the same thing. Following the positivist approach, most schools and universities became highly mathematical in their presentation of economics and finance.

This is the path that led to the loss of jobs, homes, and trillions of dollars. Even by its own measure—that of exact prediction—the attempt to force economics into the realm of the physical sciences has been an abject failure. The economic meltdown that began in 2007—which the "rigorous" methodologies of modern economics failed to predict—clearly reveals the problems associated with going down that path. The economic collapse prompted the blunt questions we considered at the opening of this chapter. Again, however, the problems lie not with economics properly understood but rather with the path down which modern economics has traveled.

There was a second path that modern economics could have taken. It is the path economics should have taken earlier, and the one we need to take now if we hope to avoid another economic disaster in the future.

The Second Path

The second path represents a road back—back to the traditional position of economics among the sciences of human action. Striving to match the methodologies of the physical sciences has only pulled economics away from its core competencies and led to economic catastrophe.

Aristotle pointed out the fatal flaw in trying to force economics into the realm of the speculative sciences. Although in mathematical sciences we can operate with a great deal of precision, in matters of human action, he wrote, "we must be satisfied to indicate the truth with a rough and general sketch: when the subject and the basis of a discussion consist of matters that hold good only as a general rule, but not always, the conclusions reached must be of the same order."[14]

Economics is, as Aristotle knew, most certainly a science of human action. In fact, the term *economics* comes to us from the ancient Greek *oikonomia*, which refers to the management of a household, that core element of human life. From the management of the family and the home, economics expanded outward.[15]

For nearly 150 years the Austrian School of economics has argued for taking the second path. Austrian economists have repeatedly denounced efforts to emulate the methods and ambitions of the hard sciences, calling attention to the dangers of ignoring crucial social contexts.

Decades before F. A. Hayek wrote of the "tyranny" of the physical sciences, Austrian School pioneer Friedrich von Wieser observed: "None of the great truths of economic theory, none of their important moral and political applications, has been justified by mathematical means. . . . If we succeed in presenting convincingly the meaning of the economy and, concurrently, the significance of the method of economic computation, we shall have accomplished far more toward understanding quantitative economic relations than the most far-reaching employment of the mathematical method could ever achieve."[16]

In the mid-twentieth century, another economist of the Austrian School, Wilhelm Röpke, deplored macroeconomics for treating the economic process "as an objective and mechanical movement of aggregate quantities, a movement being quantitatively determined and eventually predicted by appropriate mathematical and statistical methods." Röpke also condemned "the mechanistic and centrist approach in economic forecasting," declaring that its failures "are so numerous and blatant that it is astonishing that the underlying theory seems to digest these failures without losing prestige. It is even more astonishing that the protagonists of this approach are so utterly unrepentant."[17]

Several years later, Ludwig von Mises, among the most influential Austrian economists, said that "hosts of authors" were "deluded by the idea that the sciences of human action must ape the technique of the natural sciences." Trying to "imitate chemistry," these thinkers "fail to realize that in the field of human action statistics is always history and that the alleged 'correlations' and 'functions' do not describe anything else than what happened at a definite instant of time in a definite geographical area as the outcome of the actions of a definite number of people. As a method of economic analysis econometrics is a childish play with figures that does not contribute anything to the elucidation of the problems of economic reality."[18]

The idea that there is a major difference between human beings and the physical world was fundamental to Mises's approach. He used the term *methodological dualism* to refer to the distinction between the realm of the material, which can be studied by the methods of the physical sciences, and the "realm of human thought and action."[19] Drawing on Aristotle's concept of the final cause—that is, the ultimate purpose for which something is done—Mises wrote: "What distinguishes the field of human action from the field of external events as investigated by the natural sciences is the category of finality. We do not know of any final causes operating in what we call nature. But we know that man aims at definite goals chosen. In the natural sciences we search after constant relations among various events. In dealing with human action we search after the ends the actor wants or wanted to attain and after the result that his action brought about or will bring about."[20]

The Austrian School has proved remarkably consistent on the question of the place of economics among the sciences. To the Austrians, economics is an objective but *practical* science, necessarily different from the physical sciences.

The Austrian School also has been proved right in its warnings about attempts to force economics into the strictures of the physical sciences. The economic chaos that began in 2007 demonstrated the prescience of the Austrian critique of the financial and economics establishment. Suddenly the models and formulas that had seemed like magic were revealed to be the source of so much disarray in the financial sector and the broader economy.

But we shouldn't have had to wait until disaster struck to see the flaws in the modern approach to economics and finance. Plenty of failures occurred earlier that should have at least slowed the rush down the path toward strictly mathematical economics. To take just one example, the spectacular collapse of Long-Term Capital Management in 1998 revealed that not even the most sophisticated statistical models can eliminate risk, regardless of what celebrated financial minds would like to think. Long-

Term Capital Management was a hedge-fund management firm boasting some of the best mathematicians, economists (including two Nobel Prize winners), and bond traders on Wall Street. This dream team of professors and practitioners developed complex mathematical models to guide the firm's investing. The rule of thumb in finance and economics is that risk and return are twins: the more the risk, the greater the return. But the minds at Long-Term Capital Management tried to eliminate the risks of investing while generating extremely high returns.

For a while, the game worked. For four years in the mid-1990s, Long-Term Capital Management generated annual returns of more than 40 percent.[21] But then, in quick succession, financial crisis struck the Far East and the Russian government defaulted on its debt. Long-Term Capital Management's intricate equations and computerized models could not keep pace with the unexpected changes. Everything fell apart.

Although Long-Term was just one of many firms, its collapse threatened to bring down the entire financial sector. It had borrowed billions of dollars in assets from the major investment banks. Moreover, as financial journalist Roger Lowenstein notes in his account of Long-Term's rise and fall, "the firm had entered into thousands of derivative contracts, which had endlessly intertwined it with every bank on Wall Street." At one point Long-Term's exposure totaled more than $1 *trillion*.[22] Fearing that the firm would bring down the entire financial sector and even the global economy, the Federal Reserve finally stepped in to bail out Long-Term Capital Management. Virtually all the top Wall Street banks contributed to the multibillion-dollar bailout.

The fall of Long-Term Capital Management should have been a warning to the entire financial community about the dangers of embracing strictly mathematical economics. But the lessons were quickly forgotten. A decade later many of the same factors behind Long-Term's collapse— the belief that mathematical models could eliminate risk, the spread of risky derivative contracts throughout the financial system, overleveraged banks—led to a far more extensive and damaging collapse.

With our most recent disaster, the Austrian School of economics was proved right once again. The wisdom of the Austrian counsel not to force economics into the realm of hard sciences should have been obvious. Many noted thinkers have echoed these warnings over the centuries.

Aristotle, as we have seen, laid out the traditional understanding of

the sciences. Like Aristotle, the great eighteenth-century British statesman Edmund Burke understood politics, ethics, and economics to be
sciences of human action. Burke expert Peter Stanlis summarizes:
"According to Burke the chief strength of mathematics and of logical dis-
quisitions consisted in considering one thing at a time, but the best judgments and results in moral and political problems came from having in
one view the greatest number and variety of circumstances."[23]

Countless non-Austrian economists have sounded the same refrain:
economics is a human discipline that cannot be reduced to mathematical formulas or scientific theories. In the early nineteenth century, Jean-
Baptiste Say observed: "The *values* with which political economy is concerned, admitting of the application to them of the terms *plus* and *minus*,
are within the range of mathematical inquiry; but being at the same time
subject to the influence of the faculties, the wants and the desires of mankind, they are not susceptible of any rigorous appreciation, and cannot,
therefore, furnish any *data* for absolute calculations."[24]

In the early twentieth century, Alfred Marshall offered another
economist this advice: "(1) Use mathematics as a shorthand language,
rather than as an engine of inquiry. (2) Keep to them till you have done.
(3) Translate into English. (4) Then illustrate by examples that are important in real life. (5) Burn the mathematics."[25]

After initially calling for economics to use the physical sciences as a
model, Joseph Schumpeter concluded, in the words of biographer Thomas
McCraw, "that exact economics can no more be achieved than exact history, because no human story with the foreordained plot can be anything but fiction. . . . The best mathematics in the world cannot produce
a satisfactory economic proof wholly comparable to those in physics or
pure mathematics. There are too many variables, because indeterminate
human behavior is always involved."[26] Schumpeter, as we will see, studied
with the Austrian economists, and his work reflects their influence.

John Kenneth Galbraith neatly summed up the shortcomings of a
heavily mathematical approach: "The only function of economic forecasting is to make astrology respectable."[27]

Keynesian "fine-tuning" of the economy in the mid-twentieth century became the most obvious example of the conviction that economics could be a hard science. As Jane Jacobs wrote, Keynesian economists
"concentrated on creating a science of fiscal intervention—a real science,

like chemistry and physics, in which one can count on precise, quantifiable interventions yielding predictable, quantifiable results."[28] Consequently, the movement to treat economics as a physical science has often been attributed to John Maynard Keynes.

But Keynes himself expressed doubts that the methods of the physical sciences could capture "the complexity, and reflexive nature, of social life." Keynes biographer Robert Skidelsky notes that "Keynes's skepticism about the use of mathematics in economics grew rather than diminished with age." The great economist conveyed this skepticism as early as the 1920s, writing that mathematical economics breaks down because "we are faced at every turn with problems of Organic Unity, of Discreteness, of Discontinuity—the whole is not equal to the sum of the parts, comparisons of quantity fail us, small changes produce large effects, the assumptions of a uniform and homogeneous continuum are not satisfied."[29]

Although Keynes's most influential adherents did not follower this advice, the Austrian School of economics has always recognized that discreteness, that heterogeneity. Indeed, the very foundation of the Austrian theoretical approach is the concept that economics is a precise analysis of individual human action. The Austrians' contributions—and warnings about the mainstream approach—have been underappreciated for too long. Perhaps this most recent economic catastrophe will cause the establishment to recognize the Austrians' contributions and heed their warnings at last.

2

Looking at Today and Dreading Tomorrow

H ow did this happen?

That's been the question on everyone's mind since vast sectors of the worldwide economy began collapsing in 2007. Although there has been no shortage of answers offered, most accounts by economists, politicians, and pundits have failed to explain fully how the global economy fell into its most precarious state since the 1930s.

On the macroeconomic level looking at things on a large scale, rather than at individual people or companies—the economy has entered the last leg of what the Austrian School of economics calls the business cycle (or trade cycle). This occurs when large parts of the economy have fallen apart and businesses have to come to grips with the consequences of "malinvestment"—bad business decisions—financed with loans made at interest rates that the government keeps artificially low. In other words, it follows a period of false prosperity created by government intervention in the economy. The typical down leg is accompanied by bank failures, deflation, and high unemployment—all of which have been evident in recent years.

The simplest answer to the question "How did this happen?" is that the housing bubble burst. The biggest run-up of housing prices in history ended in a cataclysmic crash that left the American economy and many other economies in chaos. The carnage was extensive. Hundreds of thousands of people lost their homes, and housing prices declined nationwide by as much as 50 percent in less than two years. The Dow Jones Industrial

Average plummeted by 30 percent almost overnight in September 2008. Just about everyone who had a pension or 401(k) fund lost 30 to 50 percent of his assets. Several of the nation's largest brokerage houses went bust, including Lehman Brothers.

Like nearly all bubbles of recent memory, this one resulted from four financial curses that now beset the American economy:

1. Artificial prosperity created by the federal government through credit expansion.
2. Mathematical modeling by banks and traders.[1]
3. The extraordinary budget deficits run by federal, state, and local governments.[2]
4. The notion that time-tested, venerable market principles going back to antiquity have been replaced by new technology, government regulation, or a more enlightened humanity. (When a government official says something like, "We are in a new economic paradigm," or "The traditional concept of the business cycle is outdated," odds are that financial troubles are near.)

False Prosperity

In the case of the housing bubble, the U.S. Federal Reserve fueled false prosperity. It did so by suppressing interest rates to artificially low levels beginning in 2002. This was certainly not the first time that the Fed's manipulations led to economic dysfunction.

Congress—working with a group of New York bankers—created the Federal Reserve System in 1913, ostensibly to stabilize the currency and prevent runs on banks and the "panics" that sometimes accompanied them.[3] Over time the Fed's mission expanded from merely stabilizing the currency to overseeing the national economy through the manipulation of the money supply to find just the "right mix" of inflation (too much money) and unemployment. (The so-called Phillips curve, a staple of mainstream economics for decades, held that there was an inverse relationship between inflation and unemployment—if unemployment drops, inflation will go up, and vice versa. The high unemployment and inflation of the 1970s "stagflation," which befuddled the economics mainstream, exposed the error of this thinking.) An important step in the expansion of the Federal Reserve's mandate came in 1946, when Congress passed the Full Employment Act, empowering the Fed to expand and contract the nation's money supply to maintain employment. This mandate was based on a principle preached by John Maynard Keynes, whose thinking dominated the economics establishment. Keynes held that the federal government can "spend itself out of a recession" by lowering interest rates (increasing the money supply) or raising federal spending (stimulus) to create new demand throughout the economy.

In the decades since, politicians, mainstream economists, and the media have conditioned most people to think that it's perfectly normal for the Fed—an unelected body—continually to inflate the currency, effectively controlling the throttle on the economy. According to the media, the Fed lowers the interest rate in an effort to "fine-tune" or "jump-start" the economy. Sometimes it adjusts rates in an effort at "belt tightening" or to "cool down" the economy.

But what tamping down interest rates really does is produce "easy money," which eventually comes due at a monstrous price. With easy money comes malinvestment, since many people and businesses are tempted to borrow money and spend it in ways they never would if forced to pay the actual market-based value of the loan. This has been proved time and again.

Before the housing bubble burst, the previous crisis was the dot-com bubble, which exploded in 2000. People who had no understanding of the Internet were led to believe that companies associated with it were the "new IBMs" of the world. Companies that had nothing more than a paper prospectus raised tens of millions of dollars in stock offerings. The stock market has yet to recover from this fiasco: the NASDAQ eclipsed 5,000 in the year 2000 but never came close to that again over the next dozen years, settling at around 3,000.

After the stock market collapsed from the dot-com bubble, there was a minor recession. To "jump-start" the economy, the Fed dropped interest rates dramatically, from 6.5 to 3.5 percent within a few months.

But that Fed reaction was nothing compared with what came just a year later, following September 11. The Federal Reserve slashed the federal funds target rate, which is a key driver as the rate at which private banks lend to one another, to a mere 1 percent. Adjusted for inflation, the short-term interest rate was actually *negative* for two and a half years. What did this mean in real terms? "For bankers, in other words, money was free," as author Charles R. Morris sums it up in his book on the housing bubble, *The Two Trillion Dollar Meltdown*.[4] To keep rates so low, the Fed increased the money supply at a staggering rate. Thomas E. Woods Jr. reports in his bestselling book *Meltdown* that "more dollars [were] created between 2000 and 2007 than in the rest of the republic's history."[5]

All this easy money flooded the housing market. Interest rates remained low, and loans were easy to come by. The federal government used regulations to push banks into making imprudent loans and mortgages to expand home ownership and stimulate the building industry. The Federal Reserve also encouraged the Federal Housing Authority, plus quasi-governmental agencies like Fannie Mae and Freddie Mac, to borrow and lend heavily.[6] All these factors lured many people to buy houses they could not afford.

The government's interventions stimulated an artificial boom. Housing prices skyrocketed, and in turn the construction of new houses took off.[7] As people saw supposed profits pile up from merely owning a home, many decided to become "flippers," buying houses for the sole purpose of reselling them in short order. By 2005, 40 percent of all home purchases were either for investment or as second homes.[8] And as Morris reports, "Merrill Lynch estimated that about half of all American GDP growth in the first half of 2005 was housing-related, either directly through home-building and housing-related purchases, like new furniture, or indirectly by spending refinancing cash flows."[9]

Looking back in 2008, President George W. Bush tried to explain the causes of the housing bubble and the broader economic crisis by saying, "Wall Street got drunk."[10] What Bush didn't say was that the U.S. government knowingly distributed the noxious alcohol that brought down Wall Street—and millions of naive Americans.

Congress and the White House did this by dramatically changing the way mortgages were issued in the United States. For decades, arguing that home ownership was a "right," many politicians had fought to extend it among the population. The Community Reinvestment Act, originally passed during Jimmy Carter's presidency, applied pressure on banks to loosen lending standards so that even low-income borrowers could buy homes. The Clinton administration increased the pressure on banks in the 1990s. Fearing lawsuits alleging discriminatory lending practices, banks complied. Thomas Woods highlights a revealing statement by Bill Clinton's secretary of Housing and Urban Development (HUD), Andrew Cuomo, that reflects the attitude of many politicians on this matter. Announcing the settlement of a discrimination complaint with one mortgage lender, Cuomo acknowledged that the lender would "take a greater risk on these mortgagees, yes," and would give mortgages to families who "would not have qualified but for this affirmative action on the part of the bank, yes." He even admitted, "I am sure there will be a higher default rate on those mortgages than on the rest of the portfolio." Never mind that the mortgages in question totaled $2.1 *billion*.[11]

Tragically, both the Federal Reserve and Congress encouraged bankers to seduce people into buying houses they could never possibly afford, at no money down, and with adjustable-rate mortgages that insidiously used "teaser rates." The interest rate on a mortgage could quickly reset to double or triple the initial teaser rate. The new monthly payments frequently were higher than the borrower's total income. Rather than urging caution, Federal Reserve chairman Alan Greenspan "cheered it on," as Morris notes. In 2004, Greenspan said that families were losing "tens of thousands of dollars" by failing to take advantage of adjustable-rate mortgages that boasted teaser rates of 3.25 percent. The rate for long-term fixed mortgages was only 5.5 percent at the time. Morris writes: "In any scrapbook of bad advice from economic gurus, that should be near the top of the list."[12]

In part because the government was so strongly encouraging mortgage lending, banks—dozens of banks—got away with making obviously bogus loans totaling hundreds of billions of dollars. Some unscrupulous brokers made money in the housing bubble, but millions of trusting souls were badly damaged, even destroyed, financially.

Austrian economists have for decades pointed out that one cannot fool the market for very long. Eventually the piper gets his due.

Economic Modeling

The financial crisis also exposed a complete breakdown of mainstream economic analysis. Austrian economists have long criticized the overreliance on mathematics and econometrics, and because of that the academy frequently derides the Austrian School for a nonmathematical approach. But in the wake of the recent collapse, significant figures in the world of finance and economics have recognized the failures of mathematical modeling. Basing banking and economic decisions purely on mathematics has had disastrous consequences.

For example, many economists and analysts have observed how financial institutions became convinced that they could eliminate the risk of loss in investments by using mathematical formulas. In 2000 a talented actuary devised a new formula that supposedly allowed massively complex risks to be modeled easily and accurately. As *Wired* magazine reported, "everybody from bond investors and Wall Street banks to ratings agencies and regulators" soon began using this formula. It became the basis for tens of thousands of faulty "subprime" mortgages nationwide.[13] Relying on the formula, rating agencies such as Standard & Poor's, Fitch, and Moody's assigned AAA ratings to what we might call dodgy debt.[14] This formula and similar models dramatically oversimplified correlations and the complex workings of markets. But many in the financial community embraced the promise of such formulas—even if they didn't understand the math involved. British economic historian Robert Skidelsky, acclaimed biographer of John Maynard Keynes, points out: "Few of the bank executives and boards who were supposed to manage risk understood the mathematics of risk-management models. This did not prevent them selling [the models] to the public—or themselves."[15]

According to Nobel Prize–winning economist Joseph Stiglitz, the problem was not confined to Wall Street. Stiglitz argues that the markets depend too much on the concept of efficiency and calls for an entirely new economic approach:

> Bad models lead to bad policy: central banks, for instance, focused on the small economic inefficiencies arising from inflation, to the exclusion of the far, far greater inefficiencies arising from dysfunctional financial markets and asset price bubbles. After all, their models said that financial markets were always efficient. Remarkably, standard macroeconomic models did not even incorporate adequate analyses of banks. No wonder former Federal Reserve chairman Alan Greenspan, in his famous mea culpa, could express

his surprise that banks did not do a better job at risk management. The real surprise was his surprise: even a cursory look at the perverse incentives confronting banks and their managers would have predicted short-sighted behaviour with excessive risk-taking.[16]

This statement could easily have been made by an economist of the Austrian School. As we saw in the previous chapter, many figures are now realizing that something is terribly wrong with the teaching of economics. Their criticisms, whether they realize it or not, run parallel with the warnings of the Austrians, who have always held that the quantitative approach to economics is seriously flawed. This call for a new approach in understanding the economy should lead to a reconsideration of the teachings of the Austrian School.

The Federal Budget

The third major factor in the bursting of the bubble was runaway government debt, which reflected rapidly increasing spending. Government deficits are one of the major indicators of economic distress. State and local governments have reached a crisis stage, as their economies haven't generated sufficient tax revenues to cover spending. As for the federal government, the explosion in spending is well documented. Even in its most optimistic forecasts, the Obama administration estimated adding another $4 trillion to the national debt by 2015. The federal government is borrowing $40 of every $140 it spends.[17]

The federal budget can be most easily understood by dividing it into two constituent parts: mandatory and discretionary expenditures. Mandatory expenditures—which include deposit insurance, federal retirement, means-tested entitlements, Medicaid, Medicare, Social Security, and unemployment insurance, as well as interest paid on the national debt—involve "programs that do not come up for annual review or decision by either Congress or the President," in the words of *The Budget of the United States Government*. Because these outlays do not require an annual appropriation, they become a permanent part of federal expenditures, and each succeeding administration must carry the burden. President Ronald Reagan may have disagreed with entitlement programs enacted during the New Deal and the Great Society, but he was still held responsible for raising revenue to continue them. There is no way to rein in the spending on most of these programs, because the government is required to pay out entitlements to any eligible recipient who applies. *The Budget* concludes: "Sometimes referred to as uncontrollable, these programs are clearly out of control."[18]

Discretionary outlays, by contrast, are those the president proposes and Congress votes on. These include expenditures for programs administered by the various cabinet departments—Defense, Commerce, State, Justice, Treasury, Interior, Energy, Education, and so on. It is in these areas that budgetary restraint can take place, because the administration can change these outlays, with the cooperation of Congress. Obviously, the larger the proportion of discretionary expenditures, the easier it is to control the budget. When John F. Kennedy became president in 1961, fully 77 percent of the federal budget was discretionary; by the time Bill Clinton took office in 1993, the percentage had fallen to 63 percent; by 2009, when Barack Obama entered the White House, it had plummeted to about 30 percent.

The explosive growth of the mandatory portion of the budget reflected the institution of massive entitlement programs, most notably those of Lyndon Johnson's Great Society. LBJ's programs, such as Medicare and Medicaid, proved far more expensive than anyone had imagined. And almost every administration since the 1960s has added to these entitlements.

Moreover, Social Security outlays have radically increased over time (and will continue to do so). When Social Security was established in 1936, life expectancy was much lower, and so the projected payout was relatively modest. Because so many people were paying into the program, the system ran large surpluses. These were promptly invested into government debt, which allowed politicians to spend the "extra" money on current projects and hide the real deficit. As the "surplus" accumulated, politicians began to make the system more attractive by adding survivor and disability benefits, as well as allowing people to retire at younger ages. In truth, Americans have really been forced to invest in the ability of present-day governments to tax the future earnings of later generations of Americans.

Today there is no longer even a so-called surplus. With life expectancy increasing and not enough younger people paying into the system, Social Security collections fell short of the benefits paid out in 2010—the first time that had happened since 1983.

It has been obvious for decades that entitlement programs such as Social Security are unsustainable in their current form. Still, any suggestion of paring down the payouts has been a nonstarter politically. These programs have been considered untouchable. The very term *entitlement* conveys that these payments are owed to citizens as a matter of right. This represents a substantial cultural shift even from the early days of Social Security. The Social Security program, after all, was constructed on the idea that participant contributions to the system would fund the benefits to be collected later. Most Americans thought the program was a way to save, and they were building a fund for their old age and disability. They would have bristled at the suggestion that their Social Security payments meant, in effect, that they were accepting welfare. Today, however, the spread of "entitlement" programs has eroded the sense of a relationship between contribution and benefit.

To meet expenses it cannot control, the government is left to scramble to find the necessary funding—through taxation, borrowing, inflation, or growing the economy, or any combination of the four. The cumulative effects of carrying entitlement programs for decade after decade, essentially untouched, have devastated the federal budget. Indeed, no sober analysis can come to any conclusion other than that America is in its worst financial shape ever.

And the United States is not alone. Greece has faced massive rioting as government workers lashed out against cuts in pay and benefits. The future of the European Union has come into question as member nations have debated whether to bail out countries wracked by debt and unemployment, such as Greece, Ireland, Spain, and Portugal. Other European nations face the implosion of their massive welfare states. The benefits they pay out—which dwarf those paid by the U.S. government—simply cannot be sustained as the birthrates of these countries continue to drop.

Ignoring the Warning Signs

If the fundamental question to emerge out of the economic crisis is "How did this happen?" a second question often follows: "Why didn't we see this coming?"

It is true that the collapse stunned politicians, bureaucrats, pundits, and even economists and banking and financial authorities. But at least some economists did warn that the apparent boom times were masking fundamental problems in the economy. For years—decades, in fact—economists from the Austrian School had been calling attention to the curses bedeviling the modern economy. These warnings typically went unheeded.

If the Austrian School received attention from the mainstream at all, it was usually dismissed or mocked. Consider, for example, a blog post that a well-established economist, Tyler Cowen of George Mason University, wrote in January 2005.[19] At the time, the housing market was soaring, economic growth was strong, unemployment was low—in short, everything looked great. To Cowen, then, the warnings of Austrian economists seemed utterly misguided. He mockingly titled his post "If I believed in Austrian business cycle theory," and wrote the following:

> 1. I would think that Asian central banks, by buying U.S. dollars, have been driving a massive distortion of real exchange and interest rates.

The financial press as well the mainstream media have widely reported on the distortion of the foreign exchange markets.[20] Asian banks have aggressively bought U.S. dollars to keep the value of the dollar higher than the market would allow under normal conditions. This kept the prices for U.S.-produced goods high and thus depressed U.S. exports. It also kept the value of Asian currencies low, dropping the prices of their goods and thus favoring their exports. In the fall of 2010, the Fed prompted complaints from the Chinese when it lowered the value of the dollar, because this attempt to expand exports challenged the Asian banks' own currency manipulations.[21]

> 2. I would think that the U.S. economy is overinvested in non-export durables, most of all residential housing.

Even back in 2005 there were plenty of warnings that low interest rates were creating an unsustainable housing bubble. Yet Cowen—and many others—didn't see this.

3. I would think that we have piled on far too much debt, in both the private and public sectors.

In 2004 the U.S. government had racked up a deficit of $412.7 billion, just three years after running a *surplus* of $128.2 billion. The trend looked ominous even from the perspective of 2005, and of course in the years since, the federal government has piled additional trillions on the public debt.[22] Household debt had been soaring as well—from about 90 percent of annual disposable income in 2000 on its way to a high of 130 percent in 2007.[23]

4. I would think these trends cannot possibly continue. Asian central banks may come to their senses. Furthermore the U.S. would be like an addict who needs an ever-increasing dose of the monetary fix. This, of course, would eventually prove impossible.

Cowen may have noticed that these trends came to an abrupt halt in 2007–9, with the collapse of the housing market, the bankruptcy of Lehman Brothers, and the rest. Meanwhile, under Chairman Ben Bernanke, the Federal Reserve has provided the U.S. addict steady doses of the "monetary fix."

Lest there was any doubt that Cowen was ridiculing the Austrian School, he concluded his post by writing, "Of course that is not me."

So just what has the Austrian School said to earn such derision? And how have the Austrians been right all along, whereas their critics have been proved wrong? In the next chapter we'll look at the thinkers who have developed the Austrian School of economics. As we'll see, these include some very sharp minds steeped in the Western tradition. They have thought the problems through, in different times and circumstances.

Once we understand the contributions of the Austrian School, we will recognize that it is not at all absurd to believe that the world can live in peaceful prosperity.

3

A Short History of
the Austrian School

Ideas have consequences. This is especially true in the world of economics, where good ideas can pull nations out of poverty and lead to prosperity—and where a single bad idea can wind up being a calamity for millions.

In the mid-nineteenth century, Karl Marx was an unemployed writer scribbling in the British Museum while his family starved. Several decades later his ideas on economics—which added a toxic mix of materialism, atheism, and class warfare to the classical school's labor theory of value (the value of a product is determined by the labor that goes into it)—had come to dominate much of the world, embraced by tyrants in the Soviet Union, China, Cuba, and many other countries. Marxism led to tyrannical regimes that claimed more than one hundred million lives through political persecution, famine, warfare, purges, and much more.

How different things would have been in China and Russia had the revolutionaries adopted the concepts of free markets and liberty. These ideas guided the Founding Fathers in the United States toward the end of the eighteenth century, and produced the freest, strongest, and most prosperous nation in history. More recently, in 1948, Germany's economics minister, Ludwig Erhard, responded to economic distress by adopting free markets and sound money, bringing to the underclass a realistic hope of prosperity. The experiment succeeded. He could have chosen the same path as East Germany, which struggled.

John Maynard Keynes captured the extraordinary influence of economic ideas when he commented:

> The ideas of economists and political philosophers, both when they are right and when they are wrong, are more powerful than is commonly understood. Indeed, the world is ruled by little else. Practical men, who believe themselves to be quite exempt from any intellectual influences, are usually the slaves of some defunct economist. Madmen in authority, who hear voices in the air, are distilling their frenzy from some academic scribbler of a few years back. I am sure that the power of vested interests is vastly exaggerated compared with the gradual encroachment of ideas.[1]

Keynes's own career is a testament to this idea: no twentieth-century economist had as great an influence on the course of government economic policy as he did. And Keynes was quite right about the power of *wrong* ideas. Adding to the tragedy of Marxism is the fact that while Marx was conjuring up his faulty ideas, the Western world, which had seen warfare as far back as anyone could remember, was in the midst of a century of peace thanks to the premises of classical liberalism—simple economic ideas like the gold standard, free markets, and liberty.

By the 1970s, Keynes's own ideas had produced a seemingly intractable economic dilemma. The United States and the rest of the developed world were wracked by inflation and economic stagnation. In late 1974, accepting the Nobel Prize in Economics, F. A. Hayek surveyed this scene and concluded that economists deserved blame: "We have indeed at the moment little cause for pride: as a profession we have made a mess of things." Hayek noted that the ruinous inflation of the 1970s had been "brought about by policies which the majority of economists recommended and even urged governments to pursue."[2]

The Austrian School was not part of the economics establishment that urged such misguided policies. It is important to understand the contributions of the many thinkers—including Hayek—who have developed the substantial teaching of the Austrian School over more than a century.

The Substantial Teaching of the Austrian School

The Austrian School's influence is quite small in the American academy. Thus it may surprise the reader to discover that the Austrians' essential ideas form the foundation of modern mainstream economics.

Ludwig von Mises, who is credited with bringing the Austrian School to the United States during World War II, made this point when describing the spread of Austrian thinking in the early twentieth century:

> The number of foreign economists who applied themselves to the continuation of the work inaugurated by the "Austrians" was steadily increasing. At the beginning it sometimes happened that the endeavors of these British, American, and other non-Austrian economists met with opposition in their own countries and they were ironically called "Austrians" by their critics. But after some years all the essential ideas of the Austrian school were by and large accepted as an integral part of economic theory. [By the 1920s], one no longer distinguished between an Austrian school and other economics. The appellation "Austrian" school became the name given to an important chapter of the history of economic thought; it was no longer the name of a specific set with doctrines different from those held by other economists.[3]

But there are exceptions. The most important distinguishing characteristic of Austrian economics is its emphasis on the individual acting person. Whereas the other schools think in terms of aggregates, Austrians observe individuals participating in the marketplace, what Mises calls "methodological individualism."

Additionally, unlike the other schools, Austrians rarely speak of capital or labor as homogeneous units. It follows that Austrians don't see mathematics as essential to economic thought; at best, math is a visual or conceptual aid. One will not see many equations or graphs in an Austrian treatise. Even Lord Keynes, often considered the nemesis of the Austrian School, now and then spoke harshly of math: "Too large a proportion of the recent 'mathematical' economics are mere concoctions, as imprecise as the initial assumptions they rest on, which allow the author to lose sight of the complexities and interdependencies of the real world into maze of pretentious and unhelpful symbols."[4]

Still, many departments of economics that describe themselves as Keynesian insist on the substantial use of mathematics. Obviously, they have not read their master, or don't take him seriously! For instance, the following formula is commonly used in macroeconomics classes at both the graduate and undergraduate levels: *Y [GNP or output] = I [investment] + C [consumption] + G [government spending] + (X − M) [exports minus imports]*. This equation assumes that all forms of investment or consumption or government are the same. To the Austrians, such a formula is woefully inadequate and misleading. In real life, each unit of investment is usually different: some are more productive than others; some are long-term, some short-term; each one has a different profitability. We are all taught in elementary algebra that you can't add apples and oranges.

In the tradition of Aristotle and Thomas Aquinas, Austrians see economics as a practical science that deals with human nature and human choices. They believe that certain, very general laws of human action can be discerned by observation and deduction. The laws they deduce apply to human choice and nature in the face of scarcity.[5]

The Austrians are also fascinated with the division of labor as it has developed over time. They see the economy developing spontaneously and give great credit to entrepreneurs as the spark plugs of economic progress. Because of this observation, most Austrians are skeptical of government intervention. They tend to favor free markets and have been quite critical of socialism and planned economies. Since the Austrians hold that value begins with the individual acting person, the school comes into conflict with any objective theory of value such as those proposed by either the classical school or Marxism. There is a long history of intellectual debate between Marxists and Austrians, culminating in the predictions of Mises and Hayek that a socialist economic order was impossible and would collapse.

The best and easiest way to understand the Austrian School is to start with the contributions of its seminal thinker, Carl Menger, and trace the development of the school through other prominent Austrians to the present day.[6]

The Founder: Carl Menger

The Austrian School began in 1871 with the publication of Carl Menger's first book, *Principles of Economics*. Menger (1840–1921) ventured into economics in his mid-twenties as a newspaper reporter working at the Vienna stock exchange. He noticed that prices were not established anywhere except in the bidding contest among individuals out on the floor. This experience led to a major conclusion of *Principles of Economics*: value is determined by individual human judgment.

More specifically, Menger noted that if a person has a quantity of the same product, each unit of the product will be valued differently according to the individual's needs. The more the person has of the good, the less he will be inclined to value additional units of it. If the individual has only a limited supply of the product, he will apply what he has to the most important uses first.

Consider water. In most parts of the country it seems abundant. Yet in the summer many cities must limit water usage, since demand is so high. Activities like the watering of lawns are restricted. The value of municipal water thus varies with time—depending on the seasons of the year, and even the particular hour of the day—and with usage. Similarly, on a hot summer day a street vendor can sell a twelve-ounce bottle of (tap) water for two dollars. On a winter day there are no vendors to be seen. So what's the value of water? It depends on the individuals who want to sell it and buy it and their particular circumstances at any given time. There is no "objective" value of water. Menger's concept, therefore, is known as the subjective theory of value,

Although this observation seems obvious today (indeed, all schools of economics now accept it), it was groundbreaking in Menger's era. His subjective theory of value is closely connected to another theory that two economists, William Stanley Jevons of Britain and Leon Walras of Switzerland, articulated at almost exactly the same time: the theory of marginal utility. The latter theory holds that the value of any amount of a commodity depends on the importance of the last unit. Put more simply, in valuing a good, we have to consider how much of it we have and also how much additional satisfaction an additional quantity of the good would bring us.

The marginalists—Menger, Jevons, and Walras—solved the famous paradox of value, which can be illustrated with this question: How can diamonds be more valuable than water when water is more useful? In normal circumstances, of course, water is very abundant, and in such conditions an extra glass has very little meaning to us. But diamonds are quite rare and many people prize them; therefore an extra diamond can be exchanged for something very important. The marginalists thus recognized that the value of something is determined by the individual acting in specific circumstances. The only major difference among Jevons, Walras, and Menger is that the first two used mathematics extensively in their presentations, whereas the last eschewed such tools in explaining his theory. Menger's nonmathematical—but very practical—analysis is one of the hallmarks of the Austrian approach.

Although this concept broke new ground in economics, it really wasn't new even in Menger's day. In the Bible (Mark 12:41–44, Luke 21:1–4), Jesus tells the parable of the widow's mite, which demonstrates that the contribution of a tiny sum of money by a poor widow is more significant in God's eyes than a much larger financial contribution from a wealthy man. The tale is typically interpreted to be a denunciation of ostentatious giving by the wealthy, but it also illustrates Menger's concept of subjective value.

Menger began his argument about value by discussing scarcity. Each individual actor, he wrote, reacts to limitation by adjusting his economic activity, or economizing. In economizing, each actor must make five decisions with regard to a commodity: (1) What are the best uses to which this good can be put? (2) How can this commodity be conserved? (3) How can it be used efficiently? (4) Are there substitutes or alternatives that can be employed? (5) How can production of the commodity be increased?

Menger used the example of farmers producing greater quantities of crops. As more quantities are produced, a farmer can increase his demand for other products and services; each increase in production allows him to fulfill another need. The first fruits of the farmer's harvest are used for subsistence, the most important use. As a harvest increases, the farmer can use the extra seed corn to ensure a harvest for next year. He can use further increases in production for less important purposes. He eventually produces surpluses, which he will trade with other members of society for their surpluses. Thus, the production of surplus leads to trade. Menger established an important premise—that the process of trading takes place between two parties for mutual gain. Because each sees something better in the trade, the exchange is not between equal things; it is a win-win for both parties.

Menger distinguished between first-order goods, or consumer goods immediately available for use, and goods of a higher order, or capital goods. For example, the bread at the local grocery store is a first-order good; it comes to us by the use of higher-order goods such as trucks, baking ovens, and farm equipment. Menger showed that each unit of capital is unique, and each has its own particular contribution. This concept became the foundation of his capital theory and was later closely interwoven with the trade cycle theory.

Using his observations on subjective value, Menger realized that the foundation for the value of capital comes directly from value of the consumer goods that it produces. This is called the theory of imputation. He pointed out that to know the value of any particular factor in the production process, one can simply subtract it and calculate the loss of productivity from its absence. For example, consider the value of fertilizer to a farmer: what productivity will be lost if he does not fertilize the field? This will show how much value the fertilizer has in the productive process.

Another of Menger's important insights was that money is developed spontaneously in a market, not created by governments. Starting with a theory of the commodity—something produced for trade—Menger recognized that each item put up for sale has a specific number of people interested in purchasing it. The wider that market is, the easier it will be to find buyers. Today, we call this market liquidity. In a barter economy, market participants find it most efficient to conduct trades by obtaining the most marketable commodity—something that is desired by other people—and that commodity becomes money. Menger pointed out that this process happens without government action. Governments merely ratify the choice of the market, recognizing the most marketable commodity as money with laws regarding contracts and taxation. This certainly was the case with the creation of coins. Way back when, people on the street—farmers, craftsmen, peasants—realized that to buy things it was easier to carry little pieces of precious metal than to cart around oxen and bushels of corn and wheat. Governments incorporated the idea into local currency.

In his analysis of the division of labor, Menger made two other important contributions to economic theory. He added the development of technology to Adam Smith's three factors of the division of labor (time savings, developing the skill, and capital). Moreover, he saw that as the economy develops, greater and greater specialized knowledge is passed on, from one generation to the next. Thus, one of the important factors in developing new resources is knowledge and information.

Just as Menger owed a debt to previous thinkers,[7] generations of economists would build on Menger's insights.

Price, Capital, Interest, and Marx: Eugen von Böhm-Bawerk

Eugen von Böhm-Bawerk (1851–1914), Menger's colleague at the University of Vienna, was the second member of the original Austrian School. He is best known for three further developments of Austrian thought: an explanation of price formulation, capital and interest theory, and his repudiation of Karl Marx.

Böhm-Bawerk refined Menger's insights regarding prices. He recognized that each buyer and seller comes into a market with different intensities and is therefore willing to accept or to pay different prices. As prices move up, more sellers see an advantage to the exchange, but fewer buyers see an advantage. At high prices the number of sellers will exceed the number of buyers. This means that prices will eventually move down. On the other hand, as prices come down, sellers will become discouraged and withdraw from the marketplace, but new buyers will be attracted. In this case prices tend to rise.

The best way to see this phenomenon is to observe an auction. I once went to a machinery auction for my family's business. Before leaving for the sale I had in mind a price that I would pay for a specific press. I was looking for a bargain. As the auction began, prices started low and moved up relatively quickly. As the price rose, there were fewer bids as other buyers saw better opportunities available to them and dropped out, until at last only two of us were bidding on the press. Each of us knew that once the other dropped out, our bid would prevail. Fortunately, my competitor dropped out long before my ceiling price was reached (though I couldn't know in advance how far he was willing to go). My next bid bought the machine. In essence, two of us set the price. He set the lower limit on the price by continuing to push me up. And I set the final price with my last bid.

Now consider the case of two sellers at an auction. Each seller enters the auction with an idea of the lowest price he will accept. As prices are driven downward in the bidding, more and more sellers leave the marketplace and withdraw their product, because they see better opportunities for the use of that product. Eventually just two bidders remain. As the price drops, the second seller withdraws and the next seller's bid is accepted. In essence, the seller who drops out sets the limit on the price the successful seller obtains.

It was Böhm-Bawerk who pointed out that in every market, prices are set by the last two buyers and the last two sellers. His analysis of auctions and his market price theory remain the basis of modern practice in price setting for markets. Economists have developed many other price theories, but all are based on Böhm-Bawerk's initial observations.

Böhm-Bawerk also refined Menger's capital theory (lower-order and higher-order goods). His "roundabout method of production" described the stages of creating consumer goods. It recognized that a long process must be followed before the final product can be made. For example, we must build tools—capital goods—before we produce the ultimate product. Böhm-Bawerk described this process by using a bull's-eye figure. The production process starts at the center of the circle, with the use of original means—land and labor. Then the process moves outward, in concentric circles, as raw materials are put to new uses and more value is added. The final product, which satisfies the consumer's demands, emerges in the outermost ring; the interior circles represent the goods in process.[8]

In addition to refining capital theory, Böhm-Bawerk developed the theory of interest as time preference. This theory, which is used extensively in modern finance, holds that "interest income" is payment for time. Böhm-Bawerk laid out what has become a tenet of Austrian economics: the idea that people tend to value present goods more highly than future goods of the same quantity and quality, because goods today provide immediate satisfaction. Thus, future goods trade at a discount, while present goods trade at a premium. In order to get people to save, it is necessary to increase the value of future goods—which is accomplished through the payment of interest.

Finally, Böhm-Bawerk set the stage for future Austrians to criticize socialism by refuting the Marxist and classical school's labor theory of value. According to Marxist theory, value is determined by labor. In *Karl Marx and the Close of His System* (1896), Böhm-Bawerk argued that, contrary to Marx's position, capitalists do not exploit workers; rather, they accommodate workers by providing them with income well in advance of the revenue from the output they help to produce; sometimes those products won't reap revenue for many months, even years. Thus, the risk to workers is limited, as they know they'll get paid regardless of whether the product they work on sells.

The Austrian Socialist: Friedrich von Wieser

Friedrich von Wieser (1851–1926) is the third member of the founding Austrian economists. He is most famous for the concept of opportunity cost, in which he saw every cost as set by its next best opportunity. Every economic decision entails sacrifice: that which is given up or not chosen. For example, my decision to attend a concert rather than a movie says that the opportunity cost of attending the concert is attending a movie. I cannot have both at the same time, so one becomes the cost of having the other. The same idea can be applied to the financial sphere. Investing in my business may entail the sacrifice of investments in stocks.

Wieser's approach to the concept of imputation differed from that of Menger, who argued that the value of any production factor can be determined by subtracting it from the production process and seeing how much work is lost. Wieser pointed out that we can calculate the *increased* productivity that comes from *adding* a new factor of production. A farmer, for instance, can determine how much production rises from additional amounts of fertilizer by measuring the increased yield of crops. From this increase one can "impute" the value of the fertilizer.

Wieser is notable in another important respect: although he was a member of the Austrian School, he was inclined toward socialism or planned economies. At times he was even a member of the Fabian Society, the famous socialist movement. But his thinking started the debate among economists over whether socialism was economically feasible. Putting his theory of imputation together with his concept of cost, he argued that a socialist economy must have some system for the allocation of resources—a method of economic calculation to avoid chaos.⁹ Every economy—socialist or free—has the problem of scarce resources that have alternative uses. Planned economies, Wieser saw, are not exempt from the need to decide on the best allocation of a particular resource.

These observations would provide the basis for Hayek's criticism of socialist economies in the twentieth century.

Renegade Student: Joseph Schumpeter

The economist Joseph Schumpeter (1883–1950) is generally not considered a member of the Austrian School. But he did train at the University of Vienna under Böhm-Bawerk, and his thinking displays important commonalities with Austrian economics. Most notably, he championed the role of individual action, seeing the entrepreneur as central to a dynamic economy. His most famous contribution, his popularization of the concept of "creative destruction," reflects his emphasis on individual action. According to Schumpeter, innovations drive economic cycles. As new products and processes develop, they overthrow established systems of production and create new industries. For example, when the personal computer came along, it destroyed the typewriter industry—but this destruction was "creative" in the sense that it created a much larger and more dynamic industry and fueled long-term economic growth.

Like later Austrian economists such as Hayek and Murray Rothbard, Schumpeter saw modern economics beginning not with Adam Smith in the eighteenth century but much earlier, at Spain's University of Salamanca in the late fifteenth and earlier sixteenth centuries. The School of Salamanca included thinkers such as Dominican Francisco de Vitoria (1485–1546) and Jesuits Leonard de Leys (Lessius) (1554–1623) and Juan de Mariana (1536–1624). Schumpeter argued that they began modern economic analysis by applying Thomas Aquinas's teachings on economics, morality, and justice to public policy and everyday situations.

One might consider the School of Salamanca to be the first think tank. In their writings, the professors developed recommendations for the moral, economic, and political difficulties Spain faced in handling its far-flung empire. These were new economic times, as Spanish officials were forced to contend with two very different conditions: on one hand, the expanding commercial development in European areas they controlled, most notably the "low countries" (today Belgium and the Netherlands), and on the other hand, their newly discovered colonies, where the Spanish were dealing with native populations and issues of how to mine and transport the natural resources of the New World, such as gold and silver.

The major trend in governmental policy at the time of the School of Salamanca was an economic philosophy called mercantilism, which relied on heavy state control and was a precursor to modern planned economies. The goal of the mercantilists was to accumulate gold and silver bullion in the state coffers as the key to national power. By contrast, the School of Salamanca made the case for economic freedom based on justice and the efficacy of a free economic system in lifting overall standards of living. These thinkers argued—as the Austrians would later—that the nature of value began with individual actors, and they ardently defended private property.[10] And they did all this well over a century before Adam Smith took mercantilism to task in his book *An Inquiry into the Nature and Causes of the Wealth of Nations*, published in 1776.

Joseph Schumpeter did depart from his Austrian teachers in certain important ways; Leon Walras, among others, influenced Schumpeter deeply.[11] Still, his thinking aligned with that of Austrian economists in key areas: in his belief in the importance of individual action; his belief that value is subjective rather than objective; his emphasis on free markets and private property; his claim that democratically elected governments, responding to constant changes in the economy, will burden the market system with regulations and taxes; and his tracing of modern economics back to Thomas Aquinas through the School of Salamanca.

Coming to America: Ludwig von Mises

Ludwig von Mises's contributions to the Austrian School are incalculable. Like Schumpeter a student of Böhm-Bawerk at the University of Vienna, Mises (1881–1973) brought the Austrian School to the United States, where it has flourished, even though it is underrepresented in the academy. But he was more than just an evangelist; he contributed significantly to trade cycle theory, monetary theory, the epistemology of economics, and economic history, and predicted the failures of socialism and the eventual collapse of the communist empire.

Mises distinguished himself as an exceptional theorist in his first major work, *The Theory of Money and Credit* (1912). Böhm-Bawerk was so impressed that he used it as the basis of an entire seminar. Here Mises first wrote about the theory of the trade cycle, bringing together the capital theory of Böhm-Bawerk and the monetary theory of the Swedish economist Knut Wicksell. The theory of the trade cycle (or business cycle, as it is often called) is now central to Austrian economics. According to Mises, when banks attempt to increase credit not backed up by cash or gold—usually in combination with central bank policies to lower interest rates artificially—it produces an unsustainable boom and malinvestment. Inevitably the boom turns into bust. (A full explanation of trade cycle theory is included in chapter 13 of this book.)

As we know from the Federal Reserve today, central banks frequently increase the money supply to try to "stimulate" the economy. But expanding the money supply does not increase the amount of goods and services available or the standard of living. Therefore, such increases cause economic problems because those who receive the new money first begin to spend it, which drives up prices. Those who didn't benefit from the increase in the money supply end up suffering, because now they must pay higher prices for the same goods and services without any additional money to spend. This is inflation, which Mises fought against throughout his career.

Mises firmly established that the value of money depends on two factors: changes in the monetary stock and changes in productivity. Money, like any other commodity, is subject to the laws of supply and demand. He pointed out that prices in the marketplace start with the last price quoted the day before, and that money, to be accepted by the marketplace, must have a basis in preexisting purchasing power. We saw this principle at work with the creation of the euro, the common currency for the European Union; when the euro was introduced, its value was based on that of the preexisting currencies.

Following Menger, Mises realized that the foundations of economics are extremely important, especially concerning method. He argued forcefully against the notion that economics should follow the example of physics. In *The Ultimate Foundation of Economic Science* (1962), he contended that economics is part of a larger science of human action, which is not measurable by the physical sciences. Because human action always starts with a purpose—or a "final cause," in the language of Aristotle—economics should belong to a group of sciences known as *praxeology*, or the study of human action. Mises argued that human beings are special and completely different from material things. He called his approach "methodological dualism." To Mises, economics is an integral science based on a logical, step-by-step analysis of individual human action.

Mises built on Wieser's contributions as well as Menger's. Wieser pointed out that socialism needs a decision-making process for the allocation of resources, and Mises insisted that market prices form the basis for the decision process. Market prices are a contradiction to socialism, since they must be formed in free markets based on private property. Anticipating Hayek's arguments, Mises saw that prices—as the expression of value set by alternative bidding—represent the best way to evaluate how to allocate a particular resource. In fact, one of Mises's greatest achievements was to note that socialism makes true economic calculation impossible. A socialist society, he showed, cannot effectively allocate resources to the best possible uses because without market prices, there is no way of knowing what that use is. The result? Planned chaos, as Mises put it in the title of one of his most important books. His predictions were borne out with the collapse of the Soviet Union.

Mises critiqued all forms of state intervention, subsidies, price control, social tax policy, and inflation. He argued that whenever governments intervene in the economy to solve a problem, invariably they not only fail to solve the problem but also create new problems, each crying out for further government intervention.

Mises's analysis is as important today as ever. The problems he detected were precisely those that led to the recent economic collapse. The U.S. government, trying to make housing affordable to the poor, pressured banks to give home mortgages to low-income (sometimes jobless) families, sometimes without a down payment. The result was the meltdown of the housing industry in 2008, which in turn led to the collapse of the U.S. economy and widespread unemployment.

The Popularizer: Henry Hazlitt

Henry Hazlitt (1894–1993) is perhaps the best-known popularizer of the Austrian School. Describing himself as a "working newspaperman," he was published in a wide variety of major publications, including the *New York Times*, the *Wall Street Journal*, *Newsweek*, and *The Freeman*. He was also directly responsible for bringing the Austrian School to the United States, as he helped Mises secure academic employment at New York University.

Hazlitt's best-known work, *Economics in One Lesson* (1946), remains a wonderful introduction to economics. He carefully analyzed the effects of government interventions in a number of areas—labor, agriculture, and so on—and showed that all such interventions not only violate the rights and property of others but actually wreak more havoc than the original problems. He cautioned that economists are too often shortsighted: "The art of economics consists in looking not merely at the immediate but at the longer effects of any act or policy; it consists in tracing the consequences of that policy, not merely for one group, but for all groups."[12]

Although not an economic theorist per se, Hazlitt cogently argued that throughout history, enormous gains in living standards have followed the introduction of free markets, while poverty and economic dislocation have resulted from interventionism. Hazlitt predicted the consequences of the expansion of the welfare state starting with Woodrow Wilson and continuing through the 1990s. He correctly predicted that U.S. federal agriculture programs would create tremendous shortages in some areas and excessive surpluses in others. Hazlitt also detected the frailties of the international monetary system established at the 1944 Bretton Woods conference, where economists from the Allied nations gathered to construct a stable postwar economy. The Bretton Woods system established fixed exchange rates based on the U.S. dollar as the reserve currency; foreign central banks could convert the dollar into gold at thirty-five dollars per ounce. Hazlitt showed that this system would lead to inflation and the eventual breakdown of the dollar. He was a prominent proponent of a return to the convertible gold standard.

For a time Hazlitt was one of the lone voices pointing out the inconsistencies and errors of the interventionist government policies of the twentieth century. Not surprisingly, he was very critical of the reigning Keynesian economics and wrote a point-by-point critique entitled *The Failure of the "New Economics": An Analysis of the Keynesian Fallacies.*

The Nobel Prize Winner: Friedrich August von Hayek

Along with his mentor, Ludwig von Mises, Nobel laureate F. A. Hayek (1899–1992) is perhaps the most influential of the Austrian economists. He is best known for his 1944 book *The Road to Serfdom* (which Henry Hazlitt was instrumental in bringing to publication in America). That landmark book documented the dangers of centrally planned economies—not only to prosperity but to individual liberty as well.

In addition to highlighting the dangers of a planned economy, Hayek clearly explained the Austrian theory of the trade cycle. In his explanation, he did not see the value in aggregate statistics. During the 1920s (as in our own time), the economics "establishment" claimed that there could be no inflation because the general price level was stable. These mainstream figures also referred to economic statistics that indicated, in the aggregate, continuing growth. Needless to say, they were as bewildered by the coming of the Great Depression as present-day economists were by the recent economic downturn.

Looking at the trade cycle in a different way, Hayek saw that it is not overall price statistics that matter but price differentials between capital goods and consumer goods. He showed that when central banks expand bank credit and lower interest rates, causing prices to go up, the prices of capital goods rise much faster than those of consumer goods—and then fall much more drastically in the recession that inevitably follows. We saw this phenomenon when housing prices skyrocketed from 2003 to 2008, and when dot-com stocks soared from 1994 to 1999.

This concept of the trade cycle followed very closely that of Mises. The main difference between the two was that Hayek saw the trade cycle as a natural outcome of the fractional-reserve banking system (which allows banks to lend out far more money than they actually hold in their reserves). He pointed out that during the initial phases of a boom, banks will continue to extend credit in order to increase their profits. In contrast, Mises argued that the trade cycle begins with a deliberate policy of the central bank to lower interest rates artificially. Both, however, agreed on the deleterious effects of credit expansion and artificially low interest rates. Needless to say, neither would have been surprised at the current downturn.

Hayek is also known for his analysis of the structure of capital in the economy. Building on the work of Böhm-Bawerk and Menger, he saw that the capital structure expands in time—that is, resources must be committed now to achieve value in the future—and depends on interest rates. As interest rates are lowered, either through increased savings or injections of credit by central banks, businessmen are inclined to invest in longer and longer processes of production. For example, an automobile company, seeing that interest rates are low, will tend to develop new technologies as it perceives new profit opportunities. Conversely, as interest rates rise, companies will attempt to get goods to consumers as quickly as possible and thus hold off on investing in longer periods of production. A vintner faced with high interest rates will tend to get his wine to the market as soon as possible. With lower interest rates, he might let the wine season longer in anticipation of an increase in profits.

Hayek's criticism of socialism drew on Friedrich von Wieser's observation that even a planned economy needs a mechanism for calculating the best allocation of economic resources, as well as Mises's argument that socialism cannot make accurate economic calculations, because its prices are not formed in free markets. The essence of Hayek's criticism is contained in the essay "The Use of Knowledge in Society."[13] Here he points out that an effective economic system depends on knowledge— not scientific or technical knowledge but the understanding that only individual actors can possess. For example, a manager of a factory knows which employee to match with each machine in order to achieve maximum productivity. This is not knowledge open to statistics, but it is crucial to the efficient operation of the economy at the most basic level.

In other words, Hayek understood that the governing officials in charge of a centrally planned economy can't allocate economic resources as well or as accurately as the far more numerous businesspeople, entrepreneurs, and consumers making economic decisions every day. Prices set freely in the market most accurately indicate the proper allocation of resources because they draw upon a vastly greater range of knowledge, skill, and experience.

Hayek's criticisms of the planned society, articulated in such books as *The Road to Serfdom* and *The Fatal Conceit* (1988), also derived from his emphasis on the "spontaneous order" of society. In the tradition of Edmund Burke, Hayek saw society as developing from a whole stream of human action, one generation to the next, all the while developing technology, law, and social organization. Central planning, or any top-down management, ran counter to this natural organization of society, Hayek argued.

The American Austrian: Frank A. Fetter

Frank Fetter (1863–1949) has been recognized as the American Austrian economist. Like the other members of the Austrian School, Fetter supported the idea of marginal utility. He argued that the last use to which any commodity is put indicates how an economy values that commodity. For example, if one comes to a country and sees that gold is used for common, ordinary things, whereas iron is used sparingly, for only jewelry and money, one could conclude that gold is abundant and iron scarce.

Moreover, like Böhm-Bawerk and other Austrian economists, Fetter traced economic laws to individual human action. He examined interest payments as a way to compensate for the extra value people tend to place on satisfactions today over satisfactions tomorrow. Such observations allowed him to contribute to the modern science of finance. He recognized the role of interest rates in determining the value of capital goods. How do we discount today for something that will generate cash flow in the future?

To understand this issue, consider a person who will receive a bequest of $1 million ten years hence. He can sell that bequest on the open market today, but he won't be able to get $1 million for it: the buyer would get no benefit from surrendering his use of $1 million now. So the seller must offer a discount off the face value in order to sell the bequest today. How much of a discount? The answer lies in the rate of interest. The sell price is the figure that when multiplied by the interest rate and the number of years equals $1 million. Say the market interest rate is 5 percent annually rate: the face amount of the bequest would then be discounted from $1 million to just shy of $614,000, since that amount, earning 5 percent interest per year, would be worth $1 million after ten years. Fetter recognized that the interest rate is what connects the values of the asset over a period of time. This observation is a fundamental principle of modern finance.

Following the other Austrians, Fetter examined the role of money expansion in the trade cycle. He saw that the trade cycle had three distinct phases: prosperity, crisis, and depression. He also argued that a society could pull itself out of poverty if it had a high enough savings rate. In being champions of savings, Fetter and other Austrians departed from the dominant school of Keynesianism, which tended to be critical of savings while favoring spending, or consumption, as the key driver of an economy. (In the most recent economic crisis, Austrian economists have similarly challenged government programs intended to stimulate consumer spending; they would favor actions to promote capital investment through savings.)

Taking on Keynes: William H. Hutt

William Hutt (1899–1988) is best known for his analysis of Say's Law, which can be very simply stated: "The supply of X creates the demand for Y." In 1936, John Maynard Keynes published his most famous work, *The General Theory of Employment, Interest, and Money*, in which he built his entire concept of effective supply and aggregate demand based on his interpretation of Say's Law. Hutt disagreed with Keynes's analysis.

In explaining the Great Depression, Keynes constantly referred to the lack of effective demand and took issue with Say's doctrine:

> From the time of Say and Ricardo the classical economists have taught that supply creates its own demand;—meaning by this in some significant, but not clearly defined, sense that the whole of the costs of production must necessarily be spent in the aggregate, directly or indirectly, on purchasing the product. . . .
>
> Thus Say's Law, that the aggregate demand price of output as a whole is equal to its aggregate supply price for all volumes of output, is equivalent to the proposition that there is no obstacle to full employment.[14]

Hutt argued that Keynes misinterpreted Say's Law, particularly in reference to "the aggregate" and full employment. Hutt pointed out that it was not the aggregate supply that created demand. Say argued that producing goods and services allowed an *individual* to trade for the goods and services of others. He believed that supplier production was the mainspring of prosperity and that money merely facilitated commerce but did not actually create wealth.[15]

Hutt confronted Keynesianism with these principles in his work *Keynesianism—Retrospect and Prospect: A Critical Restatement of Basic Economic Principles* (1963). There he explained that the economy generates demand and income through increased production. Keynes, by contrast, looked at income as a monetary phenomenon. Hutt was critical of cartels, particularly trade unions, that prevent the price system from balancing supply and demand. The cartel effect of trade unions cannot raise wage rates for all workers, he said; unions can only transfer benefits from consumers, or other workers, to their members. A political cartoonist captured this concept during a General Motors strike in the 1990s. In the cartoon, a management representative says, "We can survive the strike." At the same time, union picket signs declare, "We can survive the strike." But off to the side, a lady selling hamburgers says, "I can't survive the strike." When high demand for wages leads workers to lose their jobs, they become unproductive, and thus, in perfect accord with Say's Law, they cannot purchase other people's production.

The solution to unemployment, Hutt said, is to recognize this cartel effect, which causes wages to be out of sync with the market and takes workers out of production. Labor union policies simply cover over these problems, he argued. Continuing them will lead to inflation and depreciation of the currency, and can never solve the problem. Hutt argued that an effective price system keeps all resources employed and contributes to maximum demand in the economy.

Ideas in Practice: Wilhelm Röpke

Like so many other economists of the first half of the twentieth century—both Austrian and not—Wilhelm Röpke (1899–1966) was profoundly shaped by the experiences of World War I. He and the others had experienced the world of classical liberalism prior to the Great War—and as such, had seen a beautiful world that came to a tragic end.

Röpke was a soldier in the trenches during World War I, and his opposition to collectivism was largely shaped by his experiences then. He wrote:

> As soldiers too we had learnt what it meant to be crammed for years into a machine in which the individual had no other life than that of the mass, a life determined by force, unconditional obedience and constraint. Even outside the army the war brought with it a hitherto unknown degree of restriction upon elementary freedoms. Waging war did not only mean killing and being killed, inconceivable hardships, mud, vermin, hunger, thirst and disease, destroying, lying and hating; it also meant militarism, giving and obeying orders, the unchaining of brutal thirst for power, the triumph of unbridled ambition, the exploitation of uncontrollable positions of power, the degradation of the human being, mass existence, by day and night, mass feeding, spiritual stagnation, restriction of the most primary freedoms. It meant never being alone, never being one's own master, never to think or to question. . . .
>
> If we ever examined ourselves rightly, our revolt against war amounted to a passionate protest against the intolerable domination of the State.[16]

Another profound experience occurred when Röpke lived in Switzerland as a refugee from Nazi Germany. (In Switzerland, he taught with Ludwig von Mises.) According to Röpke biographer John Zmirak: "Switzerland constituted for him living proof that the market economy and liberal society were still viable in contemporary Europe. With their traditions of decentralized government, freedom of thought, participatory democracy, middle class virtue, and economic self-reliance, Switzerland had managed to avoid most of the ethnic polarization and class hatred, mass impoverishment, and harsh financial inequality which had torn apart other nations in the wake of World War I."[17]

Given these experiences, it is perhaps not surprising that Röpke's work stressed the social structure of freedom. He emphasized the value of the individual over the "masses" of society. He examined the deleterious effects of the welfare state on individual character, and showed how it destroys not only individual initiative but moral strength as well. The key to preserving liberty against governmental tendencies to totalitarianism, he argued, comes from maintaining strong mediating institutions, such as the family, civic groups, and local government. Although Röpke strongly opposed the welfare state, his emphasis on these mediating institutions has made him known as a proponent of a "Third Way." According to this economic view, the structure of the economy should rest on free trade and a gold standard but should provide temporary assistance to maintain small businesses, families, and small communities.

Röpke stood out from the Austrians in other ways as well. For example, he was the only Austrian economist who expressed concerns about overpopulation. Hayek, by contrast, argued that more people meant more productivity, since labor is heterogeneous.[18]

Despite these differences, Röpke should properly be considered part of the Austrian School, not least for the contributions he made to trade cycle theory. In his book *Crises and Cycles* (1936), he gave a wonderful description of the state of the economy in a time of recession, when businessmen are neither willing nor able to borrow, and often banks are too nervous to lend. Röpke's insightful analysis of bank lending and borrowing added significantly to the outline of the cycle given by Hayek and Mises. He put meat on the skeleton of the theory, making it much more understandable.[19]

And Röpke's contributions were not confined to theory. He played a profound role in the post–World War II revitalization of West Germany. Writing from Switzerland during the war, he published books and articles on what should be the foundation of a new German economic order. He advocated a complete break from statism, calling for a repudiation of the disastrous economic policies of Bismarck and Hitler. Röpke's views influenced Ludwig Erhard, who became German finance minister and, later, chancellor.[20] Following Röpke's recommendations, Germany stabilized the mark by tying it to the Bretton Woods agreement, linking it to gold. In addition, the government established free markets by abruptly removing all wage and price controls. It also sold off numerous state industries, including the famous Volkswagen Automobile Works. Erhard lowered tariff barriers and campaigned for free trade. It was a huge success, as Germany became the locomotive that pulled Europe from the economic doldrums of World War II, and prevented the expansion of communism.

The "German Miracle" put Röpke squarely in the winner's circle of international finance.

Last of the Vienna Line: Richard von Strigl

Richard von Strigl (1891–1942) was the last of the Austrian School to actually teach at the University of Vienna. His premature death in 1942 ended the line that began with Carl Menger seventy years earlier.

Strigl specialized in the study of capital and the trade cycle. To form and maintain capital, he pointed out, requires a subsistence fund, or savings. As people save money, they give up their ability to purchase consumer goods; in exchange, they receive interest income. Entrepreneurs borrow from this "subsistence fund" to pay workers to build capital goods. All workers need to be paid today to produce capital goods that will be more valuable in the future. Strigl argued that the subsistence fund is "capital in potency." It can be transformed into any type of capital good during the production process, as it can be used to pay workers to build railroads, construct buildings, add inventory, and so on. The greater the savings, the greater the amount of capital goods potentially available.

"Anarcho-Capitalism": Murray Rothbard

Murray Rothbard (1926–1995) was another protégé of Ludwig von Mises. He is best known as both an economic historian and a historian of economic thought. Perhaps most notably, his work on the Great Depression challenged the mythology that the economic devastation was caused by laissez-faire capitalism, that Herbert Hoover did nothing to alleviate it, and that Franklin Roosevelt solved the problems. In his book *America's Great Depression* (1963), Rothbard showed that the Depression followed an artificial boom created and exacerbated by constant government intervention—exactly as the Austrian theory of the trade cycle predicts. Far from being an inactive president, Hoover actually initiated many of the programs carried out in Roosevelt's New Deal, including tax increases, large government spending programs, and price support programs. In other historical works, such as *The Panic of 1819* (1962), Rothbard gave detailed accounts of the effects of government intervention throughout the nineteenth and twentieth centuries.

Rothbard made many contributions in the world of economic theory as well. He worked heavily on the concept of monopoly, for example. He argued that in the absence of governmental restrictions—or, put differently, when there is free entry into the marketplace—monopolies are not a problem. It is nonsense, he felt, to define a monopoly as a price setter; any market producer always has control over his price. The main decision for a businessman is how many products he wants to sell. Every entrepreneur assumes a downward-sloping demand curve; in other words, as prices are lowered, the more of his products will be sold.

Of all the Austrian economists, Rothbard was the most politically active and interested in political theory. He outlined the theory of "anarcho-capitalism," which, as the name implies, has a strong bent toward anarchy. Rothbard held that the spontaneous operation of the marketplace could replace governments, private markets could take the place of courts, and insurance companies could replace a public police.

In this regard, Rothbard stood far apart from Ludwig von Mises, who, along with Dietrich von Hildebrand, was a member of a committee sympathetic to the idea of restoring the Habsburg monarchy following World War II.[21]

The Austrian School Today

Although these economists represent some of the most influential members of the Austrian School, they are by no means the only figures who have contributed to Austrian economics. In fact, Austrian thinking has spread in recent decades—if not to the halls of the Ivy League or Washington, then at least among an increasingly significant contingent of economists, historians, and authors.

Much of that growth can be attributed to modern popularizers like Leonard E. Read (1898–1983), Hans F. Sennholz (1922–2007), and Llewellyn Rockwell (1944–). Read was not an academic, but he was a prolific author who wrote twenty-nine books. He also founded the Foundation for Economic Education, the first modern libertarian think tank in the United States. Read is probably best known for his remarkable essay "I, Pencil," which traces the manufacturing of the simple leaded writing instrument through its dizzying structure of production in several continents. His compelling testimony to the power of the market gained renewed fame when Nobel Prize–winning economist Milton Friedman (who is not part of the Austrian School) included the story as part of his legendary PBS television series, *Free to Choose.*

Sennholz was born and raised in Germany—he served during the Second World War—but then came to the United States, where he became the first student to earn a PhD under Ludwig von Mises in this country. A longtime professor of economics at Grove City College and later the president of the Foundation for Economic Education, he was also popular on the lecture circuit. Sennholz exerted a profound influence on one of today's best-known proponents of Austrian economics, Congressman Ron Paul. Paul has said that getting to know Sennholz and Murray Rothbard "really got me fascinated with studying economics."[22] Larry Reed, a student of Sennholz, carries on his work as president of the foundation.

Rockwell, who served as Paul's chief of staff from 1978 to 1982, is among the most influential and recognized Austrian economists today. He runs the popular website LewRockwell.com, which features essays by, and interviews with, many scholars and writers in the Austrian School. Moreover, he is the founder and chairman of the Ludwig von Mises Institute, which describes itself as "the world center of the Austrian School of economics and libertarian political and social theory."[23] Although Rockwell, Rothbard, and others have emphasized libertarianism in their teaching of the Austrian School, it should be noted that libertarianism, as a political movement emphasizing individual liberty, is distinct from Austrian economics. Most of the Austrians did their work before the coming of the libertarians, and there are many libertarians who would not consider themselves part of the Austrian School—for example, Milton Friedman.

Economists continue to develop Austrian theory. Israel Kirzner (1930–) has made significant contributions with his analysis of the entrepreneur and the role of knowledge and information in the marketplace. Kirzner presents the economy as two separate markets—one for productive services (which include all the factors of production that go into making final products), and the other for consumer goods. The entrepreneur is the liaison between the two, the master of knowledge and the creator of information.

Both Roger Garrison (1944–) and Mark Skousen (1947–) have offered valuable explanations of the Austrian theory of the trade cycle. Just as important, they present Austrian economics in terms that are common to modern-day economics. In the book *Time and Money*, for example, Garrison developed an Austrian macroeconomic point of view, bringing core Austrian concepts together with the production-possibility curve used in most economics texts today.

Skousen is best known for advancing Austrian trade cycle theory in his book *The Structure of Production*, in which he links Austrian theory to modern finance. His universal four-stage macro model accurately reflects the dynamics of the global economy, including technological changes, asset bubbles, and commodity inflation. Skousen is also one of the first Austrian economists to explain the differences in the various types of inflation and how they affect the economy (a matter we will explore in chapter 12). Moreover, he has developed a new national aggregate statistic, gross domestic expenditures (GDE), that is an advance on gross domestic product (GDP) because it accounts for economic activity at all stages of production, not just the end product. Another Skousen innovation is an alternative to the Keynesian aggregate supply-and-demand model; describing production and savings as vectors, Skousen's alternative does a better job explaining the trade cycle.

Fair Warning

Although the Austrian School is not well recognized by the academy, four factors indicate its influence and continued relevance: first, the fact that so many other modern schools of economic thought have adopted its original insights; second, its correct predictions, particularly regarding the fall of communism and socialism and the trade or business cycle; third, its relevance in diagnosing today's economic problems; and last, its insight that the overreliance on mathematical models in economic analysis is misguided and dangerous.

As we have seen, Austrian principles permeated mainstream economic thinking by the early twentieth century. One of the standard textbooks of the 1950s and 1960s, *A History of Economic Thought* by John Fred Bell, acknowledged the significant contributions of the Austrians. Describing Austrian School founders Carl Menger, Friedrich von Wieser, and Eugen von Böhm-Bawerk, the textbook noted: "The contributions of the men and the influence of their theories rank them above all others after the classical school. Indeed, a comparison of the height of the 'pinnacles of fame' for the two schools would probably give the Austrians the advantage. Certainly no other group added so much to the body of pure economic theory as did the Austrians. The intellectual debt of all economists to the body of doctrines developed in the years from 1871 to 1889 by the Austrian economists is indeed great. Their contributions provide some of the strongest warp threads in the garment of economic theory."[24]

Even where the Austrians seemingly depart from other schools, as with their theory of the trade cycle, there are more commonalities than is typically assumed. Ludwig von Mises made this point when he objected to calling his interpretation of the causes and course of the trade cycle "Austrian." In fact, he said, "the Circulation Credit Theory is a continuation, enlargement, and generalization of ideas first developed by the British Currency School and some additions to them made by later economists, among them also the Swede, Knut Wicksell."[25]

Even Keynesians accept many of the Austrians' fundamental views on the trade cycle. Keynesians share the Austrian view that business fluctuations are closely connected to imbalances between savings and investment. They disagree only on the cause of such imbalances: Austrians attribute it to malinvestment caused by credit expansion, whereas Keynesians blame a lack of entrepreneurial opportunity and a fall in consumption. Even Keynes admitted, however, that credit expansion can precipitate booms and busts. Keynesians and Austrians also agree on the importance of investment over the course of the trade cycle. They just disagree on the effectiveness of state action, with Keynesians seeing government spending as the key to making up for a shortfall in investment. Finally, Keynesians agree with Austrians that at the bottom of the cycle it is difficult to revive the economy. Keynes called this the liquidity trap: the situation in which businessmen are afraid to invest because they feel prices will continue to fall and therefore expansion of the currency will have no effect.

The U.S. government and other Western governments seized on Keynesian thinking in the Great Depression and for decades thereafter, largely ignoring Austrian warnings about state interference in markets. Austrian economists saved their sternest warnings for communism. They hammered away at central planning, predicting that this economic system was doomed to failure, mainly because it provided no reliable pricing structure to accurately relay information throughout the market. Their predictions, of course, were borne out.

Austrians also warned about problems in the U.S. economy. As noted, since the recent crisis began, many non-Austrian economists have conceded that a major source of the disaster was an overreliance on mathematic modeling among bankers, financial managers, and economists. But the Austrians warned about more fundamental problems as well—most notably, interest rates that the Federal Reserve kept artificially low and an unsustainable housing bubble. For instance, in February 2007, Peter Schiff published the book *Crash Proof: How to Profit from the Coming Economic Collapse*, in which he used Austrian theory to predict—accurately, as we now know—the collapse of the housing market and the broader economy. Similarly, throughout the 1990s and early 2000s the Ludwig von Mises Institute published essays and ran conferences focused on problems in the economy. To take just one example, in June 2004, Mises Institute resident fellow Mark Thornton published the article "Housing: Too Good to Be True," in which he wrote, "What the prophets of the new housing paradigm don't discuss is that real estate markets have experienced similar cycles in the past and that periods described as new paradigms are often followed by periods of distress in real estate markets, including foreclosure sales, bankruptcy and bank failures."[26]

Such warnings were not heeded. Nor did the U.S. government listen to Austrian prescriptions for the economic crisis as it launched a Keynesian response, with massive government spending to try to create jobs and "stimulate" the economy. More than three years into the crisis, unemployment remained stubbornly high and growth was minimal.

Meanwhile, Austrians sadly shook their heads, saying, *It didn't have to be this way.*

Part II

How We Got Here

4

The Age of Classical Liberalism

It may be hard to imagine today, but only a hundred years ago the Western world had an economic system that was probably the best in history. Inflation was nonexistent, and there was free and open trading throughout the world. There was also price stability: for a full century the price of a loaf of bread remained about the same. At every level of society in America and Europe, people saw their standards of living ratchet up continually. People lived longer, diseases were wiped out, and literacy spread. These were years of monumental technological achievement, unprecedented economic growth, and extraordinary population growth. Most important, for a century after the end of the Napoleonic Wars, peace reigned virtually everywhere. While small-scale or localized military conflicts broke out on occasion, there was nothing on the scale of previous wars.

This state of general peace and prosperity began in 1815, but it was prefigured in three major events that took place in 1776: the signing of the Declaration of Independence, the invention of the steam engine, and the publication of Adam Smith's *Wealth of Nations*.[1] These three events laid the foundations for the successes that followed in what has been called the age of classical liberalism. The first event marked the political basis for classical liberalism, standing for personal freedom, private initiative, freedom of movement, and respect for individual rights; the second represented the technological advances that ushered in the phenomenal growth of the Industrial Revolution; and the third was a landmark in the development of classical economics, which—like the Austrian School that came later—was committed to free markets, free trade, private property, stable currency, individual liberty, and a well-articulated division of labor to raise living standards. On these foundations were built the economic and political policies that sustained peaceful prosperity throughout the nineteenth century and into the twentieth.

Then, in 1914, things fell apart. The First World War came, and the world has not been the same since.

The Age of Classical Liberalism

The term *liberalism* has a number of different meanings. In the modern American experience, we typically identify liberalism with certain social and political causes, such as social justice and equal rights, and with the idea that the government should play the leading role in addressing unemployment, poverty, the lack of health care, and other social ills.[2] Classical liberalism, as it developed in the nineteenth century, was different. Committed to individual liberty and limited government, classical liberalism emphasized free trade and a free economy operating under a rule of law. From these principles flowed political and economic policies that ushered in a century of peaceful prosperity before the First World War.

Although the ideas of classical liberalism predominated in the nineteenth century, modern liberalism—or political liberalism—can trace its roots back nearly as far. If 1776 represents a useful starting point for classical liberalism, 1789 marks a watershed in the history of political liberalism. For in 1789 the French Revolution began.

The French Revolution was an uprising against the monarchical and aristocratic order. The *philosophes* who inspired the revolution emphasized progress and distrusted tradition and religion. Thus the French Revolution had a secular bent, emphasizing democratic voting and extending the franchise. After a lofty proclamation of principles at the outset, including the "Declaration of the Rights of Man and of the Citizen," the revolution quickly devolved into warfare and a bloody Reign of Terror. Nonetheless, some Europeans embraced the principles of the French Revolution. As Carlton J. H. Hayes notes in his history of modern Europe, in the early nineteenth century "a large number of intellectuals and middle-class persons and artisans were calling themselves 'liberals' and were disposed to subvert the old order of class distinctions, established religion, absolute monarchy, and dynastic states, in favor of a new order of social equality, ecclesiastical disestablishment, constitutional monarchy, and national states."[3]

These were decidedly not the principles of classical liberalism. Where political liberalism is rooted in the French Revolution, nearly every foundation of the age of classical liberalism can be located in the American Founding. Consider three crucial American documents: the Declaration of Independence, the Northwest Ordinance, and the Constitution.

The Declaration, as noted, laid out the political principles of classical liberalism, especially individual rights and liberty. But classical liberalism distinguished itself by its emphasis on economic as well as political principles. That combination of the economic and political can be seen in the Northwest Ordinance, which Thomas Jefferson initially proposed in 1784 and Congress ratified on July 13, 1787. This ordinance contained all the principles of the rule of law that would be found in the Constitution and Bill of Rights that soon followed. In addition, it prohibited the practice of slavery in the new Northwest Territories; recognized property rights, the rights of contract, and the right to a fair and open trial by jury; mandated that the courts operate according to the common law; promoted education and religion; and prohibited cruel and unjust punishments.

The U.S. Constitution, which all thirteen states had ratified by May 1790, codified the Northwest Ordinance. The Constitution put forth the major tenets of classical liberalism, both political and economic: limited government and limited taxation, the rule of law, the protection of private property, the inviolability of contract, the use of specie (gold and silver) as money, and free trade, especially among the states.[4] The American Founders, in short, not only were aware of the importance of trade and property but actually made provisions for free markets and specie-based money systems.

Of the principles outlined in America's founding documents, four would become central to the economic success and general peace that characterized the age of classical liberalism: the rule of law (including the sacredness of contracts), limited taxation and economic freedom, free trade, and a metallic-based currency.

The rule of law: The rule of law and the sanctity of contract, concepts that lie at the root of the entire Western tradition, proved central to the prosperity and peace of the nineteenth century. The concepts have been attributed to another member of the School of Salamanca, political theorist Francisco Suárez, SJ (1548–1617), who applied natural law principles to society. He believed that the actions of governments should be predictable and limited by written law, and thus he emphasized the importance of constitutions. Suárez outlined the principle of *nulla lege sine poena,* or "no punishment without law"—meaning that the actions of governments should not be arbitrary but rather should proceed only according to established law. The type of administrative law that today's bureaucracies issue was virtually unknown, and unimaginable.

In his study of classical liberalism, Professor Gottfried Dietze identifies the United States and Great Britain as leaders in the rule-of-law movement.[5] This emphasis on the rule of law and respect for contracts, along with other components of classical liberalism, helped those two countries achieve incredible prosperity in the nineteenth century. In fact, economic growth in the United States and Great Britain far outpaced that of the rest of the world. From 1820 (after Britain adopted the gold standard) until 1913, the British gross domestic product increased sixfold; the U.S. economy grew *forty-one* times over. The rest of the world's economies increased threefold during the same period.[6]

Low taxation and economic freedom: The principle of low taxation and small government was a second feature of the era of classical liberalism. America's Founders had carefully written into the Constitution provisions to limit taxation by government. Those provisions proved remarkably successful throughout the nineteenth century, as the United States did not have an income tax, an inheritance tax, or a corporate tax. Economic freedom prevailed—and not just in America. Following the Napoleonic Wars, Great Britain repealed numerous taxes, including income taxes. In 1832, Parliament actually repealed more laws than it passed. Cultural historian Christopher Dawson wrote of this phenomenon, "In England the bloodless victory of constitutional reform in 1832 inaugurated a long period of social peace and economic progress."[7] British historian A. J. P. Taylor noted that as late as 1914, "The Englishman paid taxes on a modest scale . . . rather less than 8 percent of national income."[8]

Classical liberalism's emphasis on economic freedom rested in part on the idea that the economy was self-correcting. This concept is generally attributed to a school of scholars in eighteenth-century France known as the Physiocrats, which included such notables as A. R. J. Turgot (1727–1781). It was the Physiocrats who coined the term *laissez-faire*, or "let do," conveying the idea that the government should leave things alone. They called for lower taxes, freer trade, and much less government regulation. These ideas became widespread in the nineteenth century. In fact, nearly every economist during the age of classical liberalism (at least before Karl Marx) believed that the automatic operations of the market would cure shortages and surpluses, raise living standards, correct monopolies, and allocate resources efficiently without government intervention. Like the Physiocrats before them, classical liberals called for laissez-faire, seeing the intervention of government as the most important obstacle to economic stability.

To be sure, the nineteenth century witnessed many calls for government intervention in the economy, especially in the form of tariffs and subsidies. But compared to the interventionism, regulation, and burdensome levels of taxation that have become the norm in the modern world, the age of classical liberalism was characterized by much more economic freedom and respect for the rule of law.

International free trade: A third defining principle of this era was international free trade. Although many thinkers promoted free markets, Adam Smith spearheaded the charge. In the first chapter of *The Wealth of Nations*, he presented the founding principle of modern economics, the nature of the division of labor, showing the economic efficiency of human cooperation and specialization. From this presentation he drew out his case for free trade and economic liberty, arguing that it is human cooperation under the division of labor that produces wealth, not the possession of gold and silver reserves, as the mercantilists believed.

Underlying the principles of free trade and laissez-faire is the idea that a harmony of interests is possible among all men and nations. French economist Frédéric Bastiat (1801–1850) expressed this concept in his work *Economic Harmonies*, pointing out that men better one another through trade and peaceful exchange. The harmony-of-interests doctrine became an accepted premise of the classical liberal system. (Of course,

Marx sharply contradicted Bastiat with his theory that the capitalist class exploited the worker—setting in motion forces that ultimately would end the age of classical liberalism.)

The age of classical liberalism witnessed thriving free trade. The Founders of the United States set the tone for the era. By prohibiting the states from passing tariffs against one another, the Constitution set up the largest free market at that time, and therefore put in place the most awesome economic engine in history. We have already seen how dramatically the U.S. economy grew during the nineteenth century.

Great Britain also offers a clear case of the success of free trade during this period. In 1815, Britain instituted protectionist measures known as the Corn Laws. The country was at war with Napoleon's France at the time, and British officials justified the laws on the grounds of national security, arguing for self-sufficiency in food production to protect against an economic blockade. But lobbying by large landlords and the agricultural sector kept the food tariffs in place for decades after the wars ended. Finally, in 1846, classical liberal reformers persuaded Sir Robert Peel's government to repeal the Corn Laws. That move started a trend of trade liberalization: as economic historian Jim Powell points out, "during the next three decades, England reduced the number of dutiable imports from 1,152 to 48." As a result, England prospered, Powell writes, "England became the unquestioned leader of world shipping, commerce, insurance, and finance."[9] British historian George Winter sums up the matter: "If we consider poverty stricken Great Britain and her three undeveloped Dominions at the time of the Repeal of the Corn Laws in 1846, and study them again before the outbreak of the First World War, after only 68 years of Britain's free trade policy, they present what must surely be the world's greatest example of rapid economic growth. The only comparable development is that of the United States during the same period. . . . Between 1855 and 1913 Britain's national income quadrupled, while her population and standard of living both doubled. Between 1846 and 1914 her exports were multiplied 8½ times. Never has the policy of allowing men to buy and sell just as they like, free from state interference, been more completely vindicated."[10]

The gold standard: The fourth factor in the economic success of the era of classical liberalism was the adoption of metallic standards, particularly gold, for money. Here again, the United States was an important early example, having adopted such a specie standard in the Constitution. The Founders had learned from their initial experience with a national currency. During the Revolutionary War, the Continental Congress issued paper bills of credit not backed by specie, and runaway inflation, along with counterfeiting and other abuses, quickly robbed the bills of their value. By 1779 the bills were worth ¹/₂₅ of their original value—hence the expression "not worth a Continental." Supreme Court justice Joseph Story (1779–1845), who offered some of the best commentary on the classical liberal nature of the Constitution, noted that "all public confidence was lost" in the Continental currency, and that "private evils . . . were so enormous that the whole country seemed involved in the general bankruptcy; and fraud and chicanery obtained in undisputed mastery." The Constitution fixed the problem, creating "healthy and sound currency, and solid credit which constitute the true foundation of our prosperity, industry, and enterprise."[11] Indeed, a system of metallic-based currency ushered in about one hundred years of no inflation, stable exchange rates and money, and as a result very low interest rates.

Other countries experienced similar success when they followed suit. Historians date the adoption of the international gold standard to Napoleon in 1815, or to Britain in 1819–21. Once countries established convertibility of their currencies with a specific weight of gold, the market proceeded automatically to handle the flow of goods and gold across borders. Historian John Lukacs observed that this was "one of the most extraordinary phenomena of the one hundred years before 1914," though it has received little attention. "Money continued to be good as gold, and as solid as the rock of Gibraltar. In 1900 the pound, the dollar, the franc, the florin, the crown, the mark, the lira—all of these national currencies with their names that reach back to the Middle Ages—were worth, in each other's terms, the same everywhere. Their value had not changed in decades, for some of them not in one hundred years. They were available in the form of gold pieces (except in the United States during the Civil War), silver coins, and bills, freely exchangeable at one's convenience."[12]

Even today, economists look back to that period as a golden age. Benn Steil, director of international economics for the Council on Foreign Relations, writes: "Capital flows were enormous, even by contemporary standards. . . . Currency crises occurred during this period, but they were generally shallow and short-lived. That is because money was then—as it has been throughout most of the world and most of human history— gold, or at least a credible claim on gold."[13]

These four elements—adherence to the rule of law, low taxation and economic freedom, free trade, and a specie-based currency—combined to create the golden age that was the era of classical liberalism. The age of classical liberalism had an impressive record of achievement, most of which came through individual initiative. It was the age of inventions and the application of new technology in the fields of medicine, agriculture, communications, and travel, to name a few. Population exploded largely because the infant mortality rate fell. The average standard of living doubled, and then doubled again. The average life expectancy in 1800 was about twenty-plus years of age, which was about the same as in Roman times; it increased to about forty-five years of age by 1900.

It should be noted, however, that the age of classical liberalism was not perfect from an economic standpoint. Even with these four key elements holding sway, trade cycles were a recurrent problem. That is because government interventionism is remarkably difficult to fend off. As is the case today, bank credit inflation was a problem. In the United States, the expansion and contraction of credit led to severe fluctuations.[14] In Britain, there developed two schools of economic thought to explain and tame trade cycles. The first group, called the Currency School, saw bank credit inflation as producing overexpansion and malinvestment. It was from this school that Austrian economists first began their study on the problems of the business cycle. In 1844 the Currency School convinced Sir Robert Peel's government to reform Britain's banking laws, forbidding banks to expand loans without gold reserve. The banking system, however, found a way around the law by issuing checks and money substitutes. An opposing school, called the Banking School, defended the expansion of bank credit and blamed downturns on other factors.[15] The debate has continued in various forms into our own century.

Still, the strengths of the age of classical liberalism outweighed its problems, especially in comparison with what has come after it. The era bore out one of classical liberals' chief assumptions, that free trade would promote peace among nations because commercial activity depended on economic interdependence. Between 1815 and 1914, Europe did not see a continental war, let alone a world war. Conflicts were limited to those that came from expansion, as certain European countries attempted to pacify overseas empires, or from unification efforts such as those of Germany and Italy in the 1860s and 1870s. Otherwise conflicts were local in nature, such as the Franco-Prussian War (1870–71). By 1875, even most of the European revolutionary fever following the French Revolution had run its course.

With the end of the American Civil War (1861–65), most of the advanced world settled down to what the French called *La Belle Époque*, or "The Beautiful Era" (1875–1914). It was a period of peace, prosperity, and the expectation of continued economic and social advancement. Looking back after the Great War, John Maynard Keynes called it "an extraordinary episode in the economic progress of man." During that age, Keynes wrote, "any man of capacity or character at all exceeding the average" could vault himself "into the middle and upper classes, for whom life offered, at low cost and with the least trouble, conveniences, comforts, and amenities beyond the compass of the richest and most powerful monarchs of other ages."[16]

It was also an era of individual rights, certainly compared with the experience of previous generations. During this era the Western powers effectively ended slavery, which had been a part of certain societies going back to biblical days. And, except in the case of the United States, they did so without war, largely because classical liberal thinkers strongly opposed slavery on moral as well as economic grounds. The broader society, meanwhile, enjoyed many freedoms and was generally spared the intrusions of the state. A. J. P. Taylor offered a fitting summary of this age:

Until August 1914 a sensible, law-abiding Englishman could pass through life and hardly notice the existence of the state, beyond the post office and the policeman. He could live where he liked and as he liked. He had no official number or identity card. He could travel abroad or leave his country forever without a passport of any sort of official permission. He could exchange his money for any other currency without restriction or limit. He could buy goods from any country in the world on the same terms as he bought goods at home. For that matter, a foreigner could spend his life in this country without permit and without informing the police.[17]

Foundations of the Coming New Age

Given the rapid betterment of individual lives and of society, optimism became the spirit of the age. With so much advancing so quickly, philosophers and other thinkers began to expect that social and material improvements would continue unimpeded. Many came to believe that improvements were occurring not because of specific policies and conditions in place but because mankind had arrived at a stage of history in which the march of Progress was inexorable. This view became a powerful undercurrent in the age of classical liberalism. The expectation of continuing progress was fundamental to utopian visions outlined in the nineteenth century, especially socialist visions.

Like the French Revolution, socialism and the more moderate progressivism—a movement that began to flower in the United States in the late nineteenth century—were rooted in faith in Enlightenment thinking, an emphasis on egalitarianism, and distrust of private property and traditional institutions such as the family. Also like the French Revolution, these movements often took a materialist or secularist approach (though many early progressives emphasized the "Social Gospel," using Christianity to promote their ideals).[18] Moreover, they were united in calling for expanded state power: the proper role of government, according to socialism and progressivism, was not to keep order in society but to *transform* society.[19] To fund such an active government role would require increased taxation, especially through income taxes. Increased state authority also meant more state control of the economy, particularly through regulatory bodies and an expanded role for the central bank—in other words, manipulations of the money supply.[20]

Just as the United States was a precursor and exemplar for the age of classical liberalism, Otto von Bismarck's Germany provided a model for changes to come in the twentieth century. Having founded the German Empire in 1871, Bismarck needed to establish an independent source of income for the central government. He chose to impose tariffs, thus rejecting the classical liberal idea of free trade. He found immediately that he had allies among German farmers, who needed protection from imports of less expensive food from Russia and Poland. Bismarck realized that he could protect his own power and that of the Hohenzollern monarchy by extending the franchise to the German peoples and appealing to their desires. Because socialist ideas appealed to the masses of voters, he began implementing a social welfare state, adopting a socialist program of old-age pensions, universal health care, and cartelization of German industry.[21]

Bismarck received intellectual support for this program from a group of economists belonging to the German Historical School. The most prominent of these were Adolph Wagner (1835–1917), an intimate of Bismarck, and Gustav von Schmoller (1838–1917). Known as Socialists of the Chair, they supported government interventionism, arguing that the state should play the primary role in the economy.[22] In this regard, they clearly disagreed with the Austrian School, which was emerging in the 1870s as Bismarck was remaking Germany.

Bismarck, however, did not embrace socialist views; he merely used socialist policies as the means to strengthen state power, as historian A. J. P. Taylor pointed out:

> Of course, Bismarck did not promote social reform out of love for the German workers. Sympathy and affection had never been his strong points. His object was to make the workers less discontented or, to use a harsher phrase, more subservient. He said in 1881: "Whoever has a pension for his old age is far more content and far easier to handle than one who has no such prospect. Look at the difference between a private servant and a servant in the chancellery or at court; the latter would put up with much more, because he has a pension to look forward to."

Bismarck's cynical view helps explain the resilience of the social welfare systems that were created in the twentieth century. Writing from the perspective of the 1950s, Taylor added, "Social Security has certainly made the masses less independent everywhere; yet even the most fanatic apostle of independence would hesitate to dismantle the system which Bismarck invented and which all other democratic countries have copied."[23]

Sure enough, Bismarck's welfare state was copied. The Austrian economist F. A. Hayek observed that "Germany became the center from which the ideas destined to govern the world in the twentieth century spread east and west. . . . Whether it was socialism in its more radical form or merely 'organization' or 'planning' of a less radical kind, German ideas were everywhere readily imported and German institutions imitated."[24]

German ideas soon reached west to England. In 1883—the year of Karl Marx's death—a socialist movement known as the Fabian Society was launched in Britain.[25] The society took its name from Quintus Fabius Maximus, a Roman general in the third century B.C. who avoided head-on conflict with Hannibal, instead favoring a war of attrition. As its symbol, the society chose a wolf in sheep's clothing. Both the name and the symbol were fitting, for the Fabian Society operated on the principle that the people of England would not accept socialism under its own colors but would accept it under the guise of social programs claiming to help the poor and laborers. Rather than calling for revolution, then, the Fabians committed themselves to achieving socialism in small steps. Attracting well-known intellectual leaders of English society, including George Bernard Shaw and H. G. Wells, the Fabians formed the foundation of the British Labour Party and ultimately helped nationalize many industries after World War II. In addition, they helped construct Britain's National Health Service.

Thus, in the waning years of the nineteenth century, Germany and Britain led the way in turning away from reliance on free markets and individual initiative for the overall betterment of society. Of course, classical liberal principles and policies established the prosperity that provided resources to fund the new governmental planning. But this was a lesson that leaders failed to heed when the crisis of World War I erupted; they turned away from the tried and true that had led to a century of peaceful prosperity and forged ahead with state intervention. In response to a tremendous disruption of civilized life, they embarked on a new age.

The Great War and the End of an Age

The general peace and prosperity of the age of classical liberalism came to a crashing halt on June 28, 1914, with the assassination of Archduke Franz Ferdinand, the heir to the Austrian throne. The murder set in motion a series of events that led to World War I and set the stage for the most important, and incomprehensibly tragic, events of the twentieth century.

By August 1914 the Allied Powers, made up of France, Great Britain, Russia, and Romania (they would later be joined by Italy and the United States), were at war with the Central Powers—Germany, Austria, and Turkey. In most of Europe's capital cities there was wild enthusiasm for the war, as historians Frank Chambers, Christina Phelps Grant, and Charles Bayley point out: "The British House of Commons on August 3, the German Reichstag on August 4, the French Chamber on August 4, the Russian Duma on August 8, expressed their respective wills with all but complete unanimity. For the men and women who lived through the first week of August 1914, the outstanding impression was of the cheering, singing, marching masses."[26] Nearly all parties concerned miscalculated the intensity and duration of the war.

It was not long before the savagery of modern technology began to take its toll on both soldiers and civilians. New weapons included the machine gun, the submarine, heavily armored battleships, airplanes, and poison gas. Generals ordered millions of young men into the vortex of death.

Most tragically, it did not have to be this way. Economist Wilhelm Röpke pointed out: "If all nations and their leaders had solely and with total clarity borne their economic interests in mind, the First World War—of which the Second is only a worse continuation—need never have broken out. . . . Never before had an objective and nationally developed interest in peace been greater among all peoples than at that time, never before had the bare existence of such a number of human beings been directly dependent on the preservation of peace." The fact that war did break out despite all this, Röpke maintained, demonstrated that "the spiritual and sociological foundations of the system had fallen into disorder, and thus very thoroughly and disastrously."[27]

But a miraculous reprieve occurred on Christmas Eve 1914: the troops on both sides ceased fighting, in contradiction of orders from their commanders. Soldiers hunkered down in trenches all along the five-hundred-mile Western Front began singing Christmas carols, instantly recognizable to their enemies across the way, who joined in. Recognizing their common culture, both sides left their trenches, declaring spontaneous truces up and down the front. Some truces lasted the whole week from Christmas to New Year's.

Pope Benedict XV, who had worked ceaselessly for peace, asked that the Christmas truce be extended and the war be stopped. The Germans and the Austrians accepted Benedict's offer, but the Allied Powers rejected it. In fact, when Italy joined the Allies in April 1915, the agreement affirming the alliance, the Treaty of London, decreed that the Vatican would have no part in an eventual peace treaty.[28]

This was a turning point. Had the war come to an end with the Christmas truce, many millions of lives would have been saved, and millions more would have been spared maiming. Instead, the deadly fighting lasted four more years, with each side continually escalating its use of force. The Great War was a harrowing example of "total war." Author John Barry notes that U.S. president Woodrow Wilson saw the war as "a crusade," and because of that, Wilson "intended to wage total war. Perhaps knowing himself even more than the country, he predicted, 'Once lead this people into war, and they'll forget there ever was such a thing as tolerance. To fight you must be brutal and ruthless, and the spirit of ruthless brutality will enter into the very fiber of our national life, infecting Congress, the courts, the policeman on the beat, the man in the street.' "[29]

The human cost of World War I was enormous: among all combatants, some nine million were killed, twenty-one million were wounded, and another eight million went missing or were prisoners of war. The social costs were staggering—all those lost children, husbands, and fathers, and the effects their deaths had on families and communities. The survivors, too, dealt with the consequences of the war: they have been immortalized as the Lost Generation.

Even beyond these tragic consequences, the rejected truce had economic consequences. Among the millions killed was a great deal of "human capital"—future leaders of banking, industry, government, the academy, and more. Austrian economist Benjamin Anderson gives a good example of how countries felt this loss. England, he writes, "lost an appalling percentage of her finest and best in that cruel war," including "very many of the younger men and even men no longer young who would normally become, in a short time, the leaders of industry and finance." These able leaders "ought to have been ruling the city of London," but instead they "were dead in France."[30] It is simply impossible to measure the damage done by the removal of so many young and energetic people. Every country, not just England, experienced a breaking of tradition and a loss of able leadership.

Another casualty of the rejected truce may have been the age of classical liberalism itself. After the Great War, the pillars of classical liberalism fell: the rule of law gave way to arbitrary government; taxation levels were raised to finance the war and then to pay off war debts, and economic freedom was curtailed (including by requiring passports for travel); worldwide trade was restricted, as was capital movement; and the gold standard was suspended, never to be restored.

The eventual peace treaty signed was so one-sided that it set in motion forces that would bring about another world war and worse terrors—the rise of ideology, inflation, protectionism, and nationalism. In real terms, World War I brought about Hitler, Lenin, Stalin, the Great Depression, the Holocaust, and World War II, to name just a few of its unintended consequences.[31] And so the age of classical liberalism, which began in 1815 with the Congress of Vienna, ended in 1919 with the Treaty of Versailles.

The contrast between those bookends is instructive. The Congress of Vienna, convened after Napoleon's defeat in 1814, was held to establish peace after nearly twenty-five years of continual war stemming from the French Revolution. Chaired by Austria's minister of state, Prince Metternich (1773–1859), the congress included ambassadors from virtually every European state. The hallmark of the Congress of Vienna was that the victors—Great Britain, Austria, Prussia, and Russia—sat down together with the vanquished, France, to construct a peace. Christopher Dawson wrote that these statesmen "faced the problem of European unity in a sane constructive spirit, without utopian illusions or nationalist prejudices. Their attempt to transform the old antagonistic principle of the Balance of Power into a practical system of international co-operation which was embodied in the Law of Treaties and the Concert of Europe was fundamentally sound, and it gave Europe a longer period of peace than it has ever known before or since."[32]

The Treaty of Versailles was entirely different. Tragically, there were no statesmen with the wisdom of Metternich. The victorious powers wanted to punish Germany for World War I, and they did. Rather than put together a workable peace, the winners inflicted extremely harsh terms on the German people. Germany lost a good deal of its land area, in particular its coal-producing regions. Meanwhile, the German people were saddled with enormous reparations, which for years hampered a European recovery and put the world economy off balance.

John Maynard Keynes, who attended the peace conference as an adviser to the British government, protested the treaty's terms in his book *The Economic Consequences of the Peace*, published in 1919. Calling the Treaty of Versailles a "Carthaginian Peace," Keynes argued that the German economy simply could not produce the revenues necessary to pay reparations. More to the point, he predicted that the treaty's terms would hamper economic recovery—not just for Germany but for other European economies as well. If the victorious powers end up "abusing their momentary victorious power to destroy Germany and Austria-Hungary now prostrate," he wrote, "they invite their own destruction also, being so deeply and inextricably intertwined with their victims by hidden psychic and economic bonds."[33]

The Treaty of Versailles went so far as to include a war-guilt clause, in which Germany was forced to accept total responsibility for the beginning of hostilities. Keynes rightly sensed that such vindictive terms could have devastating consequences far beyond the real of the economic. "But who can say," Keynes warned, "how much is endurable, or in what direction men will seek at last to escape from their misfortunes?"[34]

Sure enough, many Germans viewed the treaty—and the victors who forced the harsh terms upon them—with contempt. Soon the Germans would look to change the terms in the same manner that the treaty was imposed on them—by force.

5

Chaos

The Legacies of World War I

I f there is a word that most aptly describes the nearly one hundred years from 1914 to the present day, it is *chaos*.

Chaos? At first blush that might seem an unfair characterization of the past century. After all, this is a period that has brought technological innovations that even Jules Verne could not have imagined, innovations that have dramatically improved standards of living and extended human life. It is a period marked by lengthy periods of economic growth. It is a period that has featured magnificent leaders and laudable accomplishments. It is a period that has seen stupendous advances in every walk of life.

All this is true. But just as true is that, compared with the peace and prosperity of the age of classical liberalism, the world has been in a state of continual—and unnecessary—upheaval. Throughout this era we have barely recovered from one devastating war or other man-made calamity before going through another.

Chaos theory, developed by French mathematician Henri Poincaré and American meteorologist Edward Lorenz, holds that a small event can have extraordinary and completely unpredictable consequences. The classic illustration is the "butterfly effect," in which the flapping of a butterfly's wings in South America can create a hurricane in Texas. If this concept seems absurd, consider that a single bullet fired at an Austrian archduke in 1914 changed the entire world, toppling numerous governments that had ruled for centuries and creating financial mayhem that

79

continues unabated a century later. From that single bullet there followed bloodshed and cruelty on a scale mankind had never witnessed—warfare, genocide, mass executions, purges, forced famines. In the twentieth century some 169 million people were killed by *their own* governments—this compared with an estimated 133 million over the rest of recorded history.[1] Even the influenza epidemic of 1918–20, which killed as many as 100 million people worldwide, may well have been contained had it not been for the Great War. Strong evidence indicates that the influenza virus was carried to army camps in Kansas in 1918.[2] The virus became much more virulent as young men from these camps made the long voyage to fight in Europe. The first influenza outbreaks occurred precisely where American troops disembarked in France. The influenza epidemic is a perfect example of chaos theory at work.

Before the Great War, nobody could have predicted such a chain of events. Certainly the leaders of the nations that entered the war had no concept of the dark forces they were releasing. They were, after all, committing their resources in the "war to end all wars." But it didn't turn out that way. Instead, they brought the era of classical liberalism to an end and brought to the fore the murderous ideologies of communism, national socialism (Nazism), and fascism. Most of the evils of these hundred years can be traced to World War I and its aftermath. The war left in its wake enormous distortions in economic, financial, political, and moral life. The demons it unleashed spread far beyond the battlefields, into the capital cities of most nations, wreaking havoc everywhere as long-established customs and traditions were dismantled one after another. From an economic standpoint, World War I had three main consequences, all of which intermingled, worsening the damage. The first was inflation: This used to be an abstraction read about in history books, but today currencies throughout the world are worth a fraction of what they were in 1914. According to the U.S. Bureau of Labor Statistics, what cost $100 in 1913, just before the outbreak of the Great War, cost $2,202.59 in 2010. In other words, the dollar deteriorated to one-twentieth of its 1913 value. The second economic consequence of the war was the breakdown in world trade and the rise of protectionism. The third was the acceptance of greater government intervention, which swelled the size and scope of the state, curtailed individual liberty, and introduced systemic instability into the world's banking and financial structure. The combined effects of these three factors led to the economic and political crises of the 1930s and '40s.

The role of government dramatically increased in order to fight World War I, but the state's power also expanded domestically—and kept expanding long after the fighting ended. This was in keeping with the vision of the progressive movement in the United States, the Fabian Society in England, and Bismarck's welfare state in Germany. An interventionist government required new sources of financing hitherto unknown in those countries. One way central banks—including the U.S. Federal Reserve, created in 1913—secured this financing was by expanding bank credit. This became the basis of inflation in most of the world. The resulting currency instability became the basis of trade imbalances. These imbalances in turn led governments to institute protectionist policies

It must be noted that all of this economic damage—along with the horrific bloodshed of the twentieth century—has been perpetrated by government. And yet people continue to look to government for solutions to problems large and small. Today, with people across the world expecting the state to supply answers to the economic crisis, governments threaten to resurrect economic policies that led to crisis in the Great Depression.

We must understand the history of the past century—the terrible legacies of World War I and the long train of abuses by government—if we ever hope to restore the proper foundations of a free and prosperous society. It is a history that the Austrian School of economics has chronicled but that too often goes overlooked.

The First Legacy: The Age of Inflation

The first and most important issue to be considered is what the economist Jacques Rueff called the Age of Inflation.[3] Since the First World War, paper currencies have continually depreciated, leading to the disruption of both the capital market and foreign trade.

During the age of classical liberalism the world's major currencies were linked to gold. For one hundred years, therefore, inflation was practically unknown in Europe and the United States (except for the Civil War period). Because currencies were all tied to a particular reference point, they came in balance with one another, expanding and contracting in reference to gold. They were not undervalued or overvalued. Moreover, monetary policy was not subject to political decision-making. Countries could not lower the value of their currency by monetary expansion to achieve an export advantage.[4] The duty of the central bank was simply to keep the currency convertible into gold.

In the twentieth century that changed. In the United States the transition began even before World War I, when, in 1913, Congress created the Federal Reserve, a new central banking system.[5] But the experience of the war accelerated the involvement of central banks in the government budgetary process. Governments of the belligerent countries needed money to pay for the war, so most went off the gold standard. This allowed them to create money and credit to pay for the hostilities. When a government ran a deficit, the central bank stood ready to purchase the government's bonds by increasing bank credit. In essence, central banks—not an objective standard, gold—now set the value of currency. They created a new standard, statistical verification of the price level, and would announce that they had kept price increases within "acceptable" levels.[6] Even the U.S. government, which maintained convertibility to gold until the 1930s, discovered ways to manipulate money and credit that essentially superseded the gold standard.

After a hundred years of virtually no inflation—as historian Paul Johnson points out, "retail prices had actually fallen in many years, as increased productivity more than kept pace with rising demand"—the new system of monetary relativism produced inflation almost immediately. By the time of the Treaty of Versailles in 1919, Johnson observes, "wholesale prices, on a 1913 index of 100, were 212 in the USA, 242 in Britain, 357 in France and 364 in Italy. By the next year, 1920, they were two and a half times the pre-war average in the USA, three times in Britain, five times in France, and six times in Italy; in Germany the figure was 1965, nearly twenty times."[7]

Wartime inflation was only the beginning. After the war, many attempts were made to return to the gold standard, but to no avail. The world had changed: the age of classical liberalism was dead, along with the stability of the gold standard.

Soon countries were facing a second kind of inflation: that which resulted when governments simply printed money to finance government deficits. This is known as fiat money inflation. Still a third type of inflation occurred as governments expanded bank credit to try to stimulate economies.

Let's consider each of these types of inflation in turn.

The War Inflation

Why did prices shoot up so quickly during the Great War—more than doubling in the United States and Britain, and more than tripling in France and Italy? One of the best explanations for the wartime inflation comes from a study by Austrian economists C. A. Phillips, T. F. McManus, and R. W. Nelson. In *Banking and the Business Cycle*, they argue that the First World War "was probably the worst-financed war in history from the viewpoint of sound fiscal policy." In the past, the study notes, governments had received the bulk of their war financing from taxation. For example, tax revenue accounted for an estimated 63 percent of England's financing for the Napoleonic Wars, compared with just 17.5 percent for World War I.

The primary way governments covered the difference was through inflation. Phillips and his coauthors write that most nations "resorted to the age-old expedient of inflation of the note currency." Even worse, they expanded bank credit—"securing money from the banks by issuing bonds directly to them for which they pay by creating new credits in favor of the Government, or by selling bonds to individuals who cover their subscriptions by borrowing from banks the credits that are newly created for this purpose." To make the scheme work, central banks lowered local banks' reserve requirements—that is, they made "such advances to local banks as would enable them to maintain adequate reserves." This expansion of credit increased purchasing power, but it "was unaccompanied by an equal increase in production, and hence resulted in inflation." Little wonder, then, that economist Hartley Withers called the tactic of expanding bank credit "quite the worst way of raising money for war or any other purpose."[8]

How could this inflation continue in the United States, which was supposedly on the gold standard at the time? The newly created Federal Reserve System provided the U.S. government with the necessary room to manipulate credit. Phillips, McManus, and Nelson write: "Had it not been for the creation of the Federal Reserve System, . . . the ratio of reserves to deposit liabilities would have fallen to the legal minimum and prevented the further expansion of deposit credit, unless new reserves were acquired in some manner."[9] The Federal Reserve Act had cut member banks' minimum reserve requirements by about half. So, for example, under the old National Bank Act, $1 billion in reserves had supported about $5 billion of deposit credit; under the Federal Reserve Act, the same $1 billion supported about $10 billion of credit. Then, after the United States entered the Great War in 1917, Congress passed an amendment that reduced reserve requirements even further. With "its pooling and economizing of reserves," Phillips and the other economists conclude, the Federal Reserve "magnified several times" the U.S. banking system's ability to expand credit.[10]

Significantly, the government's lowering of bank reserve requirements was a process that the public generally did not understand. Thus the government could blame increased prices on the war effort rather than on its own manipulations.

As troubling as all this was, none of it could compare with what happened in Russia. In 1914, Russia had extremely high economic growth and a solid currency. In fact, the Russian currency was considered to be one of the strongest in the world, because the ruble was backed 98 percent by gold. But Russia was also one of the poorest of the belligerent countries, meaning that it had incredible difficulty financing its war effort. Historian Richard Pipes reports that Russia's war costs were equal to Britain's, while its national per capita income was barely one-sixth that of England.[11]

To pay for the war, Russia's czarist regime increased the amount of paper notes some 600 percent, dropping the gold content of the ruble from 98 percent in 1914 to 16.2 percent in January 1917.[12] Inflation soared, destroying the value of Russia's once-strong currency. By 1917 prices had increased 7.5 times over the 1913 level; by 1918 they had jumped 102 times; and by 1919 they had increased *923* times.[13] Meanwhile, industrial production fell precipitously, hollowing out Russia's economy.[14]

And who bore the burden of wartime inflation? Those holding the inflated currencies. Although wages tended to keep up with rising prices, whoever maintained fixed assets—including insurance policies, pension funds, bonds, savings accounts, and cash—saw inflation act as a massive tax that wiped out the value of such holdings. This inflation had an inordinate impact on the middle class, pensioners, religious and charitable institutions with fixed-rate endowments, and others that tended to hold their assets in fixed denominated securities. For example, a widow in the United States effectively would have been taxed approximately 60 percent on her assets, as a bond having $1,000 purchasing power in 1913 was worth only about $400 by 1919. In Great Britain this effective tax rate was 66 percent; in France, 80 percent; in Italy, 83 percent; in Germany, 95 percent; and in Russia, 999 percent.

In many cases the rate of inflation was closely correlated with the level of political instability in the country. For instance, skyrocketing inflation in Italy played a key role in bringing the fascist Benito Mussolini into power. In Germany, inflation prepared the way for the rise of Nazism. And in Russia, the resulting economic chaos provided an opening for the Bolsheviks and helped lead to the collapse of the czarist regime.

War inflation also made it much more difficult to return to a gold-backed currency once the hostilities ended, because gold reserves had to support anywhere from 2 to 5,200 percent of their prewar position. Jacques Rueff and other economists have argued that after the war there should have been a conference to revalue world currencies to a realistic level in order to support the new reserve position. This would have meant raising the price of gold to soak up the excess currency occasioned by the financing of World War I.

Fiat Inflation

Once World War I ended, a second type of inflation took hold: fiat inflation. In fact, fiat inflation—which results when a government prints money to cover its deficits, money that is not backed by gold—became one of the constant characteristics of government in the twentieth century, and is still with us today. The value of such printed money lies in the fact that it is legal tender in payment of debt and that governments promise to limit its issuance. A promise to limit its issuance also means that it is a limitation on government budgets. But as history has proved, it is extremely difficult to limit government spending.

A lack of limits is a distinguishing characteristic of fiat inflation. There is a limit when central banks expand bank credit or fiduciary credit: a central bank can literally create trillions in reserves, but banks must find people willing and able to borrow the money before the extra reserves have any effect. The public's actions thus determine—and limit—the amount of money put into circulation. With fiat inflation, however, a currency can inflate to such an extent that the monetary unit has no value whatsoever.

The most famous case of fiat inflation following World War I occurred in Germany. The great German inflation lasted from 1914 to 1923, with its most acute stage occurring between August and November of 1923. It was so sweeping that it completely wiped out the German middle class. As the German mark fell to an insignificant sliver of its value, pensions, savings accounts, and bonds became worthless. The iconic images of Germans hauling wheelbarrows full of cash capture the devastating price increases experienced during this period.[15]

Economist and educator Melchior Palyi, who was teaching at a Berlin college in 1923, gives a firsthand account of the effects of hyperinflation. Palyi recalls that his monthly salary was "raised from an inflated 10,000 marks or so in early 1922 to 10,000,000 marks by July, 1923, and the whole amount was being a paid twice a month; then, once a week; then once each day. The next step to meet the skyrocketing living cost was to pay us twice a day, in the morning and in the afternoon." By August 1923, he writes, 10 million marks "paid for a modest lunch." Palyi also recounts a conversation with fellow professor at the end of a workday: "The professor of physics overtook me. 'Are you taking the streetcar?' he asked. 'Yes,' I said. 'Let's hurry. The fare will be raised by 6 P.M. We may not be able to pay it.'"

Palyi concludes: "Galloping inflation threw the German economy into virtual chaos and demoralized large segments of the German people." As the middle-class influence vanished, it left an opening for political radicals who promised to revitalize the German economy. Palyi succinctly captures the long-term consequences of the German hyperinflation: "Adolf Hitler was the ultimate outcome."[16] It is no exaggeration to say that while Hitler was fathered by the Versailles Treaty, he was mothered by the great German inflation that wiped out the middle class.

But how did the German government allow inflation to get so out of control? Economist Costantino Bresciani-Turroni, author of the seminal study of the German inflation, provides the answer. In the immediate aftermath of the war, he writes, authorities "believed that the rapid reconstruction of German business would be helped by the incessant printing of notes." They also wished to pay off government debts more quickly. Initially, the plan showed signs of working: "The inflation retarded the crisis for some time. . . . At first inflation stimulated production because of the divergence between the internal and external value of the mark." But inevitably the fiat inflation led to disaster—decreased production, massive unemployment, and much more. Bresciani-Turroni recounts the effects of the inflation: "It annihilated thrift; it made reform of the national budget impossible for years; it obstructed the solution of the Reparations question; it destroyed incalculable moral and intellectual values. It provoked a serious revolution in social classes, a few people accumulating wealth and forming a class of usurpers of national property, whilst millions of individuals were thrown into poverty. It was a distressing preoccupation and constant torment of innumerable families; it poisoned the German people by spreading among all classes the spirit of speculation and by diverting them from proper and regular work, and it was the cause of incessant political and moral disturbance."[17]

Given all these repercussions, it is, as Bresciani-Turroni writes, "easy enough to understand why the record of the sad years of 1919 to 1923 always weighs like a nightmare on the German people." To this day the experience is emblazoned on the German memory. After the global economic crisis erupted in 2008, German chancellor Angela Merkel repeatedly warned the major economic powers not to rely on inflation or the expansion of credit.[18]

Germany is the best-known example of post–World War I fiat inflation, but it was not the only country to go through this process. Similar inflations occurred in Russia, Poland, Austria, and Hungary. In each case, political power was eventually transferred to radicals and dictators.

In Russia's case, the postwar inflation far outpaced the already staggering inflation the country had experienced during the war. Recall that at war's end, Russian prices were 923 times higher that they had been in 1913; by 1923 the price level was more than 648 *million* times greater than it had been a decade earlier. Paul Johnson writes, "About the only thing in plentiful supply was the paper rouble, which the printing presses poured out ceaselessly, and which had now fallen to little over 1 percent of its November 1917 value."[19]

Although the results of the Russian and German postwar inflations were similar, the governments had different reasons for inflating their currencies. The German government began its inflationary policies mainly so it could take care of its budget deficits. By contrast, Russia's communist regime set loose inflation as a deliberate act of destruction: the Bolsheviks wanted to eliminate any remnant of the former czarist society. The inflation allowed Lenin and his regime to consolidate their authority. It led to a centralization of state power, the elimination of the middle class, and a monstrous, diabolic dictatorship.

Bank Credit Inflation

The third type of postwar inflation, bank credit inflation, has also endured into the twenty-first century. It is the most dangerous type of inflation, because it the hardest to detect and because its effects are more far-reaching.

One of the contributions of the Austrian School is to recognize that capital is not homogeneous. In the case of inflation, this means that an increase in the money supply will not have uniform effects across the entire economy. Rather, as one of the first writers on economic theory, Richard Cantillon (1680–1734), observed, some people and institutions get access to the new money first, giving them an advantage because they can use the new money before prices increase; meanwhile, those who receive access to the money last are harmed. Because of the uneven distribution of new money, prices will rise at different rates in different sectors of the economy. This is known as the Cantillon effect. In short, inflation builds distortions into the economy. Based on this crucial observation, Austrian economists differentiate between inflations by looking at the *points of injection*—that is, where and to whom the new money goes.

The concept of points of injection helps us understand a key difference between fiat inflation and bank credit inflation. With fiat inflation, the money is distributed to the public first, as governments pay bills with newly printed bank notes. As such, funds are immediately injected into the consumer marketplace, and the prices of consumer goods begin to rise. Fiat inflation, then, becomes evident very quickly. As the prices of consumer goods rise, merchants and consumers attempt to protect themselves against the inflation they now expect to arrive.

In the case of bank credit inflation, the funds come out of the banking system, and so their point of injection is in that part of the economy where banks primarily make loans: the capital goods and real estate industries. Although the prices of capital goods and real estate move, they do not move as quickly. These changes typically have little if any immediate effect on the consumer market. In fact, with consumers and businesses not taking precautions against impending inflation, the consumer price level remains relatively stable. The effects of bank credit inflation, therefore, are much more hidden than those of fiat inflation. Where it is detected, in the business community, it is often welcomed, because it sparks some confidence and activity.

Bank credit inflation is dangerous not only because it is harder to spot but also because its effects normally are not limited to a particular country, as fiat inflation's are. Since bank credit can affect the bond markets on an international scale, it can influence financial systems around the world. As we will see, the expansion of bank credit had international consequences during the 1920s, in the lead-up to the Great Depression. But there is a much more recent example of how bank credit inflation can weaken the international financial system. The global financial crisis of 2007 erupted at least in part because so many U.S. mortgage-backed securities were sold to foreign financial institutions. All over the world, banks, mutual funds, and pension funds held the securities as assets. Because U.S. institutions rated the securities highly, the risk traveled through the financial system almost undetected.

The recent financial crisis illustrates another of the dangers involved with bank credit inflation: the downturn usually arrives as a complete surprise. Very few people expected a collapse in 2007. On the surface everything looked promising—the stock market was rising, business profits were good, economic activity was strong, and employment was high. The economic world could not have looked better. Then in a flash the downturns began and institutions found their assets to be little more than worthless. Financial systems all across the globe were gravely wounded.

As the Austrian School of economics has shown in detail, abundant bank credit is the necessary condition for booms and bubbles. Historically, an expansion of bank credit has produced a bubble—and then the inevitable bursting of that bubble.[20]

To understand why bank credit inflation is so powerful, and ultimately so damaging, it is necessary to know something of the nature of banking.

The modern banking system is premised on the fact that not everyone wants all his money at the same time. Indeed, people generally save most of their money in banks, rarely using their funds. Knowing that customers will demand to withdraw only a small amount of their total deposits at any one time, the banking system can lend out a multiple of the funds it has on hand. For example, if a bank has deposits of $1 million, it may feel safe in lending out $10 million. Put another way, banks need to keep as a reserve against deposits just a small fraction of the amount they lend out. Hence we call this system fractional-reserve banking.

Normally, banks should receive their reserves from the savings of the public. As people make more deposits into the system, reserves increase. Any growth in reserves is important because it allows banks to increase the number of loans they make, and banks earn their profits from the interest paid on loans. But the advent of central banking changed this arrangement. Banks no longer had to rely solely on funds from their own depositors. If a bank needed to honor withdrawals that exceeded its reserves, it could turn to the central bank for a loan to increase its reserves. With the central bank there as a safety net, local banks discovered that they could keep an even smaller fraction as a reserve against lending. The minimum reserve dropped as low as 2.5 percent.

In this way, central banking is by its very nature inflationary. When the central bank allows for decreases in bank reserves, it generates bank credit inflation.[21] Once credit is generated, it has to go someplace. As the central bank increases credit to local banks, local banks then increase credit to businesses and individuals (provided the public will borrow the money). Loans allow increased spending on capital goods, affording businesses the chance to invest in new equipment and produce new products, families to buy bigger and more expensive homes, and so on. The expanded credit, though not as obviously inflationary as a fiat expansion of the money supply, creates the perception of strong business conditions. That perception influences industries, government, the public, and even banks themselves. As banks expand their lending, they naturally must extend beyond the lowest-risk loans. The more confidence banks have in the strength of the economy, the more willing they will be to extend credit to lower-quality borrowers.

This is how bank credit inflation leads to bubbles: The central bank artificially creates credit, which flows to local banks and then into the broader economy. This artificial credit creates the perception of growth and overall economic health, even though the underlying fundamentals of the economy did not change.

As Austrian economists have documented, this process of bank credit inflation is exactly what generated the boom of the 1920s and the bust that followed with the Great Depression.

The Bank Credit Inflation of the 1920s

Austrian economists, most notably Murray Rothbard, have extensively investigated the causes of the Great Depression. Rothbard, in his book *America's Great Depression*, argued that the Federal Reserve's inordinate credit expansion during the Roaring Twenties was a primary factor behind the Depression. Following the Austrian theory of the trade cycle, he showed how banks increased the supply of credit far beyond the gold supply. This increase fueled bubbles as well as overexpansion of business.

The founding of the Federal Reserve System in 1913 ended one of the chief characteristics of the gold standard—the discipline over monetary expansion. The Fed now could manipulate interest rates independently of market forces—lowering rates by expanding credit, especially in the short-term money markets, and raising rates by contracting credit.

Three times in the 1920s, the Fed consciously intervened in the marketplace to inject credit: in 1922, 1924, and 1927. This credit inflation had very real consequences, as can be seen from five bubbles that the inflation created: the Florida land boom, the foreign bond bubble, the stock market bonanza, the housing and construction bubble, and the capital goods boom.

The Florida land boom, 1924–26: One of the first outcomes of the credit expansion was a land boom in Florida. Lasting only two years and collapsing in 1926, it should have sent a warning about an economy that appeared to be roaring, as it showed what massive credit expansion did and how the boom would inevitably go bust.

With credit plentiful after the Fed's bank credit expansions, demand for Florida property soared, and so did prices. Cities and developers went heavily into debt to finance large building and infrastructure projects, expecting to pay off the debts by selling at higher prices. At the height of the boom, there were two thousand real estate offices and twenty-five thousand agents marketing housing lots or acreage in Miami. Prices rose to dizzying heights. Frederick Lewis Allen sets the scene in his history of the 1920s:

> A lot in the business center of Miami Beach had sold for $800 in the early days of the development and had resold for $150,000 in 1924. For a strip of land in Palm Beach a New York lawyer had been offered $240,000 some eight or ten years before the boom; in 1923 he finally accepted $800,000 for it; the next year the strip of land was broken up into building lots and disposed of at an aggregate price of $1,500,000; and in 1925 there were those who claimed that its value had risen to $4 million. A poor woman who had bought a piece of land near Miami in 1896 for $25 was able to sell it in 1925 for $150,000. Such tales were legion; every visitor to the Gold Coast could pick them by the dozen; and many if not most of them were quite true—though the profits were largely on paper.[22]

Those paper profits disappeared in 1926. The Florida land boom went bust, partially because of severe hurricanes and partially because at such dizzyingly high prices the market simply dried up. Speculators and local governments were left holding tremendous debt. By 1928, Florida was littered with abandoned subdivisions, unoccupied houses, governments that could not pay their bonds, and failed banks. By 1930, twenty-six Florida cities had gone into default, unable to pay the interest on their bonds.[23]

Some eighty years later, another Florida land boom was eerily similar. The years 2005–2007 brought a boom that saw buyers purchasing Florida property with no intention of living there, but rather with the intent of "flipping" the properties to other buyers. This was reminiscent of a practice common in the 1920s: purchasing "binders" on property. In his book *The Great Crash, 1929*, John Kenneth Galbraith described this form of speculation: "In the Florida land boom the trading was in 'binders.' Not the land itself but the right to buy the land at a stated price was traded. This right to buy—which was obtained by a down payment of 10 percent of the purchase price—could be sold. It thus conferred on the speculators full benefit of the increase in values. After the value of the lot had risen he could resell the binder for what he had paid plus the full amount of the increase in price."[24]

The major difference between these two land booms is that, in the more recent frenzy, the bust reached far beyond Florida. When property values collapsed, the borrowers weren't the only ones who suffered. The banks were hit too—and so were all the financial institutions worldwide that had bought securities backed by these mortgages. The default became an international financial problem.

The foreign bond bubble: The 1920s credit expansion also produced a bubble in foreign bonds. In 1922, Congress passed the Fordney-McCumber Tariff, raising tariff rates substantially. This had the practical effect of reducing foreign purchases of U.S. exports. By inhibiting foreign countries from selling their goods in America, the tariff hampered their ability to earn dollars. The United States was the world's largest economy at that time, meaning that many countries already carried trade imbalances and other debts. Without dollars to pay off their debts, foreign countries either would not or could not buy U.S. exports to the extent that they had previously—all because of a tariff intended to "protect" American industry and farming.

Farmers, in particular, suffered immediately, as the U.S. agricultural sector depended heavily on exports. In an attempt to keep tariffs high and yet satisfy the overseas market for U.S. food and thereby help the farmers, the Federal Reserve embarked on a policy of credit expansion, lending foreign countries dollars to buy our food.[25] In essence, the United States financed its customers by expanding bank credit.

The Federal Reserve's easy credit sparked a bubble in the purchasing of foreign bonds. Economists Phillips, McManus, and Nelson write that the Fed's flood of cheap credit floated "huge foreign loans in the United States from 1922 to 1928. These foreign loans in turn stimulated an investment inflation abroad, notably in Germany and certain South American countries." Some economists saw the dangers inherent in this American policy. In 1927, Bertil Ohlin of Sweden warned that the Federal Reserve's expansion of credit had effectively overwhelmed the gold standard. "This," he wrote, "implies nothing less than a revolution in the monetary system not only of the United States but of all countries with the gold standard. The control of the development of the world price level has passed entirely into the hands of the Federal Reserve Board and Governors."[26]

The effects of this "revolution" were incredible. The volume of foreign securities in the United States jumped from $631 million in 1922 to $1.56 billion in 1927.[27] To put this in perspective, in 1927 the amount of foreign bonds issued was greater than the total borrowing of all American states, counties, townships, districts, towns, boroughs, and cities combined.[28]

Then, of course, it all fell apart. Foreign countries had come to depend on increasing amounts of American money to continue their economic expansions. When the bank credit expansion stopped in 1928 and 1929, the foreign loans stopped too, and so did the investment booms overseas. After the stock market crashed, purchasing power was shattered and debts went into default. America's exports dropped dramatically, and American institutions and citizens who held the bonds found themselves in distress.[29] By 1932 the size of the private debt that Europeans owed to American citizens exceeded the war debts European governments had owed to the United States at the time of the armistice in 1918.[30]

Although economic historians do not often cite the foreign bond crisis, it revealed weaknesses in the American economy. First, because the United States had a high tariff in place at the same time it was issuing easy credit, foreign governments and borrowers could not use exports to the United States to repay their debts. As economist Benjamin Anderson put it, for a foreign loan to be good, the foreign country "must be in a position to obtain dollars with which to make it good, and to obtain these dollars, she must be able to sell goods in adequate volume in foreign countries, including the United States."[31] But instead of accepting foreign goods to pay off the bonds, the U.S. government actually *increased* tariffs. As a result, many of the bonds went insolvent, and American farmers suffered from reduced shipments overseas.

Second, the 1920s crisis showed the instability that results when foreign bonds become a major part of the U.S. financial system. When the foreign bonds defaulted, U.S. bank reserves shrank. But it wasn't just banks that bought foreign bonds; all classes of people in the United States purchased them.[32] Thus the effects of the defaults were far-reaching.

A similar problem emerged in the recent financial crisis. In the 1920s, U.S. banks and financial institutions used foreign bonds as reserves and counted them as assets. In the 2000s, foreign pension funds and banks bought U.S. bonds (public and private) and counted them as assets. In both cases the securities were financed by increasing amounts of credit coming from the central banks. And in both cases this credit expansion and the consequent lowering of interest rates created the bubbles that later burst.

The stock market craze: Credit inflation in the 1920s directly influenced the stock market as well. First, companies began floating a great number of new stock issues, and second, stock prices rose quickly.

Companies have a tendency to issue new securities after credit becomes available, because as they begin to grow they aim to raise funds for further expansion. Benjamin Anderson shows that the number of new public issues of securities increased steadily through the 1920s and then jumped up dramatically toward the end of the boom. Between 1926 and 1927 the number rose from 6,344 to 7,791, nearly a 23 percent increase. Then, between 1928 and 1929—the last year of the boom—the figure soared from 8,114 to 10,195, more than a 25 percent increase.[33]

As stock issues rose, so did the Dow Jones Industrial Average. In the two years leading up to the October 1929 crash, the Dow had doubled, from 191 in early 1928 to a peak of 381 in September 1929. The bubble was building. Trading activity became frenetic during this period. The number of shares traded in a day peaked at 4 million in March 1928; a new height of 6.9 million was reached in November; then, in March 1929, yet a new record was set, with 8.2 million shares turned over in a day—more than double the peak set just a year earlier. Economist Charles Kindleberger points out that price-to-earnings ratios rose from "a conservative 10 or 12 to 20, and higher for the market's favorites." These stock prices were based on expectations more than anything else—"anticipation of continued increases in earnings and dividends."

But the Dow Jones peak of 381 in 1929 did not by itself indicate problems. The market would reach similar levels (when adjusted for inflation) numerous times in the decades ahead. Kindleberger observes, "The danger posed by the market was not inherent in the level of prices and turnover so much as in the precarious credit mechanism that supported it and the pressure it exerted on credit throughout the United States and the world."[34]

Benjamin Anderson documents how that credit mechanism came

about. In 1927 the governors of the central banks of the United States, Great Britain, Germany, and France held a conference at which they decided to expand bank credit. Following the meeting the Federal Reserve took steps to do just that, Anderson shows. This new credit set off the frenzied last stage of the run-up in stock prices.[35]

The housing and construction boom: Excessive credit also flooded the real estate market, resulting in a massive building boom. Florida was an extreme case, but it was hardly alone in experiencing a real estate bubble. When the housing boom turned into a bust, a mortgage crisis resulted. In an analysis that could easily describe what happened in the 2000s, Anderson writes that many mortgages had been "based on very exaggerated real estate prices." He concludes: "Many smaller banks fell into grave difficulties because they had bought such mortgages in too great a volume and too uncritically when they had excess funds and didn't know how to use them."[36] In fact, Kindleberger and fellow economist Robert Aliber report, "Real estate loans in default, not failed stockbrokers' accounts, were the largest single element in the failure of 4,800 banks in the years from 1930 to 1933."[37]

The capital goods boom: The prosperity during the Roaring Twenties is legendary. During this period the economy grew faster than ever before. The capital goods market saw extraordinary growth, thanks to technological advances and to the bank credit that was floating everything. Historians Larry Schweikart and Michael Allen recount, "Improved productivity in the brokerage and investment firms expanded their ability to provide capital for the growing number of auto factories, glassworks, cement plants, tire manufacturers, and dozens of other complementary industries." This explosive growth in capital goods in turn produced spikes in the sales of consumer goods—automobiles, most notably, but also new technologies like radios and electrical appliances.[38] All this activity created the expectation of increased profits going forward, which drove a good deal of the stock market frenzy. A modern-day parallel was the so-called dot-com boom of the 1990s. In both cases, the unrealistic expectation of perpetual prosperity led to collapse.

The Second Legacy:
The Collapse of Free Trade and Global Markets

Another economic development of the post–World War I era was the collapse of free trade. The numbers tell the story. In 1928, at the height of the boom, world trade was valued at $114.4 billion; by 1932 the value had dropped fully 60 percent, to $45.5 billion; by 1935 it had fallen even lower, to $40.3 billion.

The problem was that when the economic crisis began, countries all over the world resorted to "economic nationalism." Rather than embracing the free trade that had led to prosperity during the age of classical liberalism, governments resorted to a host of protectionist measures—as historian Carroll Quigley reports: "tariff increases; licensing of imports; import quotas; sumptuary laws restricting imports; laws placing national origin, trade-mark, health, or quarantine restrictions on imports; foreign-exchange controls; competitive depreciation of currencies; export subsidies; dumping of exports; and so on."[39] The United States was one of the first to embrace protectionist measures. Since 1922, the Fordney-McCumber Tariff had been in place. As noted, this tariff seriously inhibited the ability of foreigners to sell their goods in America and hence earn dollars to pay off their debts. It also depressed U.S. exports. Then, in 1930, Congress passed the new Smoot-Hawley Tariff, which raised tariff rates again and made the economic situation considerably worse.

Movement on Smoot-Hawley began even before the crash. When campaigning for president in 1928, Herbert Hoover had promised to help America's farmers by increasing tariffs. In his March 1929 inaugural address, Hoover showed he was serious about the campaign pledge, declaring that "in justice to our farmers, our labor, and our manufacturers," the U.S. government could not postpone action on "further agricultural relief and limited changes in the tariff."[40] The Senate soon took up the charge. In the popular book *The Way the World Works*, Jude Wanniski traces the progress of the tariff through the legislative process. The markets, he shows, were reliably opposed to protectionism. Each time it looked as if the bill would pass, the stock market went down. When it seemed that the tariff would die, the market advanced.[41] Despite the stock market crash of 1929, Congress pushed forward with the tariff bill, with the Senate finally passing it in March 1930. Even then, more than a thousand economists signed a petition pleading with President Hoover not to sign the bill. Hoover did sign it, in June.

As the world's largest economy, the United States was certain to inspire other countries either to imitate its trade restrictions or to retaliate against them. Sure enough, protectionist measures were widespread by 1931. The chain reaction depressed export industries everywhere. Because countries could not export, they were unable to meet their debt obligations and then could not receive further credit. Investment overseas stopped. Trade came to a halt. The foreign bonds held in the United States became practically worthless. Farmers, who were heavily mortgaged, could no longer make their payments. Since farmers accounted for 25 percent of U.S. employment, this crisis reverberated throughout the entire economy.[42] With exports in severe contraction, industries suffering, and credit dried up, unemployment skyrocketed worldwide. The Great Depression had begun.

It is often said that most major disasters are the result of many factors coming together at the wrong time. This was the case with the Great Depression. To be sure, the Fed's credit expansion was a primary cause of the Depression, creating unsustainable booms in many areas of the U.S. and world economy. But the rise of protectionism and the resulting collapse of worldwide markets was a major contributing factor as well. Had there been only a false credit boom, or had there just been protectionist legislation, the economy certainly would have suffered, but the situation would not have been as dire as it became in the Great Depression. The worldwide economy imploded in a way never seen before or since because these two factors came together simultaneously, along with a number of other serious issues, such as farm overexpansion and the foreign bond bubble. One might say that credit inflation blew up the bubble and the Smoot-Hawley pin burst it.

The high tariff rates of Smoot-Hawley were especially damaging at this moment in history because the United States was in a new position as a creditor nation. Prior to the Great War, the United States had been a debtor nation. This did not pose a big problem at the time, because most of the world—and most importantly Britain, then the global center for trade and finance—had adopted free-trade policies.[43] The sale of exports allowed the United States to generate the cash flow needed to pay off the bonds. Even the relatively high tariff policy in effect from the time of the

Lincoln administration did little economic harm, since the United States was exporting goods and services and importing capital. This vital process of using exports to pay off debts is, as we have seen, precisely what the United States denied to foreign countries when it became a creditor nation after the First World War and built ever higher protectionist barriers.

Following World War I, the Allied nations and Germany already owed huge debts to the United States. The foreign bond bubble, inflated by the Federal Reserve's easy credit, only added to other countries' debt burden. It was as if the United States drilled a hole in a boat that was already taking on water—and then took away the buckets the countries needed to bail themselves out. Except it wasn't just other countries that were sinking; all those American citizens and institutions that held the suddenly worthless foreign bonds were brought down as well.

Just as the United States took the lead on protectionism, it also played a key role in scuttling the opportunity to revive international trade. On June 12, 1933, the World Economic Conference began in London. The conference had two goals: to restore world trade and to reestablish a stable international monetary order. The American secretary of state, Cordell Hull, went to London to lobby for a reduction of tariffs. There was only one problem: just days after the conference began, President Franklin D. Roosevelt signed the National Industrial Recovery Act, which permitted the U.S. government to institute further restrictions on imports. With this act indicating that the U.S. government emphasized protections for American industry over a revival of global trade, the World Economic Conference arrived at no agreement on reducing tariffs.[44]

The Roosevelt administration also subverted the second goal of the conference, currency stabilization. As Roosevelt adviser (and later critic) Raymond Moley recalled, Britain, France, and Italy tried to get the American president to agree to a "wholly innocuous" statement that "gold would ultimately be reestablished as a measure of international exchange value, but that each nation reserved the right to decide when it would return to a gold standard and undertake stabilization." Roosevelt would not agree to this. In fact, on July 3 he sent a cable explicitly rejecting the conference's attempt to stabilize world currencies. In his statement, Roosevelt said that he would consider it a "catastrophe" if the conference focused on "a purely artificial and temporary experiment" at stabilizing currencies.[45] With this blunt message, Roosevelt effectively torpedoed the conference. It adjourned a few weeks later without reaching any agreements on the major questions it had been convened to address.[46]

With the London conference, the world had an opportunity to reinstate two of the most important pillars of the age of classical liberalism, free trade and a stable world currency system. It was a huge opportunity lost.

The Third Legacy: Relying on Government Intervention

Although the world was left to solve its economic problems, economist John Maynard Keynes applauded Roosevelt's decision. According to Robert Skidelsky, the eminent biographer of Lord Keynes, "Despite the fact that Roosevelt's message scuppered his own plan, Keynes proclaimed that 'President Roosevelt is Magnificently Right' in choosing the path of national currency management."[47] This is because they both wanted to promote an expansion of government activities. An open market and a gold standard would run counter to this agenda.[48]

The drive toward state intervention had been increasing for some time. Since the late nineteenth century the American progressive movement had been calling on the government to play a more active role. The progressives achieved three major reforms in 1913 alone: the creation of the Federal Reserve, the institution of a federal income tax, and the move to the direct (popular) election of senators. Then World War I brought, in the words of historian Robert Higgs, "an enormous and wholly unprecedented intervention of the federal government in the nation's economic affairs." Higgs writes: "By the time of the armistice, the government had taken over the ocean-shipping, railroad, telephone, and telegraph industries; commandeered hundreds of manufacturing plants; entered into massive economic enterprises on its own account in such varied departments as shipbuilding, wheat trading, and building construction; undertaken to lend huge sums to business directly or indirectly and to regulate the private issuance of securities; established official priorities for the use of transportation facilities, food, fuel, and many raw materials; fixed the prices of dozens of important commodities; intervened in hundreds of labor disputes; and conscripted millions of men for service in the armed forces."[49]

The experience of World War I prepared the United States and western Europe to accept, and indeed expect, increasing governmental activity in any emergency. So it is no surprise that when economic crisis hit, the public did not oppose government interventions. The argument was that government had won the war, and now government would beat the Depression. This notion had bipartisan appeal: as Murray Rothbard shows in *America's Great Depression*, Republican Herbert Hoover's administration tried many of the programs that Democrat Franklin Roosevelt later continued in the New Deal.

In the academic world, however, there was no overall theoretical justification for government intervention in the economy. The trends were already established, waiting for the theory to catch up. It was Keynes who provided intellectual legitimacy for government control, with his book *The General Theory of Employment, Interest, and Money.*

Breaking with many economists before him, Keynes thought the economy was neither capable of self-correction, in the case of unemployment, nor able to operate efficiently without government aid. He based his theory on the premise that the economy would not consume all that is produced; this theory held that unemployment was inevitable. Keynes believed that government should act as a balance wheel to the economy by intervening in economic slowdowns but withdrawing during good times.

The major objection to Keynesian economics during this time came from Friedrich A. von Hayek, an Austrian economist who moved to Britain in the early 1930s and took a position at the London School of Economics. Hayek argued that increased government intervention would only make the economic problems worse. He advocated a hands-off policy by which government would remove barriers to trade and let the economy work off the exuberance of the credit expansion of the 1920s. In 1944, Hayek published his most famous work, *The Road to Serfdom.* Although largely ignored by the academy, it became a bestseller.

In this book, Hayek argued that economic planning by government requires a constant increase in state activity. Drawing from his experience in Austria and from the history of Germany, Hayek asserted that government expansion in the economy leads to a type of tyranny. A growing state, he said, makes the rule of law impossible, necessitates further intervention, leads to the rise of a political elite, and ends democratic rule.

George Orwell's review of the book aptly summarizes Hayek's argument: "By bringing the whole of life under the control of the State, Socialism necessarily gives power to an inner ring of bureaucrats, who in almost every case will be men who want power for its own sake and will stick at nothing in order to retain it. . . . The only salvation lies in returning to an unplanned economy, free competition, and emphasis on liberty rather than security."[50] Objecting to Keynes's views, Hayek said that it was government intervention in the first place that caused the dislocation of the 1930s. The removal of government intervention, Hayek argued, would allow the market to readjust and solve the Depression.

In this debate, Keynes had the rhetorical advantage. To the general public, he promised a "quick fix" to the problem of unemployment. To politicians, he provided a way to gain popularity by increasing government spending, influence, and jobs. And to academic economists, he promised positions in society as social and economic engineers. Hayek had to contend with the fact that his solution would require time and a reversal of the government intervention that was the cause of the crisis. After resonating so strongly in the 1930s, Keynes's ideas would influence the teaching of economics for decades to come. For at least the next forty years both politicians and academics relied on his theories to support government spending programs and high tax policies.

But whatever rhetorical advantage Keynes had, the fact is that his policies did little to lower unemployment during the Great Depression. For all the New Deal's activist measures, the median unemployment rate from 1934 to 1940 was 17.2 percent. Never in the 1930s did unemployment go below 14 percent—a rate several points higher than what was experienced in the brutal recessions of the early 1980s and of 2008–10.[51] Even Henry Morgenthau, Roosevelt's longtime secretary of the treasury, confessed that the New Deal didn't work: "We have tried spending money. We are spending more than we ever spent before and it does not work. . . . We have never made good on promises. . . . I say after eight years of this Administration we have just as much unemployment as when we started and enormous debt to boot."[52] More recently, Keynes biographer Robert Skidelsky has acknowledged: "It is now increasingly recognized that Hitler's was the only New Deal that actually succeeded in eliminating unemployment. Roosevelt's certainly didn't. There were 15 million Americans out of work when he took office in March 1933. There were still 11 million four years later and the economy properly recovered only with rearmament and war."[53]

As Skidelsky suggests, Keynesian interventionism continued unimpeded until another world war interrupted the flow of events. Added to all the awful legacies of the First World War was the fact that it had not even been the "war to end all wars"; just twenty years after the Treaty of Versailles, Europe exploded in conflict again.

The world would have to wait for that global war to be settled before the economic mistakes made after World War I could be addressed. As World War II entered its final year, the Allied nations—the eventual victors—gathered at a hotel in New Hampshire to map out what the postwar international economic order would look like. That conference would lay the foundation for what would be one of the longest periods of economic prosperity in human history.

6

The Age of Bretton Woods

I n July 1944, representatives of forty-four Allied nations gathered at the Mount Washington Hotel in Bretton Woods, New Hampshire. After years of carnage and punishing battles, World War II was entering its final phases (V-E Day would come ten months later). The Allied powers assembled to set up international monetary and trade arrangements for the postwar world. To do so, they moved decisively to correct mistakes made after the First World War.

In fact, the Bretton Woods Conference reclaimed the opportunity lost at the World Economic Conference in London eleven years earlier. That 1933 conference ended with no significant action on its two key goals: a relatively stable international currency system and a movement toward worldwide free trade.[1] Those were precisely the goals achieved in New Hampshire in 1944.

Given the prosperity that followed the Bretton Woods agreement, some scholars have argued that had the London conference succeeded, the Great Depression would have ended much more quickly and World War II may have been avoided. For example, Austrian economist Melchior Palyi writes that after the United States, the world's economic leader, adopted strong protectionist stances and "torpedoed" the World Economic Conference, "Hitler's answer . . . was to tighten the 'strait jacket' around Germany's foreign trade and to maximize domestic self-sufficiency. For both Germany and Japan, territorial expansion was the ultimate alternative to genuine foreign trade." Palyi goes on:

It is of interest to speculate about the possible course of Hitler's policies *if* the London conference of 1933 had been even a partial success. With some relaxation on the international economic front, it is possible that Germany could have corrected her raw material shortage without going to war. Unwittingly President Roosevelt had strengthened the hand of the hard-core anti-internationalist Nazis by breaking, temporarily, with the best liberal traditions of the Western world.[2]

Germany and Japan's economies had always depended on exports and foreign trade. The protectionist walls built after World War I, and especially during the 1930s, robbed them of the raw materials and agricultural produce they needed. In short, the conflict that followed the rise of protectionism epitomized an adage attributed to economist Frédéric Bastiat: "When goods don't cross borders, soldiers will."

Comeback

The agreements instituted at the Bretton Woods Conference helped revive foreign trade and stabilize the currency after World War II. Specifically, the conference put forth resolutions to establish the General Agreement on Trade and Tariffs (GATT) and the International Monetary Fund (IMF). Although these agreements were far from perfect, they at last pushed the world closer to the pre-1914 economic order.

GATT, which would be set up at a conference held in 1947 and refined at future meetings, lowered trade barriers enough to undo the damage done by the protectionism of recent decades. Both Harry Truman's and Dwight Eisenhower's administrations supported GATT and pressed for freer trade throughout the 1940s and 1950s. By contrast, the Roosevelt administration had fortified protectionist walls (though Secretary of State Cordell Hull mitigated some of the protectionist problems by negotiating bilateral agreements).

The goal of the IMF was to mimic the gold standard by producing stable exchange rates between currencies. That is not to say that Bretton Woods actually reinstituted the gold standard. Under the gold standard, the stability of exchange rates was automatic, set by market forces; it did not require interventions by governments or monetary authorities. By contrast, Bretton Woods made it necessary for the IMF and the world's central banks to manipulate currencies constantly to keep exchange rates stable and in place. The system was not as effective as the gold standard had been: over the twenty-five years after Bretton Woods, the dollar lost about 50 percent of its purchasing power.[3]

Nevertheless, the Bretton Woods arrangement provided a degree of monetary discipline, and certainly more than had been in place at any time since World War I. It did so by making the U.S. dollar the world's reserve currency. Under the new system, foreign central banks were able to convert dollars into gold at thirty-five dollars per ounce. This plan recognized a simple fact: the United States had the vast majority of the world's gold supply. So rather than linking directly to gold—which foreign central banks did not have—the other major currencies of the world were linked to the dollar at fixed exchange rates.[4] The IMF's job was to keep the exchange rates stable and in place. The United States, meanwhile, needed to maintain the value of the dollar. In practice, this meant that the U.S. government had to maintain relatively balanced budgets and refrain from expanding its money stock to stimulate the economy.

Whatever its imperfections, Bretton Woods played a key role in lifting the world economy out of its doldrums. Economists and historians across a range of perspectives agree that Bretton Woods brought prosperity.[5] For example, Keynesian economic historian Robert Skidelsky, in his book *Keynes: The Return of the Master*, sets up the Bretton Woods era as a "golden age" in comparison with the growth of the Reagan years. After noting that the average growth rate from 1951 to 1973 outpaced that of the 1980s—4.8 percent versus 3.2 percent—Skidelsky writes: "Had the world economy grown at 4.8% growth rather than 3.2% from 1980 until today, it would have been 50% larger, something we shall achieve only in 2022 with the 1980–2009 average."[6] This endorsement of Bretton Woods may seem odd, given that (as we will see) Keynesian thinking ultimately led the U.S. government to topple the gold-backed international currency system. But in 1944, John Maynard Keynes was one of the dominant figures at the Bretton Woods conference, along with U.S. treasury official Harry Dexter White.

Nobel Prize–winning economist Robert Mundell, the father of supply-side economics, has challenged many tenets of Keynesianism. But like Skidelsky, he praises the Bretton Woods arrangement. Mundell writes that Bretton Woods produced a quarter century that was "exemplary in its stability, growth, and economic development, perhaps unmatched at any time outside an imperium, such as the Roman Empire."[7] Historian Brian Domitrovic, in his monumental study of the supply-side school and its contributions to the economic growth of the 1980s, observes that the Bretton Woods system finally restored in the United States "sustained high growth, low unemployment, low inflation, and sound money—the kind of economic performance that enabled the nation to come into its own in the decades before 1914." Domitrovic adds: "The guarantee, under Bretton Woods, to foreign central banks of $35 gold was not incidental. It ensured that there would not be too many dollars chasing goods, even in the home market."[8]

Judy Shelton, a devotee of the gold standard and longtime monetary columnist for the *Wall Street Journal*, underscores the impact of the Bretton Woods agreement on both trade and currency:

> With the dollar stabilizing price levels around the world, productivity began to soar in the 1950s. International trade flourished as restrictions were steadily reduced. . . . With the dollar providing outside monetary discipline, governments were forced to act responsibly in implementing economic policies for their nations. For the most part, they did so, and the 1950s marked an extraordinarily successful economic era characterized by stable prices, high productivity, and free trade.[9]

The European Recovery: Triumph of the Austrians

As all these scholars suggest, the revival of trade and monetary stability under Bretton Woods provided the umbrella under which Europe and Japan began to recover from the devastation of the world wars and the Great Depression.

The first highlight of the postwar economic revival was the *Wirtschaftswunder* or German economic miracle.[10] As we have seen, this recovery was largely the work of Ludwig Erhard and his adviser Wilhelm Röpke, both devotees of the Austrian School of economics.

Erhard, Chancellor Konrad Adenauer's minister for economic affairs, followed an exceedingly simple path to prosperity: free markets and stable currency. Erhard's policy repealed wage and price controls, lowered tariff barriers, reduced taxes, linked the mark to gold (following the Bretton Woods agreement), and sold off state industries. In essence, Germany adopted the major parts of the classical liberal program.

The resulting turnaround was remarkable. Germany had been devastated by war and inflation. The cities were bombed out, the industries were in shambles, government intervention was rampant, and the country was flooded with refugees. French economist Jacques Rueff describes how quickly the recovery came. By early 1948, just three years after Germany's crushing defeat in the war, "There was a sudden change. All the graphs were skyrocketing. Agricultural and industrial productions came to life at the same time. Homes began to rise from the ruins, and reconstruction soon set a pace that left neighboring countries gasping. German exports increased sixfold from 1948 to 1952. The national income in nonmonetary terms increased 40% between 1948 and 1950. . . . Everywhere the clatter of construction replaced the stillness of the ruins."[11] By the mid-1960s, Germany was the world's third-largest economy.

It also became the engine that pulled the rest of the European train, with prosperity following in France, Italy, Belgium, the Netherlands, and Luxembourg.

Jacques Rueff (1896–1978), who was heavily influenced by the Austrian School and was a friend of both Röpke and Erhard, played a pivotal role in France's economic recovery. When Charles de Gaulle became president of the French Republic in 1959, he appointed Rueff as his economic adviser. Committed to free markets and the gold standard, Rueff laid out a recovery plan that stabilized the franc, slashed government spending, and eliminated tariffs, quotas, and other protectionist barriers. The French economy quickly took off. As historian Paul Johnson reports, France's gross national product (GNP) rose by 3 percent in the second half of 1959, then jumped by 7.9 percent in 1960, another 4.6 percent in 1961, and 6.8 percent in 1962. Living standards improved as well, increasing at an annual rate of 4 percent.[12]

Economic policies such as those Erhard and Rueff developed proved central to the European recovery. They do not, however, receive nearly as much attention as the massive reconstruction plan the United States administered after World War II. The Marshall Plan, named for U.S. secretary of state George Marshall, included billions of dollars in American aid and credit help to the war-devastated nations of Europe. To be sure, this much-lauded plan helped speed the European recovery. But it alone did not drive the economic revival. In fact, the results of the Marshall Plan were mixed. Countries that did not enact free-market-oriented recovery plans of their own did not see their fortunes turn as dramatically as those of West Germany and France. For example, Great Britain generally followed Keynesian and socialist solutions, nationalizing industries, raising taxes, establishing entitlements, and using other forms of government intervention, and its economy did not take off.

Jane Jacobs, the great chronicler of urban development, makes the point clearly in *Cities and the Wealth of Nations*:

> The Marshall Plan did not, of course, metamorphose stagnant or declining European economies into developing, expanding, self-generating economies. Some of the aided economies, such as the Netherlands, West Germany, parts of France, and parts of Italy, did proceed to expand and develop—as San Francisco did after its disaster. But others did nothing of the kind. Britain received Marshall Plan equipment, as West Germany did, but this bounty did not make Britain's economy behave like West Germany's.[13]

The Japanese recovery likewise shows the importance of free-market policies. After World War II ended, the Allied Powers, led by the United States, occupied Japan. The United States dismantled industrial cartels and monopolies, and GATT opened up free trade. Paul Johnson observes that there was nothing miraculous about Japan's postwar economic "miracle." Rather, he writes, "It was a straightforward case of Adam Smith's economics with no more than a touch of Keynesianism."[14] Under the leadership of Prime Minister Shigeru Yoshida, Japan adopted a program of moderate taxation and reduced government spending. Meanwhile, the Japanese people saved at a high rate, and the banking system allowed these funds to be channeled into industry.[15]

The Fall of Bretton Woods

By moving away from the mistakes made after World War I, the Bretton Woods agreements laid the groundwork for economic recovery after the Second World War. But inherent in these agreements were certain weaknesses that would ultimately undo the Bretton Woods system.

Austrian economist Henry Hazlitt was a prominent critic of Bretton Woods. Even as the Allied delegates were convening in New Hampshire in 1944, Hazlitt wrote editorials for the *New York Times* questioning the decisions that John Maynard Keynes and others were making.[16] Most important, he warned that the agreements would prove inflationary. Foreseeing huge entitlement spending by Western governments, Hazlitt said that it would be impossible for states to maintain a peg to gold or to other currencies and also support enormous government expenditures. He predicted that to pay for budget deficits, governments would monetize their debts—that is, print money. Rather than merely mimicking a gold standard, Hazlitt said, the United States should actually reconstitute the gold standard.

Hazlitt also pointed out that governments would be forced to subsidize their fellow states. For example, if Great Britain wanted to enact huge spending programs and monetize its debt, the pound sterling would fall in worldwide markets. To maintain the peg, other governments would have to come in and either purchase pounds to hold up the price or make loans to Britain.[17] In 2010 a similar instance occurred when German taxpayers were asked to support a Greek government drowning in debt. The key difference was that both Germany and Greece used the same currency, the euro.

Another advocate of free markets, Jacques Rueff, foresaw major difficulties with Bretton Woods as well. Rueff warned that as the U.S. government increased the supply of dollars to finance its deficits, some of those dollars would be deposited in foreign central banks. Since the U.S. dollar was the reserve currency under the Bretton Woods system, a central bank could use deposited dollars as backing for loans. These deposited dollars then would create credit inflation in that country, because as the central bank expands its reserves, it can lend out more money. In addition, the central bank could use the same currency to purchase U.S. Treasury bonds to earn interest; by buying those bonds, the foreign bank would be lending money back to the U.S. government, which would lower interest rates in the United States. Inflation, therefore, would be felt both in the United States and in the central bank of the country where the dollar deposits were made.

The Bretton Woods system was predicated on the fact that the United States held by far the world's largest gold supply. But Rueff saw that eventually the U.S. gold supply would dwindle, because foreign banks holding dollars also had the option of redeeming the dollars for gold. This, he said, would undercut the entire system. Rueff suggested that the system could be repaired by going back to the gold standard. Under a true gold standard, the United States could not simply expand the money supply when it ran a deficit in the balance of trade. To settle that deficit, the United States would have to transfer gold to foreign central banks, which would reduce U.S. reserves and thereby limit the potential money supply.

The situation that has recently developed with the United States and China shows that Rueff was right. The United States now runs a balance-of-trade deficit with China. As a result, U.S. dollars are deposited in the central bank of China. Because the dollar is a reserve currency, the banks in China can use these dollars as reserves, which inflates the Chinese currency. They use the dollars as backing for loans. The Chinese also use the dollars to lend to the U.S. government by purchasing Treasury bonds, which enables the United States to keep its interest rate relatively low. The Chinese then use the American bonds as reserves. In other words, dollars are used twice as reserves: once as bonds backing up loans made in China, and once as loans back to the U.S. government. Charles de Gaulle said that the United States was granted an "exorbitant privilege" by virtue of having its dollars used as the international reserve currency. Indeed, the system has enabled the United States to live at an artificially high standard of living. This would not be possible under a gold standard, because such a system requires that gold can be used only *once* as reserves.

The warnings of Hazlitt, Rueff, and other critics proved prescient. Over the past several decades Western governments have dramatically increased their spending, particularly on entitlement programs such as old-age benefits and medical care. In the United States, Social Security, Medicare, Medicaid, welfare, and other entitlement programs now account for the majority of government spending. These are categorized as "mandatory" expenditures, meaning that they cannot be curtailed in the federal budget process. Government deficits have soared. The U.S. government has responded to the deficits precisely as Hazlitt predicted it would: by monetizing the debt. That is to say, administrations have pressured the supposedly nonpolitical Federal Reserve to purchase government bonds, thus increasing the supply of money in circulation and lowering the value of the dollar internationally.

Under the Bretton Woods agreement, the United States needed to maintain a fixed relationship between the dollar and gold. The agreement also required the United States to pay out gold to foreign central banks on demand when presented with dollars. Printing too many dollars led to one of two consequences, or often both. First, the newly expanded supply of dollars increased the free-market price of gold, which presented foreign central banks with a profit opportunity. Say the market price of gold rose to forty-five dollars per ounce; foreign banks could withdraw gold from the United States at thirty-five dollars and then sell it on the commodity market at a profit of ten dollars per ounce. This did not happen very often in practice, thanks to gentlemen's agreements among central bankers. But foreign banks could take advantage of a second opportunity: Through trade, some of the increased supply of U.S. dollars would reach foreign central banks. Well aware that gold was increasing in value vis-à-vis the dollar, bankers could go to the United States and demand gold. As a result, the U.S. supply of gold dwindled, exactly as Rueff predicted it would.

By 1971 the U.S. government had arrived at a monetary crisis. During the 1960s the Federal Reserve had expanded the money supply considerably to finance the massive spending increases necessitated by Lyndon Johnson's Great Society and the Vietnam War. Gold was flowing out of the country to such an extent that the entire gold reserve was in danger of being depleted. The Bretton Woods system had always obligated the United States to maintain the value of the dollar in order to keep its gold stock. This meant restricting the rate of domestic inflation by tightening the money supply and raising interest rates. At higher interest rates, dollars became more attractive than gold to central bankers and other investors. The reason for that is simple: dollars could be invested in higher-yielding bonds, whereas holding gold alone yielded no profit or interest. Bretton Woods thus represented an external discipline on the monetary activities of the U.S. government.

President Richard Nixon saw that inflation was rising and gold was disappearing, but he decided that tightening monetary policy was not a palatable option. A tight money policy, he knew, would protect the dollar but raise interest rates, which would lead to a recession. A recession on his watch was out of the question, since 1972 was an election year.

Instead, Nixon went in another direction. His fateful decision spelled the end of the Bretton Woods system, dismantled any external disciplines on U.S. fiscal policies, and set the stage for the grinding years of stagflation.

7

Nixon's Folly

The crisis the Nixon administration confronted in 1971 had arisen, oddly enough, because of America's preeminent position in the world. As the leading economic power and the holder of the world's reserve currency, the United States had long been considered a safe place to invest. This preeminence allowed the United States to borrow huge sums abroad at low interest rates. It also enabled the U.S. government to pursue imprudent fiscal policies, building large debt and inflating the currency without incurring a penalty of high interest rates and/or a collapsing dollar. Or at least that was the case until the exploding spending of the Great Society and the Vietnam War pushed the United States to the brink. The increased spending and deficits brought about rising inflation in the late 1960s and early 1970s, causing foreign governments and investors to doubt the stability of the U.S. dollar.

Economists of the Austrian School had been warning of a coming crisis since the late 1950s and early 1960s. In an analysis of U.S. balance of payments from 1946 to 1959, Melchior Palyi showed conclusively that government and private loans and payments from the United States to foreign countries—especially foreign aid and military expenditures—canceled out the U.S. trade surplus. This left the deficit, which was covered in many cases by the outflow of gold.[1] Wilhelm Röpke, meanwhile, warned consistently that the growing welfare state would lead to two things: a corruption of morals in society and constant inflation—the latter because governments would need to inflate the currency to support the continual extension of benefits to the people.[2] Röpke died in 1966, just as Lyndon Johnson's administration began imposing the Great Society on the American people.

In short, the monetary crisis of 1971 developed from bad policies practiced over a period of years and even decades. The policies led to raids on the U.S. gold supply and the fall of the dollar on world currency markets. To respond to the problems, Richard Nixon could either continue with bad policy of his own or attempt the politically less popular route of trying to stop the process once and for all. Facing a reelection campaign in 1972, he chose the more expedient path.

In mid-August 1971, with inflation and unemployment on the rise, President Nixon retreated to Camp David with his key economic advisers to decide what to do. He emerged from the weekend session to lay out a series of economic measures that have become known as the "Nixon Shock." Some economists have referred to the president's action as "Nixon's Folly," a fitting name given the long-term consequences of his hasty decision.

President Nixon's first and most important move was to "close the gold window." That is to say, he declared that the United States would no long allow foreign central banks to redeem dollars for gold. He had unilaterally scrapped the Bretton Woods agreement that had been the anchor of the international monetary system since World War II. With no gold backing, the dollar's value was tied simply to its legal tender status and to the hope that politicians would not print too much money. In other words, the value of the dollar became a political matter.

It was clear that this devaluation of the dollar would lead to inflation, so Nixon trotted out another measure to try to keep the dollar stable: price controls. By pairing these policies, writes historian Brian Domitrovic in his excellent account of the 1970s economy, the president "saw before him the best of both worlds. He would have low unemployment as a result of inflationary pressures, and low inflation because of price controls."[3]

The Austrian economists were quick to respond. Murray Rothbard recalled that when Nixon imposed a price-wage freeze, "I went ballistic, denouncing the controls everywhere I could. That winter, I debated Presidential economic adviser Herbert Stein before the Metropolitan Republican Club of Washington, D.C." The Austrian case was clear and to the point: price controls would not work because they had *never* worked. Rothbard wrote: "Price controls, that is, the fixing of prices below the market level, have been tried since ancient Rome; in the French Revolution, in its notorious 'Law of the Maximum' that was responsible for most of the victims of the guillotine; in the Soviet Union, ruthlessly trying to suppress black markets. In every age, in every culture, price controls have never worked. They have always been a disaster. . . . They don't check inflation, they only create shortages, rationing, declines in quality, black markets, and terrible economic distortions."[4]

Having cut the link to gold, the Nixon administration allowed the value of the dollar to "float" in international currency markets, with supply and demand setting exchange rates on a day-to-day basis. Henry Kissinger, Nixon's national security adviser and later secretary of state, recalls the thinking behind the new arrangement: "It took us nearly two years to get a fully floating exchange-rate system accepted by our allies. Its advocates thought it would avoid the periodic crises in which fixed rates were devalued when currency reserves ran out or revalued in the face of surpluses. There would be 'painless' daily adjustments; speculators would disappear; exchange rates would more faithfully reflect underlying economic strengths; countries would not be bankrupted of their gold and currency reserves supporting 'artificial rates.'"[5]

That was the thinking, anyway. As Kissinger notes, "It has not quite worked out that way." The value of the dollar did not float; it sank. By 2010 it took well over five dollars to purchase what one dollar had bought in 1971.[6] Nixon's price controls did nothing to tamp down inflation. As the dollar's value fell in world markets, the prices of imports rose to the holders of dollars. Most notably, the falling value of the dollar led to major increases in the price of oil imports from the Organization of Petroleum Exporting Countries (OPEC). Writing in 1979, Kissinger said that "problems of the dollar, the OPEC balances, and the whole system of international payments will, I suspect, remain on the international agenda for the indefinite future."[7] He was absolutely right.

Arthur Laffer, who was chief economist at the White House Office of Management and Budget in 1971, describes the Nixon Shock as a "panic decision," an overreaction to a "silly one-month inflation number" that was actually lower than inflation spikes from 1970. This decision, says Laffer, had "far-reaching deleterious consequences that would last for years to come—inflation surged and unemployment rose as output fell."[8] Domitrovic agrees: "Price controls were an artificial device through and through, meant to paper over Federal Reserve overprinting in the absence of a dollar link to gold. Even if controls could in fact keep inflation at bay, it would have to be at the expense of output, innovation, and wage growth. In a word, the price was stagnation."[9] Even Keynesians acknowledge that the Nixon Shock led to inflation and slowed economic growth.[10]

In fact, it was under the banner of Keynesianism that President Nixon devalued the dollar. "I am now a Keynesian in economics," he famously said in January 1971.[11] This is ironic in two respects. First, by closing the gold window, Nixon destroyed the international monetary system that John Maynard Keynes had spearheaded at Bretton Woods. Second, his economic measures produced a condition that was supposedly impossible under Keynesian theory: high inflation combined with high unemployment. According to Keynesian logic, there was a trade-off between inflation and unemployment: Keynesian stimulus of demand through deficit spending or monetary expansion would cause a rise in prices, but this was tolerable—even welcome—because meanwhile the stimulus would provide enough purchasing power to take up the slack of vital resources and restore full employment. The Phillips curve, named for a New Zealand economist, purported to document the inverse relationship between inflation and unemployment. By the 1960s that inverse relationship had acquired "received-truth status" in economics, in Domitrovic's words.[12]

The experience of the 1970s exploded that supposed truth. Economists were forced to come up with a new indicator to gauge the unprecedented conditions: the "misery index," which added up the inflation rate and the unemployment rate. The misery index had been below 8 when Nixon took office in 1969; it was above 17 when he resigned the presidency in 1974; by 1980, the last year of Jimmy Carter's presidency, it had hit a sky-high 21.[13] This was the era of "stagflation," a neologism that combined stagnation and inflation. The Keynesians who had long dominated mainstream economic thinking could find no way to explain what was happening.

This was the era in which Austrian economist F. A. Hayek, accepting the Nobel Prize, declared that economists had "made a mess of things."

In 1975, a year after winning the Nobel, Hayek published a paper that explained why increased inflation leads inevitably to increased unemployment, contrary to Keynesian orthodoxy. He wrote: "The argument is often advanced that inflation merely produces a *redistribution* of the social product, while employment *reduces* it and therefore represents a worse evil. The argument is false, because *inflation becomes the cause of increased unemployment.*" One problem, Hayek observed, is that government stimulus tries to address unemployment in the short run, but even to reach those short-term goals requires such inflation to "*accelerate* constantly." This accelerating inflation will "sooner or later reach a degree that makes all effective order of a market economy impossible." More important, "in the long run such inflation inevitably creates much *more* unemployment than the amount it was originally designed to prevent [emphasis in original]."[14] That is because the government's intervention misdirects production in the economy.

To Hayek, the Nixon Shock was only another step toward a total world fiat money system. The experience of the twentieth century since World War I convinced him that government could not and would not issue a stable money. In 1976, Hayek suggested that the currency should be completely separated from the political process. He proposed a free-market money system, one in which market participants chose among competing currencies. Sound currencies would perforce carry lower interest rates because they would protect the parties against inflation and devaluation. Competition would keep the currencies strong. Hayek concluded: "As in other connections, I have come to the conclusion that the best the state can do with respect to money is to provide a framework of legal rules within which the people can develop the monetary institutions that best suit them. It seems to me that if we could prevent governments from meddling with money, we would do more good than any government has ever done in this regard. And private enterprise would probably have done better than the best they have ever done."[15]

What government had done, in the most recent case, was to dismantle the Bretton Woods system. By doing so, Richard Nixon had sent shock waves through the U.S. economy and, indeed, through the global economy.

Stagflation

Although stagflation flummoxed most economists, the damaging effects of the Nixon Shock should not have been a surprise. Nixon's closing of the gold window may have delivered the death blow to the Bretton Woods system, but Hayek was correct to see the move as only the latest in a long line of decisions that eroded the value of the dollar. Over the course of seven decades, the U.S. government had been moving away from a metallic-based currency to fiat money. The progression occurred in six steps:

* **1913:** The Federal Reserve System is created, allowing the U.S. government to manipulate credit independent of market forces and therefore opening the door to inflation.
* **1933:** In a flurry of executive orders and legislative acts, President Franklin Roosevelt and Congress prohibit the private ownership of gold, making it much more difficult for citizens to cope with inflation when the government manipulates the currency.
* **1945:** Congress lowers the minimum gold reserve requirement for Federal Reserve notes from 35 percent to 25 percent, giving monetary authorities more leeway to expand the supply of dollars.
* **1964:** The federal government ceases minting of coins with 90 percent silver content for general circulation.
* **1968:** Congress eliminates even the 25 percent reserve requirement of gold certificates against Federal Reserve notes. In other words, gold reserve requirements are abolished altogether, allowing the U.S. dollar to become a completely fiat currency at home.
* **1971:** President Nixon severs the link to gold, blocking foreign central banks from redeeming Federal Reserve notes for gold.[16] This last step puts the world's currency on a completely fiat basis, opening the door for even more rampant inflation.

The end of silver coinage was a harbinger of what was to come. In 1966 investment expert and journalist William F. Rickenbacker sounded a warning about the move away from silver:

Silver was never the backbone of our monetary system, but nevertheless in recent years it did serve in its minor fashion to measure the speed of our monetary debauch. Now it is gone, and the United States is on a completely fiat basis (the trivial connection between gold and that 20 percent of our money supply that is composed of Federal Reserve notes can be, and will be, ignored). That is, for the first time since 1792 we are out of money backed by nothing better than the politician's pledge. The stage is set for the final inflationary blow-off if that is what our money managers desire. The shelves of the libraries groan under the weight of the evidence that wealth cannot be created through the printing of paper money. . . . Our leaders have not learned from history. We cannot bid farewell to silver without profound foreboding.[17]

Rickenbacker's warnings about fiat money would become all the more relevant when the U.S. government eradicated all ties to gold. With Bretton Woods no longer acting as an external discipline on monetary activities, the U.S. government had a freer hand to expand the money supply and engage in deficit spending. These tools became popular among politicians unwilling to raise taxes.

The inflationary effects of the Nixon Shock were profound. During the twenty-five years between 1946 and 1971, the dollar's value declined by about half: what $100 had purchased in 1946 took $207 to purchase in 1971. After Nixon delinked from gold, the dollar's value was cut in half again, but in just *nine* years this time: in 1980 it took $203 to buy what $100 had purchased in 1971.[18]

To keep pace with this rampant inflation, in 1975 the federal government began using cost-of-living adjustments (COLAs) to increase payments to Social Security recipients. The year-by-year COLAs give an excellent picture of the state of inflation in this brutal era: in 1975 the COLA increased payments fully 8 percent; after dropping to around 6 percent for a few years, the COLA jumped to 9.9 percent in 1979; then, in 1980, it soared to 14.3 percent.[19]

Even when wages kept up with inflation, people often saw their standard of living suffer. The problem was that if someone's earnings were merely adjusted for inflation, with no real gain in income, that person could be propelled into a higher tax bracket and have even more of his pay seized. This was the phenomenon known as "bracket creep."[20]

Still others did not see their incomes adjusted for inflation.

Rickenbacker warned about this problem in 1966, citing the example of a man "who took out a retirement-type insurance policy in the mid-1930s when $150 a month was enough to retire on," then found in the 1960s that this money "didn't go so far as it used to or as he had thought it would." As Rickenbacker rightly observed, the man "had incurred a genuine intangible loss, which he could trace back to the depreciation of the money."[21] In the 1970s, those on fixed incomes or living on their assets saw the value of their holdings fall by half in nine years.

Savings and investment became precarious as well. Domitrovic describes the situation in the stagflation era: "Those who tried to wait out the chaos by saving money were brutally punished. The greatest inflation since the Revolutionary War destroyed the value of funds in bank accounts, the stock market was in free fall, and municipal-bond issuers missed payments."[22] Just to avoid losing capital, an investor had to make sure that the returns on his portfolio equaled the inflation rate. That meant achieving a return on investments of anywhere from 6 to 14 percent *annually*—and this merely to tread water.

The Austrian School helps us understand what was happening here. Ludwig von Mises points out that two factors influence the purchasing power of the monetary unit: *cash-induced changes* and *goods-induced changes*.[23] Cash-induced changes refer to the influence of increases in the supply of money. Although the money supply had been increasing significantly before 1971, monetary expansion really took off once Nixon removed the external discipline of gold convertibility. According to Federal Reserve economic data, the U.S. money supply increased from $459.2 billion in August 1971 to $650.4 billion in August 1975—an increase of nearly 42 percent in just four years.[24] This expansion of the money supply, or cash-induced change, overwhelmed the goods-induced changes that were occurring simultaneously—namely, the increase in productivity. Whereas the growth rate of real gross national product averaged 4.12 percent per year from 1961 to 1970, it averaged only 3.16 percent from 1971 to 1980.[25]

Flexible Exchange Rates

Richard Nixon identified himself as a Keynesian, but in fact the idea for flexible exchange rates originated with the monetarist school. The leading proponent of monetarism, Milton Friedman of the University of Chicago, proposed a system of freely floating exchange rates in his 1962 book *Capitalism and Freedom.*

Like the Austrians, monetarists are critical of government intervention in the economy and thus oppose Keynesian efforts to "stimulate" demand. But Friedman's proposal for flexible exchange rates signals a crucial difference between monetarism and Austrian economics. Monetarists hold that the most powerful influence in the economy is money: if the money supply is stable, the rest of the economy will automatically adjust. It follows that inflation is a monetary phenomenon: stabilize the money and you will stabilize inflation. Operating from these fundamental premises, Friedman argued that governments should increase the money supply at a constant rate over time. That rate should be announced to the public, which can then adjust its economic activity accordingly.

Flexible exchange rates, Friedman writes in *Capitalism and Freedom*, are the only viable mechanism that is "consistent with a free market and free trade." He acknowledges that the gold standard also would be consistent with free markets, but he makes the case that such a system—a "real gold standard," which is fully automatic and independent of government actions—is not "feasible," and that "in any event we cannot adopt it by ourselves." Denouncing the "pseudo gold standard" that Bretton Woods codified, Friedman calls for "a system of freely floating exchange rates determined in the market by private transactions without governmental intervention." He warns that "if we do not adopt [a flexible-exchange-rate system], we shall inevitably fail to expand the area of free trade and shall sooner or later be induced to impose widespread direct controls over trade."[26]

Friedman was one of several University of Chicago economists earning attention and respect for his work, and especially for challenging Keynesian orthodoxy. Friedman was making his name not only with *Capitalism and Freedom* but also with his 1963 follow-up, *A Monetary History of the United States, 1867–1960*, written with Anna J. Schwartz. This monumental work argues that changes in the money supply always accompany trade-cycle fluctuations. Friedman and Schwartz show that in the run-up to the Great Depression, 1929–33, the Federal Reserve's excessively tight monetary policy allowed bank reserves to shrink by about a third. This collapse of the money supply, they write, turned a recession into the economic cataclysm of the 1930s.[27] *A Monetary History of the United States* forced historians and economists alike to rethink the causes of the Depression. In a 2004 speech, Federal Reserve chairman Benjamin Bernanke paid tribute to Friedman and Schwartz's work, saying that it "transformed the debate about the Great Depression."[28] It is no coincidence that in late 2008, when another economic crisis hit, Bernanke's Federal Reserve pumped trillions of dollars of reserves into the system.

Friedman won the Nobel Prize in Economics in 1976 and became perhaps the most influential economist of the second half of the twentieth century. But when it came to his system of freely floating exchange rates, he made a mistake. His mistake was trusting politicians not to tamper with the money supply. Austrian economists such as Hayek and Hans Sennholz have shown that when the value of the monetary unit is left in the hands of the political class, currency depreciation or inflation follows.[29]

Friedman was naive in suggesting that the values of currencies could be determined "in the market by private transactions without governmental intervention." As any student of history quickly learns, leaders too often lack the will or discipline not to manipulate currencies. There is no free market in currencies when government, through a central bank, can increase or decrease the amount of money in circulation at will.

For Friedman's system to operate correctly, the money supply needs to match the rate of growth in the economy. The "monetary rule" that Friedman envisioned the Federal Reserve adopting—that is, the constant rate at which it would increase the supply of dollars—did not square with political reality. As has been shown repeatedly over the past four decades, the insatiable demands for government spending put pressure on the Fed to abandon any monetary rule.

One of the major problems with the flexible-exchange-rate system is the lack of a standard of international value for individual currencies aside from the willingness of nations to maintain a certain exchange rate. When governments can change the value of currencies at will, they are free to engage in a kind of monetary warfare, or nationalism, wreaking havoc on their trading partners. Under the current system, a nation may affect its balance of imports and exports simply by changing the value of its currency. Lowering the value of the currency makes a country's products cheaper for other countries to buy. Raising the value of the currency makes the country's products more expensive, while at the same time allowing the country more power to purchase imports.

Such machinations cannot occur if currencies are tied to an objective standard such as gold. Politicians lose control over monetary policy. As a result, there are no overvalued or undervalued currencies, and international trade follows competition, not monetary manipulation.[30]

The problems with a flexible-exchange-rate system became apparent during the decade that followed Nixon's decision to close the gold window. Without an objective standard to follow, the Fed increased the money supply dramatically, sending the United States on a wild ride of inflation.

Federal Reserve Watching

Markets quickly responded to the fact that the value of the dollar had become a political determination. A new industry sprang up: Federal Reserve watching. Everyone wanted to know what the Fed was going to do and how it would affect the long- and short-term value of the dollar. In addition, speculation in the value of the dollar on foreign exchange markets started in earnest.

This is a fundamental problem with a fiat currency: its value in world markets largely reflects the public's confidence that the supply of the currency will be restrained. The public must be convinced that the government is willing to risk a cash crunch or a recession to protect the value of the currency. The U.S. federal government has had a difficult time preserving such credibility. Most administrations find it easier to give in to rising prices and expand the money supply than to take the political heat.

As the government loses credibility, inflationary expectations begin to appear. All elements of the economy soon recognize that they must take future inflation into account. To protect against expected inflation, manufacturers and retailers increase prices, unions push for increased wages, landlords increase rents, banks increase interest rates, and so on.

Imagine the case of a gas station owner who is paying $3 a gallon wholesale for gasoline. To earn a 10 percent profit, he sells his product at $3.30. But then he receives a notice from his wholesaler that future deliveries will be $4 per gallon. Suddenly, the cost to fill his inventory of ten thousand gallons has jumped from $30,000 to $40,000. To maintain his profit margin, he must immediately raise the price of gas to $4.40. If he kept his price the same, he would not only fail to earn a profit but would actually fall $10,000 short when it came time replace the supply. A retailer must always be able to sell this product for at least enough to replenish the inventory. Otherwise, he will consume his capital and be forced out of business. Similarly, a landlord must anticipate what his future costs will be in agreeing to long-term leases, and labor leaders must try to anticipate inflationary effects when they negotiate long-term contracts for union members. Investors, too, must anticipate future inflation. Every financial planner must calculate future depreciation of the dollar to ensure that his client will have sufficient funds for retirement.

Of course, markets cannot anticipate precisely how much inflation will come. In certain sectors, in fact, prices actually race ahead of the expansion of the money supply. That eventually pushes up prices across the board. Rising costs then become a way of life. If the central bank prints new money to keep up with inflation, the government in effect validates the higher prices seen on the market (which is why economists call the process of creating new money to match higher prices *validation*). But if the central bank does not provide the new money, high prices will discourage purchases and demand will fall. Unemployment will result, and in the ensuing recession, prices will drop as unions, manufacturers, and investors are forced to give concessions.

To see how this pattern plays out, consider the economic events of 1978 and 1979. During the summer of 1978, prices surged to annualized double-digit rates. President Jimmy Carter's administration faced a choice: it could create new money to validate the higher prices, or it could take a hard line against monetary expansion, adopting a new policy signaling that prices must be lower—and that the government was willing to accept a recession. Carter took the latter course. Inflation was now the number-one political problem. In December 1978, *Time* magazine reported: "The President, who began the year trying to prod the economy to faster growth, shifted gradually to a tight-budget policy and proclaimed wage-price guidelines that stop just short of mandatory controls. When even those measures failed to stop inflation and the sickening plunge of the dollar, President Carter on Nov. 1 welcomed a sharp increase in interest rates that normally would have violated his populist principles."[31]

In 1979, President Carter called on Paul Volcker, who had a reputation for endorsing hard-money policies to combat inflation, to be chairman of the Federal Reserve. To adjust the market's inflationary expectations, Carter publicized his intention not to validate rising prices, talking openly of the need to fight inflation. The Fed likewise showed that it was serious about taming inflation, allowing both short-term and long-term interest rates to soar. The prime rate, which stood at 11.75 percent at the beginning of 1979, jumped to 20 percent by the spring of 1980.[32]

The Carter administration also turned to deregulation to try to kill inflation. Carter advisers argued that the United States was experiencing *cost-push inflation*, meaning that burdensome federal regulations were increasing the costs of production, and those costs were being passed on to consumers in the form of higher prices. Carter's "inflation czar" was Alfred E. Kahn, who came to the administration from the New York Public Service Commission, where he had pioneered reforms that lowered costs significantly. Kahn is best known for his work to deregulate the airlines. During his tenure as chair of the Civil Aeronautics Board, deregulation led airfares to fall and ridership to increase dramatically: airline profits rose from $409 million in 1977 to $905 million in 1978. Kahn's deregulatory work opened up the skies to millions of Americans who could now afford to travel quickly and efficiently.[33] And the work on airline deregulation was just part of a broader Carter administration effort to reduce regulations. A number of other industries, including banking, stock exchanges, railroads, busing, and telecommunications, benefited from the decrease in the regulatory burden.

In short, Democrat Jimmy Carter put in place effective anti-inflation programs after his two Republican predecessors had failed to develop successful strategies (Richard Nixon's price controls and Gerald Ford's "Whip Inflation Now" appeal had both proved feckless). Unfortunately for Carter, his previous efforts to stimulate the economy made the market wary of his approaches, even when he signaled a new hard line against inflation. Inflation kept rising in 1979, and the price of gold, always an indicator of the market's judgment about future inflation, jumped to more than $800 an ounce. It can take a while for inflationary expectations to catch up with new policies, and this is what happened late in the Carter administration.

Finally, by 1980, the Fed's tight money policies began to take hold and the economy started to slow. If the Nixon Shock had started the United States on a wild ride of inflation, Paul Volcker's Federal Reserve finally slammed on the brakes, pushing interest rates above 20 percent. The result was a deliberate, government-induced recession that was one of the worst business downturns of the twentieth century. With unemployment rising and stagflation persisting, Republican presidential candidate Ronald Reagan could slam the Carter administration for its handling of the economy. The relevant economic statistics became worse and worse as the 1980 election approached. Carter appeared totally ineffective. Reagan was an easy choice for voters battered by nine years of chaos since "Nixon's Folly."

As brutal as the effects of the Fed's hard-line policies were, they ultimately did end the inflation and monetary expansion. That said, these monetary policies were no substitute for reinstituting the gold standard, as the Austrian School pointed out. Reinstating a gold standard had stopped inflation dead in its tracks before. One famous instance occurred in Napoleon Bonaparte's France. Confronting the fiat inflation that had raged since the French Revolution began, Napoleon announced that gold would back the French currency. This move stopped the price spiral almost immediately. Later, when his ministers pushed him to inflate the currency again, he declared, "While I live I will never resort to irredeemable paper."[34] Similarly, the great German inflation after the First World War ended once Germany issued a new currency that was backed by a gold reserve of $33\frac{1}{3}$ percent (the United States loaned the gold under the so-called Dawes Plan) and made bank notes redeemable in gold.[35] In those and other instances, the recovery was almost immediate, because instituting the gold standard caused inflationary expectations to disappear.[36]

The Fed policies of the late 1970s and early 1980s led to a more protracted and painful recovery. It would take a few years for Volcker's austerity measures to rein in inflation. Eventually, however, the new monetary policy worked. Over time, the market finally became convinced that the government was serious—serious enough that it would risk a recession. Eventually investors lowered interest-rate expectations, manufacturers and others cut costs, unions considered concessions and moderated wage demands, and real estate prices fell off.

The policies begun under the Carter administration paved the way for the end of stagflation. The next step was to restore economic growth.

The Reagan administration did this by employing supply-side economics, which arose as a direct response to the Keynesian establishment's
failure to handle—or even properly explain—the brutal economic conditions of the 1970s.

Like Austrian economists, supply-siders recognized the relationship
between taxes and incentives—specifically, that taxes impose a large cost
on the economy and discourage investment—and called for deregulation
to remove government fetters on the economy. Similarly, supply-siders
generally agreed with Austrians on the advantages of a gold or fixed-
exchange-rate standard and the need to balance the budget. The Reagan
administration would achieve the first two goals and set off a remarkable
economic run. But its failures to achieve the last two goals would under-
mine those achievements in the long run.

8

Reagan's Rally

The 1970s were the worst economic decade since the 1930s—indeed, the second-worst decade in American economic history.[1] This ten years saw three presidents, none of whom served out two terms; the first unsuccessful finish to an American war; peacetime wage and price controls; and extremely high inflation. At the time, the academic economics establishment offered little by way of solutions to the stagflation crisis that resulted from policies this mainstream had championed. F. A. Hayek's memorable comment that "as a profession we have made a mess of things" was not the only public acknowledgment of economists' failings. In 1978 one of the most influential academic economists, future Nobel Prize winner Robert E. Lucas of the University of Chicago, admitted that Keynesian predictions had been "wildly incorrect" and that "the doctrine on which they were based is fundamentally flawed." Lucas added that "the task now facing contemporary students of the business cycle is to sort through the wreckage." Doing so, he said, would require "the reopening of basic issues" that had long been viewed as closed.[2]

Challenges to the Keynesian orthodoxy were already developing in certain pockets of the academy, most notably at Lucas's University of Chicago. In addition to Milton Friedman and monetarism, Chicago was home to Lucas and the school of "rational expectations." Building on the work of John Fraser Muth, Lucas disputed the Keynesian view that the central bank could adopt easy-money policies to spur employment. The school of rational expectations held that high inflation and high

131

unemployment existed simultaneously—contrary to what Keynesian doctrine said was possible—because the market recognized the central bank's monetary manipulations and workers would began to push for salary increases to offset expected inflation.[3]

Another new school of economics emerged at the University of Virginia in the 1960s, led by future Nobel Prize winner James Buchanan (who had studied at the University of Chicago) and Gordon Tullock. The "public choice" school of economics helped explain the practical difficulties with the Keynesian idea of "fine-tuning" the economy, which has the government playing an active role during economic downturns and then backing off during periods of prosperity. The problem, Buchanan and Tullock showed, is that the government is not a neutral observer but rather expands its own interest. Given the nature of politics and bureaucracy, a new government program put into place "temporarily" to solve a particular problem often is impossible to end once the crisis passes.[4]

In the face of Keynesianism's fundamental flaws, what new economic paradigm could be followed to spur a recovery from stagflation?

As a presidential candidate, Ronald Reagan promoted "supply-side" economics as the key to recovery. This was yet another challenge to Keynesianism that could trace its roots to the University of Chicago: both Robert Mundell, the most significant supply-side theorist, and Arthur Laffer, who explained these ideas to people in power, had taught in the Chicago economics department. With Reagan serving as apostle, supply-side economics gained widespread attention and soon shaped a host of government economic policies. Reagan promised that supply-side economics would bring jobs and economic growth at last, while also ending inflation, lowering taxation, and balancing the federal budget.

Supply-Side Economics

Supply-siders saw eye to eye with Austrian economists in their criticisms of government intervention in the economy (although they departed from the Austrians in analyzing the economy from a macro standpoint). Like the Austrians, supply-siders argued that excessive taxation, regulation, and manipulation of the money supply caused problems ranging from inflation to unemployment to stagnation to international currency crises.

Supply-siders believed, along with Austrian economists, that the U.S. government took a fateful step in 1913 by creating the Federal Reserve and installing a federal income tax. These two institutions represented the government's most powerful means of intrusion into the economy. The supply-siders argued, in fact, that excessive taxation and manipulation of the money supply are the primary causes of *any* economic crisis.[5] For example, the Fed's policies and tax rates led to stagflation in the 1970s, as historian Brian Domitrovic explains: "First, the government had taken to destabilizing the means of exchange—the dollar—by printing it with abandon. This was the origin of inflation. Second, the government had jacked up tax rates, particularly on income that people earned as they got richer. This brought about disincentives to work and poisoned the well of capital formation. Unemployment was the necessary result."[6]

The term *supply-side economics* reflects the fact that this school stood opposed to Keynesianism, which might be called "demand-side economics." Keynesianism is all about using government intervention to increase demand in the economy, either through the printing of money or through increased government spending. This is the thinking that produced the federal "stimulus" package in 2009 as well as "quantitative easing," which is the new name for a central bank's expansion of the money supply.[7]

But supply-siders traced their intellectual heritage much farther back, all the way to the French economist Jean-Baptiste Say (1767–1832). Say challenged economic thinking that blamed downturns on a lack of money. When he published his book *A Treatise on Political Economy* in 1803, many economists were calling for the government to turn out more money or "purchasing power" to remove the gluts of unsold goods on markets (at the time, economists spoke of gluts rather than recessions or depressions). In his famous chapter "On the Demand or Market for Products," Say responded that supply or production—not demand, and not money—was the mainspring of prosperity. He argued that the marketplace allowed an exchange of goods and services for other goods and services; money was merely the facilitator. According to Say, a person would be anxious to sell his product on the market. That person would be equally anxious to use the money received to buy other products. The ultimate use of money is to buy another product. So it followed that the *supply* of one product created the demand for another. This has become known as Say's Law ("The mere circumstance of creation of one product immediately opens a vent for other products").[8] Say realized that each man's prosperity is linked to everyone else's; the more prosperous one person becomes, the better customer he is for other's goods and services, and vice versa.

Following Say's insight, the supply-siders of the twentieth century argued that the economy could be stimulated by increasing productivity and lowering cost—that is, by focusing on supply, not demand. They formulated an economic program based on removing obstacles to economic initiative and stabilizing the currency in order to stimulate investment and production. Their program had four parts: (1) much lower marginal tax rates, (2) a return to a gold standard (which would lower inflationary expectations and, thus, interest rates),[9] (3) deregulation of the economy, and (4) balanced federal budgets.

In the popular imagination, supply-side economics is associated with the first of those four planks: tax cuts. This is an oversimplification of supply-side thinking, though tax cuts were undoubtedly central to the supply-siders' case. Since at least the 1960s, Robert Mundell, a future Nobel Prize winner, had been doing the theoretical work supporting a policy mix of low taxes and tight money.[10] In a now-famous incident from 1974, Arthur Laffer made the case for tax reductions to Ford administration officials by sketching a curve on a restaurant napkin.[11]

The "Laffer Curve" illustrated the argument that tax rates, like all other economic factors, have a point of diminishing returns. Up to a certain point raising rates will boost government revenue, but after that point increasing taxes will be counterproductive—providing disincentives to work harder and invest more—and federal collections will fall off. At the same time, the government could actually *increase* revenues by lowering tax rates enough to encourage economic activity and growth. Supply-siders pointed to the experience of the John F. Kennedy and Warren G. Harding administrations, both of which cut tax rates substantially, producing upturns in business activity and increases in government revenues.[12]

The supply-side argument was not so simple as to suggest that cutting taxes would, in itself, solve the problem of federal deficits. The very week Laffer drew his napkin sketch, the *Wall Street Journal*'s Jude Wanniski, an early advocate of supply-side economics, published an editorial explaining the connection between taxes and government revenue. Citing

Mundell extensively, Wanniski's piece laid out the supply-side position: (1) tax cuts might actually reduce government revenue, but they would also reduce *expenditures*, since the economic activity spurred by the tax cuts would lower the state's welfare and unemployment obligations; and (2) even if government deficits occurred, they would be easily financed, given, Domitrovic writes, "the new excitement for dollar-denominated assets that would result from tight money and tax cuts."[13]

These finer points of supply-side theory were not, however, typically part of the broader message of the supply-siders, which was politically powerful in the hands of Ronald Reagan. Reagan promised to grow the economy, reduce unemployment, end inflation, lower taxation, and balance the federal budget. The promise of economic growth helped Reagan dominate the 1980 election.

The Reagan Program

After a triumphant campaign, Reagan began the difficult task of trying to keep his word. On February 18, 1981, less than a month after his inauguration, Reagan submitted to Congress his administration's program for economic recovery. It proposed:

* A budget reform plan to cut the rate of growth in federal spending.
* Regulatory relief.
* A series of proposals to reduce personal income tax rates by 10 percent a year over three years and create jobs by accelerating depreciation for business investment plans and equipment.
* A commitment to monetary policy that would restore stable currency and healthy financial markets. In practice, this meant that the Reagan administration supported Federal Reserve chairman Paul Volcker's effort to wring inflationary expectations out of the economy through high interest rates.[14]

President Reagan made his most significant move to end the ongoing recession when, in August, he signed into law the Economic Recovery and Tax Act of 1981. The new law embodied the hopes of supply-side economists by drastically lowering marginal tax rates and abolishing the inheritance tax for most Americans. The bill also indexed the progressive tax rates to account for inflation; this ended "bracket creep," which occurred when taxpayers whose incomes merely kept up with inflation were pushed into higher tax brackets.

With the tax cuts in place, by November 1982 the economy started moving into warp speed, achieving economic growth not seen since the 1960s. Just as had occurred after the Harding and Kennedy tax cuts, federal revenues surged, unemployment declined markedly (from 7.1 percent to 5.5 percent), and the economy entered a boom phase. Inflation fell from an average of 12.5 percent in the last year of Carter's presidency to 4.4 percent in 1988, the last year of Reagan's. The boom created some eighteen million new jobs. It was, in the words of Reagan biographer Lou Cannon—a frequent critic of Reagan's policies—"by far the longest peacetime expansion in United States history."[15] The success of the Reagan program was undeniable, but the failure to push for a balanced budget or a restoration of the gold standard—two other key elements of the supply-side agenda—eventually worked against the plan. Despite Reagan's campaign pledge to balance the federal budget by 1984, the deficit grew larger than ever. Tax revenues did actually increase; the problem was spending, which outpaced new revenues. Entitlements grew, defense spending grew, interest payments on the national debt grew. The supply-siders failed to rein in spending in part because they were so enthusiastic about their program's ability to produce revenue. Congressional proponents such as Jack Kemp of New York promised that there would be no cuts in entitlement programs. This attitude eviscerated any attempt on the part of Congress to reduce federal spending. Economic growth promised to carry the increasing burden of entitlement programs while improving standards of living for Americans.

Austrian economists were shocked when administration officials began to use Keynesian terms to justify the deficit. In his 1987 book *Debts and Deficits*, Hans Sennholz observed, "Politicians and officials in high places are pointing to the fact that the Federal debt has actually declined in terms of purchasing power as well as relative value. They are supported by 'supply side' economists who point to the shrinkage of debt. They all are convinced that federal deficits no longer matter."[16] Sennholz criticized inflation, the lowering of the value of the dollar, as a species of debt repudiation.

The constant deficits brought cries for tax increases from Congress and the establishment members of Reagan's administration. Proponents of tax increases spoke of "revenue enhancement." Austrian economist Murray Rothbard pointed out that tax increases rarely solve budget difficulties. Increased revenue simply becomes an excuse for more government spending.[17] Sure enough, tax increases in 1982, 1983, and 1984 did not close the deficit. Confirming Rothbard's analysis, Reagan biographer Steven Hayward reports that the 1982 tax increase bill actually resulted in $1.14 of spending for each extra tax dollar.[18]

Growing deficits were one problem, but what ultimately tore out the foundation of the supply-side program was the failure to achieve a gold standard. The Reagan administration missed the last chance to reverse Richard Nixon's fateful decision to end any connection to gold. That opportunity presented itself after Congress, at the behest of Senator Jesse Helms, passed a law calling for a "gold commission." The commission began meeting in 1981, after Reagan took office. Members of the monetarist school were in charge of the commission.[19] Not surprisingly, then, the commission came out against reinstituting a specie-backed currency, instead favoring Milton Friedman's formula of slow monetary growth controlled by the Federal Reserve.

With that, the proposal to go back to the gold standard died, and the possibility of stopping inflation, keeping interest rates low, stabilizing world currency markets, and balancing the budget expired along with it. From the time of the commission, inflation in the United States continued on its way. What cost $1,000 in 1982 cost more than $2,263 in 2010.[20] The federal debt exploded and the dollar lost any permanent anchor. Worldwide currencies had no intrinsic value, and governments manipulated them to gain export advantage. The world has been treated to asset bubbles and crashes of increasing intensity ever since.

Bill Clinton's administration, interestingly enough, showed that borrowing at low interest rates—a major feature under the gold standard—could help balance the budget. Robert Rubin, Clinton's secretary of the treasury, argued that if the federal government was not in the capital market, then it would leave more capital available for private investors.[21] As the government borrowed less, the demand for funds would drop and so would long-term interest rates. Consequently, the Clinton administration moved the federal debt into short-term markets to take advantage of lower interest rates. This move did involve some risk, as short-term interest rates can shoot up quickly. But in this case the decision significantly lowered federal borrowing costs. The resulting savings helped balance the budget. Also, because the federal government needed to borrow less, more capital was available in the private market, and interest rates fell for all sectors of the economy.

Still, without a gold standard, inflation continued. By the end of the Clinton administration, in 2001, it cost approximately 25 percent more to purchase things than it had when Clinton took office in 1993.[22]

The supply-siders explained that this ongoing inflation was particularly problematic because it inflated the federal debt. In the nineteenth century the great Austrian economist Eugen Böhm-Bawerk had shown that interest rates are payment for time. Supply-siders and Austrians both recognized that before lending money, people and institutions account not only for time but also for inflationary expectations in setting interest rates. In the absence of inflationary expectations, naturally, interest rates are lower. Consider the most prominent risk-free investment of the nineteenth century, the British government bond known as the consol. The yield on the British consol fell steadily from 4.42 percent in 1820 to 2.54 percent in 1900. Why? Because in 1819, Britain adopted the gold standard, and effectively there was no inflation in the ensuing decades. When governments adopt a monetary standard that is perceived to be inflation proof, interest rates will drop significantly. That is precisely what happened in Britain: long-term interest rates fell continually after 1819.[23]

The magic of gold is the absence of inflationary expectations. People are willing to lend at low rates, knowing that their principle will not deteriorate. Those low interest rates mean that the federal government can fund its debt cheaply, borrowing money at a rate of 2–3 percent, participating in both long- and short-term markets. That 2–3 percent, not coincidentally, is the interest rate paid on gold in short- and especially in long-term markets. Imagine the difference in the federal debt had the gold commission persuaded the U.S. government to adopt the gold standard in 1981. Interest alone added a total of nearly $1.9 trillion to that debt between 1981 and 1993. During this time, the interest rate paid on the debt averaged more than 6 percent annually (before the Clinton administration took a different approach). An interest rate of 2–3 percent would have amounted to huge savings on the debt—even without cuts in government spending.

Nor is the federal budget the only area in which the gold standard would have helped. Every other sector of the economy—local governments, state governments, businesses, individuals—would have been able to finance debt at lower interest rates. Lower interest rates would have meant lower costs, such as mortgage rates. This is one of the reasons why economic growth under a gold standard is consistently higher than under a fiat standard.

In addition, a strong case can be made that the United States could have avoided both the housing bubble and the dot-com bubble had a gold standard been adopted. Writing in the *Wall Street Journal*, economist Charles Kadlec notes that the "high and highly volatile interest rates" we have seen ever since President Nixon closed the gold window "are symptomatic of the monetary uncertainty that has reduced the economy's ability to recover from external shocks and led directly to one financial crisis after another. During these four decades of discretionary monetary policies, the world suffered no fewer than 10 major financial crises, beginning with the oil crisis of 1973 and culminating in the financial crisis of 2008–09." Kadlec concludes with an undeniable fact from the historical record: "There were no world-wide financial crises of similar magnitude between 1947 and 1971," the Bretton Woods era.[24]

The Protectionist Trap

During the 1980s, the Reagan administration faced another political problem—intense pressure for protectionism. U.S. manufacturers and their unions were struggling with foreign competition, and an array of interest groups demanded higher tariffs, quotas, and other protectionist restrictions.

The cry for protectionism grew louder as the Federal Reserve tried to halt inflation. By ceasing to print money, Paul Volcker's Fed caused the U.S. dollar to rise significantly in world markets. As a result, U.S. exports became more expensive on world markets, while imports from other countries became relatively cheap. This was one of the results of the floating-exchange-rate system Milton Friedman had devised.

The trouble with protectionism is that when a country restricts imports, it also restricts exports. The only way foreigners can purchase U.S.-made products is to earn dollars by selling goods and services to Americans. One of the reasons for the high trade deficit was that foreigners were buying plenty of things in the United States—mainly government bonds to finance the federal deficit.

In September 1985, in New York City, Secretary of the Treasury James Baker headed a conference of the so-called G5 nations: the United States, Great Britain, France, West Germany, and Japan. Baker hoped that by lowering the value of the U.S. dollar, he could mollify the protectionist sentiment without actually turning to protectionism. He reasoned that the United States could lower the value of the dollar in foreign markets, causing the prices of U.S. goods to fall and thus increasing the demand for U.S.-made products.[25] Baker orchestrated an agreement called the Plaza Accord, named after the hotel where the conference took place. The five nations agreed to intervene in currency markets to weaken the U.S. dollar and strengthen the currencies of the other members. The plan achieved the desired effect: by late 1987 the dollar had fallen 54 percent against both the deutsche mark and the yen.[26] U.S. automobile companies and exporters were thrilled, but they failed to take into account that the move made American assets cheaper for foreigners. GM, Ford, and Chrysler found that the Japanese auto firms could build plants in the United States at a much lower cost than American companies could. Suddenly foreign-owned, low-cost competitors were setting up right next door.

Even more dangerous was that the Federal Reserve helped lower the value of the dollar by increasing bank credit. This was the start of an inflation of bank credit. As always, this credit inflation stimulated a boom. In the end, the bursting of those bubbles—that is, the ultimate failure to account for the realities of the trade cycle that Austrian economists had documented over and over again—undercut the legitimate achievements of Ronald Reagan and supply-side economics. To be sure, supply-side policies increased employment, federal revenues, and assets. But the failure to adopt a meaningful, gold-based currency produced the bubbles and the international currency disorder that wreaked havoc in later decades.

The Austrians Were Right:
The Collapse of the Planned Economies

The course of the U.S. economy through the twentieth century and into the twenty-first confirmed again and again the analyses and predictions of the Austrian School. Events on the world stage validated Austrian predictions as well. Specifically, the collapse of communism showed that Ludwig von Mises, F. A. Hayek, Wilhelm Röpke, and other Austrian economists had been precisely right about the fate of centrally planned economies.

In the mid-twentieth century the expectation was that socialism, or the planned economy, was the wave of the future. The academy taught very little about the virtues of free markets. Both academics and the press mistakenly identified free markets as the cause of the Great Depression.[27] Subsequent events only seemed to confirm these views, as socialist revolutions roiled Latin America, Asia, and Africa into the 1970s and 1980s. Prominent Western economists, such as Paul Samuelson in his famous economics text, estimated that it would be only a matter of time before the planned economies surpassed the market economies of the West. In the 1980s the CIA estimated that the Soviet Union's rates of economic growth dwarfed those of the United States, and that consequently the USSR could someday catch up to the U.S. economy. Of course, after the Soviet Union collapsed, we learned that the Soviet economy had been dramatically smaller than the CIA estimated, with its central planners managing an economy perhaps one-eighth the size of the U.S. market economy.[28]

Austrian economists were among the few who foresaw the coming collapse of the planned economies. Mises, Hayek, and Röpke all perceived serious problems with both the practice and theory of trying to plan economic activity and production.

Mises wrote of the "impossibility" of socialism. He argued that socialist economies could not provide for a true price system and thus would face chaos as they attempted to allocate resources. By destroying the price system, Mises said, socialism destroys the very thing that allows people to make rational economic decisions. After the fall of communism, mainstream economists were forced to concede that Mises had been on the mark. In 1990, Robert Heilbroner, author of the famous economics book *The Worldly Philosophers*, admitted that when he encountered Mises's argument at the beginning of his career, he did not see it as "a particularly cogent reason to reject socialism, given the irrationalities and incoherence of capitalism during the Great Depression." But Heilbroner now acknowledged: "It turns out, of course, that Mises was right. The Soviet system has long been dogged by a method of pricing that produced grotesque misallocations of effort. . . . As Mises foresaw, setting prices became a hopeless problem, because the economy never stood still long enough for anyone to decide anything correctly."[29]

Hayek noted that economic planners do not have sufficient knowledge to run an entire economy. That is to say, they simply do not have access to all the myriad pieces of economic information that arise at all different times and in all different places. Only those on the ground, working in real time, have sufficient knowledge to make decisions about the best and most efficient use of resources. Crucially, none of those individuals decides about the allocation of scarce resources for the economy as a whole. Rather, many thousands or even millions of people make economic decisions every day. Those countless decisions and transactions are reflected in prices set in the free market. The sheer range of information occurring simultaneously all over the place makes central planning highly inefficient and ultimately untenable, Hayek said.[30]

Röpke saw that communism's entire structure was built on force and that it had lost any moral foundation. He pointed to the brutal suppression of worker demonstrations in both Poland and Hungary in 1956 as evidence. He predicted that such systems predicated on force could not endure.[31]

All these predictions were borne out beginning in 1989, the year Ronald Reagan left the White House. After the Cold War had raged for nearly a half century, the collapse of communism was swift and stunning. By the time 1989 was over, the Berlin Wall had been torn down, Ceausescu had been ousted in Romania, Bulgaria's communist leadership had resigned, the Czechs had launched their Velvet Revolution, Solidarity had scored remarkable electoral wins in Poland, and Hungary had dismantled its barbed-wire border fence to Austria.

The Austrian economists correctly saw that the fall of the centrally planned economies was inevitable, but the collapse occurred more quickly than anyone could have imagined. It took political genius to bring about such a sudden turn of events. Specifically, the leaders of the free world, and especially Ronald Reagan and Margaret Thatcher, saw the opportunity to deal a significant blow to Soviet power. The Reagan administration put together a plan that led to the collapse of the Soviet Union, all without a shot being fired.[32]

Another figure played a crucial role during this time: Pope John Paul II, the first modern pope to turn the Vatican into a full-fledged power in world affairs.[33] The Polish-born pope came from behind the Iron Curtain and clearly understood the theory and practice of communism, and especially its weaknesses.

Significantly, as a philosopher, John Paul II drew from the same roots as the Austrian economists. emphasizing the nature of the human person. The philosopher that both drew from was Franz Brentano (1838–1917). Brentano was a colleague and friend of, and an important philosophical influence on, Austrian School founder Carl Menger.[34] The *Mises Review* sums up Brentano's position: "The nature of the world is 'read off' directly, using both external observation and introspection. Not only is it held that we know the actual world: sometimes, just by operating in a commonsense way, we can see how the world must be."[35] Most notably, Brentano's views influenced Menger's concept of subjective value.

John Paul II was aware of Brentano's influence from his studies of Edmund Husserl, a student of Brentano. Like Austrian economists, the pope focused on the individual acting person. In fact, in 1967 he published a book entitled *The Acting Person*. The pope's philosophy of personalism, as it is known, teaches that each person is unique and has free will, and should never be used as a means to the end of another person. Clearly, then, John Paul II's thinking stood opposed to totalitarianism and any economic system that used people to achieve a "greater good."[36]

And this, ultimately, was the view of the Austrians. They argued against centrally planned economies not merely on grounds of economic efficiency. In fact, in *The Road to Serfdom*, Hayek acknowledged that the planned economies dangled the prospect of a greater standard of living for all; the problem was that in the hope of achieving such material gain, people would have to sacrifice their civil liberties and their "individualism." By doing so, Hayek said, we sacrifice "independence, self-reliance, and the willingness to bear risks, the readiness to back one's own conviction against a majority, and the willingness to voluntary cooperation with one's neighbors."[37]

Critiques of communism, then, were no mere footnote in Austrian economic analysis; they were of a piece with the Austrians' fundamental belief in individual liberty and in economics as being centered on the individual acting person. The Austrian School's economic guidelines are all built on these philosophical foundations. As the history of the past century reveals, those guidelines have too often been ignored, and the penalty has been economic turmoil and even war.

Having reviewed that history, let us now look more carefully at the Austrian School's economic tenets to see how they might pave the way for peaceful prosperity in the future.

Part III

A Reconstruction of Economics

9

The Division of Labor

Few principles are so common in nature as cooperation among diverse parts. Every living thing proclaims it. Aristotle makes it the foundation of all human society. The Bible, in the Book of Genesis, speaks of it in referring to Adam and Eve as helpmates. Adam Smith writes about it in the first chapter of *The Wealth of Nations*.

St. Paul, in his first letter to the Corinthians, offered a good description of this principle. Dealing with a group of early Christians wracked by turmoil, he diagnosed the problem as lack of cooperation and confusion as to each person's role. Paul appealed to the analogy of the human body to demonstrate that in a successful community, each person has a role to play based on his or her talents, and that those roles are interdependent:

> Now the body is not one member, it is many. If the foot should say, "Because I am not a hand I do not belong to the body," would it no longer belong to the body? If the ear should say, "Because I am not an eye I do not belong to the body," would it no longer belong to the body? If the body were all eye, what would happen to hearing? If it were all ear, what would happen to smelling? As it is, God has set each member of the body in the place he wanted it to be. If all members were alike, where would the body be? The eye cannot say to the hand, "I do not need you," any more than the head can say to the feet, "I do not need you." Even those members of the body which we deem less important are in fact indispensable.[1]

The principle of cooperation that Paul outlined is fundamental to all walks of life. Within any community, each subgroup—be it the family, the military, business, the academy, the government, the healing professions, or the church—has a specific purpose and necessary autonomy. Generally, when one subgroup invades the work of another, it does a poor job. Government, for example, normally fails in its attempts to raise children or run businesses. A community is successful when all these groups operate in harmony, fulfilling their own distinct purposes. This is a matter not just of efficiency but of social justice as well. The political philosopher Russell Kirk, drawing on Socrates, pointed out that "the happy society is the just society"—a society in which every person is "free to do the work for which he is best suited," receives "the rewards which that work deserves," and is confident "that no one will meddle with him."[2]

What St. Paul described is known in economics as the division of labor. Although the ultimate goal in an economy is to produce goods and services of value, it would be a mistake to see the division of labor as nothing but a mechanism to produce those goods and services more efficiently and inexpensively (though it does do that). The belief that human relationships are primarily economic is an error all too common in contemporary economics.[3] The Austrian School combats this error by reminding us that economics is a science of human action, that the economy is only part of the larger society. Human behavior and human interactions cannot be reduced to mere commercial exchanges. As Ludwig von Mises wrote, human cooperation not only is necessary to achieving common goals but also produces "feelings of sympathy and friendship and a sense of belonging together [that] are the source of man's most delightful and most sublime experiences. They are the most precious adornment of life; they lift the animal species man to the heights of a really human existence."[4]

To the Austrians, the division of labor is "the fundamental social phenomenon," as Mises put it. It is the "counterpart" to the principle of human cooperation. Jeffrey Tucker, formerly of the Ludwig von Mises Institute, has called the division of labor "an essential part of the case for freedom," "probably the single greatest contribution that economics has made to human understanding," and "the most important idea in the history of social analysis."[5]

Foundation

Some 1,600 years after St. Paul wrote his epistle to the Corinthians, Adam Smith reiterated the principle of the division of labor. The eighteenth-century economist saw that a lack of cooperation plagued the reigning mercantilist economy.

Mercantilists were convinced that the way to a strong national economy was to possess a large store of specie. Given the military and political success of the Spanish Empire, they associated prosperity and power with the abundant flow of gold and silver from the New World. Selling manufactured goods and raw materials abroad in return for gold produced what was called a positive balance of payments. Nations came to discourage foreign trade so as not to deplete their gold supply. They set up planned economies, instituting tariffs and subsidies to favored industries. The object was to attain self-sufficiency, so that a nation did not depend on other economies.[6]

Naturally, many nations also sought to expand into colonies to ensure a source of raw materials and an outlet for goods. This led to intense competition, and wars, for overseas possessions. An especially bitter aspect of the mercantilist system was the institution of slavery, as nations tried to cut the costs of their products to be competitive in world markets.

Smith struck at the heart of the mercantilist system in his first chapter of *An Inquiry into the Nature and Causes of Wealth of Nations*, entitled "Of the Division of Labour." Here he argued that the state and intricacy of the division of labor explained why some societies are prosperous and others impoverished. To illustrate the power of the division of labor, he described visiting a pin factory where specialization produced higher and higher levels of productivity. If one person made the entire pin, his production would be hardly 20 pins per day. But if each person specialized in only one or two of the eighteen operations required to make a pin, production would increase to *4,800* pins per person per day.[7] Smith attributed the huge increase in productivity to three factors: (1) as a person does only one task, he saves time; (2) through specialization the worker refines his skill; and (3) the division of labor allows for the development of specialized tools.

Smith's argument has been borne out endlessly over the past two centuries. Probably the most famous example is the Ford Motor Company's use of the assembly line in the early twentieth century. Henry Ford and his staff divided the production of the automobile into thousands of small operations. Before this change, Ford workers wasted time moving from one task to another and picking up and putting away different sets of tools. The line process allowed each worker to develop the skills necessary for fast, accurate, and easy assembly. The workers discovered better and faster ways of doing the work, while Ford discovered ways to mechanize or automate production.

After the introduction of the assembly line, production exploded. In 1904–5, the year after its founding, the Ford Motor Company produced 1,700 cars. By 1906–7 the company was producing about 8,500 units.[8] By 1916 the company was selling more than 577,000 cars.[9]

In *The Wealth of Nations*, Adam Smith argued that efficiencies spread through the whole economy, improving standards of living for workers and customers alike. The increase in the supply of goods makes more and better products and services available to customers at lower prices, while reduced production costs allow workers to receive higher wages. This is exactly what happened in the case of Ford, which brought prices down and wages up. Ford priced its model at $850 in 1906–7 (more than $19,000 in 2011 dollars); by 1916 the price had dropped to $360 (about $7,000 in 2011 dollars). A product that originally was available only to the upper-income consumer came to serve a mass market. Ford also increased wages substantially. On January 5, 1914, Henry Ford famously doubled the pay of his workers.[10]

The Ford case is a good example of what is known as the principle of regressivity. This principle states that the less income or wealth a person has, the more changes in prices affect him; he benefits more when prices fall and suffers more when prices increase. Put another way, the benefits of the division of labor are distributed first to those on the lower end of the income/wealth scale. Say that the price of gasoline suddenly dropped to one dollar per gallon. Who would be helped more, the person working at a low-wage job or multibillionaire Bill Gates? Both would pay the same price for gas, but Gates's overall budget would hardly be affected, whereas the low-wage earner would see his spending power increase dramatically. The worker could afford better food, have an easier time supporting his family, or add to his savings. On the other hand, if the price of gas shot up to ten dollars per gallon, the wage earner might now have to pay 10 percent of his budget just to get to work. With an increase of that magnitude, he must cut back severely, even on necessities like food and clothing. For Gates, though, purchasing gasoline would still account for only a fraction of a percent of his overall budget.

Although Adam Smith did not cite the principle of regressivity in *The Wealth of Nations*, he did explain how wealth is passed on to the broader society:

> It is the great multiplication of the productions of all the different arts, in consequence of the division of labour, which occasions, in a well-governed society, that universal opulence which extends itself to the lowest ranks of the people. Every workman has a great quantity of his own work to dispose of beyond what he himself has occasion for; and every other workman being exactly in the same situation, he is enabled to exchange a great quantity of his own goods for a great quantity, or, what comes to the same thing, for the price of a great quantity of theirs. He supplies them abundantly with what they have occasion for, and they accommodate him as amply with what he has occasion for, and a general plenty diffuses itself through all the different ranks of the society.[11]

Here, then, we see the flaw in the mercantilist systems that Smith critiqued. Governments that attempted to establish economic "self-sufficiency" only limited the goods and services their people could access, increasing prices for individuals and businesses alike. Government tariffs and regulations imposed costs that harmed businesses, especially those that did not receive government subsidies. The smaller companies were harmed the most, for the principle of regressivity applies to businesses as well as individuals. Increased costs were spread over the number of units a company produced. Companies that produced a small volume of goods found their costs per unit much higher than those of a large concern.

More recent examples illustrate the unequal impact of government interventions in the economy. For many years government programs propped up the ethanol industry by using subsidies, tax credits, and protective tariffs to encourage the fermentation of corn for fuel. Because the ethanol industry requires so much corn, the cost of corn soared. That sent "shock waves through the food system," as *Foreign Affairs* magazine reported in 2007. Whom have the corn-price increases affected most? "Consumers, especially in poor developing countries," *Foreign Affairs* noted. The world's poorest people—including nearly three billion people who live on less than two dollars a day—"already spend 50 to 80 percent of their total household income on food," meaning that "even marginal increases in the cost of staple grains could be devastating."[12] The economic burden falls most heavily on those least able to afford it.

Adam Smith recognized the division of labor as crucial to avoiding such burdens and spreading economic blessings throughout society. He summarized his argument in the very first sentence of *The Wealth of Nations*: "The greatest improvement in the productive powers of labour and the greater part of the skill, dexterity, and judgment with which it is any where directed, or applied, seem to have been the effects of the division of labour."[13] This perceptive sentence articulates a foundational principle of economic liberty and prosperity.

Knowledge and Technology

Nearly a century after Smith published *The Wealth of Nations*, the Austrian School expanded on the fundamental concept of the division of labor. Carl Menger, the father of the Austrian School, explained how knowledge and technology factor in. Like Smith before him, Menger understood that as people work at a task, they increase their knowledge of what they are working at. Thus the development of technology follows increased specialization. But Menger pointed out that advances in technology benefit more than just those who develop the technology.

Ideas and inventions cross-pollinate, reaching unrelated fields. The laboratories that first developed the laser, for example, could not have anticipated all the uses to which lasers have been put to use, from surgery to measurement to cutting metal. Similarly, advances in computers have reshaped—and created—countless industries.

In *Principles of Economics* (1871), Menger summed up:

> Increasing understanding of the causal connections between things and human welfare, and increasing control of the less proximate conditions responsible for human welfare, have led mankind, there-

fore, from a state of barbarism and the deepest misery to its present stage of civilization and well-being, and have changed vast regions inhabited by a few miserable, excessively poor, men into densely populated civilized countries. Nothing is more certain than that the degree of economic progress of mankind will still, in future epochs, be commensurate with the degree of progress of human knowledge.[14]

The process of applying human knowledge and skill over time to develop new technologies cannot be planned. No one knows what new inventions will come about in the future. Myriads of people are working on ideas, and although many will fail, some will open up doors to the unforeseen. We simply don't know what some mind will come up with, nor can any government or corporation plan it. Imagine having tried to plan the twentieth-century economy before knowing about automobiles, aviation, or computers, or the twenty-first-century economy before knowing about the Internet or wireless communications.

Population

One of the major components of the division of labor is, of course, population. Each person is unique, possessing special talents that no one else has. The division of labor allows people to develop their natural endowments, making more and better products and services available to all the participants in the marketplace. As more people are added to the process, the output usually increases at a greater and greater rate.

That is why rising populations lead to higher standards of living. Many thinkers, from Thomas Malthus in the 1790s to Paul Ehrlich in the 1960s, have predicted that the world's growing population will outstrip the available resources, resulting in scarcity. But history has proved their warnings wrong. Austrian economist Wilhelm Röpke observed that the century after Malthus issued his dire warnings witnessed "the greatest population increase in history." Instead of the "misery, want, and famine" Malthus predicted, industrial countries experienced massive increases in their standards of living. Meanwhile, Röpke wrote, "the agricultural production of the world has increased in many countries to an extent where there is more concern about the problems of overproduction than of insufficiency."[15]

Per the principle of regressivity, the poorer members of society have the greatest interest in the proper working of the division of labor, because they will benefit the most from increasing quality and decreasing costs. That goes for poor and underdeveloped countries. As they join the international marketplace, they gain access to products that would take years and copious amounts of capital to produce by themselves. Consider that most of the world is now benefiting from vaccines, innovative surgeries, and other medical advances developed in the industrial nations as well as from technologies such as cell phones.

As underdeveloped countries see their economies improve, they can expand their own industries. China is the classic example. With the opening up of international markets and the demise of its planned economy, China began to supply all sorts of consumer goods to the world. People who were involved with subsistence farming sought new jobs in the cities and expanding industry. Standards of living rose quickly. China has overcome enormous poverty.[16]

Productive nations, or people or companies for that matter, should not fear or resent the rise of other productive outfits. Recall Say's Law, enunciated by the French economist Jean-Baptiste Say (1767–1832), which, simply put, states that the supply of x creates the demand for y. The operation of Say's Law rests on three foundations: (1) prices must be flexible and respond to demand; (2) producers must add value to their products; and (3) other participants in the marketplace must also be productive.

That last point is essential to understanding the division of labor. As Say explained, someone who creates an object of value "can not expect such a value to be appreciated and paid for, unless where other men have the means of purchasing it."[17] In other words, each producer's prosperity is tied to the prosperity of all other producers. A major reason 1930's Smoot-Hawley Tariff exacerbated the economic crisis was that it killed overseas markets for American farmers. As a result, the farmers themselves became unproductive, unable to purchase goods from other producers. At that time farming accounted for fully 25 percent of the U.S. economy. Naturally, the depression spread.

The Division of Labor, from Micro to Macro

The division of labor can be seen in, and analyzed in the context of, anything from a single business to the total economy. Ford's assembly line showed how one company could use the division of labor to produce better, lower-priced products while raising wages. At the same time, many schools of economics present the division of labor as a massive flowchart showing how households, business, government, and the foreign sector work together.

When the principles of economy are applied to the larger social structure, the study is referred to as macroeconomics. Macroeconomic analysis has largely been the method of Keynesian economics, focusing on employment, economic growth, and the flow of money among the various sectors of the economy.

Many Austrian economists, as we have seen, disdain macroeconomics for adopting a strictly quantitative analytical approach that overlooks human actors. Wilhelm Röpke saw the economy divided into the industrial and the social realms.[18] Even when looking at the industrial sector, Röpke emphasized the role of human actors. He did so by arguing that an analysis of the industrial realm properly studies the operations of the single firm. The present-day academy calls this study microeconomics. But as Hayek and other Austrians showed, efficient management and direction of any firm requires a complete knowledge of the various members of the firm and the alternatives open to the entrepreneur. As such, it covers cost, market structure, and, most important, pricing.

Austrian economists from Menger to the present day have accounted for the division of labor by following the productive process—the mechanics of how goods and services come into existence. As seen in chapter 3, Menger distinguished between first-order goods, meaning those immediately available to the consumer, and higher-order goods, meaning those that are used to produce consumer goods.[19] By drawing this distinction, Menger recognized the simple but important fact that production takes place in time. It may take years to bring a product, the first-order good, to market.

Eugen von Böhm-Bawerk built on the foundation his University of Vienna colleague had laid with his insight that production is a *roundabout process*. Böhm-Bawerk observed that as the tools needed to produce consumer goods, higher-order goods must be made *first*. Very few products are made directly. Most industrial processes are immensely complicated. When an automobile manufacturer decides to bring a new product to market, it can't just start rolling the new cars off the line. The design must be completed, tested, and approved. Then the firm must build the tools necessary for making the new car and organize the production process, all before a single vehicle can be manufactured. Auto companies plan new models several years in advance.

In his book *The Structure of Production*, Mark Skousen, an American economist of the Austrian School, demonstrates that the roundabout production process takes time. At each stage of the process, value is added, as raw materials are slowly transformed into higher-order goods and ultimately final products that reach the consumer.[20] Skousen calls the process *longitudinal*, as one step develops and sets the stage for the next.

In the classic 1958 essay "I, Pencil," Leonard E. Read of the Foundation for Economic Education illustrated the interplay between first-order and higher-order goods, and the way the productive process develops over time. The essay traces the production of a simple lead pencil from the jungles where rubber is produced, to mines contributing steel and graphite, to forests whence comes the wood. He sums up: "I, Pencil, am a complex combination of miracles: a tree, zinc, copper, graphite, and so on. But to these miracles which manifest themselves in Nature an even more extraordinary miracle has been added: the configuration of creative human energy—millions of tiny know-hows configurating naturally and spontaneously in response to human necessity and desire and *in the absence of any human master-minding!* [emphasis in original]"[21]

Read's last point speaks to an essential element of the division of labor, and a centerpiece of Austrian economics: spontaneous order. The division of labor does not result because the government passes a law ordering a certain number of people to be engineers and a certain number to be mechanics. It occurs naturally—spontaneously. To F. A. Hayek, the "fatal conceit" of socialism was the notion that government could manage the economy and society efficiently. Such top-down planning utterly ignores the fact that society—its traditions, customs, laws, goods, technologies, markets, and so on—evolved naturally over many generations, not from any plan. When Leonard Read marvels at the "extraordinary miracle" of spontaneous order, he recognizes, with Hayek and other

Austrian economists, that markets allocate resources more efficiently than central planners ever could.

Writing at a time when Communist governments around the world stubbornly engaged in central planning, Wilhelm Röpke explained why the participants in a free market know better than any bureaucrat what should be produced, how and where goods should be made, and how they should be priced. Röpke wrote: "Who is charged with seeing to it that the economic gears of society mesh properly? Nobody. No dictator rules the economy, deciding who shall perform the needed work and prescribing what goods and how much shall be brought to market. . . . *The modern economic system, an extraordinarily complex mechanism, functions without conscious central control by any agency whatsoever* [emphasis in original]."[22]

A tale about a college that had a generous alumnus and a wise president illustrates how top-down and bottom-up organizations diverge. The wealthy alumnus, grateful for the education the college had given him, donated enough money to build a brand-new campus. One of the country's top architectural firms designed the campus, complete with all-new buildings and a system of sidewalks connecting them. But when the campus was nearly ready, the college president ordered the builders not to install the sidewalks. He reasoned that the students would create pathways in the grass that would show the actual—and best—traffic patterns between the buildings. After a year, sidewalks were placed over the paths.

The architectural firm's design represented top-down management. Everything was organized to fit a pattern, and students were expected to follow the plan. The president's decision allowed for bottom-up management. In essence, he thought, "We don't know the shortest way between the buildings or the traffic patterns, so let the students [the market] show us the most efficient way to do things and we'll follow them."

The bottom-up approach—the free market—has shown remarkable efficiency and generated huge increases in standards of living.[23]

Four Influences on the Division of Labor

Four types of change affect the division of labor in any economy, be it local, state, national, or international. Those four influences are: seasonal, frictional, structural, and cyclical. All these types of change occur simultaneously, interacting with one another.

Seasonal change: Seasonal changes are the simplest and therefore the easiest to understand. Natural seasons affect the economy because of changes in weather. The winter months spur increases in snowmobiling, skiing, and trips to warmer climes. Summer brings boating, light clothing, and beach-house rentals. Since the seasons follow a natural rhythm, manufacturers, travel agencies, and retailers can all plan to have the necessary goods and services available for purchase at the appropriate times. In addition, the financial community can make credit available before the season and expect repayment at the end of the season.

A second type of seasonal change follows society's conventions. These so-called conventional changes include all the shopping spikes that occur at Christmas, Valentine's Day, Mother's Day, and the like. These predictable selling seasons shape the plans of retailers, manufacturers, and many other businesses. Florists, for example, count on huge sales on February 14 and Mother's Day. If sales fall far below expectations at those times, it will be an unprofitable year. Similarly, retailers look to the Christmas shopping season as their make-or-break period. The day after Thanksgiving has come to be known as "Black Friday" at least in part because that busiest day of the shopping year marks the switch from red ink to black ink in a retailer's books.

The state of hiring follows seasonal changes. Teachers, resort workers, ski instructors, farm laborers—these and many other workers often prepare to take two separate jobs, one for the season and one for the off-season. Because the seasons (natural and conventional) are predictable, the division of labor will react accordingly.

Frictional change: Economists use the term *frictional unemployment* to refer to the period after a person leaves one job but before he or she can find another. For instance, someone may be so dissatisfied with pay or working conditions that he quits before lining up another job. But the concept of frictional change can be extended beyond unemployment to other aspects of the economy, such as investment and capital allocation. Sometimes the financial rewards available in one line of work or industry are not enough to justify keeping resources in it. Investors may determine that the risk of a specific investment may be too high to justify the potential return; they pull their investment out without knowing where they will invest their capital next. Or they could pull back from the stock market altogether because of uncertain economic conditions that they fear will lead to a bear market. In either case, they hold out until a good opportunity comes along.

Whereas seasonal changes are highly predictable, frictional changes are much harder to read. One can try to guess how frictional changes are playing out by watching certain economic indicators such as interest rates on Treasury bills or business closures. But because other complicating factors are often involved, it is difficult to pinpoint how frictional change will play out.

Structural change: Of the four types of change affecting the division of labor, the most powerful is structural, which is nearly irreversible, at least in the short term. This type of change affects the fundamental structure of the economy. The most significant structural change the world economy has experienced is the transition from agricultural to manufacturing and service. At the time of the founding of the United States, nearly half the population was involved in farming. Today that figure is about 2 percent. As technology improved, better methods were applied to food production, and large segments of the population were released to seek positions elsewhere in the economy. The increased efficiency allowed industries to develop. Imagine what industries would be lost if suddenly farms needed half the U.S. population.

Many factors work together to bring about structural change. Henry Ford and the automobile—an innovative businessman and a new invention—changed the world economy. These factors also combined with others to remake the economy of the American Midwest. These states benefited from Ford's revolution, the availability of cheap water transportation with the Great Lakes, and huge iron ore and coal deposits, which made steel production economical. These factors combined to attract a huge network of skilled workers to the major cities of Michigan and Ohio to man the new industries.

Moreover, the construction of the Erie Canal, connecting the Hudson River to the Great Lakes, made New York City the hub of transportation between Europe and the interior of the United States. New York thus became the financial and business center of the United States, leap-frogging over Philadelphia. In short, geographic and demographic factors combined with the work of dynamic entrepreneurs to make dramatic change happen.

Or think of how legal and policy decisions can lead to structural change. Industries—and individuals—often move from high-tax, high-regulation areas to low-tax, low-regulation areas. Therefore a low-tax haven like Hong Kong has become home to many industries, allowing standard of livings to soar. This same effect has been seen within the United States. Political analyst Michael Barone has shown that the greatest population growth between 2000 and 2010 occurred in low-tax states. "Seven of the nine states that do not levy an income tax grew faster than the national average," Barone writes. "The other two, South Dakota and New Hampshire, had the fastest growth in their regions." Meanwhile, sunny California, with its high taxes, burdensome regulations, and nearly bankrupt big government, has seen residents leave in droves; only the inflow of immigrants has offset this domestic outflow.[24]

Predicting and following structural change is one of the most exciting and profitable parts of economics. It is the least susceptible to statistical methods, because structural developments are new, whereas statistical analysis generally relies on historical data. Because structural change is so unpredictable, one prepares for it through diversification. One must also be flexible enough to adapt to change as it happens. Structural change can lead to tremendous profit opportunities, but those who are unprepared for change, or unable or unwilling to adapt, go extinct, sometimes quickly.

Cyclical change: The fourth and final type of change affecting the division of labor is cyclical change. Cycles generally refer to the ups and downs of business activity: recessions and depressions, booms and busts. We have already seen how the Austrian theory of the trade cycle explains bubbles and why they burst. We have also seen how, since the creation of the Federal Reserve in 1913, government has tried to smooth out the trade cycle, only to make busts worse.

Cyclical change is also evident within various sectors of the economy. At any given time, some industries will be booming, others experiencing a downturn. For the most part, changes in the business climate that follow the ups and down of the trade cycle are reversible, and they do reverse. So an industry that goes through a downturn and is forced to lay off employees and abandon projects usually will see an increase in business over time. Employees will be called back and new projects undertaken.

Up until the 1980s the automobile business followed this pattern of cyclical change. There would be a boom—high employment, robust sales of cars, and lots of overtime and good benefits for the workers. Then the bust would inevitably follow; companies would begin to lose money as sales dropped. Work hours and overtime would be cut, and layoffs would ensue. A short time later, the entire process would reverse, workers would be called back, and production would increase. The pattern stopped only when structural change affected the underlying business conditions. Detroit automakers, once dominant, steadily lost market share to foreign car companies such as Toyota and Honda. Not only autoworkers but also employees in countless small supporting industries were affected as the structure of production moved out of the Midwest, shifting to the American South and overseas.

The Four Factors of Production

Following the productive process also entails looking at the factors that affect how goods and services are produced. Each division of labor uses four factors of production: land, labor, capital, and entrepreneurship. Of these four, the Austrian School has made significant contributions to the theory of capital and the theory of the entrepreneur.

The theory of the entrepreneur: Israel Kirzner, a modern-day Austrian economist, took concepts his predecessors had advanced and developed an intricate theory of the entrepreneur. His argument begins with the concept of arbitrage. Simply put, arbitrage is buying an item with the intention of immediately selling it to take advantage of price differences between markets. For example, if gold is selling in London for $1,000 an ounce and in New York for $1,050 an ounce, the arbitrage opportunity is to buy in London and sell in New York. As entrepreneurs exploit this opportunity, the price in London will rise and the price in New York will fall until the two prices are equalized and the profit opportunity disappears.

Kirzner used the idea of arbitrage to explain entrepreneurship generally. The entrepreneur looks to move resources from positions of lower value to positions of higher value. In essence, profit can be defined as increasing value in the marketplace. A firm that is running profits is really moving resources to a position that the market regards as having higher value. Firms that are losing money, on the other hand, are moving resources to a position that the market sees as having less value. That is the risk the entrepreneur takes in moving resources: there is never a guarantee that the new position will increase in value or that the old position *won't* increase in value.

Kirzner observed that entrepreneurs are constantly looking at the market for productive services and imagining how these can be put together or taken apart to make new products at a profit. Following the principle of arbitrage, entrepreneurs often assemble a whole that is more valuable than the parts taken separately. For instance, a new building is a combination of steel, concrete, bricks, and design. The total value of each part separately is far less than the value of the building if the entrepreneur has successfully assessed the final market price. Likewise, companies merge on the theory that the resulting new organization will be more profitable than the two separately.

Sometimes, though, things become more valuable when they are taken apart. Once I had a car stolen and I asked the police officer why someone would want such an old vehicle. He said that that particular model had many parts that could be dismantled and sold at a much higher price.

Kirzner saw that to find profit opportunities, the entrepreneur must continually add to his knowledge of cost, products, prices, and new technologies. This process of searching and then organizing resources helps advance the division of labor.

The theory of capital: The Austrian theory of capital is one of the school's most important contributions to economic thought. Even today, most economists employ the Austrians' insights and explanations of the productive process.

Working from ideas Menger had articulated, Böhm-Bawerk advanced the Austrian theory of capital. This theory developed in tandem with his concept of production as a roundabout process. Böhm-Bawerk pointed out that the productive process involves not only human labor but also the tools used to make consumer goods. Those tools, he saw, are really a means of harnessing the forces of nature. The steam engine, which powered the Industrial Revolution, was a contraption for harnessing the energy inherent in petrochemicals and putting it to work for us. Creating and employing tools to harness nature requires substantial investment. Böhm-Bawerk called these devices capital. As he wrote, the term *capital* signifies "a complex of goods that originate in the previous process of production, and are destined, not for immediate consumption, but to serve as a means of acquiring further goods."[25]

Although capital investment means sacrificing immediate gain—in the form of money or consumer goods—it increases output and adds value in the longer term. *The Concise Encyclopedia of Economics* offers a good illustration of the point: "As the leader of a primitive fishing village, you are able to send out the townspeople to catch enough fish, with their bare hands, to ensure the village's survival for one day. But if you forgo consumption of fish for one day and use that labor to produce nets, hooks, and lines—capital—each fisherman can catch more fish the following day and the days thereafter. Capital is productive."[26]

Böhm-Bawerk added significantly to our understanding of the division of labor. He refuted the widely accepted labor theory of value, which held that the amount of human labor that goes into making a product determines that product's value. Instead, he showed that entrepreneurs and businesspeople can *add* value through the productive process and that they respond to the demands of the market in allocating their resources. If labor alone determined value, entrepreneurs would have little incentive to invest in capital goods.

Austrian theory recognizes the forces that make the free economy so dynamic.

The Way the Economy Works

The division of labor can be seen at all different levels of the economy, from the family to a single business to the entire global marketplace. In fact, the division of labor really *is* the economy. This organization makes possible the many products and services that constitute a standard of living. The more efficient the division of labor is, the better off all its participants will be. What the Austrian School of economics has shown is that the division of labor operates at its best when people are free to harness their natural talents, when entrepreneurs are free to invest capital in such a way that adds value, and when government does not interfere with the spontaneous order that leads to economic and social progress.

10

The Prerequisites of Prosperity

Economic activity, especially the activity of a market economy, . . . presupposes sure guarantees of individual freedom and private property, as well as a stable currency and efficient public services. Hence the principal task of the state is to guarantee this security, so that those who work and produce can enjoy the fruits of their labors and thus feel encouraged to work efficiently and honestly.
   —*Pope John Paul II,* Centesimus Annus *(1991)*

The Austrian School's tenet of spontaneous order holds that a free, prosperous, and humane society is the by-product of the operations of free individuals. This is not to say, however, that a free, prosperous, and humane society will always and everywhere result. It is a mistake to think of a free-enterprise system as independent of the broader culture. Social orders develop organically over time, as different organizations, businesses, and political systems are established. The market is not a stand-alone system; it is inextricably linked to all these other systems, organizations, and associations. In their prescient critiques of central planning, Ludwig von Mises and F. A. Hayek pointed out the ways in which the political system can effectively—and intentionally—destroy markets.

But communism is only one example of how cultural conditions affect prosperity. Consider what happened *after* the collapse of communism.

Free markets did not suddenly flourish in the former Soviet Union once the communist regime was gone. Why? One major reason was that the decades of totalitarian communist rule had robbed Russian culture of a tradition of laws and contracts. As the Austrian School shows, a tradition in which the rule of law reigns and contracts are held sacred is one of the foundations on which a free-market economy arises.[1]

These foundations cannot be overlooked. The Austrian School teaches that a prosperous economy and harmonious society can develop only when crucial preconditions are met.

Cornerstone: Private Property

Managing risk is one of the most important elements of the productive process. An element of risk is unavoidable in human activity, because the future is always uncertain. When a manufacturer begins making a product, he cannot know for certain whether the public will accept it, what the selling price will be, or what other obstacles he must overcome. When a farmer begins planting seeds in April, he takes the risk that the price of the food come harvest time in October will cover his costs and produce a profit. Naturally, the goal of all economic actors is to reduce risk as much as possible. The more uncertain the outcome, the more difficult it is to entice someone to invest.

Insurance policies are the most familiar set of risk-management strategies. There is a dizzying array of such policies, from the life, health, and auto insurance that individuals own to complex mechanisms such as "credit default swaps" that international investors purchase to manage the risks inherent in currency and other markets. But before any of these forms of insurance come certain societal preconditions. A society that hopes to achieve material abundance must foster peace and predictability of institutions. Most important of all, society must ensure the protection of private property.

For millennia before Karl Marx launched his (failed) revolution against private property, philosophers, political scientists, statesmen, and economists recognized the protection of property rights as a pillar of society and a prosperous economy. More than two thousand years ago, Aristotle noted that property should be, "as a general rule, private."[2] In the Judeo-Christian tradition, two of the Ten Commandments deal with protecting private property: the eighth, "Thou shalt not steal," and the tenth, "Thou shalt not covet thy neighbor's goods." Property rights also play a prominent role in the Anglo-Saxon legal tradition, dating back to Magna Carta in 1215.[3]

Why are property rights so important? For starters, the concept of private property is broader than merely the possession of physical things. Paul Heyne explains in *The Economic Way of Thinking*: "When economists speak of property rights, they have in mind something closely akin to what we have called 'the rules of the game.' *Property rights are rights to control the way in which particular resources will be used and to assign the resulting cost and benefits* [emphasis in original]."[4] If humans can't make those decisions for themselves, they lose a stake in, and thus the incentive to work toward, a positive outcome. This concept applies not only to entrepreneurship and investments but also to something as basic as one's job. If a boss unduly interferes with his employees' work, their work is no longer theirs; they have no motivation to devote the time and thought needed to excel and innovate, because the boss micromanages everything. When a property right is interfered with, the benefits of that property will be compromised.

The Austrian School of economics understands that prosperity depends on private property. But more than that, Austrian thinkers have long identified property rights as necessary to preserving *liberty*. Hayek conceived of private property rights as a set of "general rules governing the conditions under which objects or circumstances become part of the protected sphere of a person or persons." He stressed, "We must not think of this sphere as consisting exclusively, or even chiefly, of material things," for property rights also secure "certain uses of things" and protect "against interference with our actions." Hayek added:

> The recognition of private or several property is thus an essential condition for the prevention of coercion, though by no means the only one. We are rarely in a position to carry out a coherent plan of action unless we are certain of our exclusive control of some material objects; and where we do not control them, it is necessary that we know who does if we are to collaborate with others. The recognition of property is clearly the first step in the delimitation of the

private sphere which protects us against coercion; and it has long been recognized that "a people averse to the institution of private property is without the first element of freedom."[5]

Pope John XXIII made much the same point in 1961 when he argued that "the right of private individuals to act freely in economic affairs is recognized in vain, unless they are at the same time given an opportunity of freely selecting and using things necessary for the exercise of this right. Moreover, experience and history testify that where political regimes do not allow to private individuals the possession also of productive goods, the exercise of human liberty is violated or completely destroyed in matters of primary importance. Thus it becomes clear that in the right of property, the exercise of liberty finds both a safeguard and a stimulus."[6]

In short, without private property, there is no liberty.

Property rights also have very practical connections to a prosperous economy and harmonious society. Aristotle and Thomas Aquinas are among the many thinkers who have noted such connections. Aquinas identified three reasons why "it is lawful for man to possess property." First, he observed that "every man is more careful to procure what is for himself alone than that which is common to many or all: since each one would shirk the labor and leave to another that which concerns the community, as happens where there is a great number of servants."[7] In other words, that which belongs to everyone really belongs to no one. No one will take care of it, because absent property rights, no one has an *incentive* to take care of it. People can reasonably expect that they will be able to enjoy the rewards of their labor only when society installs firm protections for property rights.

Second, Aquinas perceived that property rights help establish social order. He wrote that "human affairs are conducted in more orderly fashion if each man is charged with taking care of some particular thing himself, whereas there would be confusion if everyone had to look after any one thing indeterminately."[8] Aristotle made a similar point when he argued that "when every one has a distinct interest, men will not complain of one another, and they will make more progress, because every one will be attending to his own business."[9] Even at the foundational level of society, the family, establishing a form of property rights—enforcing boundaries to teach children what belongs to them and what belongs to others—allows kids to know what to expect and thus to function with safety and assurance, even happiness.

Third, Aquinas said, "a more peaceful state is ensured to man if each one is contented with his own. Hence it is to be observed that quarrels arise more frequently where there is no division of the things possessed."[10] To illustrate the disharmony that can result from communal property, Aristotle told the story of a group of travelers who shared a common purse, which only led to disputes. Again, that which belongs to everyone really belongs to no one.

Contrary to what is often heard, private property does not stand at odds with charity and social responsibility. In fact, the question of generosity relies on private property: most charitable acts require a sacrifice on the part of the giver, and if there is no private property, there is nothing to sacrifice. Even as Aristotle and Aquinas laid out the basis for property rights, both took care to explain that private property did not preclude generosity. Aristotle wrote: "By reason of goodness, and in respect of use, 'Friends,' as the proverb says, 'will have all things common.'" He added that "well-ordered states" honor the principle that "although every man has his own property, some things he will place at the disposal of his friends, while of others he shares the use with them."[11] Similarly, Aquinas maintained that when it comes to using his possessions, a person must be "ready to communicate them to others in their need."[12]

In the 1950s and '60s a common rallying cry was: "Human rights are more important than property rights!" But property rights *are* a human right. Moreover, when governments refuse to defend property rights, they ensure that other human rights are violated as well. The city of Detroit is a monument to the refusal of public authorities to defend property rights. Block after block of the city is nothing but abandoned and burned-out buildings. Anyone who has owned property in Detroit knows a major contributing factor to this blight. One of my brightest and most entrepreneurial students went into the real estate business, refurbishing and then renting out grand old apartment buildings. At one point, he and his business partner unknowingly rented an apartment to drug dealers. They were unable to evict the undesirable tenants, because the city enforces landlord/tenant laws in such a way that practically denies building owners their property rights. Understandably, the law-abiding tenants started to move out, for their own safety. The building quickly became uninhabitable, the cash flow stopped, and my student was unable to keep up the payments. Now the building is boarded up and has suffered extensive fire damage. This story could be repeated thousands of times. As of 2010, Detroit had more than ninety thousand vacant homes or residential lots.[13]

Taxation affects private ownership of property in all its forms. Detroit not only fails to protect property rights adequately but also has high tax rates on both property and income. Those tax levels discourage new investment and make it harder to keep citizens in the city. High taxation and widespread property ownership just don't mix. Hilaire Belloc wrote in *The Restoration of Property*: "High taxation is incompatible with the general institution of property. The one kills the other. Where property is well distributed resistance to big taxation is so fierce and efficacious that big taxation breaks down. Where an effort is being made to restore well-divided property, high taxation will destroy that effect."[14]

Warnings against high taxation come from many sources. Chief Justice John Marshall, writing in the landmark Supreme Court decision *McCulloch v. Maryland* (1819), stated that "the power to tax is the power to destroy." In 1891, Pope Leo XIII recognized the same principle in his foundational work on Catholic social policy, *Rerum Novarum*. The pope described the advantages that result from the right of private property, a right that "must be regarded as sacred." "But," he added,

> these advantages can be attained only if private wealth is not drained away by crushing taxes of every kind. For since the right of possessing goods privately has been conferred not by man's law, but by nature, public authority cannot abolish it, but can only control its exercise and bring it into conformity with the commonweal. Public authority therefore would act unjustly and in an inhumane way, if in the name of taxes it should appropriate the property of private individuals more than is equitable.[15]

The government encroaches even further on property rights when it "nationalizes" businesses or even entire industries. Nationalization is simply a government takeover, which means outright seizure of private property. Protections against government seizure of property date back at least as far as the Magna Carta. As John Chamberlain observed in *The*

Roots of Capitalism, the Magna Carta "was confirmed under Edward I, with a kingly admission that no seizures of goods would be made for the crown's use; and all through the later Middle Ages judges applied the rights of the Great Charter as the 'law of the land.'" From the thirteenth century onward, Englishmen "held that rights came with birth and not from any permissive act of king or state." It was the Tudor monarchs who broke with this concept, when, during the sixteenth century, they looted churches to pay the war expenses of Henry VIII.[16]

The government seizure of church property had far-reaching consequences. When the Tudors seized monasteries and distributed them among their court retainers, Chamberlain wrote, "this lawless act not only put the property right in question, but it also saddled the state with the necessity of caring for the indigent and aged who had hitherto been supported by the contributions of churchmen."[17] Nineteenth-century British prime minister Benjamin Disraeli described the situation in England prior to the crown's theft of the monasteries: "The monks were, in short, in every district a point of refuge for all who needed succour, counsel, and protection; a body of individuals having no cares of their own, with wisdom to guide the inexperienced, with wealth to relieve the suffering, and often with power to protect the oppressed."[18] That vanished after the government took the monasteries away. Those who had been able to turn to the church for help now had to turn to government. The crown thus laid the groundwork for the modern welfare state.

For all these reasons, private property rights are a cornerstone of a stable and prosperous society. Securing these rights eliminates unnecessary uncertainty about the future, allowing human actors to make reasonable estimations of risk. With incentives to invest and to care for property, and with a stable social order, economic production will increase and prices will fall. Those increases in production and decreases in price will, by the principle of regressivity, benefit the poor most quickly.

A Sound Currency

The Austrian School upholds a sound currency as another prerequisite of prosperity. Virtually all economists agree that inflation—the devaluation of the monetary unit—is a bad idea. Austrians consider it the worst of economic crimes. The Austrian School has made a special study of inflation and its destructive influence on society.

Anyone who has lived through inflation knows that it cuts into savings and distorts production. In extreme cases it leads to chaos and poverty, as in the German hyperinflation following World War I. The fear of inflation has been an important factor since the economic collapse began in 2007. Concerns over currencies such as the euro (saddled by the massive debts of the Greek, Portuguese, and other governments) caused the value of gold to increase more than 50 percent in just fourteen months.[19]

The Austrian School, as we have seen, has long advocated the gold standard as the way to ensure a sound currency, free from government manipulation. What does a sound currency look like? It is marked by several key characteristics:

1. The "productivity dividend" is preserved: The division of labor generates efficiencies. Those efficiencies are passed along to the consumer—in the form of lower prices and better products—through what economist Donald Byrne (a former professor of mine) calls the "productivity dividend." To work properly, the productivity dividend relies on a sound currency. The principle of regressivity dictates that those with lower incomes benefit from the productivity dividend first. But when there is constant inflation, these benefits are offset. That is because inflation rewards those who receive the new money first but harms those who receive money later. Poorer people normally are not among those who receive the money first. They do not have the market power to demand increased salaries to keep up with the rising inflation, whereas the typical union or government contract includes automatic cost-of-living adjustments (COLA). In essence, inflation transfers wealth away from the poor, or those with little market power.

Economist Ruchir Sharma made this point when he showed that the Federal Reserve's programs to increase the money supply, euphemistically called "quantitative easing," were "increasing inequality." Sharma wrote, "The hope is that quantitative easing will drive up stock prices, making consumers feel richer and spend more. But this glow is felt mainly by families in the top 10 per cent of incomes, because they own 75 per cent of all stocks. Meanwhile, the poor are hit hardest by rising commodity prices: families in the bottom 20 per cent of incomes spend 8 per cent of their income on petrol and 30 per cent on food, while the top 20 per cent spend just 2 per cent on petrol and 5 per cent on food."[20]

In a sound currency system, money operates as a medium of exchange, not a mechanism to transfer wealth.

2. The currency protects savings: One of the primary uses of money is to retain purchasing power over time and place, allowing people to build up reserves during times of prosperity that can be used during the down times. If currency is inflated, the value of savings drops, which, in essence, constitutes an unfair tax on the savers.

3. Interest rates are stable: Increasing the supply of money has a marked effect on interest rates. As a central bank increases the money supply, short-term rates tend to fall. But this lowering of short-term rates can ignite inflationary fears. When investors harbor such fears, they will protect themselves by demanding higher interest rates in long-term capital markets. Long-term rates can come to exceed the increase in productivity, leading to inefficiency in the economy. Now consider what happens when there is no monetary interference in the rate of interest: if capital can be obtained at a 3 percent interest rate (historically, the market-dictated long-term rate for relatively risk-free securities under a gold standard) and invested into ventures that increase productivity by 6 percent, not only can the interest be repaid but the loan principal can be easily retired as well. A sound currency, then, allows capital to be allocated to its best use.

Recall that one of the Austrian School's most important theoretical contributions to economics involves interest rates. It was Austrian School pioneer Eugen Böhm-Bawerk who developed the theory of interest as time preference, which has become a common element of modern finance. This theory explains interest as a way to account for the fact that people tend to value immediate satisfactions over satisfactions put off into the future. Without interest payments, there is little incentive to save or invest money when that money could be used to purchase consumer goods or services today. Under a sound currency, the rate of interest reflects nothing more than this time preference, plus the premium paid to account for the risk of default. Interest rates creep higher only when market participants worry about a decline in the value of their principal—that is, when they worry about manipulations of the currency that lead to inflation.

4. The currency protects against deflation: Just as a sound currency is relatively free of inflation, it also protects against deflation. In other words, the value of a stable currency does not decrease *or* increase significantly. With deflation, prices and wages fall, but the debt contracted before the deflation does not. For example, people in Japan who went into debt to purchase houses saw the value of those houses—as well as their wages—fall significantly during the Japanese deflation of the 1990s. Their mortgage amounts, however, remained the same.

One of the characteristics of a deflation is extremely low interest rates. Extremely low rates are made possible when wealth is transferred to the government away from the private sector. When the market becomes fearful of the risks involved in private investment, those with money will seek safety in what are perceived to be risk-free securities, normally government bonds. In practical terms, this means that banks will not lend out money to small and medium-sized businesses, which leads to a drop in business activity and falling interest rates. Normally, this signals a deflation.

5. The currency operates independent of federal policy: The currency should not be tied to the federal budget. Governments often finance deficits by expanding bank credit, which usually causes inflation. Linking the currency's value to the amount governments must borrow from a central bank leads to instability, and the value of savings becomes vulnerable.

Interest rates are an important indicator of a currency's soundness. When the long-term interest rate is too low, it can be an indication of deflation; a high long-term interest rate is a probable indication of inflation. In both cases, the currency is unsound.

The Rule of Law

One of the most important preconditions for an effective economy is the rule of law. An economy can never function smoothly if participants in the market cannot anticipate what actions the government will take in the future. As Hayek pointed out, there must be some generally enforced rules of operation to ensure future planning.[21] We need to know what the rules are before we start the game, and everyone needs a level playing field. Thomas Aquinas summed up the matter well when he wrote, "Everything is uncertain when there is a departure from justice nor can anything be made stable when it depends upon the will of another, much less on his caprice."[22]

The rule of law encompasses two categories. First, governments must provide an arena of public safety. One only has to look at areas where clerks serve the public through bulletproof glass to understand that violence acts as a restraint on investment and raises the costs of shopping and insurance. It is essential to create an environment where life, liberty, and property are secure against coercion, governmental or otherwise. Second, government regulation of business and its settling of disputes must be predictable. Investment is encouraged when risk can be calculated. Following precedent is, therefore, crucial to the rule of law, for it brings a degree of certainty about how laws will be enforced. When the courts refuse to follow precedent and custom, the question arises, what standard will they use? Rulings become unpredictable, and the government becomes essentially lawless. In this case the risk premiums—insurance rates, interest rates—rise sharply while property values plummet.

The rule of law, or especially its absence, has a profound effect on property rights. The government has abused property rights by extending eminent domain laws to include the taking of private property for private use. Specifically, in the 2005 case *Kelo v. City of New London*, the U.S. Supreme Court upheld the decision by the city of New London, Connecticut, to condemn private property in order to pass it on to more affluent parties who would develop it and pay more taxes. As Justice Sandra Day O'Connor noted in a dissenting opinion, "The fallout from this decision will not be random. The beneficiaries are likely to be those citizens with disproportionate influence and power in the political process, including large corporations and development firms."[23] Meanwhile, the poor and the powerless are exposed to the predatory whim of politicians and their patrons. In a separate dissent, Justice Clarence Thomas wrote that "extending the concept of public purpose to encompass any economically beneficial goal guarantees that these losses will fall disproportionately on poor communities. Those communities are not only systematically less likely to put their lands to the highest and best social use, but are also the least politically powerful."[24] The only positive to come out of the *Kelo* ruling was that it led to a series of state laws protecting private property rights.

The government's failure to enforce the law also does damage in labor disputes. Once investors know that their rights will not be protected, investment will decline, and industries will become noncompetitive and eventually go out of business.

The Sacredness of Contracts

Another pillar of a prosperous economy and a free society is the sacredness of contracts. A contract is an agreement between two equal parties. It is a hallmark of a free society. In earlier times, the bond between men could be called hegemonic—that is, one party was superior to the other and set the terms of the deal for both parties. This implies a society based on rank, serfdom, or even slavery.[25]

Contracts allow productivity to flourish because they provide the ability to exchange things today for the promises of things to be done or given in the future. Most productivity takes place over time, and by providing that resources will be available at a later time, contracts allow individuals and businesses to plan. "Deferred exchanges," economist Harry Scherman wrote in *The Promises Men Live By*, "take place *only* because of the virtual certainty that they will be completed."[26] John Chamberlain explained the fundamental nature of contracts: "There can be markets without contracts, but it is obvious that if every trade or exchange or agreement to do something for compensation had to be completed on the spot there could be little forward-planning of production, and little round-aboutness in men's dealings with each other."[27]

Hayek captured the Austrian emphasis on contracts when he wrote: "That other people's property can be serviceable in the achievement of our aims is due mainly to the enforcibility of contracts. The whole network of rights created by contracts is as important a part of our own protected sphere, as much as the basis of our plans, as any property of our own."[28]

Once the concept of contracts is broken, no one is sure what will happen in the future and risk increases dramatically. To proceed with the bankruptcy of General Motors and Chrysler, courts allowed contracts and bonds to be superseded. This may have solved a temporary problem for labor, but investors then questioned the safety of their commitment, especially in an industry that requires huge amounts of capital.

The Free Movement of Prices

The free movement of prices represents still another prerequisite of prosperity. Since the time of Menger and Böhm-Bawerk, the Austrian School has examined price formulation and the important role prices play in the allocation of resources. As prices rise, more suppliers appear on the scene to overcome scarcity. Conversely, a fall in prices means that a particular item is abundant and there is no need to produce more. Benjamin Anderson, an American economist of the Austrian School, summarized the vital function of prices freely set in the market:

> Prices have work to do. Prices have the important function of accomplishing priorities, allocations, and rationing. That is their regular work. It is the work of free prices and freely moving wages to determine whether labor and supplies shall be drawn to the production of commodity "A" or commodity "B." Rising prices mean more production. Falling prices mean less production. Rising prices mean less consumption. Falling prices mean more consumption. With freely moving prices, commodities are divided among consumers in accordance with the relative urgencies of demand. With freely moving prices and freely moving wages, the goods in most urgent demand are produced, and the production of the less urgently demanded goods declines.[29]

Austrian economists, most notably Hayek and Mises, have shown what happens in the absence of freely moving prices. Central planning interferes with the pricing process. As a result, balancing the needs of suppliers and demanders becomes more difficult; future planning breaks down; risk increases. In the words of former Federal Reserve chairman

Alan Greenspan: "Without the help of a market pricing mechanism, Soviet economic planning had no effective feedback to guide it. Just as important, the planners did not have the signals of finance to adjust the allocation of savings to real productive investments that accommodated the population's shifting needs and tastes."[30]

Entrepreneurship

As we have seen, the Austrian School emphasizes the role of the entrepreneur. Entrepreneurship fits well with the Austrian concept that the individual is at the center of all economics. Entrepreneurs enhance standards of living by organizing resources to make new goods and services available to the market. In this sense entrepreneurship is another prerequisite of prosperity.

Ludwig von Mises explained the crucial function the entrepreneur plays in the economy:

> The driving force of the market process is provided neither by the consumers nor by the owners of the means of production—land, capital goods, and labor—but by the promoting and speculating entrepreneurs. These are people intent upon profiting by taking advantage of differences in prices. Quicker of apprehension and farther-sighted than other men, they look around for sources of profit. They buy where and when they deem prices too low, and they sell where and when they deem prices too high. They approach the owners of the factors of production, and their competition sends the prices of these factors up to the limit corresponding to their anticipation of the future prices of these products. They approach the consumers, and their competition forces the prices of consumer goods down to the point at which the whole supply can be sold.[31]

The Austrian School is not alone, of course, in highlighting the role of the entrepreneur. Entrepreneurship has long been honored in America. Eli Whitney and his cotton gin, Thomas Edison and the light bulb, Charles Goodyear and the process of vulcanizing rubber—these and countless other inventors and innovators have dramatically reshaped American life.

Family Structure

While focusing on economics as a science of individual human action, the Austrian School does not ignore the family unit. On the contrary, the Austrians show that a vigorous and productive economy relies on a healthy family structure to maintain its existence. There probably is no greater threat to a sound division of labor than the modern collapse of the family.

As families have disintegrated and fertility rates have fallen, economic distress has resulted, particularly in those societies with large welfare states. The financial health of these programs relies on a large number of people paying in and a small number collecting. The larger the number collecting and the smaller the number paying in, the more difficult it becomes to administer the program. State and city governments face growing financial crises largely because the declining number of supporters is unable to sustain their generous retirement and medical programs. The federal government confronts similar problems with Social Security, Medicare, and other transfer programs.

In many cases the nuclear family is simply collapsing. The family is the fundamental unit of society. Both Aristotle and Thomas Aquinas saw the family as arising from the nature of man and as existing prior to the state. Aristotle showed, in fact, how the state evolved from the family—as family groups formed villages and, ultimately, cities. Aristotle and Aquinas agreed, too, that the family is responsible for introducing new members into society and assisting the person to full development.[32]

The family is also an important foundation of the division of labor. The family is where the child first learns language, manners, respect for others, responsibility, and other basic values he will need to join society (and the economy).

The collapse of the family is leading to massive social and economic problems. From an economic standpoint, one result has been that more people arrive in the workforce without personal stability, diligent work habits, basic moral values, or a strong sense of how to deal with people.

Society's poor view of the family unit has created economic challenges for family businesses. A major threat to family business is the estate tax, also known as the "death tax," which has a number of ill effects. The death tax concentrates industry into larger corporations and is an impediment to the formation of family capital and tradition. If the owner of a family business dies, the family is obliged to pay out a significant amount of capital to the government. Take the case of a farm valued at $5 million. If the owner farms as an individual, when he dies, his family will receive a certain deduction and then be required to pay the government upward of 55 percent of the farm's value within nine months. If the family receives a deduction of $1 million, it must still pay a tax of $2.2 million to retain the farm. In many cases that will mean the family will be forced to pay high insurance rates, take on significant debt, or sell the farm. By contrast, a corporately owned farm never confronts the death tax. It can continually invest in the latest equipment and technology, which provides a competitive advantage over the family farm. In this way, the economy becomes increasingly concentrated into larger units that will have more market power.

Twentieth-century Austrian economist Hans Sennholz pointed out:

> Estate taxation does not raise production costs of all enterprises simultaneously, as income taxes boost the costs of profitable enterprises. The death duties fall on family enterprises at different points of time. Following hard on an enterprise affected by death, they may not leave enough productive assets to carry on production. Output is curtailed through contraction or even liquidations; competition is reduced a little at a time, which causes goods prices to rise.[33]

The undue tax and regulatory burdens placed on family-owned businesses are particularly troubling because such businesses are important engines of job creation. Small businesses comprise half the U.S. economy and created 64 percent of all new jobs from 1995 to 2010.[34] Many, if not most, of these businesses are family owned.

The death tax presents a problem that goes beyond economics. It constitutes a gross infringement on the rights of the individual. A man has the right to transfer his possessions onto his progeny without a third party taking a cut, because the individual and, indeed, the family come before the state. According to Pope Pius XI (drawing on earlier statements by Leo XIII), "Man's natural right of possessing and transmitting property by inheritance must remain intact and inviolate, cannot be taken away by the State, 'for man precedes the State' and 'the domestic household is antecedent, as well in idea as in fact, to the gathering of men into a community.' "[35]

Savings and Capital Formation

Another essential component of a well-integrated and prosperous economy is the ability of the participants to save money. The Austrian School has always stressed the necessity of saving to produce capital.[36] Austrian economists also emphasize that savings guard the independence and economic security of the participants.

Young people today are racking up substantial debt. The average debt of college graduates is the highest in history—some $24,000.[37] Calling the Class of 2011 "the most indebted ever," the *Wall Street Journal* observed that in inflation-adjusted terms, the average debt for those graduates is a whopping 47 percent higher than the debt of graduates a decade earlier.[38] In many cases these debts will take decades to pay, which will make it much more difficult for these young people to form families, buy homes, and so on.

Yet young people often don't learn about the importance of savings. When I participated in a seminar on finance for high school students, my fellow panelists, who were bankers, stressed that students should achieve a high credit rating. They made no mention of savings.

Unfortunately, savings are disparaged in Keynesian economics as well. Savings must be encouraged because it makes possible the formation of capital in a noninflationary way. Proverbs 13:22 states, "The good man leaves an inheritance to his children's children." Modern society, however, is leaving children with a negative inheritance of debt.

Leisure

Perhaps one of the most overlooked prerequisites for a prosperous, well-functioning society is leisure. So overlooked is leisure that the vast majority of Americans today, business and political leaders included, scarcely know any longer what the term means and why it is essential to the development of any healthy economy.

Leisure is not simply time away from work. It is, rather, time dedicated to the pursuit of something specific—to a consideration of the highest and most important things. It involves moving beyond the workaday world to the world of contemplation. Furthermore, leisure is neither sloth nor entertainment. Leisure is an activity, though it is an activity of the mind and soul. It is, in other words, an inward activity. As such, it is not the same as entertainment or diversion. Although entertainment can be a good of the soul, it draws the focus away from one's self toward something to relieve the demands and weariness of work.

As an activity of the mind, leisure is quite different from work. But as Aristotle observed, there is no leisure without work. If one enjoys anything worthy of the name *leisure*, then one understands resolutely that work is part of life. Work is not only inescapable but also, in its proper context, a fundamental good of life providing many other necessary goods, including food, clothing, housing, education, investment capital, and, yes, leisure.[39]

Leisure is in many ways akin to play, especially the kind of children's play that lacks any specific plan, rule, or time line. Leisure offers the entrepreneur and the manager the opportunity to think about new and better products, services, and ways of doing business. Because leisure involves a consideration of theory, principle, and practice, the entrepreneur and the manager are poised to consider and reconsider the operation of their business in light of collected information, knowledge, and wisdom from both the past and the present.

The importance of this connection cannot be emphasized enough. Economic calamities reflect a failure on the part of successive generations of business and political leaders to act on the wisdom born of experience. Just how many of our fiscal and monetary policy errors are new? How many of our so-called can't-fail capital investments and risk-free or risk-limited ventures are original? Have we not in one sense or another seen these items and patterns before? And yet here we are making so many of the same mistakes over again. Leisure, properly understood, deters misguided, utopian schemes for human behavior by linking the past and present to future-oriented efforts.

In *The Ordeal of Change*, social commentator Eric Hoffer says that leisure refreshes man's soul and results in cultural and technological progress:

Archimedes' bathtub and Newton's apple suggest that momentous trains of thought may have their inception in idle musing. The original insight is most likely to come when elements stored in different compartments of the mind drift into the open, jostle one another, and now and then coalesce to form new combinations. It is doubtful whether a mind that is pinned down and cannot drift elsewhere is capable of formulating new questions. It is true that the working out of ideas and insights requires persistent hard thinking, and the inspiration necessary for such a task is probably a by-product of single-minded application. But the sudden illumination and the flash of discovery are not likely to materialize under pressure. . . . Hence the remarkable fact that many inventions had their birth as toys. In the Occident the first machines were mechanical toys, and such crucial instruments as the telescope and microscope were first conceived as playthings.[40]

Subsidiarity

Another precondition too frequently overlooked is the principle of subsidiarity. This principle holds that the smallest, least centralized units of society are best equipped to handle most of the work society gets done. The Austrian School, in accord with its emphasis on the individual and the family and its criticisms of centralized authority, recognizes and respects the constituent institutions of society that stand between the individual and the state. Subsidiarity includes the recognition of property rights in associations, businesses, and local institutions that have been voluntarily formed over time. These institutions make up the fabric of a free and prosperous society.

As Hayek wrote, local institutions are the closest to, and most protective of, the individual. They understand the individual and the community in a way that large governments and institutions simply cannot. Hayek argued:

If we can agree that the economic problem of society is mainly one of rapid adaptation to changes in the particular circumstances of time and place, it would seem to follow that the ultimate decisions must be left to the people who are familiar with these circumstances, who know directly of the relevant changes and of the resources immediately available to meet them. We cannot expect that this problem will be solved by first communicating all this knowledge to a central board which, after integrating *all* knowledge, issues its orders. We must solve it by some form of decentralization. But this answers only part of our problem. We need decentralization because only thus can we insure that the knowledge of the particular circumstances of time and place will be promptly used.[41]

Society is complex, and it is impossible for one central government to oversee all the goings-on at every level of the community. This basic recognition allowed Hayek and other Austrians to see early on that communism simply could not last. As Hayek wrote: "Nobody has yet succeeded deliberately arranging all the activities of a complex society: there is no such thing as a fully planned society of any degree of complexity."[42]

Here again, the Austrians are not alone in highlighting a prerequisite for a successful society and economy. In crafting the Bill of Rights, the Founders tried to ensure that the national government would not usurp what local governments could or should do, and that government at any level would not usurp the functions of the individual, the family, and the private economy. The Tenth Amendment states: "The powers not delegated to the United States by the Constitution, nor prohibited by it to the States, are reserved to the States respectively, or to the people." Unfortunately, by the twentieth century, the federal government had come to ignore this stricture all too often.

In 1931, Pope Pius XI echoed the guarantees of the Tenth Amendment. He enunciated the principle of subsidiarity as a response to the rising threat of totalitarian ideologies. Coming out of World War I, communist and fascist governments had made the state the dominant aspect of human activity, with every association, business, school, employee organization, religion, university, and family becoming completely subservient to the government. Within just a few years the National Socialist regime in Germany would do the same. In *Quadragesimo Anno*, Pius XI called for political and economic activities to be done at the lowest possible level:

That most weighty principle, which cannot be set aside or changed, remains fixed and unshaken in social philosophy: Just as it is gravely wrong to take from individuals what they can accomplish by their own initiative and industry and give it to the community, so also it is an injustice and at the same time a grave evil and disturbance of right order to assign to a greater and higher association what lesser and subordinate organizations can do. For every social activity ought of its very nature to furnish help to the members of the body social, and never destroy and absorb them.[43]

The pope explicitly addressed the harm an all-encompassing state does to the economy. "To consider the State as the ultimate to which everything else should be subordinated and directed," he wrote, "cannot but fail to harm the true and lasting prosperity of nations." He continued: "If, in fact, the State lays claim to and directs private enterprise, then such private enterprises, ruled as they are by delicate and complicated internal principles which guarantee and assure the realization of their special aims, may be damaged to the detriment of the public good, by being wrenched from their natural surroundings, that is, from responsible private action."[44]

Although the communist regimes of Pius XI's era have collapsed, government interventionism in the United States and other Western countries is far more pronounced than it was when the pope wrote, in those pre–New Deal days. The most recent economic crisis brought out quite vividly the codependency of government and the economy: the government relies on the economy for revenue, while the population has come to rely on government for an array of services. Even in the face of overwhelming evidence that the private sector is more efficient in providing services than government, the expectation that the state will supply a range of services makes the situation difficult to change. (There is a reason Social Security is called the "third rail of American politics.") But to fund expansive entitlement programs and public-sector pensions, governments need more and more tax revenue. Tax revenue depends not on tax rates but on the level of overall economic activity. According to a study by Hoover Institution economist W. Kurt Hauser, the federal government's annual tax receipts have hovered right around 19 percent of gross domestic product (GDP) *since the end of World War II*—this despite the fact that the top marginal rate has ranged from 28 percent to 92 percent during that time.[45] As a result, when the economy goes into a severe recession, tax revenues drop significantly.

State and local governments feel the pinch in a recession as well. To pay for the services and pensions they are expected to provide, they must raise taxes, cut budgets, or both. Since 2008, city, county, and state governments across America have run huge deficits, laid off workers, slashed services, instituted pay freezes, and increased sales, property, income, and other taxes.

The real solution to such problems is to ensure a prosperous, well-balanced economy—and the only way to achieve that is to keep the government from interfering too much with markets. Interventionist government can throw an economy out of balance and depress economic activity, as we saw in part 2 of this book. Writing in the *Wall Street Journal*, economist Paul Godek rightly notes: "Private investment and hiring are suppressed by economic and political uncertainty. Such uncertainty is generated by unprecedented government intervention, massive increases in government spending, and anticipated tax increases. This is what the policies undertaken during the 1930s, those that sustained the Great Depression, should have taught us."[46]

The Common Good

For a tree to grow to its full height, it needs to be nurtured in an environment where certain preconditions are met—where it is provided sunlight, water, mineral-rich soil, room to spread its roots, and so forth. Society functions much the same way: when crucial preconditions are not met, it will not grow to its potential.

It is to everyone's benefit to establish the necessary preconditions for a free and prosperous society: private property, a sound currency, the rule of law, the sacredness of contract, the free movement of prices, entrepreneurship, a strong family structure, savings, leisure, and subsidiarity. These preconditions form the foundations of the common good.

The common good is that which promotes the good of everyone to the detriment of no one. The concept sounds simple enough, but in political thought it is often elusive. In modern government, lobbyists descend on state and national capitals, seeking to skew government policy in their direction. Very little thought is given to the overall direction of society.

One of the best ways to measure whether an action promotes the common good is to answer a simple question: "Whom does it harm?" If a piece of legislation benefits one group at the clear expense of another, that legislation does not serve the common good. Protectionist tariffs, for example, harm the economy by serving the interests of a small group of manufacturers and distributors at the expense of a far larger population. Emphasizing the need to serve the common good, Hayek held that laws should be general in character and not aimed toward specific groups.[47]

Critics of free-market economics might scoff at associating free markets with the common good. Since the time of the Enlightenment, a powerful (but controversial) strain of economic thought has held that rational self-interest governs all economic activity. Adam Smith put forward this idea in *The Wealth of Nations*, where he wrote: "It is not from the benevolence of the butcher, the brewer, or the baker, that we expect our dinner, but from their regard to their own self interest. We address ourselves, not to their humanity but to their self-love, and never talk to them of our own necessities but of their advantages."[48] Adherents of the classical school carried forth this idea in the nineteenth century, and more recently Ayn Rand, Milton Friedman, and many secular libertarians have popularized the concept of rational self-interest.

The Austrian School is different, however. From the start, Austrian economists have challenged the idea that rational self-interest drives all of economics. In the nineteenth century, Austrian School founder Carl Menger referred to this notion as the "dogma of self-interest." The idea that self-interest alone guides people, he argued, prohibits "the strict regularity of human action in general and economic action in particular—and thereby eliminates the possibility of a rigorous economic theory." In short, Menger criticized classical economists for being too narrow in their approach. He also observed that "in innumerable cases [people] are in error about their economic interest, or in ignorance of the economic state of affairs"—facts that economists ignored when claiming that self-interest infallibly guided economic activity.[49]

The Austrian School also recognizes that the concept of rational self-interest became a barrier to thoughtful discussions about economics. Almost from the beginning, critics used the notion of self-interest to pillory the field of economics. Clergymen, social critics, and many others derided economics as the science of greed. Even within the profession, more and more people came to see economics as a science dealing strictly with material wealth, which in turn led to overemphasis on mathematical measurement.

Israel Kirzner summed up the Austrian perspective when he wrote that the early classical economists "thought of economics as concerned with wealth understood in a more or less material sense" and regarded self-interest as "an impersonal force that extracted this wealth from the factors of production and propelled it through the distributive channels of the economy." Subsequent writers, Kirzner added, laid "greater stress" on "the force of self-interest itself as the core of economics" and consequently emphasized "maximization-patterns of behavior." Kirzner observed that the emphasis nineteenth-century economists placed on self-interest "goes hand-in-hand with a desire to turn economics into a 'science' like mechanics. This required the postulation of a pervading force manipulating 'wealth' into various configurations susceptible of analysis through the use of maximization formulae from the calculus. Self-interest was seized upon with avidity from the classical system as providing just such a plausible force."[50] Many schools of economics still try to measure utility and, as we have seen, still rely on mathematics to try to force economics into the realm of the physical sciences.

To be sure, each individual or group in the division of labor pursues his or its own end. But the Austrian School recognizes that in a society directed toward the common good, there is still overall harmony among the various parts. Others have reinforced this point. Jacques Rueff, the French free-market economist who was influenced by the Austrian School, pointed out that if men were to pursue only their private interests, the broader society would suffer. The private interest of taxpayers, for instance, "is to pay as little as possible," but if everyone followed that private interest, it would "set the public treasury on the road to bankruptcy and ruin." Similarly, "the interest of all users of public services is to pay the lowest possible rates, while the interest of those engaged in production is to obtain the highest possible remuneration." Rueff concluded: "All these forces converge upon one common objective: to put the institution to death by exhausting its resources." Putting any institution—let alone the entire society—"to death" will serve *no one's* interest. Reconciling private interests and the common good is what Rueff referred to as "the real political problem."[51]

Thomas Aquinas made a similar point when he observed:

> Where there are many men together and each one is looking after his own interest, the group would be broken up and scattered unless there were also some one to take care of what appertains to the common weal. . . . There must exist something which impels towards the common good of the many, over and above that which impels towards the private good of each individual. . . . If, therefore, a group of free men is governed by their ruler for the common good of the group, that government will be right and just, as is suitable to free men. If, however, the government is organized not for the common good of the group but for the private interest of the ruler, it will be an unjust and perverted government.[52]

Economics is the science of individual human action. But the Austrian School also recognizes that for individuals to flourish—for spontaneous order to lead to a prosperous and harmonious society—these essential cultural, political, and legal preconditions must be met.

11

The Nature of Human Action

Precise analysis of individual action has been the hallmark of Austrian economics since the time of the school's founder, Carl Menger. In the 1860s, as a newspaper reporter and then a member of the economics staff of the government publication *Wiener Zeitung*, Menger wrote market surveys and was an observer at the Vienna stock exchange. In these positions he became fascinated by how prices were formed in the marketplace. He saw that the actual pricing process, as traders explained it, did not match up with the standard textbook explanations he had learned at university. Menger concluded that the value of money (or of commodities or anything else) comes from the spontaneous actions and judgments of individual traders, not from the actions of an institution or government. That his observation seems commonplace today is a testament to the influence of Menger and the Austrian School; this foundational insight of Austrian economics has become part of the fabric of modern economics.

Still, other schools of economic thought begin their study of the economy by observing the actions of governments and corporations. The Austrian School has remained focused on individual human action. After Menger and his colleague Eugen Böhm-Bawerk built the foundation of Austrian theory, Ludwig von Mises put it all together into a new area of study he called *praxeology*, which is the study of human action. In the Austrian view, economics is a division of praxeology. Mises wrote:

No less than from the action of an individual praxeology begins its investigations from the individual action. It does not deal in vague terms with human action in general, but with concrete action which a definite man has performed at a definite date and at a definite place. But, of course, it does not concern itself with the accidental and environmental features of this action and with what distinguishes it from all other actions, but only with what is necessary and universal in its performance.[1]

Of course, praxeology was not really a new area of study in the twentieth century. Mises, like his Austrian predecessors, drew on a great tradition that extends back millennia, one that places economics in its proper context. The Austrian School recognizes what Aristotle, Aquinas, and other giants observed centuries ago: economics is a practical science that deals with human nature. And the only way to truly understand economics is to understand what motivates human action. As the Austrians have shown, many other schools of economics provide overly narrow accounts of what drives economic activity, or they fail to consider human motivations at all, preferring to reduce everything to numbers on a ledger (or a computer screen).

This chapter looks at the grand tradition of thought that informs a proper understanding of human action. We will begin by considering the three conditions necessary for any human action to take place. These three axioms of human action are: purpose, desirability, and means. One might think of the three axioms as the legs of a tripod; for it to stand, all three legs must be in place.

The First Axiom: Purpose

The first axiom of human action is purpose. Every human action is directed to a goal. This goal defines the nature of the action and guides the actor in achieving it. Thomas Aquinas held that without a purpose, or "end," intelligent action will not take place. "Every agent acts either by nature or by intellect," he wrote. Those who act by intellect, he added, "act for an end, since they act *with* an intellectual preconception of what they attain by their action, and they act *through* such a preconception."[2]

Mises observed that this notion of purpose separates the sciences of human action from the natural sciences:

> What distinguishes the field of human action from the field of external events as investigated by the natural sciences is the category of finality. We do not know of any final causes operating in what we call nature. But we know that man aims at definite goals chosen. In the natural sciences we search after constant relations among various events. In dealing with human action we search after the ends the actor wants or wanted to attain and after the result that his action brought about or will bring about.[3]

The Second Axiom: Desirability

From the fact that all conscious human action is purposeful, it follows that there must be something good or desirable in that purpose.

Fourteenth-century French philosopher Jean Buridan illustrated the importance of this axiom with his story of a donkey. Located equidistant from two identical bales of hay, the donkey couldn't decide from which bale to eat, so he starved to death. Buridan's point was that an actor makes a specific choice only when he sees a benefit in not making a different choice. Without this judgment or observation, every action becomes impossible.

Mises explained how human action flows from such judgments of desirability. "Acting man," he wrote, "is eager to substitute a more satisfactory state of affairs for a less satisfactory. . . . A man perfectly content with the state of his affairs would have no incentive to change things. He would have neither wishes nor desires; he would be perfectly happy. He would not act, he would simply live free from care."[4]

When teaching this principle to students, I have often encountered the objection, "If every action is for a good, what about criminal activity?" The answer is that there are different types of goods: short-run and long-run goods. For example, a criminal might see in his action a source for wealth, an expression of power, or some other benefit. Wealth and power are not bad in themselves, and put to good purposes, they can achieve good things. The criminal, however, concentrates only on the immediate benefit to himself and doesn't comprehend the evil effect of his actions on others.

Political scientist Edward Banfield, in his classic study *The Moral Basis of a Backward Society*, found that poverty and backwardness result largely from the inability of citizens "to act together for the common good."[5] The concept that there is a relationship between the moral state of the people and the state of society goes back to Plato's *Republic*.[6] Political philosopher Russell Kirk offered a modern-day version of this argument in *The Roots of American Order*, noting that "the 'inner order' of the soul and the 'outer order' of society" are "intimately linked." Order, he observed, is "the first need of the soul": "It is not possible to love what one ought to love, unless we recognize some principles of order by which to govern ourselves." Order is likewise "the first need of the Commonwealth": "It is not possible for us to live in peace with one another, unless we recognize some principle of order by which to do justice."[7]

Crime is hardly the only area where we see a divergence between short-term and long-term goods. All of us regularly weigh outcomes in the shorter and longer terms. If a sugary dessert is sitting right in front of us, we may indulge in the short-term good—the sweet taste—without seriously considering the long-term good, that of a healthy diet and body.

The dilemma one faces in choosing between short-term and long-term goods—or *proximate* and *ultimate* goods, as they are also known—is one of the most important considerations in economic policy. The French economist Frédéric Bastiat described the choice as between "that which is seen, and that which is not seen." According to Bastiat, the "bad economist," just like the criminal (or the idler, or the spendthrift, or the glutton), accounts only for the immediate, visible effect without considering the long-term, often dangerous consequences of his decisions.[8] Also, the bad economist sees only immediate benefits for particular interest groups but not for society as a whole—just as the criminal sees only the short-term benefit to himself. Austrian economist Henry Hazlitt made this point in his book *Economics in One Lesson*: "The art of economics consists in looking not merely at the immediate, but at the longer effects of any act or policy; it consists in tracing the consequences of that policy not merely for one group but for all groups."[9]

The concept that every agent acts for a good should not be confused with an objective standard of ethics. To make judgments, individuals must grapple with such concepts as value, choice, limitation, and time. Human choices are rarely, if ever, made in perfect circumstances. They must sort out messy complications; each alternative usually will have both positive and negative consequences. Many choices boil down to the answer to this question: "What downside am I able to cope with to gain the advantage I desire?" Take, for example, the choice of whether to accept a new job. The salary offered at one job might be higher, but taking the position could require moving to another city, or perhaps a much longer commute; another job might provide a lower salary but better working conditions. Every day we must make such choices from among the options in front of us. Resources are limited. Moreover, the options we face are competing, in that every particular choice prevents us from making some other choice.

These facts inform another central tenet of the Austrian School: that economic human action responds specifically to *scarcity*. Carl Menger first showed that how individual actors respond to scarcity affects prices; since then, Austrian economists have shown how scarcity informs all aspects of economics. Life itself is a continual series of choices dealing with scarcity. The essential challenge of economics is to reconcile unlimited wants with limited resources.

The Third Axiom: Means to Achieve the Goal

The third axiom about human action follows from the first two. It states that no human action can take place unless the actor has a means to achieve his goal. Menger first mentioned this in *Principles of Economics*, which begins, "All things are subject to the law of cause and effect." Anything can be brought into a cause-and-effect relationship to satisfy a need or want; something that achieves the end we want becomes an economic good.[10] Take oil, for example. For centuries, petroleum was considered little more than a waste product. Then people discovered how to refine it and use it as a fuel. In little more than a century and a half, oil has reshaped the entire world and become one of the most important economic goods.

Mises advanced the understanding of how purpose and means come together in his books *Human Action* and *The Ultimate Foundation of*

Economic Science. He encapsulated the matter by writing, "To act means to strive after ends, that is, to choose a goal and to resort to means to attain the goal sought."[11] Mises's protégé Murray Rothbard spelled out the process. The citizen frames "general ethical rules or goals." "But," he added, "in order to decide how to arrive at such goals, he must employ all the relevant conclusions of the various sciences, all of which are *in themselves* value-free." Rothbard offered an illustration of how this works:

> For example, let us suppose that a person's goal is to improve his health. Having arrived at this value . . . the person tries to discover how to reach his goal. To do so, he must employ the laws and findings, value-free in themselves, of the relevant sciences. He then extends the judgment of "good," as applied to his health, on to the means he believes will further that health. His end, the improvement of his health, he pronounces to be "good"; he then, let us say, adopts the findings of medical science that *x* grams of vitamin C per day will improve his health; he therefore extends the ethical pronouncement of "good"—or, more technically, of "right"—to taking vitamin C as well.[12]

Corollaries of Human Action

Following the axioms of purpose, desirability, and means, there are eight corollaries of human action that help us better understand each individual human act:

1. The actor changes and that which is acted upon changes: Every time we perform an action we build a habit or skill. For example, each time I read, I learn to read faster. If I play tennis with someone better than me, I become better. The second part of this corollary is that reality changes. Every time we act, we bring about some change in the world around us.[13]

2. The actor gains knowledge with each action: This is an extension of the first corollary. A reason that industries develop in specific locations is that over time a region builds up a reservoir of knowledge and expertise in certain fields. For instance, even though many manufacturing facilities have left the Detroit area, engineering firms from around the world are moving in, because they can take advantage of the knowledge accumulated over more than a hundred years of making cars.

3. Every human action is future-oriented: Each human act has a purpose, which is the goal to be achieved. Ethics, politics, and economics are all future-oriented and as such involve factors that cannot be foreseen. This means that risk and speculation are necessary elements of our lives.

4. Each action has unintended consequences: In a sense, each action opens up a new adventure. Some unintended consequences are very good, whereas others lead to new problems. The inventor of the wheel did not foresee the modern automobile. The politicians who directed World War I had very little idea of the evils that the conflict would unleash through the rest of the twentieth century. Who could have imagined Hitler, Stalin, Mao, and the Great Depression, all of which had their origins in the world's response to the shooting of a single archduke?

In focusing on human action rather than mathematical models and formulas, the Austrian School takes special notice of the uncertainty inherent in virtually every choice we make. Ludwig von Mises summed up: "Every action is a speculation, i.e. guided by a definite opinion concerning the uncertain conditions of the future. Even in short-run activities this uncertainty prevails. Nobody can know whether some unexpected fact will not render vain all that he has provided for the next day or the next hour."[14]

5. Each action takes place in time and is irreversible: There's an old saying, "You can't take words back." In the same way, one cannot change a decision on the stock market or an investment once it is done. How many times have we said to ourselves, "I shouldn't have done that"?

6. Each action is historically unique: Key to the Austrian School perspective is that studying history can expand our understanding of the present and inform our decisions for the future. As Mises put it, the study of history makes a man "understand the situation in which he has to act," and it also "increases wisdom."[15] But this is not to say that studying history can ever allow us to have perfect knowledge of how to act and what the effects of that action will be. History can give us principles to follow, certainly, but as Mises pointed out, each action is unique and unrepeatable.[16] The harder we try, the more we learn that there is no way to perfectly replicate the past. New circumstances, new ideas, new actors come on the scene all the time.

7. Every action involves an opportunity cost: With each action we take, we are sacrificing something else we could have done. If I go to Europe this summer, I cannot at the same time go to California. A government that spends money on schools cannot spend the same resources repairing bridges. This is simply another way to say that action constantly responds to scarcity. All the human sciences have to wrestle with this fact.

8. Every action involves valuation at the margin: Say that a young man has an important exam tomorrow he must study for, and his girlfriend asks him to go out tonight. He must now make a concrete choice between the three hours of study or the three hours of companionship. If he chooses to forego the date to pass the exam, it's not because he is choosing between the love of his girlfriend and his academic success. No, he is merely choosing how we will spend three hours on one particular night—deciding that the time spent will ensure a higher score on the exam, which in turn could improve his chances for a scholarship.

Every human action takes place with regard to a particular choice and a particular circumstance. The action we choose to take is often informed by the theory of marginal utility—which is to say that how we value something depends on how much of it we have. So, for example, if the young man has an entire week to study for his exam instead of just one night, the three hours of study time won't be as valuable to him, and he probably will choose to go out with his girlfriend. Once again, we see the prominent role of scarcity in influencing human action.

How Do We Judge the Good?

It is one thing to say that every human action is aimed at some purpose that is desirable. But how do individuals judge "the good"?

As we saw in the previous chapter, the concept of rational self-interest comes up short in explaining how economic decisions are made. Adam Smith and the classical economists championed this viewpoint, but as the Austrians (and many others) have pointed out, the perspective is overly narrow. It fails to account for charitable instincts, decisions made to benefit one's family or community, and other factors that inform human action. The focus on self-interest also obscures the true role and ambitions of economics. It helped lead to a strictly mathematical approach to economics. Such an approach attempts to apply methods from theoretical sciences, which study things over which we have no control (such as the motion of the planets and the structure of the atom), to the study of human action—those things which we can control. Pablo Triana, in his book *Lecturing Birds on Flying*, identifies a key cause of the recent financial crisis: "our blind devotion to theoretical concoctions (especially if sponsored by rigorous-looking individuals with PhDs from prestigious universities)."[17] Triana notes simply: "The math had its chance, and couldn't have gone any wronger."[18]

So on what basis should economic decisions be made?

Triana suggests a solution: returning to a reliance on "good old human judgment."[19] His deceptively simple counsel links back up with the great tradition of thought that the field of economics has so often ignored. What is called for here is a proper understanding of human action.

This sort of understanding is precisely what has animated the Austrian School of economics. Setting a template for other Austrian thinkers, Carl Menger not only cited economists but also drew extensively on philosophers including Plato, Aristotle, Bacon, and Hobbes. Murray Rothbard wrote an important essay on the "prehistory of the Austrian School" in which he cited "a long and mighty tradition of proto-Austrian Scholastic economics, founded on Aristotle, continuing through the Middle Ages and the later Italian and Spanish Scholastics, and then influencing the French and Italian economists before and up till the day of Adam Smith." Rothbard concluded, "The achievement of Carl Menger and the Austrians was not so much to found a totally new system on the framework of British classical political economy as to revive and elaborate upon the older tradition that had been shunted aside by the classical school."[20]

What do the great philosophers and political philosophers tell us about the primary virtues that should guide human action? There is a consistent thread that runs through the works of thinkers ranging from Aristotle to Aquinas and on to Edmund Burke and Russell Kirk: that experience and good judgment—prudential judgment—should guide people in their actions.

To emphasize the practicality of the human sciences, Aristotle distinguished between demonstration and deliberation. The theoretical sciences rely on demonstration, as in the proofs a mathematician provides. The sciences of human action, meanwhile, rely on deliberation, which is a process of rational inquiry. Prudence is an essential part of deliberation. Prudential judgment can come only from experience, Aristotle showed. In the *Nicomachean Ethics* he wrote:

> While young men become geometricians and mathematicians and wise in matters like these, it is thought that a young man of practical wisdom cannot be found. The cause is that such wisdom is concerned not only with universals but with particulars, which become familiar from experience, but a young man has no experience, for it is length of time that gives experience; indeed one might ask this question too, why a boy may become a mathematician, but not a philosopher or a physicist. It is because the objects of mathematics exist by abstraction, while the first principles of these other subjects come from experience, and because young men have no conviction about the latter but merely use the proper language, while the essence of mathematical objects is plain enough to them?[21]

Aristotle could well have been writing about the young men and women on Wall Street in the lead-up to the financial crisis. Their skills at mathematical modeling and numerical analysis were no substitute for practical wisdom and prudential judgment.

Thomas Aquinas, too, saw that prudence stems from knowledge and experience, not emotion. He defined prudence as the ability of the intellect to find the right way to do things for the right time and for the right purpose. It is an intellectual virtue that guides individual action in specific circumstances.[22]

To Aquinas, prudence is the main virtue on which other virtues depend. He described prudence as enabling us first to assess what means are available to achieve our goals, then to judge which means to employ, and finally to take the right course of action.[23] Pablo Triana is right when he says that we need "good old human judgment." Aquinas's analysis of the elements of prudential decision-making apply to economic and financial decision-making today. In the *Summa Theologica*, Aquinas identified eight essential parts of prudence:

1. Memory: A knowledge of history can help us avoid mistakes of the past. In *This Time Is Different: Eight Centuries of Financial Folly*, economists Carmen Reinhart and Kenneth Rogoff note: "No matter how different the latest financial frenzy or crisis always appears, there are usually more remarkable similarities with past experience from other countries and from history. Recognizing these analogies and precedents is an essential step toward improving our global financial system, both to reduce the risk of future crisis and to better handle catastrophes when they happen."[24] Unfortunately, economists and financiers generally do not have a good grasp of history. They are unfamiliar with what caused economic fluctuations in the past and how those fluctuations were handled. Investors, too, need to know a good deal of history about the financial instruments in which they wish to invest. Although knowing history can never guarantee that our actions will achieve "the good," failing to heed the lessons of the past will almost surely mean we will fall into similar traps.

2. Insight: Knowing history is not sufficient. One must be able to see exactly how that history applies in the present case. By using insight, one is able to see the underlying principle. For example, one might take a look at interest-rate differentials to see what they indicate about market conditions. One might study the effects that some government intervention, such as price controls, might have in particular markets.

3. Docility: From the Latin word *docere*, docility means "teachability." It enables us to keep an open mind to new information and incorporate that information in the decision-making process.

4. Shrewdness: Shrewdness allows one to come up with a plan of action that takes into account the present situation and keep emotions out of the picture. In economic and financial matters, shrewdness means not getting caught up in the mob mania that accompanies economic ups and downs.

5. Reason: The ability to reason gives us the ability to "take good counsel," as Aquinas put it. Through reasoning, one can assess the nature of the information at hand and draw conclusions about the decision that needs to be made.[25] One might, for example, look at the price/earnings ratio of a particular stock and conclude that it is simply unsustainable. In that situation, one concludes that the best course of action is to sell the stock or perhaps sell short, depending on the circumstances.

6. Foresight: In the economic and financial arena, foresight is the ability to see how various principles and conditions will play out and to take quick corrective action. The United States and most Western governments have displayed a glaring lack of foresight by building up huge entitlement programs without establishing the financial means to support them. Politicians have avoided dealing with the long-term consequences of these unsustainable debt burdens to achieve short-term political success.

7. Circumspection: From the Latin meaning "to look around," circumspection refers to the ability to see what is going on around you—that is, to take into account the present defining circumstances. In economics and finance, circumspection can involve examining such signals as price/earnings ratios, yield curve configurations, and government and private debt ratios.

8. Caution: Every course of action involves certain obstacles. Caution is required to avoid charging into these obstacles without a plan to surmount them. For example, before starting a business, one should know the legal and economic problems that could crop up. Caution allows a decision maker to assess the risk of a particular course of action.

Together with Aristotle and Aquinas, Edmund Burke recognized the proper distinction between the speculative sciences and the practical sciences. This recognition was closely connected to Burke's emphasis on prudence, which he called "the God of this lower world." Burke scholar Peter Stanlis pointed out that "the distinction of Aristotle and St. Thomas Aquinas between speculative and practical reason is fundamental to Burke's principle of prudence."[26]

Significantly, the thought of Edmund Burke profoundly influenced Carl Menger. Menger praised Burke for emphasizing "with full awareness the significance of the organic structures of social life and the partly unintended origin of these." His esteem for Burke clearly informed his criticisms of the German Historical School of economics. Menger noted "how little the . . . mental sphere of the historical school of German economists agrees with that of [Burke]."[27] When Burke—like Aristotle, Aquinas, and others before him—highlighted the importance of prudence, Menger took note.

Other Austrian economists have taken note as well. Most notably, when Ludwig von Mises wrote about praxeology, he was discussing the prudential judgments that characterize human action. Like Aquinas and others, Mises viewed knowledge and experience, not emotion, as informing human action. He wrote: "Seen from an activist point of view, knowledge is a tool of action. Its function is to advise man how to proceed in his endeavors to remove uneasiness."[28]

Principles and Theory

The Austrian School forces us to reconsider the most fundamental aspects of economics. In this and the two preceding chapters we have studied the principles at the core of Austrian economics. We covered the foundations of the economy or division of labor, identified the necessary conditions for the economy to operate successfully, and finally explored the nature of human action.

Putting economics back on proper foundations by reclaiming the wisdom of the ages remains an essential contribution of the Austrian School. But epistemology is by no means the only area in which we can learn from the Austrians. They have contributed substantially to economic theory as well. In the next two chapters we will consider the Austrian School's most important theoretical contributions: in the areas of inflation and deflation, and the trade cycle.

12

Inflation and Deflation

Often has it crossed my fancy, that the city loves to deal
With the very best and noblest members of her commonweal,
Just as with our ancient coinage, and the newly minted gold.
Yea for these, our sterling pieces, all of pure Athenian mould,
All of perfect die and metal, all the fairest of the fair,
All of workmanship unequalled, proved and valued everywhere
Both amongst our own Hellenes and Barbarians far away,
These we use not: but the worthless pinchbeck coins of yesterday,
Vilest die and basest metal, now we always use instead.
——*Aristophanes,* The Frogs

There is hardly a country in history that has not experimented with debasing its currency. For millennia, debasement was literally what emperors, kings, and government bureaucrats did to inflate currency: they would mix a base metal in with gold or silver to produce more coins and preserve their supply of precious metals. The practice began in the sixth century B.C. under King Croesus of Lydia, in the region of modern-day Turkey. The first king in recorded history to mint coins, Croesus used them to help finance wars of empire. Economics professor Christopher Westley writes: "Croesus soon learned that his wars were more easily funded when he debased his coins, allowing him to create more currency than his supply of precious metal would otherwise allow."[1]

In ancient Rome, emperor after emperor made the same discovery, issuing currency with less and less specie content. Any cursory look at the history of the Roman Empire shows continuous inflation. The debasement started with Nero in the middle of the first century and quickly escalated. By the end of the first century, Roman coins were 93 percent silver; less than a century later, the coins were 50 percent silver; by the year 268—exactly two centuries after Nero's death—the silver content of Roman coins had dropped to *0.02* percent.[2] Naturally, the value of Roman money plunged: the silver coin known as the denarius was worth 15 cents in the middle of the first century; it was worth 0.5 cents by the end of the third century.[3] And prices rose. Why? Because, as Westley aptly summarizes, "increases in the money supply do not magically increase the store of real wealth, so that when the new money is spent, prices are bid upward."[4]

Although the same inflationary pattern recurred whenever debasement happened, governments debased their currencies again and again in the centuries that followed. We have even seen debasement in America—but for a different reason. When I was a boy, most U.S. coins were 90 percent silver, and the pennies were solid copper. Today we have pennies that are not copper, and dimes, quarters, half dollars, and dollars that are not silver. But unlike the Roman emperors, the U.S. government didn't debase coins to make more. The debasement came about indirectly. As the government expanded the money supply during the 1960s, the price of precious metals rose above the face value of the coin. In other words, the precious metals making up the currency were worth more when melted down. Once the market discovered that there was more value in a silver dollar than a dollar, the currency disappeared.

This case illustrates one type of inflation: credit inflation, which occurs when governments monetize debts (create money) through the banking system to finance deficits. Credit inflation is one of several types of inflation we will consider in this chapter. No matter the cause of the inflation, the results are almost invariably the same. The pattern goes something like this: The government has trouble balancing its expenditures with revenues (often because of war). It raises taxes, and when that isn't enough, it borrows from private markets. But the demands for government expenditures exceed its ability to borrow, as the government's needs overwhelm the capital markets. Then someone has the bright idea to expand the currency to meet the increased expenditures.

Ludwig von Mises pointed out why this approach appeals to a government regime. "Inflation," he wrote, "becomes the most important psychological resource of any economic policy whose consequences have to be concealed." A government resorts to inflationary measures "when it cannot negotiate loans and dare not levy taxes, because it has reason to fear that it will forfeit approval of the policy it is following if it reveals too soon the financial and general economic consequences of that policy." This is why Mises called inflation "an instrument of *unpopular*, i.e. of anti-democratic, policy," for "by misleading public opinion it makes possible the continued existence of a system of government that would have no hope of the consent of the people if the circumstances were clearly laid before them." Inflation, he noted, "has always been an important resource of policies of war and revolution," and "we find it in the service of socialism" as well.[5]

The Austrian School has been particularly incisive, and prescient, in its explanations of inflation. In his book *The Theory of Money and Credit*, published in 1911, Mises clearly outlined how inflation unfolds and the results thereof. He explained that interest rates eventually reflect expected inflation; that people flee into goods to avoid the consequent price increases; that increases in the money supply stimulate the economy for only a very short time; and that such increases do not affect all sectors of the economy equally but actually redistribute wealth.[6] Within a decade, the great German inflation was playing out exactly as Mises assessed, as Costantino Bresciani-Turroni pointed out in the classic study of that inflation, *The Economics of Inflation: A Study of Currency Depreciation in Post-War Germany*.[7]

A half century after Mises wrote *The Theory of Money and Credit*, fellow Austrian economist Wilhelm Röpke warned of the dangers associated with the growing welfare state and inflation, which were closely connected. In *A Humane Economy*, published in 1961, he wrote:

> Among these slowly spreading cancers of our Western Economy and society, two stand out: the apparently irresistible advance of the welfare state and the erosion of the value of money, which is called creeping inflation. There is a close link between the two through their common causes and mutual reinforcement. Both start slowly, but after a while their pace quickens until the deterioration is hard

to arrest, and this multiplies the danger. If people knew what awaits them in the end, they would perhaps stop in good time. But the trouble is . . . that it is extraordinarily difficult to make the voice of reason heard while there is still time. Social demagogues use the promises of the welfare state and inflationary policy to seduce the masses, and it is hard to warn people convincingly of the price ultimately to be paid by all.[8]

We can see the inflationary process going on all around us today. The U.S. Federal Reserve and the central banks of Europe have repeatedly expanded the currency. We even see the pattern in the budgets of states such as California, the only difference being that states cannot print money.

What is shocking about all this is the lack of historical perspective it displays. Perhaps financial and political leaders wish to convince themselves that *this time* will be different, but such an approach violates a number of the aspects of prudence: memory, insight, docility, foresight, and circumspection.

So what does history tell us? The inflationary pattern has ended in disaster over and over again, from ancient Rome to the Turkish Empire, from France, England, and Germany to the nations of South America and Africa. The relentless inflationary pressures on our own financial system will similarly end in disaster unless reversed.

What Is Inflation, and How Does It Work?

The dynamics of inflation are crucial to understand. Modern economists redefined inflation to mean an increase in the general price level. But what *causes* price increases? This is the question that must be answered.

Mises explained inflation simply: "An increase in the quantity of money reduces the purchasing power of the monetary unit."[9] An increase in the money supply therefore cause price increases. We don't have to go all the way back to ancient Rome to find examples of increases to the money supply. They are all too familiar from the U.S. Federal Reserve.

In November 2010, to take only one example, the Fed announced that it would engage in quantitative easing. News reports typically described this initiative as an effort to "jump-start" the recovery by "pumping billions of dollars into the economy."[10] How does the Fed "pump" money into the economy? Many times in the past it has simply lowered the interest rate, but in November 2010 the interest rate was already so low that it couldn't drop any further. So with "quantitative easing," the Fed bought $600 billion in long-term Treasury bonds. The purchases expanded the credit reserves of banks. Although this boost to reserves allowed banks to increase their lending, lending can occur only when the public is willing and able to borrow and the banks reassured of repayment. If the public cannot or will not borrow, the economy will not move. In this case, the billions in new dollars the Fed created did not "stimulate" the economy, because, after the bursting of the housing bubble, the public was unwilling or unable to borrow the money and banks were reluctant to lend for fear of default.

Again, Mises captured the problem:

> The dearth of credit which marks the crisis is caused not by contraction but by the abstention from further credit expansion. It hurts all enterprises—not only those which are doomed at any rate, but no less those whose business is sound and could flourish if appropriate credit were available. As the outstanding debts are not paid back, the banks lack the means to grant credits even to the most solid firms. The crisis becomes general and forces all branches of business and all firms to restrict the scope of their activities. But there is no means of avoiding these secondary consequences of the preceding boom.[11]

The Fed's efforts reflect, once again, the persistent influence of Keynesian thinking. Keynes argued that inflation will not occur when an economy is hampered by high unemployment or idle resources. In essence, a lack of demand in the private sector gives the government a window of opportunity to increase the money supply without seriously affecting prices. But that "window" is very small indeed. International commodity and currency markets are extremely sensitive to changes in central bank policies and closely monitor the central banks' actions. When an action such as quantitative easing occurs, inflationary expectations will set in almost immediately. That means the public on the market will take measures to protect themselves. For example, lenders will start to employ what is called an interest-rate premium, which is a premium to account for expected inflation over time. Contracts involving wages will be written to account for inflation. Merchants, who must charge enough to replace inventory, will price products with expected inflation in mind. The financial markets will immediately calculate inflationary expectations into long-term interest rates. Gold and silver prices will soar.

Inflationary expectations began to haunt markets after the Federal Reserve's November 2010 announcement. Almost immediately, the dollar fell on foreign exchange markets, while the prices of commodities, particularly oil and gold, rose. The German government, remembering its own terrible history of inflation, warned the Federal Reserve not to proceed. The French foreign minister also criticized the Fed's decision, fearing the impact it would have on the euro. And the European Central Bank declined to follow the Fed in "stimulus" injection, with officials expressing doubts that stimulus measures could do anything to address structural problems in the economy.[12]

To understand why markets are leery of monetary expansion, recall the Austrian School's insight that capital is not homogeneous. This means that when the money supply is increased, some people and institutions get access to the new money more quickly than others. Those who get the money first benefit because they spend the new money before prices have risen. Those receiving the money last, after markets have taken account of the effects of the expanded money supply, are forced to pay much higher prices without any increase in income. Although the injection of money into an economy is meant to stimulate a recovery, and usually to help those struggling the most, it changes patterns of wealth and income in such a way as to allow some to benefit at the expense of others.

Who Benefits?

Who benefits? Often it is not the struggling groups the government intends to help. One determinant of who wins or loses is market power, which is the ability to pass on one's increased costs to customers. Every product and commodity elicits a different response from consumers with respect to price changes. If two products see their prices increase by the same percentage, one might experience very little drop in demand, while sales of the other product could fall dramatically. This is what economists refer to as elasticity of demand. An *elastic* product is generally one for which many substitutes are available and to which there is little consumer loyalty. The producer of such a good is, therefore, in a much more difficult position with respect to inflation, since it cannot raise prices to offset the increase in costs.

A good example occurred after the Bush administration imposed steel tariffs in 2002. As economist David Breuhan points out, the tariffs drove up the price of hot rolled steel "roughly ninety percent in seven months." That sounds great for the U.S. steel industry, but it was a disaster for all those American *purchasers* of steel. Suppliers to the auto industry suffered the most. They couldn't pass the cost increases along to their customers because, Breuhan writes, "the big three Detroit automakers and other major purchasers had mandated that in order to keep their contracts, these suppliers had to cut their costs roughly five percent per year to maintain their relationship." The results were predictable: many auto suppliers borrowed heavily to try to keep up, but soon "the manufacturing sector began to implode."[13] As a result, in one year industries *using* steel lost more jobs than were lost in the entire steel industry.

Inflation also disproportionately harms those parts of the economy that depend on foreign markets for supply. As a country inflates its currency, the value of that currency falls on foreign exchange markets. The value of the dollar, for example, has frequently dropped in response to U.S. monetary expansion. When the value of the dollar drops, U.S. industries must pay more to buy foreign goods. It is no accident that when the value of the dollar falls, oil prices typically rise. That has a cascade effect. Gasoline and home heating prices rise, and so do costs for industries dependent on oil, such as trucking, rail, and air transportation, and even plastics. Either those costs get passed on to the final customers or the industries suffer significant losses—or both, as is often the case.

Some industries have difficulty covering cost increases from inflation not because they offer elastic goods but simply because consumers have become habituated to paying a certain fixed price. Churches are a prime example of this. Parishioners become used to giving a certain fixed amount every Sunday—say, five dollars. During the period of inflation, the value of that five dollars continues to fall, meaning that churches must continually play catch-up.

Even when companies find that they can pass cost increases along to consumers, this advantage cannot last. Andrew Dickson White made this point in his famous study of the inflation accompanying the French Revolution: "The mercantile classes at first thought themselves exempt from the general misfortune. They were delighted at the apparent advance of the value of the goods upon their shelves but they soon found that, as they increased prices to cover the inflation of the currency and the risk from fluctuation and uncertainty, purchases became less in amount and payments less sure; a feeling of insecurity spread throughout the country; enterprise was dead and stagnation followed."[14]

The "general misfortune" White referenced is what we generally think of in economic downturns. Governments frequently justify their interventions in the economy by saying they must help the middle class and the poor. But the resulting inflation harms rather than helps these people.

Middle-class workers pay a steep price for inflation. Although wages do rise in inflationary periods, the increase often lags behind the rise in costs. This was the case during the French Revolution, for example. White observed: "Prices of the necessities of life increased . . . and, while prices of products thus rose, wages which had at first gone up, under the general stimulus lagged behind."[15]

The ultimate problem is not that employers can't keep increasing wages but that they won't be able to pay wages at all. If inflation keeps curbing demand, many businesses will be forced to lay off workers, and some companies will go out of business. Again, White revealed the example of France: "Under the universal doubt and discouragement, commerce and manufactures were checked or destroyed. As a consequence the demand for labor was diminished; laboring men were thrown out of employment, and, under the operation of the simplest law of supply and demand, the price of labor—the daily wages of the laboring class— went down until, at a time when the prices of food, clothing and various articles of consumption were enormous, wages were nearly as low as at the time preceding the first issue of irredeemable currency."[16]

Welfare recipients are harmed as well. The size of a welfare grant (either from the federal government to the states or, especially, from a state to an individual) is normally determined based on what was given out in previous years, not on projections of future inflation. Anyone on welfare will face rising prices with no increase in income.

It is obvious, too, that any kind of fixed asset (fixed in the amount of currency, that is), such as a bond, a savings account, or a defined-benefit pension, will constantly lose value during a period of inflation. That's why financial advisers must figure in an inflationary premium when planning for their clients' retirements. White summed up the situation in France: "As to the people at large, the classes living on fixed incomes and small salaries felt the pressure first, as soon as the purchasing power of their fixed incomes was reduced."[17] During the great German inflation ending in 1923, Bresciani-Turroni reported, the working classes suffered not so much because of the difference between the *average* real wage during the inflation and average real wage before World War I as because the inflation caused real wages to fluctuate wildly from week to week. Bresciani-Turroni added that those who lived on fixed incomes "were reduced to the most abject poverty."[18]

In fact, the poor and the middle classes might suffer the most during times of inflation. Wealthier citizens have market power and can protect against inflation by putting savings in nonfinancial assets, such as real estate, stocks, and small businesses. Most people at the lower income levels of society, however, save in terms of currency. As a result, they find that whatever savings they have are losing purchasing power. Over a period of inflation the middle class will tend to be weakened, leaving a small group of very rich and a large number of very poor. In short, inflation is a mechanism by which wealth and resources are transferred from those who get the money last to those who get the money first. It silently transfers wealth and changes the structure of an economy.

The Types of Inflation

If inflation results from an expansion of the money supply, the particular type of inflation in play depends on the medium of exchange. For much of history, specie—gold or silver—was the dominant medium of exchange, and therefore debasement was the way kings and emperors expanded their money supplies. Today, of course, almost nothing is paid in coin, so debasement is not the big problem. Since the collapse of the gold standard, there have been two primary types of inflation: *fiat inflation*, which is associated with irredeemable paper money produced by government, and *bank credit inflation*, which is the most common (and pernicious) form of inflation, because credit issued by the banking system is overwhelmingly the medium of exchange in our global economy.

Let's take a look at each type of inflation.

Debasement

As we have seen, Roman emperors made a habit of debasing their currency. Christopher Westley notes that "desperate Caesars" did damage by spending "lavishly on themselves and the politically well-connected factions in society, as well as on their far-flung military empire." The debasement of the Roman currency led not only to price increases but also to hoarding. Westley writes: "Those who held silver now had strong incentives to hoard it, since the debased currency with Caesar's image on it was considered legal tender. When coins of the same face value but with different quantities of precious metal are flowing freely in society, market actors will remove whatever coinage is not debased. Thus, we observe in Rome what would later be identified as an example of Gresham's Law: Bad money drives out good."[19]

The problems of inflation and an expensive imperial government led to still other issues. As the classical scholar Michael Rostovtzeff points out, prices raced ahead of wages, creating a desperate labor situation; the banking system collapsed as banks refused to accept the imperial currency; the business environment grew more insecure, sending interest rates soaring and decreasing incentives for entrepreneurs; and the unsound currency led to the collapse of commerce with India.[20] The government bureaucracy metastasized and welfare expenditures increased. Harold Mattingly, a classical scholar and expert on coinage, notes that by the time of the emperor Diocletian (A.D. 244–311), Rome had become a massive socialist economy, with government owning most of the businesses and acting as a chief financier and banker. An estimated 50 percent of the working population was on the payroll of the state.[21]

The crowning blow to the Roman economy came when Diocletian imposed wage and price controls in the year 301. Production declined. Many businesses closed. Food riots occurred in the face of shortages. The glory of Rome had passed.[22]

Of course, as Rostovtzeff reports, fixing prices was "no novelty" in Rome. "The same expedient had been tried before him and was often tried after him. . . . Diocletian shared the pernicious belief of the ancient world in the omnipotence of the state, a belief which many modern theorists continue to share with him and with it."[23]

For Rome, inflation was both a cause and a symptom. It was a symptom because it indicated that the Roman economy could not keep up with the increasing demands of the state. The emperors' policy of bread and circuses had bankrupted the budget. To compensate, the Roman administration resorted to inflation. At this point, inflation became a cause of the dislocation of the Roman economy. With the growing bureaucracy and the increasing socialization of the economy, the empire ran out of options, became inflexible and overburdened with costs, and collapsed.

Other sovereigns failed to learn from the experience of the Roman emperors. The Tudor monarchs of fifteenth- and sixteenth-century England were notable examples. Thomas P. Gore, the famous Oklahoma senator of the early twentieth century, said it best: "Henry VIII approached total depravity, as nearly as the imperfections of human nature would allow. But the vilest thing that Henry ever did was to debase the coin of the realm!"[24]

The story begins with the accession to the throne of Henry's father, Henry VII, in 1485. In his comprehensive study of the Tudor reign, historian G. J. Meyer presents a picture of a government constantly expanding, raising taxes, confiscating private property, and debasing the currency. The Tudors' actions resulted in rampant inflation and poverty in England. Prices increased 500 percent during the Tudor century.[25] Meyer writes: "Tudor England was a world in which the rich got richer while the poor got not only poorer but much, much more numerous. Twenty years into Elizabeth's reign she had so many seriously poor subjects, and the situation of many of them was so desperate, that figuring out what to do with them had become one of the challenges of the age." There were many reasons for the poverty—for example, in destroying so many churches and monasteries, the Tudors disrupted "the ecclesiastical social welfare system that for centuries had reached out from the monasteries and parish churches into every corner of the kingdom." But chief among these reasons was the "toxic mix of economic forces that caused real wages to fall decade after decade even as prices relentlessly rose."[26]

The story of Tudor England represents a classic case of what happens during a period of inflation.

Specie Inflation

Many people believe it is not possible to experience inflation under gold and silver standards. Sure enough, during the age of classical liberalism, there was little concern about inflation. But it is possible, albeit rare, to have specie inflation.

The most famous inflation of specie currency occurred during the Spanish colonization of the New World, which overlapped with the Tudor reign in England. The conquistadors discovered vast deposits of gold and silver in the Americas and quickly established mints in the New World. It was a windfall for the Spanish. The problem was that the government acted as if it had discovered the source of infinite wealth. It went heavily into debt on the assumption that it could pay off the debts with new discoveries of gold and silver. Within a few decades, however, the Spanish ran out of lands to conquer. At that point they stepped up their efforts to mine silver and gold from the deposits they had already discovered. Jack Weathersford notes in his *History of Money* that the mines of the New World "made Spain the richest nation on earth, but these riches came at what ultimately proved to be a very high price."[27]

The pattern was predictable. All the gold and silver coins flooding back from the New World caused prices in Spain to rise. Despite doing everything possible to pull more precious metals out of the earth, the Spanish government soon saw its debts exceed the flow of income. The Spanish had become so reliant on this source of money that they did not invest in basic industries and structure. Eventually the Spanish government found itself bankrupt.[28]

Specie inflation is not only rare but also, as inflations go, mild. In the Spanish case, a commodity selling for $40 rose to $140 over the hundred years in which gold and silver were imported to Europe from the New World.[29]

The Spanish case did, however, accelerate another inflation. In the sixteenth century, the Ottoman Empire stood as the world's major power. Technologically ahead of Europe, it produced multiple goods and services, and its navy completely controlled the Mediterranean. But in the Battle of Lepanto (1571), the Ottomans lost a major naval engagement to the combined fleets of Spain, Venice, the Papal States, and the Italian city-states. Rebuilding the Ottoman fleet was a massively expensive effort, and funding the ongoing naval warfare proved costly as well. The

Ottoman sultan increased taxes to pay for the military buildup. While all this was happening, historian Roger Crowley reports, "the influx of bullion from the Americas was beginning to hole the Ottoman economy below the water line, in ways that were barely understood." The Ottomans could not defend against "rising European prices and the inflationary effects of gold."[30]

What did the sultan do? He resorted to the same trick the Tudors were using in England and so many Roman emperors had deployed centuries earlier: debasement. In fact, the Ottomans had started debasing the currency several years before Lepanto, after the failed siege of Malta in 1565. Crowley notes that in 1566 "the gold mint at Cairo—the only one in the Ottoman world, producing coins from limited supplies of African gold—devalued its coinage by 30 percent." The debasement only accelerated after that. Ottoman silver coins grew so thin that, in the words of a contemporary Ottoman historian Crowley cites, they became "as light as the leaves of the almond tree and as worthless as drops of dew."[31]

You can guess the rest of the story: Prices soared. Shortages resulted. In Crowley's words, "Raw materials and bullion were being sucked out of the empire by Christian Europe's higher prices and lower production costs."[32] The Ottomans' once-strong manufacturing base eroded. Inflation wore away at Ottoman power.

Fiat Money Inflation

Fiat inflation is probably the most common type of inflation. Fiat money is legal tender. When the government prints up more banknotes to pay its bills, the currency loses value. Everything denominated in that legal tender—savings accounts, bonds, insurance policies, pension funds, and so on—loses values too. In effect, when government prints new money to cover its budget deficits, this really constitutes a tax on people holding such financial instruments. That means Social Security recipients; people invested in government and municipal bonds; hospitals, universities, churches, and other organizations with endowment funds held in debt instruments; insurance companies holding either government or corporate bonds; and many others. In the worst cases of fiat inflation, such as in Germany and Russia after World War I, savings are wiped out altogether.

It is legal for governments to satisfy debt obligations with worthless paper. That doesn't mean it is moral. Austrian economists F. A. Hayek and Murray Rothbard have suggested a repeal of legal tender laws to protect the public from rapacious governments. Hayek made the case:

> But why should we not let people choose freely what money they want to use? . . . I have no objection to governments issuing money, but I believe their claim to a *monopoly*, or their power to *limit* the kinds of money in which contracts may be concluded within their territory, or to determine the *rates* at which monies can be exchanged, to be wholly harmful. . . . There could be no more effective check against the abuse of money by the government than if people were free to refuse any money they distrusted and to prefer money in which they had confidence.[33]

Credit Inflation

As previous chapters have demonstrated, credit inflation has become ubiquitous since the First World War. Ludwig von Mises described the process: "Political and institutional convenience sometimes makes it expedient for a government to take advantage of the facilities of banking as a substitute for issuing government fiat money. The treasury borrows from the bank and the bank provides the funds needed by issuing additional banknotes or crediting the government on a deposit account."[34]

Credit inflation also has the most influence in the modern economy. That is because credit issued by banks—so-called fiduciary currency—makes up about 93 percent of the media of exchange in this country.[35] The next chapter will detail exactly what credit inflation does to an economy—how, as the Austrian School has identified, it causes the trade cycle. What is essential to note here is that credit inflation follows the pattern of every other inflation: It transfers wealth. Those who receive the money first benefit. It is a tax. When it collapses, it leaves a trail of debt in its wake.

In the monumental study *The Rise and Fall of the Great Powers*, Paul Kennedy writes that what he calls the financial revolution began with the founding of the Bank of England in 1694. Initially a wartime expedient, the Bank of England ushered in the use of central banking as a means for governments to raise money.[36] The system works like this: The central bank buys government bonds, thereby lending the government money. Although this expansion of credit tends to cause prices to rise, the central bank then sells the bonds to the public to offset inflation. (By selling the bonds to the public, the bank is effectively reducing the amount of money in the economy again.) This is really a way for government to acquire resources from the public without raising taxes. It does, however, obligate future generations to raise tax revenue to pay interest on the public debt. For example, the American public will be obligated to pay interest on the $600 billion of "quantitative easing" the Federal Reserve granted the U.S. government in 2010 and 2011.

The great downside of this system is that it produces booms and busts. The dynamics of credit-induced inflation can be seen clearly in two periods of American history: the so-called Roaring '20s and the period from the end of the Bretton Woods agreement on August 15, 1971, to the collapse of 2008. In each case, after a long bank credit inflation, wealth became concentrated and a massive downturn occurred.

Let's take the 1920s first. Murray Rothbard of the Austrian School, in his magisterial work *America's Great Depression*, pointed out that "the prime factor in generating the inflation of the 1920s was the increase in total bank reserves." Total reserves, Rothbard observed, increased 47.5 percent, from $1.6 billion to $2.36 billion. This credit increase was primarily responsible for the 62 percent increase in the total money supply, from $45.3 billion to $73.3 billion. That is how powerful the government-controlled banking system is: "A mere $760 million increase in reserves . . . could roughly generate a $28 billion increase in the money supply."[37]

With so much new money injected into the system, one would expect price levels to have jumped during the 1920s. In fact, the price level remained stable through the decade, rising only slightly from 1921 to 1925 and falling slightly thereafter.[38] Most economists of the time therefore did not see any inflationary threat. That might seem to be a reasonable conclusion, given the price stability. But to observe the true dynamics of inflation we must dig beneath the surface.

If the money supply increased so much in the 1920s, why didn't the price level increase also? To answer that, we must recognize that the increase in the money supply was accompanied by a similar boom in productivity. As Robert S. McElvaine reports in his study of the events leading up to the Great Depression, productivity increased "astronomically," with output per person-hour rising 63 percent between 1920 and 1929.[39] The point that most economists missed was that the tremendous increase in productivity should have been passed on to the consumer in terms of price *decreases.*

The Austrian School has identified the inflationary effects that the stability of the price level masked in the lead-up to the Great Depression. Rothbard's work stands as the definitive assessment of the inflationary pressures on the economy in the 1920s. "Bank credit expansion creates its mischievous effects," Rothbard observed, "by distorting price relations and by raising and altering prices compared to what they would have been without the expansion. Statistically, therefore, we can only identify the increase in money supply, a simple fact. We cannot prove inflation by pointing to price increases." By lowering production costs and increasing the supply of goods, the increase in productivity during the 1920s essentially offset the monetary inflation. But, Rothbard concluded, "this 'offset' was only *statistical*; it did not eliminate the boom-bust cycle, it only *obscured* it."[40]

So where did all the increased productivity go? Who benefited? Remember that those who receive the money first will benefit. Citing the famous Brookings Institution study *America's Capacity to Consume,* McElvaine tells the story of who reaped the benefits in the 1920s. Income did increase across the board, with American per capita income rising 9 percent between 1920 and 1929. But the top 1 percent of income recipients saw their disposable income increase *75 percent*; their share of disposable income, meanwhile, jumped from 12 percent to 19 percent. Wealth was distributed more unevenly than income: by 1929, the top 0.5 percent owned 32.4 percent of *all* the net wealth among individuals in America. This was, as McElvaine notes, one of the highest concentrations of wealth in American history.[41]

Now let's turn to the long bank credit inflation that began with the end of the Bretton Woods system. Once President Nixon severed the dollar's link to gold, inflation took off. What cost $1,000 in 1972 cost more than $5,215 in 2010.[42] In other words, in less than forty years the dollar lost about 80 percent of its value.

Robert McElvaine, Keynes biographer Robert Skidelsky, and other critics of free markets have characterized the 1920s and the post–Bretton Woods era as free-market periods, complete with deregulation, free trade, and privatization.[43] To make this claim is to ignore the very nature of inflation. When you have inflation, you do not have free markets. As we have seen, a sound currency is a necessary precondition of a stable and prosperous economy. If the 1920s had truly been an example of the free market, the benefits of increasing productivity would have been passed forward to the consumer, and stringent protectionist policies would have disappeared. (Interestingly, the same people who regularly call for increasing regulations on the economy either ignore or disparage the one "regulation" that is most important: the disciplining of the money supply.)

Critics of free markets would not agree with the Austrian School's diagnosis of the causes of bubbles and busts. The facts they marshal, however, often back up the Austrian case. For example, Skidelsky demonstrates how much poorer economic performance was after the United States severed the gold link than it was during the Bretton Woods era. He points out that the average economic growth rate for the United States during the Bretton Woods years was 4.8 percent, versus 3.2 percent after 1980. That 1.6-percentage-point difference "might not seem very big," Skidelsky writes, but "had the world economy grown at 4.8 percent rather than 3.2 percent from 1980 until today, it would have been more than 50 percent larger."[44] Using the IMF's definition of a global economic recession as occurring in a year with less than 3 percent growth, he also observes that the Bretton Woods era witnessed no global recessions but that after 1980 there were five.[45] Likewise, the Bretton Woods era performed better when it came to unemployment rates and exchange-rate volatility.[46]

To all of which Austrian economists would reply: *exactly.* Keep in mind that the Bretton Woods system provided a type of gold standard, as it established the convertibility of the U.S. dollar to gold at thirty-five dollars per ounce. The Bretton Woods system was not ideal, but it provided some discipline to the money supply. The Austrians have consistently argued that the money supply must be disciplined by market forces, preferably a true gold standard. They could easily cite Robert Skidelsky's arguments to make the case for a return to a type of Bretton Woods system.

Deflation

Clearly, inflation can wreak havoc on an economy and on society. Deflation can do real damage as well. In some ways, in fact, it is more serious than inflation, and it is more difficult to overcome.

Modern economists define deflation as a decrease in the general price level. As with inflation, we need to dig deeper to understand the dynamics involved. The usual definition of deflation suggests that it is the converse of inflation, but as the Austrian School has shown, the cause of both is the same: overexpansion of credit.

Deflation, in essence, is a collapse of bank portfolios. As noted, bank credit accounts for about 93 percent of the liquidity in the economy. This bank credit is supported by the loans that banks make, which means that the banks' deposits depend on the quality of those loans. If banks make loans that cause significant losses to their portfolios, the banking system's reserves will shrink. As a result, banks will be reluctant, or unable, to make loans even if there are willing borrowers. The amount of credit decreases, and the savings-investment mechanism—the process by which savings are used to finance new projects, such as home building and business expansion—breaks down.

This is what happened in the Great Depression of the 1930s. As Milton Friedman and Anna Schwartz pointed out in their landmark *Monetary History of the United States*, in 1931 "banks started strengthening their reserve position, liquidating available assets in order to meet both the public's demand for currency and their own desire for liquidity." The banks' efforts to build up reserves, combined with depositors' attempt to convert deposits into currency, created "downward pressure on the money supply." From 1929 to 1933, the money stock fell by more than a third.[47]

A drop in prices may not seem like a bad thing. But in a deflationary situation, wages drop as well, often faster than prices do. That means debt compiled during an inflationary period becomes much harder to pay off once deflation goes into effect. The debts do not decrease, but one's earnings do.

We need look no further than the housing bubble of the 2000s to see how punishing deflation can be. People who purchased houses in the middle of the decade, at or near the peak of the housing market, took on expensive mortgages. When the collapse came, the value of their houses plummeted, but the cost of those high-priced mortgages stayed as high as ever. In many cases the costs actually shot higher: people who had secured adjustable-rate mortgages saw their monthly payments jump when their interest rates increased. Millions of Americans couldn't pay off their home loans and ended up "under water." Many were subject to foreclosure. In 2010 alone, a record 3.8 million foreclosures were filed in the United States.[48]

The bad debt associated with the housing bubble piled up throughout the economy. The (apparent) increase in the value of real estate allowed homeowners to finance increased consumer spending. More and more people took out home equity loans or second mortgages to give them extra disposable income, and many others refinanced their homes to take advantage of lower interest rates. Easy credit and lowered lending standards allowed millions of people to put little or no money down when they signed their mortgages. They had little equity in the homes and also secured mortgages that went well beyond what they should have been able to afford. When the bubble burst and millions were unable to pay their mortgages, lenders were left with huge debt burdens. Nor were the original lenders the only ones exposed. Using the most advanced mathematical models, banks had employed complex new financial instruments such as mortgage-backed securities to take advantage of the housing boom. The bursting of the housing bubble had a cascade effect through the entire financial system.

It is extremely difficult to turn the economy around when lending and borrowing dry up. This is what happened after our recent collapse and in the 1930s. Nervous banks lend out very little. Potential borrowers become reluctant to take out loans, even if they are able, because the high cost of doing business and the lack of attractive opportunities discourage investment. So the economy is stuck; economic expansion stops. The Austrian School of economics has demonstrated that this is all part of the trade cycle, as we will see in detail in the next chapter.

The Sorcerer's Apprentice

So now we return to the question with which we began chapter 2: *How did this happen?* Having considered the economic dynamics of the past 150 years and the insights of the Austrian School, we are ready to see exactly what the Austrian theory of the trade cycle says and how it applies to the economic crises of the past century—including our most recent crisis.

Few have delved as deep into the causes and effects of trade cycles as have the Austrians. Fundamental to their analysis is the role of credit

expansion—the role central banks play in creating bubbles and ultimately busts. What is interesting to note here is that none other than
Alan Greenspan, the longtime chairman of the Federal Reserve whom
many Americans viewed as an oracle during the boom years of the 1990s
and 2000s, admits that the Fed started the trade cycle that led to the bust
in 2007–8. In his memoir he describes a June 2003 meeting of the Federal
Open Market Committee (FOMC), the body that decides on the Federal Reserve's monetary policy. At that meeting, he writes, the committee "voted to reduce interest rates still further, to 1 percent . . . despite
our consensus that the economy probably did not need yet another rate
cut." Why did the FOMC go ahead with the reduction even though, as
Greenspan writes, "the stock market had finally begun to revive, and our
forecast called for much stronger GDP growth in the year's second half"?
Greenspan explains: "We wanted to shut down the possibility of corro-
sive deflation; we were willing to chance that by cutting rates we might
foster a bubble, an inflationary boom of some sort, which we would sub-
sequently have to address. I was pleased at the way we'd weighed the con-
tending factors. Time will tell if it was the right decision, but it was a
decision done right."[49]

Here Greenspan admits that the lowering of interest rates was not
needed *and* that he and his colleagues knew the move could foster a
bubble. But then he says he was confident that the Fed would be able to
"address" it—that is, control it. Reading this account calls to mind the
story of the sorcerer's apprentice, who thinks he can direct the forces he
releases. But just as in that story, where the apprentice loses control of
the spirits, the forces of inflation follow their own rules. No bureaucratic
sorcerer can ever fully control them, no matter what central bankers and
politicians would like to think.

Such misjudgments, such arrogance, lie at the root of economic chaos.

13

Faustian Bargain

The Trade Cycle

The gates of hell are open night and day;
Smooth the descent, and easy is the way:
But to return, and view the cheerful skies,
In this the task and mighty labor lies.
    —*Virgil*, The Aeneid

The poet Virgil's portrayal of hell could easily describe the operation of the trade cycle in an economy. When the cycle begins, everything is rosy. "Easy is the way" to prosperity—or so it seems. In reality, the prosperity is an illusion that credit expansion creates. The lack of real savings and capital will eventually reassert itself; interest rates will rise and a massive downturn will inevitably occur. Digging out from the collapse becomes the "mighty labor."

There is perhaps no more complicated problem in economics than the trade cycle. Economists from all schools have wrestled with it at one time or another. John Maynard Keynes took many different positions on the business cycle. In one instance he supported the view that expanding the money supply created the initial problems. In another place he saw the downturn as a result of diminishing entrepreneurial opportunities.

Although Austrian School theory undergirds much of economics as it is taught today, the mainstream largely ignores the Austrian theory of the trade cycle (or the business cycle, as it is also known).[1] The Austrian perspective is not so much dismissed as it is overlooked. I have interviewed candidates with PhDs in economics who have never studied or even heard of the Austrian explanation of the trade cycle.

This is a shame, for the Austrian theory of the trade cycle offers a potent explanation for why economies go bust. Mainstream economics failed to head off economic meltdown, and it failed to turn things around once the collapse occurred. We should be searching desperately for alternative explanations and solutions. Austrian theory provides both.

In the Austrian view, the trade cycle always starts with an expansion of the supply of credit, which lowers interest rates. This sets off an apparent boom, but in fact the credit expansion, because it does not spread equally throughout the economy, creates distortions that will lead to a bust. The immediate distortion occurs in the production structure. The boom begins in the capital goods sector, which takes advantage of low interest rates to fund major and long-term projects. The artificially low interest rates and appearance of prosperity lure these industries into making malinvestments, which will be exposed when the bust inevitably comes.

The effects of credit expansion spread well beyond banks and capital goods industries to other businesses, the stock and bond markets, mortgages, consumers, governments, and much more. Throughout the economy the credit expansion leads individuals, businesses, and governments to make economic decisions based on false expectations. These decisions are analogues of malinvestment that might be called *misinvestments*. Think of an investor who, at the peak of a housing bubble, buys a new house with plans to "flip" it, on the assumption that prices will keep going up. Or consider a government whose revenue projections assume continuing boom times for years to come.[2] These misinvestments become widespread during the boom cycle. Austrian economists point out that the distortions caused by credit expansion generate "clusters of errors."[3]

Let's review the trade cycle step by step from the Austrian perspective.

The Beginning of the Trade Cycle: Lowering Interest Rates

According to Austrian theory, the trade cycle begins when a central bank decides to lower interest rates. To keep interest rates low, monetary authorities must increase the supply of credit.[4]

Central banks have a few ways to inject funds into the system. One is to enter the marketplace and purchase large amounts of bonds. This process is called open-market operations; it is the method the U.S. Federal Reserve uses most frequently. Another method is to lower reserve and capital requirements, which gives banks more latitude to make loans and increase the supply of credit in the economy. This approach is not used much today because it is considered clumsy and hard to adjust on a day-to-day basis.[5] A third method is to increase loans to member banks so they, in turn, increase the amount of credit available to their customers. More recently, the Federal Reserve has deployed still another method. As my colleague Matthew Fisher points out, the Fed pays interest on bank deposits with the central bank so as to compete with the private market for loans.

Foreign investment also presents an opening for credit expansion. Since the passing of the gold standard, countries have been able to expand or contract their money supply at will. The expansion or contraction of money in one country, especially if it is a major financial power, can affect economic conditions worldwide. Because the U.S. dollar is held as the world's reserve currency, American monetary policies have pronounced effects worldwide. In a 1961 article in *Fortune*, French economist Jacques Rueff prophetically warned that the United States' continual balance of payments deficit would eventually lead to worldwide inflation and then a worldwide recession. Rueff explained the ripple effects of U.S. monetary expansion:

> When the U.S. has an unfavorable balance with another country (let us take as an example France), it settles up in dollars. The Frenchmen who receive these dollars sell them to the central bank, the Banque de France, taking their own national money, francs, in exchange. The Banque de France, in effect, creates these francs against the dollars. But then it turns around and invests the dollars back into the U.S. Thus the very same dollars expand the credit system of France, while still underpinning the credit system in the U.S.[6]

The same process is at work today. The United States has run up tremendous trade deficits. To close this deficit, the United States has given its trading partners dollars. If trading partners sell those dollars on world markets, it lowers the value of the dollar, increases the demand for their currencies, and therefore makes their goods and services more expensive. So to maintain their volume of exports, the countries deposit the dollars in their central banks rather than sell them. These deposits increase their reserves, which allows their banks to increase domestic loans. That creates a boom with all the effects of inflation, including misinvestment.

The story does not end there. The central banks holding these dollars earn interest by lending dollars out on U.S. capital markets, which further depresses interest rates in American loan markets. As interest rates decline, American governments, corporations, and individuals go on a borrowing binge, which leads to misinvestment in the United States as well.[7]

Central banks know that lower interest rates spur business activity. As we saw at the end of the previous chapter, Alan Greenspan readily admits that under his leadership the Federal Reserve slashed interest rates, even knowing that the move "might foster a bubble, an inflationary boom of some sort."

Using credit expansion to lower interest rates is indeed inflationary. When the central bank artificially increases the supply of credit, it creates a false impression that savings are abundant and that low interest rates will continue indefinitely. This affects economic decisions across the entire economy, causing individuals and businesses to undertake projects that normally they would not consider. These projects become the essence of the misinvestment problem.

To understand why this is so, we need to understand that in a balanced and healthy economy, the interaction of savers and investors sets the interest rate. Swedish economist Knut Wicksell calls this the *natural rate of interest*. Savers produce a surplus but forgo spending. Through the financial system they can transfer this spending power to investors, who transform the savings into actual projects—new equipment, real estate, inventory, personnel training, research, and so on. The savers receive claims to future income while the investors receive the ability to build capital goods today.

The price of this transaction is the interest rate. Naturally, there are many demands for scarce savings over time, and the interest rate tends to allocate these resources to their best use or greatest economic benefit. Under normal conditions, if interest rates are falling, it means that more savings are available to be invested. Conversely, rising interest rates indicate that savings are scarcer. When savings increase, more people are willing to give up funds today for a return in the future. In essence, they become more patient. Demand for immediate consumption goods falls, freeing up more resources for investments and capital projects. These changes do not exert inflationary pressure, because any increased demand for capital goods is offset by a decreased demand for consumer goods.

But when injecting credit into the system *artificially* lowers interest rates, the demand for capital goods increases even as the demand for consumer goods stays strong. This sets up a tug of war for resources. The expansion of credit is not an expansion of goods and services. It creates the impression of an abundance of savings, with credit available at low rates. Thus it temporarily creates more purchasing power. The increase in purchasing power competes with the natural purchasing power of the savers as it flows through the financial system.

At this stage of the cycle, banks scramble to lend money to boost returns (and therefore their stock prices). Remember, under credit expansion certain sectors of the economy get funds before others. The first sectors to get the newly created credit are those that borrow from banks—mainly capital goods industries, then industries such as construction and real estate, and then semi-finished and wholesale goods after that.[8] Because the financial system normally lends to capital goods projects first, booms start in the capital goods industry. Increased demand starts to push up prices of capital goods and real estate. As prices spiral upward, borrowers soon need more credit to purchase housing, factories, and other capital goods.

This point—that capital goods industries form the leading edge of the boom-bust cycle—is fundamental to the Austrian theory of the trade cycle.

Disequilibrium, or Disharmony

The banking system's artificial infusion of new money introduces disequilibrium, or disharmony, into the economic picture.[9] Something in the economy becomes unbalanced. The situation is unsustainable, but people mistake the conditions for something normal, which leads to errors in judgment. During the housing bubble, for instance, the artificial lowering of interest rates led people to invest in housing that they could not financially sustain over the long run. When the realistic economic picture reasserted itself, many could no longer maintain their houses because they were faced with job loss, falling equity, or high interest rates.

In their study *Banking and the Business Cycle*, Austrian economists C. A. Phillips, T. F. McManus, and R. W. Nelson identified three distinct types of disequilibrium that occur in the trade cycle:

1. The disequilibrium between the market rate of interest and a natural rate of interest.
2. Disequilibrium between investment and saving.
3. Disequilibrium in the cost/price relationship.[10]

All three are related, as one leads to the next. The first type of disequilibrium is that of a false signal. Prices are signals. They serve as guides to allocation, use, and production. For example, when the price of gasoline soars, most people take care in planning trips and cut back on travel. But when gas prices are low, drivers give less thought to efficiency. The interest rate is a price and, as such, a signal. If interest rates are low, we are generally less cautious about debt. We make plans based on the projected level of interest rates.

Let's look at these three types of disequilibrium.

Disequilibrium between Natural and Market Interest Rates

What Knut Wicksell called the natural rate of interest occurs when savings and investment are in equilibrium. There are no inflationary pressures, and business conditions are sustainable because firms have the funds available to carry the demands of doing business at realistic rates of interest.

In addition to the natural rate of interest, there is the *market* rate of interest. The latter is the actual rate at which the loan takes place. Under normal conditions, the natural and market rates are equal. But by increasing the supply of loanable funds, the central bank artificially lowers the market rate of interest below the natural rate. This creates disequilibrium. The artificially low interest rate sparks a flurry of investment, as businesses and individuals increase their indebtedness, anticipating the rate of return on their investment to easily exceed the interest payments they will have to make on their loans.[11] Without enough savers, banks will lack the funds to carry the increased economic activity. The rush on investment will increase demand for precious capital and thus send interest rates back up. Investors will have higher expenses than they initially anticipated. Worse, the disequilibrium typically causes the economy to slow down and lowers the returns on their investments. Investors feel the pinch both on the expense side and on the income side.

Think of the real estate sector. When central bank intervention produces a low interest rate, creating an apparent boom, real estate firms will see prospects for a good return on their investments in commercial property. Many firms will therefore increase their investment. That puts more and more floor space onto the marketplace, and when the economy slows—as it surely will, given that such artificial booms cannot be sustained—rents will fall.

Keep in mind that the normal duration for commercial loans is two to five years. Interest rates are subject to change during that period—either because the flurry of investment (caused by the artificially lowered interest rates) increases demand for capital or because banks will increase the interest rate to hedge against greater risk as the economy slows down. Also, if the buildings financed do not have sufficient cash flow, banks will probably ask the lender to invest more equity.

Let's say that I build a strip mall and base the project on an interest rate of 5 percent while calculating that my rents from the project will return 7 percent. As long as there is positive equity, the bank is happy. But if the real estate market turns sour and rents fall, suddenly I'm faced with paying a mortgage of 5 percent when my income from rents produces only a 3 percent return. The value of the property has fallen drastically. The bank will be reluctant to renew the mortgage at the old amount and will probably increase the interest rate to cover the cost of increased risk. They may demand that I increase the amount of equity in the building as a condition of renewal. If I cannot pay, a foreclosure probably will occur.

Disequilibrium between Investment and Savings

The second type of disequilibrium follows from the first. A central bank's infusion of credit into the system has the effect of increasing, at least apparently, the supply of capital available. This imbalance lowers the market rate of interest below the natural rate, as we have just seen.

That results in another type of disequilibrium, that between savings and investment. This second disequilibrium affects the structure of production. Because capital is now seen as inexpensive, businesses see profit potential in investing in capital-intensive projects.[12] As F. A. Hayek pointed out, this type of disequilibrium extends out the productive process and therefore affects the structure of capital in time.

For example, a vineyard perceives that it can increase its margins by adding new technology to the wine-making process. As interest rates decrease, business opportunities increase. But when interest rates rise, the new stages to the productive process become unprofitable, and the vineyard may even be forced to abandon the project. In short, the artificially low interest rates produce malinvestment.

We often see malinvestment in the building of skyscrapers and other massive, long-range projects. Economist Andrew Lawrence developed something called the "skyscraper index," which shows that a boom in skyscrapers has preceded almost every recession or depression. Austrian economist Mark Thornton has written extensively on the skyscraper index, linking it to the Austrian theory of the trade cycle and showing that the correlation is not merely coincidental.[13] In 1997, for example, many huge construction projects were left unfinished when the real estate boom in the Far East, which the Asian countries' credit expansion brought on, came to a sudden halt. In August 2007, noting a skyscraper boom in the United Arab Emirates, Thornton cited the ability of the skyscraper index to predict "economic depression and/or stock market collapses."[14] The worldwide economic crisis began not long thereafter.

So Hayek and other Austrians have identified credit expansion as causing this disequilibrium between savings and investment. None other than Keynes offered arguments in support of this view. According to biographer Robert Skidelsky, Keynes argued that "the seeds of disaster lay in the ability of the banks to create credit in excess of what the community voluntarily wish to save—by encroaching, as he put it, on the 'community's reserve of free resources' held in the banking system 'to be spent or saved as future circumstances may determine.'" Keynes himself put it this way: "If in any year the amount invested exceeds the amount saved, this establishes a scale of investment from which there must necessarily be a reaction."[15] That is why, he said, banks' ability to create credit causes booms to turn into busts.

Let's summarize: Both Hayek and Keynes agree that the second type of disequilibrium occurs when an infusion of credit is not backed by savings. Under normal conditions, savings—the savings of individuals and businesses, government surplus, and foreign investment—makes investing in new projects possible. There is equilibrium when the resources that banks make available to investors equal the amount saved. Such a situation can be sustained over the long term.

But when there is disequilibrium—when savers, under an artificially low interest rate, do not make available the resources necessary to finance investment projects—the banking system at some point will not be able to sustain the increased outflow of funds. Banks either run out of reserves or recognize that the financed projects are unprofitable. Interest rates then rise, making unprofitable the projects of investors who were counting on low interest rates. That is when the crisis begins.

Disequilibrium in the Cost/Price Relationship

The third disequilibrium is cost/price distortion. The sectors of the economy that first see funds from the credit expansion experience increased demand that results in higher prices. This demand and the concurrent price level depend completely on a continuing increase in credit. Once the credit flow stops, the demand dries up and prices have to fall.

Hayek points out that in every trade cycle the prices of capital goods rise much faster than the prices of consumer goods and that in the downturn the prices of capital goods *fall* much faster than those of consumer goods. That is because capital goods are mainly financed by banks. In the most recent collapse, the prices of housing and commercial buildings—both heavily influenced by bank financing before the downturn—fell 30 to 50 percent, while the prices of consumer goods hardly changed at all.

Credit expansion does, however, affect industries that produce consumer goods. As new money increases demand, the factory prices of labor and materials are bid up to a point much higher than it would be without credit expansion. In these industries prices and wages must fall to restore equilibrium. Also bid up beyond normal are asset prices—housing, stock prices, industrial real estate, capital goods, and so on. Austrian economist Melchior Palyi describes the "self-aggravating effect of the outpouring of credit," citing the experience of the Great Depression specifically:

Mortgage loans, excessive in relation to actual market values, helped raise real estate values; higher land values, in turn, attracted more mortgage credit; and so on. The more security values rose, the more their "usefulness" as collateral increased. Boom generates boom—by piling debts on debts. The inflation of asset values, nontaxable capital gains, was probably the better half of the profit inflation, that was both the proximate cause—as well as an effect—of the boom.[16]

Phillips, McManus, and Nelson confirmed this point when they showed that the distortion of wages during the 1920s boom was responsible in part for the high unemployment of the 1930s. Money from credit expansion went first into the capital goods industries, then to the durable goods industries, and finally into consumables—exactly as Austrian theory suggests. The influx caused wages to be pushed above market-clearing levels. When the boom ended, those wages had to readjust. But it is difficult to bring down wages once employees have become used to them. Writing in 1937, Phillips, McManus, and Nelson observed the persistent effects of the credit expansion. They cited one estimate saying that of the 14 million unemployed in 1933, "6 1/2 million were from the durable goods industries, nearly 6 million were from the 'service' industries, and only 1 1/2 million were from the consumption goods industries." They added, "It is in the capital goods industries, and in the construction industry in particular, that the greatest rigidity of wage rate appears. And it is precisely for this reason, in large part, that the construction industry and other durable goods industries are still depressed."[17]

Inflationary Psychology: Euphoria

So how does disequilibrium play out as the trade cycle proceeds?

After the artificial lowering of interest rates begins the trade cycle, the signs of a boom become more evident and inflationary psychology takes hold: more and more people exhibit euphoria.[18] As the prices of commodities, real estate, and stocks move higher, people move quickly to capitalize on the boom, convinced that prices can only go up.

The real estate bubble of the early twenty-first century is a recent example. Countless people began purchasing real estate simply to resell it, based on the expectation that the price would never fall. As Alan Green-span writes in his memoir, "The market for single-family homes in the United States had always been predominantly for home ownership, with the proportion of purchases for investment or speculation rarely more than 10 percent. But by 2005, investors accounted for 28 percent of homes bought, according to the National Association of Realtors."[19] This, of course, put pressure on the central bank to continue the credit expansion.

There are plenty of other examples. Before the real estate bubble we witnessed the dot-com bubble of the 1990s, when prices for compa-nies that existed only on paper reached unbelievable levels. Or we can go back more than 350 years, to the infamous tulip mania that gripped seventeenth-century Holland. The price of tulip bulbs rose so high that a single bulb could buy an entire farm.[20] What all these booms have in common is that people became convinced they could make enormous fortunes through speculation rather than by producing a new good or service.[21]

Fueling this speculation is leverage—the use of other people's money. The concept of leverage is one of the most important in all of finance. It also plays a key role in the trade cycle.

The best description of leverage is the famous accounting equation:

Assets = Liabilities + Owner Equity

This equation could easily be rewritten as:

What I manage and profit from = other people's money + what I own

To show how this principle works, let's take a person who purchases a condominium for $100,000 and puts $10,000 down. To complete the sale, the person borrows $90,000 of someone else's money. Now let's suppose that the price of the condo rises to $200,000. This person sells the prop-erty for that amount, pays the mortgage of $90,000, and pockets under $110,000. The original $10,000 that he spent now becomes $100,000. The interest he has paid on the $90,000 is minimal, and he has experienced a 1,000 percent gain on his original investment. This is a happy outcome of leverage.

Leverage can also work the other way, however. Suppose the condo price decreases to $50,000. In this case, the person not only loses his original $10,000 to satisfy the debt but also owes $40,000 beyond that. That is a 500 percent *loss*.

The higher the leverage ratio, the greater the opportunity for gain or loss. Leverage is a magnifier either way.

Almost every business and individual engages in a type of leverage at least some of the time. Leverage becomes especially dangerous when interest rates are held low artificially and euphoria reigns, because in these times people are more likely to leverage their investment to try to get rich quickly. The process encourages an orgy of speculation that can easily lead to multiple misinvestments. The most recent economic crisis resulted in part from extreme leveraging by banks and other financial institutions, which were making incredible profits.

Malinvestments and Misinvestments

From expansion of credit to euphoria to malinvestment and misinvestment: Austrian theory explains that this process plays out because the credit expansion falsely signals an extension in the production process time. Similar problems develop within the equities and consumer goods markets. They are not malinvestments in the strict Austrian sense, but they certainly follow on and mirror malinvestment. These decisions are made on the basis of false assumptions about future interest rates, prices, and market conditions.

In modern economies, higher mathematics lends an air of credibility to our false assumptions. In the run-up to the recent collapse, ratings agencies, using statistically sophisticated equations, felt safe in awarding high ratings to many bonds. These enticed investors—including pension funds and other institutions that are permitted to invest only in triple-A securities—into projects they would not otherwise have considered. Needless to say, it was all based on a false premise, and it has cost the world economy trillions of dollars, countless bankruptcies, and a protracted downturn.[22]

The Austrian theory teaches that the boom resulting from credit expansion is a Faustian bargain. In Goethe's famous story, Faust, a brilliant philosopher, makes a deal with Mephistopheles, receiving magical powers in exchange for his soul. In the trade cycle, credit expansion creates a kind of economic magic. Everything appears more prosperous: profits soar, the stock market reaches new highs, employment is high, wages are good, the government enjoys increased revenues, and so on. On the surface things could not be better. But just like Faust, we all must pay a dear price in the end. Few realize it during the boom: as prosperity grows, it seems that the economic magic is reality. Then comes the downturn, when we must pay our due.

Let's go through the types of malinvestments and misinvestments that occur during the boom phase.

Governments: National and Local

Governments are not immune to market mania or the gyrations of the trade cycle. The boom brings in major new tax revenue from sales and income taxes. Like everyone else, politicians and bureaucrats allow themselves to believe (or lead voters to believe) that prosperity will continue, allowing government tax revenue to cover expenditures. Politicians make themselves popular by supporting public works spending without having to raise tax rates. During a boom, so much money comes into public coffers that government has little reason to block the demands of teachers, police officers, prison guards, and other public-sector groups—especially because public employee unions provide campaign contributions, votes, and workers on Election Day. Federal, state, and local governments grant generous pensions and other benefits to public employees, often increasing spending on other government programs as well.

As long as the economy keeps expanding, everything is fine. Of course, prosperity is not eternal—certainly not when it is artificially created. Governments increase spending on the false assumption that a humming economy will provide the tax revenue needed to support all the spending. They are engaging in a type of misinvestment.

Look at what happened to state budgets after 2008. As the economy tanked and tax revenues fell, state governments were still on the hook to pay generous retirement benefits to public employees, which were guaranteed in contracts with various unions. The state of California faced massive budget shortfalls after the economic collapse—the largest in the country. Not coincidentally, the California government spent an estimated eighty cents out of every dollar on employee pay and benefits.[23]

During the boom, the state projected its budget based on the expectation of increased capital gains tax revenues and projected high returns from the public pension funds in their investment portfolios.

Governments throughout Europe face even deeper crises. Greece, Portugal, Italy, Spain, Ireland—these and other countries have seen their debt levels soar. The government misinvestment has threatened the future of the European Union and the health of the world economy.[24]

The Stock Market

Another type of misinvestment involves the stock market. Investors jump on shares of companies with little value, based on projections of the company's future earnings. The stock of those companies skyrocket, and the whole stock market rises along with them. In short, euphoria produces a bubble.

We know about the dot-com bubble and other recent stock market bubbles. In the book *Lords of Finance*, Liaquat Ahamed reminds us of the lead-up to the great crash of 1929. In the summer of 1928, he writes, the stock market "truly seemed to break free of its anchor to economic reality and began its flight into the outer reaches of make-believe." Over the next fifteen months the Dow Jones Industrial Average almost doubled in value. Ahamed continues:

> That it was so obviously a bubble was apparent not simply from the fact that stock prices were now rising out of all proportion to the rise in corporate earnings—for while stock prices were doubling, profits maintained their steady advance of 10 percent per year. The market displayed every classic symptom of a mania: the progressive narrowing of the number of stocks going up, the nationwide fascination with the activities of Wall Street, the faddish invocations of a new era, the suspension of every conventional standard of financial rationality, and the rabble enlistment of an army of amateur and ill-informed speculators betting on the basis of rumors and tip sheets.[25]

Stock market misinvestment spreads damage throughout the economy. The stock market profoundly affects pension and retirement funds, for instance. Most of these funds are heavily invested in equities to generate the high returns needed to provide adequate resources for their members. In the case of government pensions, the spending obligations are so great that the funds require near-miraculous returns to stay afloat. A 2011 study from the Stanford Institute for Economic Policy Research shows that the California Public Employees' Retirement System, known as CalPERS, would need to average returns of 12.5 percent per year for sixteen years to cover its liabilities.[26]

Stock market mania also creates opportunities for swindlers. As John Kenneth Galbraith wrote in his colorful history of the 1929 crash, "In good times people are relaxed, trusting, and money is plentiful. But even though money is plentiful, there are always many people who need more. Under these circumstances the rate of embezzlement grows, the rate of discovery falls off, and the bezzle increases rapidly."[27] The promise of extraordinary returns lures in many otherwise rational people. In our time, the Ponzi scheme of Bernard Madoff attracted major banks, hedge funds, charities, and billionaire investors.

Borrowing Short and Lending Long

Just like individuals, financial institutions can be swept up in the mania of a boom. Their false assumptions involve what is called the yield curve, which shows the relationship between long-term and short-term rates for loans. Normally the rate for short-term loans is much lower than the rate paid on long-term loans. This sets up the opportunity to profit by borrowing money on a short-term basis (say, at 2 percent) and lending in the long-term market (at 5 percent, for example). In a boom, then, many financial institutions increase the amount they borrow short and lend long, assuming that they can constantly ride the yield curve.

But there's a pitfall: depositors can withdraw their money at any time. Once investors start pulling out their money at signs of trouble, the banks face a huge challenge in meeting their commitments. Benjamin Bernanke and other analysts have traced the start of the Great Depression in 1931 to the collapse of the Credit Anstalt, the largest bank in Austria, which borrowed short to finance what Liaquat Ahamed characterizes as "long-term, highly illiquid, investments."[28] That failure set off a wave of bank panics and exchange-rate crises. American banks were ill prepared to deal with the situation. Like the Credit Anstalt, American banks had a lot of callable debt while their assets were highly illiquid. The bank runs that we associate with the Great Depression forced banks to liquidate assets hastily, which led to losses as other banks were trying to dump assets on the market at the same time.[29]

In the 2008 crisis, Bear Stearns and Lehman Brothers were caught in the same type of trap. Investors were pulling their money out on a daily basis, and the firms' long-term assets were questionable mortgage-backed securities. They could not market the securities to attain sufficient funds to pay off their investors. Both firms failed.[30]

Merger Mania

Business mergers become more common when firms believe that interest rates will remain low and business volume will remain high. Mergers with competitive or complementary businesses offer the prospect of lower costs and increased revenue, which typically translate into higher stock prices. Taking out loans to fund mergers becomes especially attractive when interest rates drop. The lower the interest rate, the greater the impetus to merge. And banks are more than willing to provide the resources, seeing the chances for high returns.

I witnessed merger mania in the automotive supplier base from 1995 to 2005. The concept was to merge a number of smaller companies to build a large company, the stock of which could be sold in an IPO on the London Stock Exchange. The organizers would sell their shares at a tremendous profit.

But larger is not always better. The smaller companies were quite efficient in their particular line of work because the owners knew the intricacies and quirks in each operation. As those owners were bought out, the new, larger companies lost institutional memory. In some cases the promised profits did not appear and the new company became inefficient. Meanwhile, the automotive industry went through a steady decline. The financials could not justify the overhead of the larger companies, and many went bankrupt.

Real Estate

A recurring feature of almost all booms is misinvestment in the real estate market.[31] Because real estate is one of the first lines for bank credit, prices in this sector move up much faster than do those in other areas in the economy. This is true in expansionary economies all over the world and throughout history. As real estate prices shoot up during a boom, the financial system becomes anxious to make loans against this inflationary equity. The false assumption is that real estate prices will never go down. With regard to commercial real estate, the perception during a boom is that such property will always create cash flow.

Risky Credit

The banking system further weakens itself by taking greater risks in its lending. Flush with cash, banks will lend out money first to their most secured and trusted customers but then, seeking to increase profits, to borrowers of lesser quality. Because banks are taking on greater risk, they charge a higher interest rate to those customers. But remember that interest rates at this point in the trade cycle are very low overall, making loans seem affordable to a huge range of individuals and businesses. You probably remember how often home equity loans were advertised on TV and radio during the housing bubble of the early twenty-first century: banks and mortgage institutions saw this as a profitable market, a sure sign of the expansion of credit.

Overextending credit is not a new phenomenon. University of Virginia business professors Robert Bruner and Sean Carr, who studied the Panic of 1907, point out that extending loans to riskier clients is a recurring feature of booms. They write: "The buoyancy of economic booms causes riskier creditors to approach banks for loans—a problem of adverse selection. Some banks succumb to the temptation to make loans to these creditors, perhaps in the belief that luck or a bank clearing house will see them through—this is a problem of moral hazard."[32] These problems ultimately lead to an economic slump.

Inventory Loans

Loans on inventory can also be a form of misinvestment. These loans are especially common when builders overextend themselves by building on speculation, whether it is houses, apartments, industrial buildings, or commercial property, or when businesses expand their inventory, expecting an exuberant economy. When the economy turns down, builders and businesses face severe losses as the goods are sold far below cost. Many builders have gone bankrupt because they could not sell their properties to cover the debts.

Student Loans

Even something as common as student loans can become a form of mis-investment. Taking on student loan debt is akin to a business's extending the process of production in time. Easy credit can encourage students to extend their time in school in anticipation of increasing their productivity and becoming attractive to employers. To obtain their degrees, they take on debt. But when the downturn arrives, they find that they are not as marketable as they had expected. They are left with considerable debt and little income to meet the payments.[33]

Consumer Goods Boom

The trade cycle may begin in capital goods industries, but as the cycle continues on the up slope, the capital goods boom spills over into consumer goods. Salaries and benefits, particularly in the capital goods industries, create plenty of income for people employed there. And because people are feeling more prosperous, spending on consumer goods begins. Prices are still low and wages are rising. Euphoria is spreading throughout the economy.

The wealth effect then kicks in.[34] As people see prices of their stocks and real estate zoom, they think they are rich. Too often they forget that you are not richer until you sell the asset and the check clears the bank. Many consumers are led to borrow on paper equity. During the housing bubble, home equity loans became a popular way to increase spending streams. Consumers decide to spend not only today's income but tomorrow's as well, going into debt so they can enjoy tomorrow's benefits today. This attitude leads to an explosion of spending on consumer and durable goods. One feature of this stage of the cycle is that savings decrease. People begin to think that the boom is permanent, and with interest rates low, they do not see much need or incentive for saving. The spending spree, which generates serious misinvestment, is financed mainly on credit.

Although spending on credit has an immediate inflationary impact, it also has a longer-term deflationary impact. Those buying on credit now will need to decrease future purchases to pay off debt. Consumers who commit themselves to long-term payments are left with little flexibility in the declining times.

The Turning Point

To this point we have considered only the boom phase of the trade cycle. At a certain juncture this phase ends.

One sign that the downturn may be approaching comes, paradoxically, when officials start declaring that there is no danger of a downturn. In 1929, just months before the stock market crash, President Calvin Coolidge declared that stocks were "cheap at current prices."[35] Leaders have often pronounced that a "new era" in economics has arrived, that volatility has finally been tamed.[36] Bill Clinton was more restrained than Coolidge, but he clearly signaled a belief that the old rules were not as important in what he called the "new economy."[37] The February 2000 *Economic Report of the President* noted, "Some observers have argued that the economy in the 1990s has fundamentally changed and that the concept of the traditional business cycle is outdated." The report concluded, "Evidence supports the notion that business cycle fluctuations have diminished over time."[38] Two months later, on April 3, Clinton told the Democratic Leadership Council, "I'm not sure that you've repealed the laws of supply and demand or even totally abolished the business cycle, but I am quite sure you have made them more elastic, less predictable, and that there is more potential for sustained growth."[39] The very next day, the NASDAQ fell more than 600 points before rallying. The dot-com bubble was starting to burst.

People may try to convince themselves otherwise, but booms created by credit expansion must come to an end. To keep going, such a boom requires the banking system to supply ever more credit. That is largely because savings decrease, meaning that the public is not releasing real resources for investment. As the public reduces savings and pulls in the direction of consumer goods, businesses tend to abandon long-term projects in favor of moving resources to the earlier stages of production. For example, an automaker facing increasing consumer demand for its cars will put less emphasis on developing future vehicles to get present vehicles out the door. If consumers were saving, there would not be such demand for the production of immediate products. The increase in savings would lower interest rates naturally and spur investment in long-term projects.

The expansion of credit can't last forever. The boom sets off a scramble for funds as more and more people need money. As Hayek put it, the public's time preference has changed: people want resources now rather than in the future. The demand becomes such that banks begin to ration credit.

One of the clearest explanations of this turning point comes not from an Austrian economist but from John Maynard Keynes himself: "A point will come . . . when the banking system is no longer able to supply the necessary volume of money consistently with its principles and traditions." Keynes chronicled the effects: Interest rates rise. Prices go up. Wages fall. Unemployment spreads. He wrote:

> Thus the collapse will come in the end as a result of the piling up of several weighty causes—the evaporation of the attractions of new investment, the faltering of financial sentiment, the reaction in the price level of consumption goods, and the growing inability of the banking system to keep pace with the increasing requirements, first of the industrial circulation and later of the financial circulation also.[40]

At this stage the banking system experiences the results of misinvestment. Banks begin to see lots of red ink on customers' financial statements and to question the value of the portfolios. When the central bank tightens the supply of credit, short-term interest rates move up quickly. Typically the yield curve begins to flatten and finally inverts. In other words, short-term rates rise above long-term rates.

For the trade cycle the inversion of the yield curve is a danger sign—a sign that the turning point is coming.[41] A yield curve inversion has preceded every recession and depression since World War II. Writing in the publication of the Federal Reserve Bank of New York, economists Arturo Estrella and Frederic S. Mishkin note that using the yield curve, "anyone can compute a probability forecast of recession almost instantaneously." They add that such a simple financial indicator can flag problems "that might otherwise have gone unidentified" by more complex econometric models.[42]

The yield curve can invert for several reasons. Some we have already discussed—the tightening of credit by the central bank, the cash crunch that results during a scramble for liquidity, and the downward effect on long-term rates that occurs as long-term projects are canceled. Beyond those reasons, short-term rates can rise because monetary expansion weakens the value of the currency on foreign exchange markets and the prices of imports begin to rise. This can be especially difficult for those industries relying on imports in their production process. Finally, the perception of inflation can put pressure on the central bank to raise interest rates.

Signs of a Downturn

Once the turning point in the trade cycle arrives, problems mount. Debt increases. The economy becomes less liquid. Banks start to deny credit to potential borrowers. Economic activity slows. Rising interest rates translate into increasing costs, especially for those who have signed loans that are not fixed but rather fluctuate with the market.

A cash crunch is one of the common signs of a downturn. Firms that began projects based on the assumption that interest rates would remain low are now unable to obtain credit to finish the projects. Companies begin to conserve cash to avoid going out of business or to satisfy bank loan committees. Many start paying bills more slowly.

Another indication of the downturn is a strong upward movement in factor prices—that is, labor rates and component costs. These squeeze profit margins and put firms in a difficult situation.

The bad news about the economy piles up quickly. The stock market, which during the boom climbs ever higher on the expectation of super-normal profits, starts to decline as the market realizes the ride is over. The pressure to reduce costs leads businesses to cancel projects, lay off employees, seek mergers or spinoffs—anything to keep their heads above water.

The wealth effect that played a role in the boom has a corollary during the downturn. One of my former students, Paul Brent, spent years in the securities markets. He points out that although people feel wealthier as their assets gain value on paper, their feeling of getting poorer when those assets lose value is much more acute. There is a good reason for the psychological pain investors experience with losses: it is much harder to gain than to lose. Suppose a person has assets worth $240,000. If the value of those assets in the market falls by $80,000, that is a drop of 33 percent. But to gain back the $80,000 requires a *50* percent increase in value (from a base of $160,000). Feeling poorer, some people will pull back from the market, cut down spending, pay off debt, and increase saving. This can be part of the natural healing process, but in the short run it acts as a brake on future investment and present spending.

The Recession Begins

This unwinding is the recession. Governments find themselves with declining revenues as unemployment increases. Demands for state funding to take care of the unemployed increase drastically. Retail sales drop, thereby cutting into sales tax revenue. The unemployed cease paying income taxes. Declining property values mean declining property tax revenue for local governments. To maintain their level of spending, all levels of government must either increase taxes or go into capital markets and borrow. The deteriorating situation puts pressure on the central bank to increase the money supply. At this stage, however, monetary policy will have little effect, because so many people have lost asset value and banks have no collateral to lend against.[43]

Banks and other financial institutions that borrowed short to finance long-term debt find their situation turned upside down. Many individuals end up in the same position. For example, people who depend on short-term (variable) mortgage rates now face rapidly rising interest costs. If the costs rise above their income level, they amass debt. In many cases this debt is unsustainable, and people must turn to bankruptcy or suffer foreclosure. Those who used leverage to pile up (apparent) gains— think again of house flippers—feel the terrible weight of leverage on the way down, as property values drop but the debt owed does not.

During the euphoria, the stock market kept rising on the perception that there was no top. Now it plummets on the perception that there is no bottom. As the stock market falls, so does the value of retirement funds, IRAs, and much more.

Companies that grew quickly by merger and acquisition begin to lose money and start selling assets in hopes of raising cash for operations or to cover losses. As Charles Kindleberger and Robert Aliber write in *Manias, Panics, and Crashes*, the decline in the prices of assets and commodities "leads to a reduction in the value of collateral and induces banks to call loans or refuse new ones; firms sell commodities and inventories because their prices are in decline; and the decline in prices causes more and more firms to fail." Businesses struggle even more because households cut back on spending. The failure of those businesses means further losses for banks, and even bank failures.[44]

Responding to the Downturn: Two Choices

As business slows, firms have two options: cut costs or attempt to increase sales. These approaches are not mutually exclusive; prudent business practice calls for a combination of the two. Still, businesses tend to emphasize one over the other.

The same options apply to restoring the health of the general economy. But which approach is most effective? It is on this question that the schools of economic thought, especially the Keynesians and the Austrians, diverge the most. We have seen some agreement between the two schools on the causes of business fluctuations. But on the solutions they disagree. In a nutshell: Austrians favor cost cutting, lowering of government regulations, and saving; the Keynesians look to increasing sales, or economic stimulation, especially through governmental action.

The Keynesian Approach: Stimulus

Keynesians take the second approach to dealing with an economic downturn. Key to the Keynesian case for increasing sales is the fact that consumption expenditures make up about 70 percent of the spending in the economy. Among Keynesians, different camps call for different means of increasing sales, but the end result is the same: fiscal stimulus.

One camp might be called liberal Keynesians. They favor ramping up government spending to stimulate sales in the economy. George W. Bush's administration took a liberal Keynesian approach in earlier 2008 when it called for sending out checks to taxpayers to head off the recession. Edward Lazear, chairman of Bush's Council of Economic Advisers, said the fiscal stimulus would help on both the "consumption side" and the "investment side." Investment, Lazear said, "is the way that we create demand for labor," which "means more jobs and more wages." Treasury Secretary Henry Paulson seconded Lazear, saying, "There's plenty of evidence you give money to people quickly, they're going to spend it, and they're going to spend a reasonable percentage of that. . . . When you look at putting incentives in place for business to invest quickly and grow and hire people, that will work."[45]

The next year's "Cash for Clunkers" program, which the Obama administration initiated, was another good example of the U.S. government's effort to stimulate consumer spending. This $3 billion federal program gave car buyers a rebate of $4,000 (on average) if they traded in their old cars for new, fuel-efficient vehicles. The idea was to give the economy a boost by spurring consumer spending and help the struggling auto companies by stimulating car sales. This initiative was specially designed to induce sales in hopes of stopping layoffs and restoring auto companies to profitability.

The other camp might be called conservative Keynesians. They argue for creating fiscal stimulus by cutting taxes. The Kennedy administration (1961–63) took this approach, lowering tax rates significantly. The administration did not, however, decrease federal spending, and deficits resulted. Nor did President Kennedy significantly cut government intervention and regulation (though government regulation at the time was much less burdensome than it is today). After these changes were implemented, the U.S. economy embarked on a long period of expansion, providing an argument for what would later be called supply-side economics.

As these examples suggest, the Keynesian approach, in either manifestation, is a bipartisan phenomenon. Keynesianism has been the dominant government policy for years. Only during the Clinton administration did federal spending fall as percentage of gross domestic product (GDP), to about 19 percent. Today, federal expenditures are in the neighborhood of 25 percent of GDP.[46]

In addition to spending, most recent administrations have substantially increased regulation and costs to business. Economists Nicole V. Crain and W. Mark Crain point out that by 2008, the annual cost of federal regulations had risen to more than $1.75 trillion, an increase of 3 percent in real terms in just five years. They write, "One out of every three dollars earned in the U.S. goes to pay for or comply with federal laws and regulations." And all this was before the health-care overhaul and other new policies and regulations were enacted. The Crains add that this burden falls disproportionately on smaller businesses: "Small businesses—those with fewer than 20 employees—incur regulatory costs 42% greater than firms with between 20 and 499 employees, and 36% greater than firms with more than 500 employees. The regulatory cost per employee for small businesses was $10,585, compared to $7,454 for medium firms and $7,755 for large firms." Individuals and families are hit hard too: the combined burden of regulation and taxes is $37,962 per household.[47]

The Austrian Approach:
Cutting Costs, Taxes, Regulations, and Spending

In contrast to the Keynesians, Austrians argue that when an economy is in a downturn, cost cutting is much more powerful than government stimulus. They say that the fastest way out of a recession or depression is to bring down the cost to business.

Consider a company that makes a gross margin of 25 percent on its product. This means that the cost of producing the good—labor and material, mainly—eats up 75 percent of the revenue earned on the product. The company's overhead expenses must come out of the remaining 25 percent. This is the break-even point. Only after those are paid does the company begin to make profits. Say that the firm's overhead expenses amount to $10,000 a month. Just to break even, the company must sell $40,000 worth of products per month ($30,000 pays labor and material, and $10,000 pays the overhead cost).

Now assume that the economy is in a downturn and the company is losing money. Again, the business can focus on cutting costs or attempting to increase sales. The latter approach usually proves difficult during a downturn, when consumers are cutting back on spending. But even if a firm can boost sales, the gains are only marginal: as the Austrian School points out, the company will retain only twenty-five cents for every dollar of increased sales. By contrast, the company keeps every dollar it saves by lowering administrative costs. Cutting a single dollar of costs, then, is equivalent to achieving an additional *four dollars* in sales.

Cutting costs gives a company in trouble a much greater *multiplier* than does increasing sales. In the current example the multiplier is four times. This is not some magical accounting trick; cost cutting allows a company to operate profitably with lower sales. Of course, no one wants his salary cut or his department's budget slashed. Looking people in the eye and telling them there is a cut—especially when it means someone is losing his job—is extremely difficult. Nevertheless, cost cutting is a necessity during a business downturn.

Cost cutting is essential for the broader economy as well, Austrians argue. Some costs of doing business are beyond a firm's control. The Austrian School points out that if government lowers the cost of business by simplifying the tax code and reducing the regulatory burden on businesses, profitability will return much more quickly. Taxes reduce a business's cash flow, and if the government brings down taxes, a firm achieves the same multiplier as it would by cutting costs on its end. This is why, Austrians say, government is more effective in stimulating the economy by lowering costs and taxes than by trying to stimulate sales. In addition, cutting governmental costs to business reduces the need to lay off employees. A firm will be able to keep trusted and valuable employees, preserving institutional memory and the organization's internal division of labor. As a result, it will be able to bounce back more quickly when the economy recovers.

Let's look again at Cash for Clunkers. According to the Austrians, the auto companies could have achieved profitability much faster had the government helped lower their costs rather than fashioned special programs to induce sales. Also, these federal programs did not follow the principle that in determining economic policy, government should consider the consequences for all groups, not for particular segments.

The numbers support the Austrian case. For all the hoopla surrounding Cash for Clunkers, an independent analysis found that the overwhelming majority of the vehicles sold under the program would have been purchased anyway. According to Edmunds.com, the respected automotive website, only 125,000 of the 690,000 sales credited to Cash for Clunkers—fewer than 1 in 5—would not have occurred without the program. The taxpayers' price tag for each of those extra sales? About $24,000.[48]

The Austrian Multiplier

The Austrian solution to an economic downturn is to cut both government spending and tax rates. In this way the Austrians differ markedly from the supply-siders, who (as we saw in chapter 7) focused so relentlessly on tax cuts that they failed to rein in government deficits. A prime example of how the Austrian-favored policy works can be found during the Harding administration (1921–23). President Warren Harding entered office facing a severe recession: in 1920 unemployment had tripled, from 4 percent to 12 percent, and gross national product fell 17 percent. The Harding administration did not simply cut taxes while leaving government spending alone, as the Kennedy administration later would. Instead it cut both spending and taxes by about 25 percent. The government slashed tax rates for all income levels, and by reducing spending, it cut the national debt by a third.

By the summer of 1921 the turnaround had already started. By 1922 unemployment had dropped below 7 percent; by 1923 it was at 2.4 percent. This was one of the quickest and most successful responses to a business downturn in U.S. history.[49]

The 1921 turnaround offers evidence of the Austrian multiplier. Remember that the Austrian multiplier brings savings that, given gross margins, are actually worth much more than a corresponding increase in sales or consumer spending would be. This multiplier also helps explains why government regulation and taxes are such a drain on business. Say the government implements an expensive round of new regulations. To pay for that regulation, a firm operating at a 33 percent gross margin will need to increase its sales by three times the cost of regulation, or it will need to cut other business expenses. Often companies will try to pass the expense on to the consumer through price increases.[50] Because of the multiplier, the Austrian School observes that reducing regulations and other government activities that add significantly to business costs have an outsized effect in stimulating business while having little effect on the federal budget. If anything, the resulting increase in business will raise tax collections.

The situation is similar with taxes and consumption. Let's assume that I'm in a 35 percent tax bracket; for every dollar I earn over a certain amount, various levels of government collect 35 cents in taxes. If I wish to buy something, I must earn the funds to pay the taxes as well as buy the product: to purchase an item for $100, I have to earn $135. Lowering of tax rates also lowers the price that I pay. This is one reason that the Austrians favor tax cutting rather than Keynesian stimulus. For every percentage point that taxes are cut, prices are also cut, which consequently stimulates demand.

Finally, the Austrian multiplier has the advantage of immediacy: it does not go through a government bureaucracy or depend on the spending habits of the public.

Credit Contraction: Messrs. Willing and Able Are on Vacation

One of the most significant problems associated with a serious recession or depression is credit contraction. During the credit expansion, the balance sheets of both lenders and borrowers become distorted. As a result, when the downturn comes, many consumers and businesses are not willing or able to borrow funds from the banking system: they may want and even need to borrow money to stay afloat but can't find financial institutions willing to lend to them. A complementary problem is that banks are not willing or able to lend money to consumers and businesses: a bank may really want to make a loan to a strong borrower, but the firm will hold back from taking the loan, for fear of deteriorating business conditions.

At this point, it doesn't matter how much reserves the Fed pumps into the system. Banks can expand credit only if Mr. Willing and Mr. Able are present on both sides. This is why monetary policy is impotent during business downturns.

The key at this stage of the cycle is to restore the health of balance sheets so that investors feel comfortable lending money to businesses. Any increased regulation or cost raises the break-even point of business and makes a firm less competitive. That makes banks reluctant to lend to businesses. It also makes businessmen, seeing decreased profit margins, uncertain about going into debt and expanding. Adding government regulation only causes balance sheets to deteriorate further.

The economy becomes stuck because savings are insufficient; the investment cycle is stalled. It is not unusual to see huge amounts of savings sitting on the sidelines or being invested in government bonds.

The Destruction of Savings and Capital

An important point to be made in any discussion of the business cycle is that there are many businesses in good condition—that have not overinvested or malinvested—that are nevertheless pulled into the vortex of the declining economy. They find that inflation destroys their profit margins, credit becomes unavailable, or business volume drops below the break-even point. They are innocent bystanders, sometimes destroyed by the general crisis.

It should also be noted that most capital is very specific, so that when a firm has invested savings into particular projects, it may not be possible to shift that capital to other usages. Take, for example, the skeleton of a skyscraper abandoned when a downturn comes. When such a project is abandoned, the people who invested in it simply lose their savings. This capital cannot be put to other productive uses. In this way the false expansion leads to a great destruction of savings and capital.

Deflation

The credit collapse can go so far as to lead to a monetary contraction. Deflation makes debt far harder to carry. Although the cost of raw materials comes down, these prices do not generally fall as fast as wages. As a result, mainstream economists fear deflation more than inflation.

The Great Depression was in general a period of great deflation. Benjamin Bernanke has pointed out that debtor insolvency was pervasive during the Depression because "the protracted fall in prices and money incomes greatly increased debt burdens." Specifically, he notes that "the ratio of debt service to national income went from 9 percent in 1929 to 19.8 percent in 1932–1933."[51]

Similarly, as we saw in the previous chapter, the housing bubble of the 2000s demonstrates the punishing effects of a deflation in prices: the value of homes collapsed but the debt did not drop at all, making the debt burden much greater.

The Prescience of the Austrian School

The economics establishment generally overlooks the Austrian School, and it usually disagrees with the Austrians on the effects of capital markets and various monetary and fiscal policies. But as we have seen, mainstream scholars actually endorse some core Austrian precepts, even if unknowingly. For example, Keynes acknowledged that the banking system's expansion of credit marks the beginning of the trade cycle; some of his devotees, such as Hyman Philip Minsky, agree, as do prominent historians such as Charles Kindleberger. No less a mainstream authority than Ben Bernanke has identified a major cause of the Great Depression as "the credit expansion of the predepression decade." Bernanke cites the explosion of debt during that time: "Outstanding corporate bonds and notes increased from $26.1 billion in 1922 to $47.1 billion in 1928 and . . . nonfederal public securities grew from $11.8 billion to $33.6 billion over the same period. . . . Perhaps more significantly, during the 1920s small borrowers, such as households and unincorporated businesses, greatly increased their debts. For example, the value of urban real estate mortgages outstanding increased from $11 billion in 1920 to $27 billion in 1929."[52]

The Austrian School, more than any other, has shined a light on the insidious effects of credit expansion. Its theory of the trade cycle offers a persuasive explanation for the busts that have recurred over the past century. Yet this comprehensive account gets little notice in the halls of academia or government.

Meanwhile, the theories and policies to which the economics establishment stubbornly clings have proved ineffective in heading off or recovering from economic crisis. The manifest failures of the economics establishment should lead to some humility and a willingness to consider other ideas—especially ideas, like those of Austrian economics, that have a clear track record of prescience and effectiveness.

The depression of 1920–21, as we have seen, is a specific instance in which the government took precisely the steps the Austrian School would advise, and the recovery was swift and dramatic. Author Thomas E. Woods Jr. calls it a "forgotten depression," noting that few officials or economists ever mention what happened in 1920–21. "And no wonder," he says. "That historical experience deflates the ambitions of those who promise us political solutions to the real imbalances at the heart of economic busts." Woods adds, "The conventional wisdom holds that in the absence of government countercyclical policy, whether fiscal or monetary (or both), we cannot expect economic recovery—at least, not without an intolerably long delay. Yet the very opposite policies were followed during the depression of 1920–21, and recovery was in fact not long in coming."[53] Toward the end of that decade, as most observers were reveling in the "Roaring '20s," both Mises and Hayek predicted a significant downturn. In February 1929, in fact, Hayek warned, "The boom will collapse within the next few months."[54]

I have been studying Austrian economics for forty years and have followed its precepts in my business career. During that time I have found it to be quite accurate in describing, and even forecasting, the economy. By following Austrian economics, I was able to get out of the stock market in both 1999 and 2007, before deep market downturns. Austrian thinking also guided my family in the decision to sell our business in 2005. Some students have contacted me thanking me for introducing them to Austrian theory; in a couple of cases, following Austrian precepts saved them hundreds of thousands of dollars in their IRAs.

To paraphrase Scripture, no one can know the day or the hour when the downturn will come. But with the guidance of Austrian economics, we can read the signs and at least gauge when the season is near.

Conclusion

The Austrian Moment

John Maynard Keynes and F. A. Hayek first met in 1928. The world economy was humming. Keynes, a professor at the University of Cambridge, was already world renowned for his role in the negotiations at the 1919 Paris Peace Conference, while Hayek, still in his twenties, was little known even to academic specialists. The worldwide economic collapse that soon followed only raised Keynes's stature, as economists and government officials, especially in the United States, clamored to hear his views. This did not stop Hayek, newly installed at the London School of Economics, from publishing a devastating review of Keynes's two-volume *Treatise on Money* in 1931. The harsh review sparked sharp public exchanges and private correspondence between the two economists. As they debated the causes of and solutions to the Great Depression, Keynes and Hayek clashed over fundamental questions: How much should government intervene in markets? And what role do its interventions play in the boom and bust of the business cycle?

The Keynes-Hayek debate was, as one biographer puts it, "the clash that defined modern economics."[1] For four decades that clash seemed one-sided, as governments throughout the West adopted Keynesian policies. But this would not be the last word. In 1974, nearly thirty years after Keynes's death, Hayek accepted the Nobel Prize as inflation and stagnation crippled the world economy. Soon leaders influenced by Hayek's work, including Ronald Reagan, Margaret Thatcher, and postcommunist figures in the former Iron Curtain, were instituting free-market reforms.

After the most recent economic crisis, Keynesianism came back in force. Governments rolled out massive "stimulus" packages and credit expansions to try to get the economy moving again. But the resurgence of Keynesianism only reignited the debate. Hayek's classic book *The Road to Serfdom* surged back onto bestseller lists. The BBC aired a Hayek-versus-Keynes debate held at the London School of Economics, with contemporary scholars playing the roles of the legendary economists. A filmmaker and an economist teamed up to produce, of all things, rap videos in which Hayek and Keynes squared off; the first video has been viewed more than three and a half million times online.[2]

More than eighty years after the initial Keynes-Hayek clash, the debate over the role of government in the economy still rages. Of course, the Austrian perspective that Hayek did so much to advance is still largely misunderstood, or simply overlooked, in the academy, the media, and government. Although Austrian ideas undergird much of present-day economic theory regarding finance, capital and interest rates, and prices, many economists have only a meager understanding of the Austrian School's contributions. These economists seem unaware of the Austrians' analysis of communism and their accurate prediction of its inevitable collapse; they seem unaware that the nearly overnight rebuilding of Germany's economy after World War II was based on Austrian principles; they seem unaware of Austrian predictions of devastating financial bubbles; they seem unaware of how the Austrian business cycle theory powerfully explains—and suggests solutions to—the most recent economic crisis.

Since that crisis began, pillars of the economics establishment have acknowledged the failings of mainstream economic thinking—its failure to predict or head off the collapse, its overreliance on mathematical modeling, its misguided attempts to put economics on par with the hard sciences. These mainstream thinkers are echoing criticisms that Austrians have long leveled at the economics establishment. Meanwhile, events and studies have validated Austrian teachings, especially regarding the insidious effects of credit expansion.

So there is reason to hope that Austrian thinking, too often discounted, will finally get the consideration it deserves. The Keynesian reliance on government spending to jump-start the economy has spawned a long list of permanent entitlement programs. Keynesian "solutions" have also proved ineffective: In the 1970s, Keynesians admitted to having no response to stagflation. (Only the free-market-oriented supply-siders broke through the problem.) Then, in response to the 2008 crisis, the U.S. government spent nearly a trillion dollars on a "stimulus" plan that, even after three years, did little to bring down unemployment or boost prosperity.

Perhaps most remarkably, calls for reestablishing a gold standard have grown louder in recent years. Congressman Ron Paul, a two-time Republican presidential candidate, has long argued for a return to the gold standard. But it is telling that establishment figures such as World Bank president Robert Zoellick,[3] former Federal Reserve chairman Alan Greenspan,[4] financial analyst James Grant,[5] and Keynes biographer Robert Skidelsky[6] have joined in the call for a new yardstick of gold. These and many other observers have highlighted the problems associated with fiat currencies. And like the Austrians, they point to the peace and prosperity that reigned for the century before 1914, and even under the modified gold standard of Bretton Woods.

These are positive signs, because another free-market revolution, that of supply-side economics, was ultimately undone by its failure to restore a sound currency and rein in government spending. As the Austrian School has explained (and as we saw in chapter 10), none of the foundations of a free and prosperous society can be ignored.[7]

With this book, I have aimed to illuminate those crucial preconditions for prosperity. Any student of history can see that through the nineteenth and into the twentieth century, prosperity and peace did reign when those preconditions were met. As we look around at a world still struggling to recover from economic cataclysm, we must remind ourselves that it didn't have to be this way. By following Austrian economics, we may reclaim the free, prosperous, and humane society we all desire.

Notes

For full publication details on books cited, please see bibliography.

Chapter 1: A Science of Human Action

1 Quoted in "The Other-worldly Philosophers," *The Economist*, July 18, 2009, 65–67.
2 Scott Patterson, *The Quants*. See also Charles Morris, *The Two Trillion Dollar Meltdown*, 37–38.
3 "The Other-worldly Philosophers."
4 Quoted in David Segal, "In Letter, Warren Buffett Concedes a Tough Year," *New York Times*, February 28, 2009.
5 Claes Ryn, "From Civilization to Manipulation: The Discrediting and Replacement of the Western Elite," *Humanitas* 22, nos. 1–2 (2009).
6 F. A. Hayek, *The Counter-Revolution of Science*, 13–14.
7 Ibid.
8 Mortimer J. Adler, *Aristotle for Everybody*, chap. 3.
9 Bernard Wuellner, SJ, *The Dictionary of Scholastic Philosophy*, 112; *The New Merriam-Webster Dictionary*, 650.
10 Fulton J. Sheen, *The Philosophy of Science*, 87.
11 Milton Friedman, *Essays in Positive Economics*, 8–9.
12 Uskali Mäki, ed., *The Methodology of Positive Economics: Reflections on the Milton Friedman Legacy* (Cambridge: Cambridge University Press, 2009).
13 Johan Van Overtveldt, *The Chicago School*, 93–94.
14 Aristotle, *Nicomachean Ethics*, bk. 1, chap. 3, 18–27.
15 In the introduction to Xenophon's work *Oeconomicus*, translated as *The Estate Manager*, Robin Waterfield writes: "The Latinized Greek title of the *Estate Manager* is *Oeconomicus*. The Greek *oikonomikos* means 'one skilled at managing an *oikos*,' where *oikos* means first a 'house,' and then by extension all the people and things which occupy a house—'a household'—and then by a little further extension

all one's property—an 'estate.'" Xenophon, *Conversations of Socrates*, trans. Hugh Tredennick and Robin Waterfield, 271.

16   Friedrich von Wieser, *Social Economics*, 13.

17   Wilhelm Röpke, *A Humane Economy*, 247, 254.

18   Ludwig von Mises, *The Ultimate Foundation of Economic Science*, 63.

19   Ludwig von Mises, *Theory and History*. See also Ludwig von Mises, *Human Action*, 17.

20   Mises, *Ultimate Foundation of Economic Science*, 36.

21   Roger Lowenstein, *When Genius Failed: The Rise and Fall of Long-Term Capital Management* (New York: Random House, 2000), xix.

22   Ibid.

23   Peter J. Stanlis, *Edmund Burke and the Natural Law*, 110.

24   Jean Baptiste Say, *A Treatise on Political Economy*, xxvi.

25   Alfred Marshall, *Principles of Economics*, vol. 2, 775.

26   Thomas McCraw, *Prophet of Innovation*, 504–5.

27   Quoted in Pablo Triana, *Lecturing Birds on Flying*, 32.

28   Jane Jacobs, *Cities and the Wealth of Nations*, 17–18.

29   Robert Skidelsky, *John Maynard Keynes: The Economist as Savior, 1920–1937*, 412–13.

Chapter 2: Looking at Today and Dreading Tomorrow

1   See Scott Patterson, *The Quants*; Charles R. Morris, *The Two Trillion Dollar Meltdown*, 44–46, 56–58.

2   See Amity Shlaes, "How Government Unions Became So Powerful," *Wall Street Journal*, September 4–5, 2010, A15; Arnold Schwarzenegger, "Public Pensions and Our Fiscal Future," *Wall Street Journal*, August 27, 2010, A17; Mortimer Zuckerman, "The Bankrupting of America," *Wall Street Journal*, May 21, 2010, A15; R. Eden Martin, "Unfunded Public Pensions," *Wall Street Journal*, August 19, 2010.

3   G. Edward Griffin, *The Creature from Jekyll Island*, chap. 1

4   Morris, *Two Trillion Dollar Meltdown*, chap. 4.

5   Thomas E. Woods Jr., *Meltdown*, 26.

6   See Alex J. Pollock, "Fan and Fred: What Would Andrew Jackson Do?" *Wall Street Journal*, July 23, 2010, A15.

7   Woods, *Meltdown*, 66

8   Morris, *Two Trillion Dollar Meltdown*, 68.

9   Ibid., 66.

10   Reported in Heidi N. Moore, "Was Wall Street Drunk, Stupid, or Evil?" *Wall Street Journal* blog, July 23, 2008.

11   Woods, *Meltdown*, 21–22

12   Morris, *Two Trillion Dollar Meltdown*, 69

13   Felix Salmon, "Recipe for Disaster: The Formula That Killed Wall Street," *Wired*, February 23, 2009, www.wired.com/techbiz/it/magazine/17–03/wp_quant.

14   Robert Skidelsky, *Keynes: The Return of the Master*, 25.

15   Ibid., 41.

16   Joseph Stiglitz, "Needed: A New Economic Paradigm," *Financial Times*, August 20, 2010, 7.

17 See "Federal Budget Receipts and Outlays: Coolidge–Obama," The American Presidency Project, www.presidency.ucsb.edu/data/budget.php.

18 *Budget of the United States Government 1993*, 15.

19 Tyler Cowen, "If I Believed in Austrian Business Cycle Theory," *Marginal Revolution*, January 2005, www.marginalrevolution.com/marginalrevolution/2005/01/if_i_believed_i.html.

20 See, e.g., Chris Giles and Alan Beattie, "Global Clash over Economy," *Financial Times*, October 11, 2010.

21 See Giles and Beattie, "Global Clash Over Economy"; Judy Shelton, "The Weekend Interview with Robert Mundell; Currency Chaos: Where Do We Go from Here?" *Wall Street Journal*, October 16–17, 2010, A15.

22 "Federal Budget Receipts and Outlays: Coolidge–Obama."

23 Justin Lahart and Mark Whitehouse, "Families Slice Debt to Lowest in 6 Years," *Wall Street Journal*, March 11, 2011.

Chapter 3: A Short History of the Austrian School

1 Skidelsky, *John Maynard Keynes*, 520. See also John Maynard Keynes, *The General Theory*, 383–84.

2 F. A. Hayek, "The Pretence of Knowledge," Nobel Prize Lecture, December 11, 1974, quoted in Mark Skousen, *Economic Logic*, 652.

3 Ludwig von Mises, *The Historical Setting of the Austrian School of Economics*, 46.

4 Keynes, *General Theory*, 298.

5 This emphasis on deduction was first put forth by Aquinas in speaking about the method of the human sciences. St. Thomas Aquinas, *Commentary on the Nicomachean Ethics*, 1.53.C35.

6 The reader should be cautioned that I am presenting only the basic thought of the Austrian School. The development of economic thought is quite complex and involves many thinkers. I am focusing on the most important of Austrian thinkers, though of course many other economists have made contributions to Austrian thought as well.

7 The most notable influence on Menger's thought was Edmund Burke, the great British statesman who argued that society develops spontaneously, without any master plan. See Carl Menger, *Investigations into the Methods of the Social Sciences with Special Reference to Economics*, xvii, 7.

8 Eugen von Böhm-Bawerk, *Capital and Interest*, vol. 2, *The Positive Theory of Capital*, chap. 5.

9 Friedrich von Weiser, *Natural Value*, 163–64.

10 See Joseph Schumpeter, *History of Economic Analysis*, chap. 1.

11 See Murray N. Rothbard, "Breaking Out of the Walrasian Box: The Cases of Schumpeter and Hansen," *Review of Austrian Economics* 1, no. 1 (1987), mises.org/journals/rae/pdf/R1_6.PDF.

12 Henry Hazlitt, *Economics in One Lesson*, chap. 1.

13 See F. A. Hayek, *Individualism and Economic Order*, chap. 4.

14 Keynes, *General Theory*, 18, 26.

15 Say explained that unsold goods, or "gluts," resulted for three reasons: (1) Prices are set

too high; (2) entrepreneurs overproduce goods, misreading what consumers want; and (3) sellers enter a poor market—that is, the market is not as productive or prosperous. Say believed that the first two problems are self-correcting: high prices will eventually be lowered, thus clearing the market of oversupply, and entrepreneurs who produce unwanted goods will soon go out of business. The third point simply reflects the fact that selling in depressed or unproductive markets will find very few customers. This concept explains why American dollars are so sought after by Third World countries: the dollar entitles one to purchase in prosperous markets worldwide. See W. H. Hutt, *A Rehabilitation of Say's Law*, and Say, *A Treatise on Political Economy*, chap. 15.

16   Wilhelm Röpke, *International Order and Economic Integration*, 6–7.
17   John Zmirak, *Wilhelm Röpke: Swiss Localist, Global Economist*, 45.
18   See F. A. Hayek, *The Fatal Conceit*, chap. 8.
19   Wilhelm Röpke, *Crises and Cycles*, chap. 4.
20   William Henry Chamberlain, *The German Phoenix*, 72.
21   Joerg Guido Hulsmann, *Mises: The Last Knight of Liberalism*, 804.
22   "In Defense of our 'Unalienable Rights': An Interview with Congressman Ron Paul," *J Taylor's Gold and Technology Stocks* 19, no. 5, reprinted at www.usagold.com/gildedopinion/taylorpaulintrvw.html.
23   "About the Mises Institute," Mises.org.
24   John Fred Bell, *A History of Economic Thought*, 419. This author gives a thorough presentation of the Austrian School and its teachings. His criticism of the school seems somewhat conflicted in the last part of the chapter.
25   Mises, *Historical Setting of the Austrian School of Economics*, 47.
26   Mark Thornton, "Housing: Too Good to Be True," *Mises Daily*, June 4, 2004, mises.org/daily/1533.

Chapter 4: The Age of Classical Liberalism

1   James H. Billington, *Fire in the Minds of Men*, 93–99.
2   F. A. Hayek, *The Constitution of Liberty*, chap. 1
3   Carlton J. H. Hayes, *Modern Europe to 1870*, 607.
4   See the Constitution of the United States, Article I, Section 8 (limited government and limited taxation); Article I, Section 9 (rule of law); Article VI and Amendments IV and V (private property); Article I, Section 8 (contract); Article I, Section 10 (specie); and Article I, Section 9 (free trade).
5   Gottfried Dietze, *Liberalism Proper and Proper Liberalism*, 22.
6   Statistics rounded and taken from www.theworldeconomy.org/MaddisonTables.
7   Christopher Dawson, *Understanding Europe*, 46.
8   A. J. P. Taylor, *English History: 1914–1945*, i.
9   Jim Powell, "Richard Cobden's Triumphant Crusade for Free Trade and Peace: With Trade Liberalization, England Prospered," *The Freeman* 45, no. 6 (June 1995).
10   George Winder, "Great Britain's Age of Economic Growth," *The Freeman* 13, no. 10 (October 1963).
11   Joseph Story, *A Familiar Exposition of the Constitution of the United States*, 192.
12   John Lukacs, *The Passing of the Modern Age*, 85.
13   Benn Steil, "The End of National Currency," *Foreign Affairs*, May/June 2007.

14 See O. M. V. Sprague, *History of Crises under the National Banking System*. For an excellent presentation of the problems in bank overexpansion, see Ron Paul and Lewis E. Lehrman, *The Case for Gold*.

15 See Ludwig von Mises, *The Theory of Money and Credit*, 368–73.

16 J. M. Keynes, *The Economic Consequences of the Peace*, 10–12.

17 Taylor, *English History: 1914–1945*, i.

18 See Richard Gamble, *The War for Righteousness*.

19 For a fuller development of this idea, see Thomas Molnar, *Utopia: The Perennial Heresy*, especially chaps. 6 and 7.

20 Benjamin Anderson, *Economics and the Public Welfare*, chap. 1.

21 Ludwig von Mises, *Omnipotent Government*, 69–81.

22 John Fred Bell, *A History of Economic Thought*, chap. 16.

23 A. J. P. Taylor, *Bismarck: The Man and the Statesman*, 203.

24 F. A. Hayek, *The Road to Serfdom*, 25.

25 A. M. McBriar, *Fabian Socialism and English Politics 1884–1918*, 8.

26 Frank P. Chambers, Christina Phelps Grant, and Charles C. Bayley, *This Age of Conflict*, 9.

27 Röpke, *International Order and Economic Integration*, 137.

28 Malcolm Brown and Shirley Seaton, *The Christmas Truce*, 37. On the Treaty of London, see Walter H. Peters, *The Life of Benedict XV*, 114; Charles Pichon, *The Vatican and Its Role in World Affairs*, 126–27.

29 John M. Barry, *The Great Influenza*, 121.

30 Anderson, *Economics and the Public Welfare*, 165–66.

31 Powell, *Wilson's War*, chaps. 6–11.

32 Dawson, *Understanding Europe*, 45.

33 Keynes, *Economic Consequences of the Peace*, 5.

34 Ibid., 251.

Chapter 5: Chaos: The Legacies of World War I

1 R. J. Rummel, *Death by Government*, chaps. 1–3.

2 Barry, *Great Influenza*, 169–75, 397.

3 Jacques Rueff, *The Age of Inflation*, chap. 1.

4 For a good explanation of this process in the present day, see Michael Pettis, "Protectionism Is Gaining Currency," *Financial Times*, December 2, 2009.

5 The importance of the Federal Reserve in American economic history cannot be overstated. Because both the Federal Reserve and another major reform of the progressive movement, the federal income tax, were created in 1913, historian Brian Domitrovic writes that "1913 may well be the most important year in modern American—if not modern world—history." Brian Domitrovic, *Econoclasts*, 27.

6 Anderson, *Economics and the Public Welfare*. The Federal Reserve Act explicitly stated that one of the duties of the Fed was to ensure price stability.

7 Paul Johnson, *Modern Times*, 35.

8 C. A. Phillips, T. F. McManus, and R. W. Nelson, *Banking and the Business Cycle*, 14–15, 19.

9 Ibid., 23.

10 Ibid., 23–24.

11 Richard Pipes, *The Russian Revolution*, 234.

12 Ibid., 235.

13 Ibid., 687.

14 Ibid., 698.

15 See Hans Sennholz, *The Age of Inflation*, chap. 3.

16 Melchior Palyi, *An Inflation Primer*, 1.

17 Costantino Bresciani-Turroni, *The Economics of Inflation*, 404.

18 Joseph Joffe, "I Come to Praise Ms. Merkel Not to Bury Her," *Financial Times*, June 20, 2012; Martin Wolfe, "A Bitter Fallout from a Hasty Union," *Financial Times*, June 20, 2012.

19 Johnson, *Modern Times*, 93.

20 Charles Kindleberger and Robert Aliber, *Manias, Panics, and Crashes*, chaps. 1–2.

21 Phillips et al., *Banking and the Business Cycle*, chap. 2. See also Murray N. Rothbard, *The Mystery of Banking*, especially chaps. 11–16.

22 Frederick Lewis Allen, *Only Yesterday: An Informal History of the 1920s*, 230.

23 Ibid., 232–35.

24 John Kenneth Galbraith, *The Great Crash, 1929*, 18–19.

25 See Anderson, *Economics and the Public Welfare*, 90, 116.

26 Phillips et al., *Banking and the Business Cycle*, 197–98.

27 Anderson, *Economics and the Public Welfare*, 154, quoting *Chase Economic Bulletin*, March 14, 1930, 8.

28 Garet Garrett, *The Bubble That Broke the World*, 8, reprinted in Murray Rothbard and Garet Garrett, *The Great Depression and New Deal Economic Policy*.

29 Phillips et al., *Banking and the Business Cycle*, 197–98.

30 Garrett, *The Bubble That Broke the World*, 2.

31 Anderson, *Economics and the Public Welfare*, 226.

32 See Garrett, *The Bubble That Broke the World*, 1.

33 Anderson, *Economics and the Public Welfare*, 178.

34 Charles Kindleberger, *The World in Depression*, 95–96.

35 Anderson, *Economics and the Public Welfare*, chaps. 24–27.

36 Ibid., 219. See also chap. 36.

37 Kindleberger and Aliber, *Manias, Panics, and Crashes*, 118.

38 Larry Schweikart and Michael Allen, *A Patriot's History of the United States*, 542–45.

39 Carroll Quigley, *Tragedy and Hope*, 353.

40 President Herbert Hoover, Inaugural Address, March 4, 1929, www.bartleby.com/124/pres48.html.

41 Jude Wanniski, *The Way the World Works*, 136–52.

42 Kindleberger, *World in Depression*, 73–84.

43 Benjamin Anderson describes the relatively free trade that prevailed before the First World War: "There were protective tariffs in the United States, France, Germany, and many other weaker countries. England held to a free trade policy, as did Holland, the Scandinavian countries, and Switzerland. But tariffs of those days were moderate in comparison to postwar tariffs. They were subject to infrequent change, and trade lines were sufficiently open so that countries under pressure to pay debts could do so by shipping out an increased volume of commodities." Anderson, *Economics and the Public Welfare*, 5.

44 See figure 25–1, "Average U.S. Tariffs: Duties Collected as a % of All Imports," in Arthur B. Laffer and Stephen Moore, *Return to Prosperity*, 270. Source: U.S. International Trade Commission.

45 President Franklin D. Roosevelt, "Roosevelt to William Phillips, Acting Secretary of State," July 2, 1993, in Justus D. Doenecke and Mark A. Stoler, *Debating Franklin D. Roosevelt's Foreign Policies, 1933–1945*, 93–94.

46 Charles Cullen Tansill, *Back Door to War*, 43.

47 Skidelsky, *John Maynard Keynes*, 481.

48 Anderson, *Economics and the Public Welfare*, 302.

49 Robert Higgs, *Crisis and Leviathan*, 123.

50 Sonia Orwell and Ian Angus, eds., *George Orwell: As I Please: The Collected Essays, Journalism, and Letters, 1943–1945*, 117–19.

51 Jim Powell, *FDR's Folly*, vii.

52 John Morton Blum, *From the Morgenthau Diaries: Years of Crisis*.

53 Skidelsky, *John Maynard Keynes*, 38.

Chapter 6: The Age of Bretton Woods

1 Kindleberger, *World in Depression*, 7.

2 Melchior Palyi, *The Twilight of Gold, 1914–1936: Myths and Realities*, 282–83.

3 *Statistical Abstract of the United States*, Inflation Tables.

4 Domitrovic, *Econoclasts*, 56–57.

5 See Larry Schweikart and Michael Allen, *A Patriot's History of the United States*, chap. 18 (general view); Robert Skidelsky, *Keynes: The Return of the Master*, 119 (Keynesian viewpoint); Judy Shelton, *Money Meltdown*, 52–55 (free-market and gold-standard perspective); Domitrovic, *Econoclasts*, 62–63 (supply-side view).

6 Skidelsky, *Keynes: The Return of the Master*, 118–19.

7 Quoted in Domitrovic, *Econoclasts*, 51.

8 Domitrovic, *Econoclasts*, 63.

9 Shelton, *Money Meltdown*, 55.

10 For details, see Ludwig Erhard, *The Economics of Success*; Ludwig Erhard, *Germany's Comeback in the World Market*; Ludwig Erhard, *Prosperity through Competition*; William Henry Chamberlain, *The German Phoenix*; Zmirak, *Wilhelm Röpke*, chap. 5; Antony Fisher, *Fisher's Concise History of Economic Bungling*, 45–48.

11 Rueff, *Age of Inflation*, 86–87. See also Paul Kennedy, *The Rise and Fall of the Great Powers*, 426.

12 Johnson, *Modern Times*, 596. See also Kennedy, *Rise and Fall of the Great Powers*, 427–28.

13 Jacobs, *Cities and the Wealth of Nations*, 8.

14 Johnson, *Modern Times*, 720–21.

15 See Kennedy, *Rise and Fall of the Great Powers*, 458–68; Wanniski, *Way the World Works*, 205–7; Quigley, *Tragedy and Hope*, 1147–43.

16 "An Interview with Henry Hazlitt," *Austrian Economics Newsletter*, Spring 1984, mises.org/journals/aen/aen5_1_1.asp.

17 Henry Hazlitt, *From Bretton Woods to World Inflation*, chaps. 11–24.

Chapter 7: Nixon's Folly

1   Palyi, *Inflation Primer*, chap. 12.
2   See Wilhelm Röpke, "Reflections on the Welfare State," *Welfare, Freedom, and Inflation*; see also Wilhelm Röpke, *Against the Tide*, chap. 14, and Röpke, *A Humane Economy*, chap. 4.
3   Domitrovic, *Econoclasts*, 16.
4   Murray N. Rothbard, *Making Economic Sense*, 124–25.
5   Henry Kissinger, *The White House Years*, 956.
6   Bureau of Labor Statistics, Inflation Calculator.
7   Kissinger, *White House Years*, 956.
8   Arthur Laffer and Stephen Moore, *Return to Prosperity*, 4.
9   Domitrovic, *Econoclasts*, 97.
10 See Skidelsky, *Keynes*, 119–20.
11 Leonard S. Silko, "Nixon's Program: 'I Am Now a Keynesian,'" *New York Times*, January 10, 1971.
12 See Domitrovic, *Econoclasts*, 15–16, 93–94.
13 "The U.S. Misery Index by President, January 1948 to December 2010," www.miseryindex.us/indexbypresident.asp; Domitrovic, *Econoclasts*, 2.
14 F. A. Hayek, *Unemployment and Monetary Policy*, chap. 4.
15 F. A. Hayek, *Choice in Currency: A Way to Stop Inflation*, 22.
16 *Durell Journal of Money and Banking*, November 1989, 12. See also Murray N. Rothbard, "The Monetary Breakdown of the West," mises.org/daily/4728.
17 William F. Rickenbacker, *Wooden Nickels: Or, The Decline and Fall of Silver Coins*, 156–57.
18 Bureau of Labor Statistics, Inflation Calculator.
19 www.socialsecurity.gov/OACT/COLA/colaseries.html.
20 See Domitrovic, *Econoclasts*, 13.
21 Rickenbacker, *Wooden Nickels*, 143.
22 Domitrovic, *Econoclasts*, 3
23 Mises, *Human Action*, 416–19.
24 See research.stlouisfed.org/fred2/, especially "Graph: M2A Money Supply (M1ASL plus Time Deposits at Commercial Banks other than Large CDs) (Discontinued Series) (M2ASL)."
25 See research.stlouisfed.org/fred2/, especially "Graph: Real Gross National Product (GNPCA)"; see also www.measuringworth.com.
26 Milton Friedman, *Capitalism and Freedom*, 67.
27 Milton Friedman and Anna J. Schwartz, *A Monetary History of the United States*, chap. 7.
28 "Money, Gold, and the Great Depression: Remarks by Governor Ben S. Bernanke at the H. Parker Willis Lecture in Economic Policy, Washington and Lee University, Lexington, Virginia," March 2, 2004, www.federalreserve.gov/boarddocs/speeches/2004/200403022/default.htm.
29 See F. A. Hayek, *The Denationalization of Money*, 127; and Hans Sennholz, *Money and Freedom*, 44.
30 Palyi, *Inflation Primer*, especially chaps. 3–4.
31 "Business: 1979 Outlook: Recession," *Time*, December 25, 1978, www.time.com/time/magazine/article/0,9171,948388,00.html#ixzz1IDGuhKDX.

32 See research.stlouisfed.org/fred2/, especially "Graph: Bank Prime Loan Rate (DPRIME)."

33 Kathleen McKernan, "He Gave Airlines the All-Clear," *Investor's Business Daily*, February 15, 2008, A3.

34 See Andrew Dickson White, *Fiat Money Inflation in France.*

35 Anderson, *Economics and the Public Welfare*, chap. 15.

36 See Ron Paul and Lewis E. Lehrman, *The Case for Gold*, chap. 7.

Chapter 8: Reagan's Rally

1 For the discussion of the 1970s economy and the rise of supply-side economics, I am indebted to Brian Domitrovic's excellent account in *Econoclasts*. His book is the first and only scholarly history of supply-side economics.

2 Robert E. Lucas Jr. and Thomas J. Sargent, "After Keynesian Macroeconomics," given in 1978 at a conference sponsored by the Federal Reserve Bank of Boston, www.minneapolisfed.org/research/QR/QR321.pdf, quoted in Domitrovic, *Econoclasts*, 17–18.

3 Keynesians assumed that when the wage rate was too high to ensure full employment, the monetary authorities could adopt an easy-money policy—that is, increase bank reserves and lower interest rates—to raise aggregate demand, which would increase prices and profits and thus lead to more hiring. They reasoned that workers operated under a "money illusion," tending to focus on their nominal wages—the actual dollar amount of their pay—rather than on real wages, or what the workers could purchase with their earnings. But Lucas and other members of the rational expectations school pointed out that wage earners would recognize the central bank's attempts to "fool" the economy by inflating the currency and would fight for salary increases to offset the inflation they expected to come. This idea helped explain why unemployment stayed so high in the 1970s even as the Federal Reserve kept inflating the currency.

4 When Keynes looked to the political sector to solve economic problems, he did not take into account the fact that government operates with its own priorities, which differ from the goal of efficient guidance of the economy. Politicians, needing to appeal to voters, often choose not to alienate powerful interest groups, and bureaucrats typically seek to expand, rather than contract, their power and influence. As Samuel Brittan points out in the essay "Can Democracy Manage the Economy?" "The public sector has itself become an important lobby for increased public expenditure" (Samuel Brittan, "Can Democracy Manage the Economy?" in Robert Skidelsky, ed., *The End of the Keynesian Era*, 49). This is why government programs tend to take on a life of their own. Consider rent-control programs in New York City. These were established during World War II to keep rents down for workers in the defense industry. Following the war, it became politically impossible to repeal the rent freeze. A massive, politically powerful constituency developed, and politicians seeking reelection typically chose the easier path of maintaining the rent ceilings. Additionally, bureaucrats who enforced the law did not want to have their jobs phased out.

5 Domitrovic, *Econoclasts*, 50.

6   Ibid., 10.

7   The topic of monetary expansion has been the object of much debate since the economic crisis began in 2008. For positive takes on "quantitative easing," see Michael Woodford, "Bernanke Needs Inflation for QE2 to Sail," *Financial Times*, October 12, 2010; "Bernanke Hints at Further Stimulus," *Financial Times*, October 16–17, 2010; and "Fresh Fed Boost More Likely: Meeting Minutes Reveal Officials Near Consensus—Hope that Easing Would Aid Recovery," *Financial Times*, October 13, 2010. For the opposite view, see David Malpass, "How the Fed Is Holding Back Recovery," *Wall Street Journal*, October 19, 2010, A19; and Joseph Stiglitz, "It Is Folly to Place All Our Trust in the Fed," *Financial Times*, October 19, 2010.

8   Say, *A Treatise on Political Economy*, bk. 1, chap. 15.

9   Among those who called for a gold standard were Jude Wanniski and Congressman Jack Kemp. See Wanniski, *Way the World Works*, 173; Steven F. Hayward, *The Age of Reagan*, 91.

10   Domitrovic, *Econoclasts*, 67–69.

11   Ibid., 111–12.

12   Ibid., 34–36, 65–73.

13   Ibid., 111–15.

14   Taken from *America's New Beginning: A Program for Economic Recovery*, reported in Lou Cannon, *President Reagan: The Role of a Lifetime*, 235. On Volcker, see Cannon, *President Reagan*, 269–74.

15   Cannon, *President Reagan*, 275.

16   Hans F. Sennholz, *Debts and Deficits*, 81–82.

17   Rothbard, *Making Economic Sense*, 35

18   Hayward, *Age of Reagan*, 212.

19   Domitrovic, *Econoclasts*, 246–47.

20   Bureau of Labor Statistics, Inflation Calculator.

21   Daniel Yergin and Joseph Stanislaw, *The Commanding Heights*, 348–52.

22   Bureau of Labor Statistics, Inflation Calculator.

23   Sidney Homer, *A History of Interest Rates, 2000 B.C. to the Present*, table 19, 197. See also Ken Fisher, *The Wall Street Waltz*, chart 47, 112–13; chart 49, 116–17.

24   Charles W. Kadlec, "Gold vs. the Fed: The Record Is Clear," *Wall Street Journal*, October 28, 2010, A15.

25   Cannon, *President Reagan*, 276.

26   www.traderslog.com/plaza-accord.htm.

27   See Murray N. Rothbard, *America's Great Depression*.

28   See Brian Domitrovic, "Economic Policy and the Road to Serfdom: The Watershed of 1913," in Thomas E. Woods Jr., ed., *Back on the Road to Serfdom*, 2.

29   Robert Heilbroner, "Reflections After Communism," *New Yorker*, September 10, 1990, 91–100.

30   Hayek, *Individualism and Economic Order*, 77–91.

31   Röpke, *A Humane Economy*, 15–17.

32   See Peter Schweizer, *Victory*, especially chaps. 6–7. See also John O'Sullivan, *The President, the Pope, and the Prime Minister*.

33   Tad Szulc, *Pope John Paul II: The Biography*, chap. 20.

34   David Gordon, "The Philosophical Origins of Austrian Economics," *Mises Daily*, June 17, 2006, mises.org/daily/2200.

35 "Why the Austrian School Is Austrian," *Mises Review*, Winter 1995, mises.org/misesreview_detail.aspx?control=59.
36 See Frederick Copleston, SJ, *History of Philosophy*, vol. 9, 314–15.
37 Hayek, *Road to Serfdom*, 233–34. For a discussion of Hayek's views on the "trade-off" one makes in a centrally planned economy, see Domitrovic, "Economic Policy and the Road to Serfdom," 2–3.

Chapter 9: The Division of Labor

1   St. Paul, 1 Corinthians 12:12–26
2   Russell Kirk, *A Program for Conservatives*, 166–70.
3   This error, known as *economism*, confuses a person's pure economic *function* for his broader societal *role*. Political philosopher Chantal Delsol captures the important distinction between function and role. In an army, for example, soldiers "become indistinguishable from their functions," as they are "interchangeable actors with equal levels of required competency." Similarly, "a hospital requires a radiologist, a university requires a medieval specialist, and a business needs a sales manager." Roles, by contrast, are "personalized." For instance, "The mother in a particular family cannot be replaced by any other, nor could we find a substitute for the Czech hero Václav Havel." Roles depend sometimes on talent and temperament, sometimes on one's "irreplaceable experience" and "personal history." See Chantal Delsol, *Icarus Fallen*, 142.
4   Mises, *Human Action*, 144.
5   Jeffrey Tucker, "Cooperation: How a Free Market Benefits Everyone," *Crisis*, March 25, 2008.
6   Charles Woolsey Cole, *French Mercantilist Doctrines Before Colbert*, 6–12.
7   Adam Smith, *An Inquiry into the Nature and Causes of the Wealth of Nations*, 3.
8   Burton Folsom, "Henry Ford and the Triumph of the Auto Industry," *The Freeman*, January 1998.
9   Skousen, *Economic Logic*, 160.
10 Daniel Gross, *Greatest Business Stories of All Time*, 83–84.
11 Smith, *Wealth of Nations*, 10
12 C. Ford Runge and Benjamin Senauer, "How Biofuels Could Starve the Poor," *Foreign Affairs*, May/June 2007
13 Smith, *Wealth of Nations*, 1.
14 Carl Menger, *Principles of Economics*, 74.
15 Wilhelm Röpke, *Economics of the Free Society*, 53.
16 Daniel Yergin and Joseph Stanislaw, *The Commanding Heights: The Battle for the World Economy*, chap. 7.
17 Say, *A Treatise on Political Economy*, 133.
18 Wilhelm Röpke, *Economics of the Free Society*, chap. 3.
19 Menger, *Principles of Economics*, chap. 1.
20 Mark Skousen, *The Structure of Production*, chaps. 1–5.
21 Leonard E. Read, "I, Pencil," *The Freeman*, December 1958.
22 Röpke, *Economics of the Free Society*, 4.
23 Both Frédéric Bastiat in *Economic Harmonies* (chap. 1, "Natural and Artificial

Order") and F. A. Hayek in *Studies in Philosophy, Politics, and Economics* (chap. 6,
"The Results of Human Action but Not of Human Design") cover this topic in great
detail.

24   Michael Barone, "Census: Fast Growth in States with No Income Tax," *Washington
     Examiner*, December 21, 2010.
25   Böhm-Bawerk, *Capital and Interest*, 6.
26   "Eugen von Böhm-Bawerk," *The Concise Encyclopedia of Economics*, www.econlib.
     org/library/Enc/bios/BohmBawerk.html.

Chapter 10: The Prerequisites of Prosperity

1   F. A. Hayek, "The Kinds of Order in Society," *New Individualist Review* 3, no. 2
     (November 1964): 3–19.
2   Aristotle, *The Politics*, bk. 2, chap. 5.
3   Gottfried Dietze, *In Defense of Property*, 54–55. See also "The Magna Charta," in
     Verna M. Hall, compiler, *The Christian History of the Constitution*, 37–41.
4   Paul Heyne, *The Economic Way of Thinking*, 272.
5   Hayek, *Constitution of Liberty*, 140. Hayek here refers to a statement by Sir Henry
     Maine.
6   John XXIII, *Mater et Magistra*, Section 109.
7   Thomas Aquinas, *Summa Theologica*, Q 66, art.2.
8   Aquinas, *Summa Theologica*, Q 66, art.2.
9   Aristotle, *The Politics*, bk. 2, chap. 5.
10   Aquinas, *Summa Theologica*, Q 66, art.2.
11   Ibid.
12   Ibid.
13   Alex P. Kellogg, "Detroit Shrinks Itself, Historic Homes and All," *Wall Street Jour-
     nal*, May 14, 2010, A4.
14   Hilaire Belloc, *The Restoration of Property*, 119.
15   Leo XIII, *Rerum Novarum*, sec. 67.
16   John Chamberlain, *The Roots of Capitalism*, 28–29.
17   Ibid.
18   Disraeli, *Sybil*, bk. 2, chap. 5, quoted in William Cobbett, *A History of the Protestant
     Reformation in England and Ireland*, 112.
19   Javier Blas and Jack Farchy, "Gold Hits All-Time High as Investors Seek Haven,"
     Financial Times, May 12, 2010, 13.
20   Ruchir Sharma, "For True Stimulus, Fed Should Drop QE3," *Financial Times*, Sep-
     tember 10, 2012, 9.
21   Hayek, "The Kinds of Order in Society," 12–13.
22   Thomas Aquinas, *De Regimine Principum (On the Governance of Rulers)*, 43.
23   *Kelo v. City of New London* 545 U.S. 469 (2005).
24   *Kelo v. City of New London* 545 U.S. 469 (2005).
25   Mises, *Human Action*, 196–99.
26   Harry Scherman, *The Promises Men Live By: A New Approach to Economics*, 393.
27   Chamberlain, *The Roots of Capitalism*, 63.
28   Hayek, *The Constitution of Liberty*, 141.

29 Anderson, *Economics and the Public Welfare*, 37.

30 Alan Greenspan, *The Age of Turbulence: Adventures in a New World*, 129.

31 Mises, *Human Action*, 325.

32 See: Aristotle, *Politics*, bk. 1; Earnest Barker, *The Political Thought of Aristotle*, 397–400; Hans Meyer, *The Philosophy of St. Thomas Aquinas*, 422–25.

33 Hans F. Sennholz, *Death and Taxes*, 23.

34 Meredith Whitney, "The Small Business Credit Crunch," *Wall Street Journal*, May 17, 2010, A21.

35 Pius XI, *Quadragesimo Anno*.

36 This is also a position taken by Pope Leo XIII in *Rerum Novarum*, sec. 65.

37 Tamar Lewin, "Average College Debt Rose to $24,000 in 2009," *New York Times*, October 21, 2010.

38 Mark Whitehouse, "Number of the Week: Class of 2011, Most Indebted Ever," *Wall Street Journal*, May 7, 2011.

39 See Josef Pieper, *Leisure: The Basis of Culture*; Josef Pieper, *In Tune with the World: A Theory of Festivity*; Plato, *The Laws*, bk. 2, 653–54; and Aristotle, *Nicomachean Ethics*, bk. 10, chap. 8.

40 Eric Hoffer, *The Ordeal of Change*, 90–91.

41 Hayek, *Individualism and Economic Order*, 83–84.

42 Hayek, "The Kinds of Order in Society."

43 Pius XI, *Quadragesimo Anno*, part 2, art. 5.

44 Pius XII, *The Function of the State in the Modern World*.

45 W. Kurt Hauser, "There's No Escaping Hauser's Law," *Wall Street Journal*, November 26, 2010; David Ranson, "The Revenue Limits of Tax and Spend," *Wall Street Journal*, May 17, 2010.

46 Paul Godek, "Jobless Numbers Are Worse Than You Think," *Wall Street Journal*, July 23, 2010, A15.

47 Hayek, *Constitution of Liberty*, chap. 1.

48 Smith, *Wealth of Nations*.

49 Menger, *Investigations into the Method of the Social Sciences*, bk. 1, chap. 7.

50 Israel Kirzner, *The Economic Point of View*, 67–68.

51 Rueff, *Age of Inflation*, 42–43.

52 Aquinas, *De Regimine Principum*, bk. 1, chap. 1, 32–33.

Chapter 11: The Nature of Human Action

1 Mises, *Human Action*, 44.

2 Thomas Aquinas, *Summa Contra Gentiles*, bk. 3, chap. 2.

3 Mises, *Ultimate Foundation of Economic Science*, 36.

4 Mises, *Human Action*, 13.

5 Edward Banfield, *The Moral Basis of a Backward Society*, 10–11.

6 Plato, *The Republic*. See especially bks. 8 and 9.

7 Russell Kirk, *The Roots of American Order*, 6.

8 Frédéric Bastiat, "That Which Is Seen, and That Which Is Not Seen," *Essays on Political Economy* (London, 1853), 2.

9 Hazlitt, *Economics in One Lesson*, 17.

10 Menger, *Principles of Economics*, chap. 1.

11 Mises, *The Ultimate Foundation of Economic Science*, 4–5.

12 Murray N. Rothbard, "Praxeology, Value Judgments, and Public Policy," in Edwin G. Dolan, ed., *The Foundations of Modern Austrian Economics*, 90.

13 Aquinas, *Summa Theologica*, I-II, Q. 50–54.

14 Mises, *Ultimate Foundation of Economic Science*, 51.

15 Mises, *Theory and History*, 293.

16 Ibid., 212.

17 Pablo Triana, *Lecturing Birds on Flying: Can Mathematical Theories Destroy the Financial Markets?*, 118.

18 Ibid., 119.

19 Ibid.

20 Murray N. Rothbard, "New Light on the Prehistory of the Austrian School," in Dolan, *The Foundations of Modern Austrian Economics*.

21 Aristotle, *Nicomachean Ethics*, bk. 6, chap. 8.

22 Bernard Wuellner, SJ, *Dictionary of Scholastic Philosophy*, 101; *Webster's New Collegiate Dictionary*.

23 Aquinas, *Summa Theologica*, II-II, Q. 47–51.

24 Carmen M. Reinhart and Kenneth Rogoff, *This Time Is Different: Eight Centuries of Financial Folly*, xxv.

25 See Wuellner, *Dictionary of Scholastic Philosophy*.

26 Stanlis, *Edmund Burke and the Natural Law*, xxii, 114.

27 Menger, *Investigations into the Method of the Social Sciences*, 173, 176n.

28 Mises, *Ultimate Foundation of Economic Science*, 35.

Chapter 12: Inflation and Deflation

1 Christopher Westley, "The Debate over Money Manipulations: A Short History," *Intercollegiate Review* 45, nos. 1–2 (Fall 2010): 4.

2 "Business Review," Federal Reserve Bank of Philadelphia, January 1960.

3 H. J. Haskell, *The New Deal in Old Rome*, 241, appendix 1.

4 Westley, "The Debate over Money Manipulations," 4.

5 Mises, *Theory of Money and Credit*, 223–24.

6 Ibid., chap. 7.

7 Bresciani-Turroni, *Economics of Inflation*.

8 Wilhelm Röpke, *A Humane Economy*, 151–52.

9 Mises, *Theory of Money and Credit*, 106.

10 See, e.g., Annalyn Censky, "QE2: Fed Pulls the Trigger," *CNNMoney*, November 3, 2010.

11 Mises, *Human Action*, 566.

12 Patrick McGroarty, "Germany Criticizes Fed Move: Finance Minister Says Policy 'Doesn't Add Up,' Sees U.S. Model in 'Deep Crisis,'" *Wall Street Journal*, November 8, 2010, A3; Robin Harding, "Fed to Pump in an Extra $600 Billion," *Financial Times*, November 4, 2010; Jon Hilsenrath, "Fed Fires $600 Billion Stimulus Shot," *Wall Street Journal*, November 4, 2010; Peter Garnham, "Dollar Hits Lowest Level of Year," *Financial Times*, November 6/7, 2010; Telos Demos and Richard Milne, "Fed

Lights a Fire under Stock Prices," *Financial Times*, November, 6/7, 2010; Jon Hilsenrath, "Fed Treads into Once-Taboo Realm," *Wall Street Journal*, November 4, 2010; Alex Frangos and Kanga Kong, "U.S. Move Unleashes Currency Concerns," *Wall Street Journal*, November 5, 2010; Brian Blackstone, "ECB Parts Ways with U.S. on More Stimulus," *Wall Street Journal*, November 4, 2010; Kelly Evans, "Heard on the Street: Captain Ben Charts a Treacherous Course," *Wall Street Journal*, November 4, 2010; Dave Shellock, "Wave of Buying Follows Fed's 'QE2' Decision," *Financial Times*, November 4, 2010; Martin Feldstein, "QE2 Is Risky and Should Be Limited," *Financial Times*, November 2, 2010.

13 David Breuhan, *Spread the Wealth*, 8.

14 White, *Fiat Money Inflation in France*, 64.

15 Ibid., 64.

16 Ibid., 64.

17 Ibid., 64.

18 Bresciani-Turroni, *Economics of Inflation*, 311, 320.

19 Westley, "The Debate over Money Manipulations," 4.

20 Michael Rostovtzeff, *The Social and Economic History of the Roman Empire*, 419–21.

21 Harold Mattingly, *Roman Imperial Civilization*, 223–25.

22 Haskell, *New Deal in Old Rome*, 220.

23 Rostovtzeff, *Social and Economic History of the Roman Empire*, 463.

24 Reported in Anderson, *Economics and the Public Welfare*, 319.

25 G. J. Meyer, *The Tudors: The Complete Story of England's Most Notorious Dynasty*, 559.

26 Meyer, *The Tudors*, 517.

27 Jack Weathersford, *The History of Money*, 96.

28 See Pierre Vilar, *A History of Gold and Money, 1450–1920*, chap. 17.

29 Ibid., 80.

30 Roger Crowley, *Empires of the Sea*, 287.

31 Ibid., 287.

32 Ibid., *Empires of the Sea*, 287.

33 Hayek, *Choice in Currency*, 17–18.

34 Mises, *Human Action*, 568

35 Friedman, *A Monetary History of the United States*, 4–5.

36 Kennedy, *Rise and Fall of the Great Powers*, 76–81. Kennedy writes: "The creation of the Bank of England in 1694 (at first as a wartime expedient) and the slightly later regularization of the national debt on the one hand and the flourishing of the stock exchange and growth of the "country banks" on the other boosted the supply of money available to both governments and businessmen. This growth of paper money in various forms *without* severe inflation or the loss of credit brought many advantages in an age starved of coin. Yet the 'financial revolution' itself would scarcely have succeeded had not the obligations of the state but guaranteed by successive Parliaments with their powers to raise additional taxes."

37 Rothbard, *America's Great Depression*, 96.

38 Cited in Rothbard, *America's Great Depression*, 154.

39 Robert S. McElvaine, *The Great Depression: America, 1929–1941*, 17.

40 Rothbard, *America's Great Depression*, 153–54.

41 McElvaine, *Great Depression*, 38–39.

42   Bureau of Labor Statistics, Inflation Calculator.
43   Skidelsky, *Keynes*, 101–2.
44   Ibid., 118.
45   Ibid., 119.
46   Ibid., 120–24.
47   See Friedman and Schwartz, *Monetary History of the United States*, 314.
48   "RealtyTrac Year-End Report Finds 3.8 Million Foreclosure Filings Nationwide in 2010," NationalMortgageProfessional.com, January 13, 2011.
49   Greenspan, *Age of Turbulence*, 229.

Chapter 13: Faustian Bargain: The Trade Cycle

1   The phrase *trade cycle* is interchangeable with *business cycle* in this discussion. Some recent scholars prefer the latter, while older scholars grew up with the former.
2   See Rothbard, *America's Great Depression*, 19–21. Rothbard seems to include malinvestments and these other errors under the term *misinvestments*.
3   See Rothbard, *America's Great Depression*, 16.
4   It should be noted that falling interest rates are not always a sign of credit expansion. Interest rates can decline for a number of solid economic reasons. For example, they can fall as a result of an increase in savings, either domestically or internationally, or a decrease in the demand for investment.
5   There is, however, evidence that by lessening capital requirements, the 2004 international agreement Basel II enabled banks to expand their loans on home mortgages. Writing in *Foreign Affairs*, Marc Levinson notes that the Basel accords "did not mandate" strong liquidity rules and that they "failed the system by basing capital requirements on mistaken risk assessments." For example, "Around the world, regulators adhering to the Basel II rules required banks to hold less capital against home mortgages than against loans to big companies, which were deemed riskier. As a result, banks in many countries had too little capital to cover losses on mortgages when local housing prices collapsed and borrowers began walking away." Levinson concludes, "In the end, Basel's capital requirements destabilized the financial system by giving banks an incentive to get loans off their books by securitizing them rather than setting aside more capital to back them." See Marc Levinson, "Faulty Basel," *Foreign Affairs* 89 no. 3 (May–June 2010): 81–82.
6   Quoted in Richard Duncan, *The Dollar Crisis: Causes, Consequences, Cures*, 43.
7   See Duncan, *The Dollar Crisis*; Greenspan, *Age of Turbulence*, 13–14.
8   Skousen, *Structure of Production*, 303–7.
9   Paul Cwik of Mount Olive College suggested the use of the word *disharmony* rather than *disequilibrium* to describe this condition. The Austrians see the economy as very dynamic, so they would not see an economy in equilibrium.
10   C. A. Phillips, T. F. McManus, and R. W. Nelson, *Banking and the Business Cycle*, 73, 219.
11   See, e.g., Kindleberger and Aliber, *Manias, Panics, and Crashes*.
12   Phillips et al., *Banking and the Business Cycle*, 6–7. See also Bruce Caldwell, *Hayek's Challenge: An Intellectual Biography of F. A. Hayek*, 178.
13   Mark Thornton, "Skyscrapers and Business Cycles," *Quarterly Journal of Austrian Economics* 8, no. 1 (Spring 2005).

14   Mark Thornton, "New Record Skyscraper (and Depression?) in the Making," *Mises Economics Blog*, August 7, 2007, blog.mises.org/6948/new-record-skyscraper-and-depression-in-the-making/.

15   Skidelsky, *John Maynard Keynes*, 277.

16   Palyi, *Twilight of Gold*, 240–41.

17   Phillips et al., *Banking and the Business Cycle*, 235.

18   Kindleberger and Aliber, *Manias, Panics, and Crashes*, 11.

19   Greenspan, *Age of Turbulence*, 230–31.

20   See Charles Mackay, *Extraordinary Popular Delusions and the Madness of Crowds*, 1–97.

21   Kindleberger and Aliber, *Manias, Panics, and Crashes*, 10–11.

22   See Kevin Dowd and Martin Hutchinson, *Alchemists of Loss*, part 2, for an excellent presentation of this process and how it has influenced the present situation.

23   Michael A. Fletcher, "Amid Backlash and Budget Deficits, Government Workers' Pensions Are Targets," *Washington Post*, October 6, 2010; Danielle Kurtzleben, "10 States with the Largest Budget Shortfalls," *U.S. News and World Report*, January 14, 2011.

24   John W. Schoen, "European Debt Crisis Shifts to Spain," MSNBC.com, April 16, 2012.

25   Liaquat Ahamed, *Lords of Finance*, 308–9.

26   Joe Nation, *Pension Math: How California's Retirement Spending Is Squeezing the State Budget* (Stanford Institute for Economic Policy Research, December 2011).

27   Galbraith, *The Great Crash*, 133.

28   Ahamed, *Lords of Finance*, 404–5; Benjamin S. Bernanke, *Essays on the Great Depression*, 11.

29   Bernanke, *Essays on the Great Depression*, 44–45.

30   See Henry Paulson, *On the Brink*, for an account of the struggle to keep the firms afloat.

31   Kindleberger and Aliber, *Manias, Panics, and Crashes*, chaps. 1–2.

32   Robert F. Bruner and Sean D. Carr, *The Panic of 1907*, 161.

33   See Richard Vedder and Andrew Gillen, "Is There a Bubble in Higher Education? Cost vs. Enrollment Bubbles," *Academic Questions* 24, no. 3 (2011): 282–90.

34   Greenspan, *Age of Turbulence*, 165.

35   Robert Sobel, *Coolidge: An American Enigma*, chap. 13; Rothbard, *America's Great Depression*, 148; Anderson, *Economics and the Public Welfare*, 220.

36   Anderson, *Economics and the Public Welfare*, 504–5. Anderson catalogues several cases of this happening in U.S. history.

37   For Clinton's use of the term *new economy*, see, e.g., President Bill Clinton, Remarks at the First Session of the White House Conference on the New Economy, April 5, 2000.

38   *Economic Report of the President*, 2000, 74–75.

39   President Bill Clinton, Remarks at a Democratic Leadership Council Conference in San Jose, California, April 3, 2000.

40   Quoted in Skidelsky, *John Maynard Keynes*, 331.

41   For a full explanation of the yield curve and its place in the Austrian business cycle, see Paul Francis Cwik, Dissertation: "An Investigation of Inverted Yield Curves and Economic Downturns" (Auburn University, 2004), mises.org/etexts/cwik-dissertation.pdf; and Paul F. Cwik, "The Inverted Yield Curve and the Economic Downturn," *New Perspectives on Political Economy: A Bilingual Interdisciplinary Journal* 1, no. 1 (2005): 1–35, pcpe.libinst.cz/nppe/index.php.

42 Arturo Estrella and Frederic S. Mishkin, "The Yield Curve as Predictor of U.S. Recessions," *Current Issues in Economics and Finance* 2, no. 7 (June 1996).

43 See Robbie Whelan, "When the Home Bank Closes," *Wall Street Journal*, February 1, 2012. See also "Changes in US Family Finances from 2007–2010," *Federal Reserve Bulletin* 98, no. 2 (June 2012): 1. Median real family income before taxes fell 7.7 percent; median net worth fell 38.8 percent; and mean net worth fell 14.7 percent.

44 Kindleberger and Aliber, *Manias, Panics, and Crashes*, 110.

45 Press Briefing by Treasury Secretary Henry Paulson and Chairman of the Council of Economic Advisers Edward Lazear, January 18, 2008.

46 American Presidency Project, www.presidency.ucsb.edu; Arthur Laffer and Stephen Moore, "Obama's Real Spending Record," *Wall Street Journal*, June 12, 2012, A13.

47 Nicole V. Crain and W. Mark Crain, "The Regulation Tax Keeps Growing," *Wall Street Journal*, September 27, 2010, A17.

48 Peter Valdes-Dapena, "Clunkers: Taxpayers Paid $24,000 per Car," CNNMoney.com, October 29, 2009.

49 See Thomas E. Woods Jr., "Warren Harding and the Forgotten Depression of 1920," *Intercollegiate Review*, Fall 2009; Anderson, *Economics and the Public Welfare*, chaps. 8–11; Domitrovic, *Econoclasts*, 35.

50 Companies will try to shift the burden onto the consumers as best they can. The incidence of a tax, however, depends on the elasticities of supply and demand. Because supply is never perfectly elastic, the producer will always bear some of the burden of a tax.

51 Bernanke, *Essays on the Great Depression*, 46.

52 Ibid., 47.

53 Woods, "Warren Harding and the Forgotten Depression of 1920."

54 See Sylvia Nasar, *Grand Pursuit*, 280; Ludwig von Mises, *Notes and Recollections*, 82–83; Sobel, *Coolidge*, 360; Rothbard, *Making Economic Sense*, 377; Mark Skousen, *The Making of Modern Economics*, 295–97.

Conclusion: The Austrian Moment

1 Nicholas Wapshott, *Keynes Hayek: The Clash That Defined Modern Economics* (New York: W. W. Norton, 2011).

2 See "Fear the Boom and Bust," www.emergentorder.com.

3 Alan Beattie, "Zoellick Seeks Gold Standard Debate," *Financial Times*, November 7, 2010.

4 Quoted in Judy Shelton, "Loose Money and the Roots of the Crisis," *Wall Street Journal*, September 30, 2008.

5 James Grant, "How to Make the Dollar Sound Again," *New York Times*, November 13, 2010.

6 Robert Skidelsky, "A Golden Opportunity for Monetary Reform," *Financial Times*, November 10, 2010, 8.

7 Another positive sign: as economist Greg Kaza has catalogued, the published works of the National Bureau of Economic Research over the past ninety years show that awareness of Austrian trade cycle theory is growing. See Greg Kaza, "The Austrian School in the NBER's Business Cycle Studies," *Quarterly Journal of Austrian Economics*, Summer 2010.

Bibliography

Acton, John Emerich Edward Dalberg. *Essays in the Study and Writing of History.* Edited by J. Rufus Fears. Indianapolis: Liberty Press, 1986.

Adams, Charles. *Those Dirty Rotten Taxes: The Tax Revolts That Built America.* New York: Free Press, 1998.

Adler, Mortimer J. *Aristotle for Everybody: Difficult Thought Made Easy.* New York: Bantam Books, 1980.

Ahmed, Liaquat. *Lords of Finance: The Bankers Who Broke the World.* New York: Penguin Press, 2009.

Alchian, Armen A., and William R. Allen. *University Economics: Elements of Inquiry.* 3rd. ed. Belmont, CA: Wadsworth, 1972.

Allen, Frederick Lewis. *Only Yesterday: An Informal History of the 1920's.* New York: Harper & Row, 1964.

Anderson, Benjamin M. *Economics and the Public Welfare.* Princeton, NJ: D. Van Nostrand Co., 1949.

———. *The Value of Money.* Reprint, Grove City, PA: Libertarian Press, 1917.

Angell, Norman. *The Story of Money.* Garden City, NY: Garden City Publishing Company, 1929.

Aquinas, Thomas. *Commentary on Aristotle's Politics.* Translated by Richard J. Regan. Indianapolis: Hackett Publishing, 2007.

———. *Commentary on the Nicomachean Ethics.* Translated by C. I. Litzinger. Chicago: Henry Regnery, 1964

———. *The Division and Methods of the Sciences.* Translated by Armand Maurer. Toronto: Pontifical Institute of Medieval Studies, 1986.

———. *On Kingship: to the King of Cyrus.* Translated by Gerald B. Phelan. Toronto: Pontifical Institute of Medieval Studies, 1982.

———. *On Law, Morality, and Politics.* Translated by Richard J. Regan. Edited by Richard J. Regan and William P. Baumgarth. Indianapolis: Hackett Publishing, 2002.

———. *On the Governance of Rulers.* Translated by Gerald B. Phelan. Toronto: St. Michael's College, 1935.

————. *St. Thomas Aquinas on Politics and Ethics*. Translated and edited by Paul E. Sigmund. New York: W. W. Norton, 1988.

————. *Summa Contra Gentiles*. Translated by Vernon J. Bourke. Garden City, NY: Doubleday Image Books.

————. *Summa Theologica*. Translated by the English Dominican Friars. New York: Benziger Brothers, 1947.

————. *Treatise on Law*. In *Summa Theologica*, Questions 90–97. Chicago: Henry Regnery Company, 1970.

Aristotle. *Nicomachean Ethics*. Translated by David Ross. Oxford: Oxford University Press, 1992.

————. *The Politics*. Translated by Benjamin Jowett and S. H. Butcher. Norwalk, CT: Easton Press, 1979.

————. *The Poetics*. Translated by Benjamin Jowett and S. H. Butcher. Norwalk, CT: Easton Press, 1979.

Armentano, Dominick T. *Antitrust and Monopoly: Anatomy of a Policy Failure*. Oakland, CA: The Independent Institute, 1990.

Augustine. *The City of God*. Translated by Marcus Dods. New York: The Modern Library, 1950.

Bagehot, Walter. *Lombard Street: A Description of the Money Market*. 1897. Reprint, Sioux Falls, SD: NuVision Publications, 2008.

Bagehot, Walter. *Physics and Politics*. Chicago: Ivan R. Dee, 1999.

Bandow, Doug, and David L. Schindler, eds. *Wealth, Poverty, and Human Destiny*. Wilmington, DE: ISI Books, 2003.

Barker, Ernest. *Political Thought of Plato and Aristotle*. New York: Russell and Russell, 1959.

Barnett, Correlli. *The Lost Victory: British Dreams, British Realities, 1945–1950*. London: Macmillan Press, 1995.

Barruel, A. *Memoirs Illustrating the History of Jacobinism*. Fraser, MI: American Council on Economics and Society, 1995.

Barry, John M. *The Great Influenza: The Story of the Deadliest Pandemic in History*. New York: Penguin Books, 2005.

Barzun, Jacques. *From Dawn to Decadence: 500 Years of Western Cultural Life*. New York: Harper Collins, 2000.

Bastiat, Frédéric. *Economic Harmonies*. Princeton, NJ: D. Van Nostrand, 1964.

————. *Economic Sophisms*. Princeton, NJ: D. Van Nostrand, 1964.

————. *The Law*. New York: The Foundation for Economic Education, 1998.

Bell, John Fred. *A History of Economic Thought*. New York: Ronald Press, 1953.

Belloc, Hilaire. *Economics for Helen*. Hampshire, England: St. George Educational Trust, n.d.

————. *A History of England*. New York: G. P. Putnam & Sons, 1928.

————. *The Servile State*. 1913. Reprint, Indianapolis: Liberty Fund, 1977.

————. *A Shorter History of England*. New York: MacMillan, 1934.

Bénéton, Philippe. *Equality by Default: An Essay on Modernity as Confinement*. Translated by Ralph Hancock. Wilmington, DE: ISI Books, 2004.

Bennett, William J. *Patriot Sage: George Washington and the American Political Tradition*. Wilmington, DE: ISI Books, 1999.

Bernanke, Ben S., et al. *Essays on the Great Depression*. Princeton, NJ: Princeton University Press, 2000.

Bernstein, Peter L. *The Power of Gold: The History of an Obsession*. New York: John Wiley & Sons, 2000.

Bethell, Tom. *The Noblest Triumph: Property and Prosperity through the Ages.* New York: St. Martin's Press, 1998.

Billington, James H. *Fire in the Minds of Men: Origins of the Revolutionary Faith.* New Brunswick, NJ: Transaction, 1999.

Boettke, Peter J., ed. *The Elgar Companion to Austrian Economics.* Northampton, MA: Edward Elgar, 1998.

Böhm-Bawerk, Eugen von. *Basic Principles of Economic Value.* 1886. Reprinted with translation by Hans F. Sennholz. Grove City, PA: Libertarian Press, 2005.

———. *Capital and Interest.* 1914. Reprinted with translation by Hans Sennholz and George H. Huncke. South Holland, IL: Libertarian Press, 1959.

———. *Control or Economic Law.* Translated by John Richard Mez. 1914. Reprint, Auburn, AL: Ludwig von Mises Institute, 2010.

———. *Karl Marx and the Close of His System.* 1949. Reprint, Auburn, AL: Ludwig von Mises Institute, 2007.

Bonner, Bill, and Addison Wiggin. *Empire of Debt: The Rise of an Epic Financial Crisis.* Hoboken, NJ: John Wiley & Sons, 2006.

Bonner, William, and Lila Rajiva. *Mobs, Messiahs, and Markets: Surviving the Public Spectacle in Finance and Politics.* Hoboken, NJ: John Wiley & Sons, 2007.

Bookstaber, Richard. *A Demon of Our Own Design: Markets, Hedge Funds, and the Perils of Financial Innovation.* Hoboken, NJ: John Wiley & Sons, 2007.

Bowen, Catherine Drinker. *Miracle at Philadelphia: The Story of the Constitutional Convention May to September 1787.* Boston: Little, Brown, 1966.

Bresciani-Turroni, Costantino. *The Economics of Inflation: A Study of Currency Depreciation in Post-War Germany.* London: George Allen, 1937.

Breuhan, David R. *Spread the Wealth: More Haves Fewer Have-Nots.* Lanham, MD: Hamilton Books, 2010.

Brookes, Warren T. *The Economy in Mind.* New York: Universe Books, 1982.

Brooks, Arthur C. *The Battle: How the Fight between Free Enterprise and Big Government Will Shape America's Future.* New York: Basic Books, 2010.

Brown, Malcolm, and Shirley Seaton. *Christmas Truce: The Western Front, December 1914.* London: Pan Books, 2001.

Bruner, Robert F., and Sean D. Carr. *The Panic of 1907: Lessons Learned from the Market's Perfect Storm.* Hoboken, NJ: John Wiley & Sons, 2007.

Buchanan, Patrick J. *Churchill, Hitler, and the Unnecessary War: How Britain Lost Its Empire and the West Lost the World.* New York: Three Rivers Press, 2008.

———. *The Great Betrayal.* Boston: Little, Brown, 1998.

Burke, Edmund. *Reflections on the Revolution in France.* 1790. Reprint, New Rochelle, NY: Arlington House, n.d.

Burnham, James. *Suicide of the West: The Meaning and Destiny of Liberalism.* New York: John Day, 1964.

Caldwell, Bruce, ed. *Socialism and War: The Collected Works of F. A. Hayek.* Indianapolis: Liberty Fund, 1997.

———. *Hayek's Challenge: An Intellectual Biography of F. A. Hayek.* Chicago: University of Chicago Press, 2004.

Canavan, Francis. *The Political Economy of Edmund Burke: The Role of Property in His Thought.* New York: Fordham University Press, 1995.

Carabini, Louis E. *Inclined to Liberty: The Futile Attempt to Suppress the Human Spirit.* Auburn, AL: Ludwig von Mises Institute, 2008.

Carson, Clarence B. *America in Gridlock, 1985–1995*. Wadley, AL: American Textbook Committee, 1996.

———. *The American Tradition*. Irvington-on-Hudson, NY: Foundation for Economic Education, 1979.

———. *The Beginning of the Republic, 1775–1825*. Wadley, AL: American Textbook Committee, 1984.

———. *The Fateful Turn: From Individualism to Collectivism 1880–1960*. Irvington-on-Hudson, NY: Foundation for Economic Education, 1963.

———. *The Flight from Reality*. Irvington-on-Hudson, NY: Foundation for Economic Education, 1969.

———. *The Growth of America, 1878–1928*. Wadley, AL: American Textbook Committee, 1985.

———. *The Welfare State, 1929–1985*. Wadley, AL: American Textbook Committee, 1986.

Cashill, Jack. *Popes and Bankers: A Cultural History of Credit and Debt, from Aristotle to AIG*. Nashville, TN: Nelson, 2010.

Chafuen, Alejandro A. *Faith and Liberty: The Economic Thought of the Late Scholastics*. Lanham, MD: Lexington Books, 2003.

Chamberlain, John. *The Roots of Capitalism*. Princeton, NJ: D. Van Nostrand, 1959.

Chamberlain, William Henry. *The German Phoenix: Up from the Ashes—The Rise of Western Germany*. New York: Duell, Sloan and Pearce, 1963.

Chambers, Frank P, Christina Phelps Grant and Charles C. Bayley. *The Age of Conflict: A Contemporary World History, 1914–1943*. New York: Harcourt, Brace, 1945.

Chandler, Lester V. *America's Greatest Depression: 1929–1941*. New York: Harper & Row, 1970.

Chernow, Ron. *Alexander Hamilton*. New York: Penguin Press, 2004.

Chesterton, G. K. *St. Thomas Aquinas*. New York: Sheed & Ward, 1933.

Chivvis, Christopher S. *The Monetary Conservative: Jacques Rueff and the Twentieth-Century Free Market Thought*. Dekalb, IL: Northern Illinois University Press, 2010.

Clark, Colin. *Population Growth: The Advantages*. Santa Ana, CA: Life Quality, 1975.

Clay, Henry. *Economics for the General Reader*. London: Macmillan, 1926.

Cobbett, William. *A History of the Protestant Reformation in England and Ireland*. 1896. Reprint, Rockford, IL: Tan Books, 1988.

Cole, Charles Woolsey. *French Mercantilist Doctrines before Colbert*. New York: Octagon Books, 1969.

Cole, Margaret. *The Story of Fabian Socialism*. Stanford, CA: Stanford University Press, 1961.

Copleston, F. C. *Aquinas*. New York: Penguin, 1975.

Corwin, Edward S. *The Constitution and What It Means Today*. Princeton, NJ: Princeton University Press, 1937.

Coughlin, Charles E. *Money: Questions and Answers*. Independent printing.

Crowley, Roger. *Empires of the Sea*. New York: Random House, 2008.

D'Arcy, M. C. *St. Thomas Aquinas*. Westminster, MD: Newman Press, 1954.

Daugherty, Harry M. *The Inside Story of the Harding Tragedy*. 1932. Reprint, Boston: Western Islands, 1975.

Dawson, Christopher. *Understanding Europe*. Garden City, NY: Image Books, 1960.

Dawson, William Harbutt. *Bismark and State Socialism: An Exposition of the Social and Economic Legislation since 1870*. London: Swan Sonnenschein, 1890.

De Konick, Charles. *The Hollow Universe.* London: Oxford University Press, 1960.

Del Mar, Alexander. *Money and Civilization.* 1886. Reprint, Hawthorne, CA: Omni Publications, 1975.

——— *The Science of Money.* 1885. Reprint, Hawthorne, CA: Omni, 1967

Delsol, Chantal. *Icarus Fallen: The Search for Meaning in an Uncertain World.* Wilmington, DE: ISI Books, 2003.

Denson, James V. *A Century of War: Lincoln, Wilson, and Roosevelt.* Auburn, AL: Ludwig von Mises Institute, 2008.

Denson, John V., ed. *The Costs of War: America's Pyrrhic Victories.* New Brunswick, NJ: Transaction, 1999.

D'Entreves, A. P., ed. *Aquinas: Selected Political Writings.* Translated by J. G. Dawson. New York: Macmillan, 1959.

De Soto, Hernando. *The Mystery of Capital: Why Capitalism Triumphs in the West and Fails Everywhere Else.* New York: Basic Books, 2000.

De Soto, Jesús Huerta. *Money, Bank Credit, and Economic Cycles.* Translated by Melinda A. Stroup. Auburn AL: Ludwig von Mises Institute, 2006.

Dietze, Gottfried. *In Defense of Property.* Chicago: Henry Regnery, 1963.

Disraeli, Benjamin. *Sybil.* 1845. Reprint, Hertfordshire, England: Wadsworth, 1995.

DiLorenzo, Thomas J. *Hamilton's Curse.* New York: Crown Forum, 2008.

Domitrovic, Brian. *Econoclasts: The Rebels Who Sparked the Supply-Side Revolution and Restored American Prosperity.* Wilmington, DE: ISI Books, 2009.

Dowd, Kevin, and Richard H. Timberlake Jr., eds. *Money and the State: The Financial Revolution, Government and the World Monetary System.* Oakland, CA: The Independent Institute, 1998.

Duncan, Richard. *The Dollar Crisis: Causes, Consequences, Cures.* Hoboken, NJ: John Wiley & Sons, 2003.

Ebeling, Richard, ed. *Money, Method, and the Market Processes: Essays by Ludwig von Mises.* Norwell, MA: Kluwer Academic, 1990.

Ebeling, Richard M., ed. *The Austrian Theory of the Trade Cycle and Other Essays.* Auburn, AL: Ludwig von Mises Institute, 1996.

Eberly, Don. *The Rise of Global Civil Society: Building Communities and Nations from the Bottom Up.* New York: Encounter Books, 2008.

Edwards, Lee. *The Conservative Revolution: The Movement That Remade America.* New York: Free Press, 1999.

Ekelund, Robert B., Jr., and Robert F. Hébert. *A History of Economic Theory and Method.* 5th ed. Long Grove, IL: Waveland Press, 2007.

Eland, Ivan. *The Empire Has No Clothes: U.S. Foreign Policy Exposed.* Oakland, CA: The Independent Institute, 2004.

Ellis, Joseph J. *His Excellency: George Washington.* New York: Alfred A. Knopf, 2004.

Erhard, Antony. *Germany's Comeback in the World Market.* Translated by W. H. Johnston. London: George Allen & Unwin, 1954.

Erhard, Ludwig. *Prosperity through Competition.* Translated by Edith Temple Roberts and John B. Woods. London: Thames and Hudson, 1958.

Erhard, Ludwig. *The Economics of Success.* Princeton, NJ: D. Van Nostrand, 1963.

Eucken, Walter. *The Foundations of Economics.* Chicago: University of Chicago Press, 1951.

Farrell, Walter. *The Fullness of Life.* Vol. 3 of *A Companion to the Summa.* New York: Sheed & Ward, 1940.

Ferguson, Niall. *The Ascent of Money: A Financial History of the World.* New York: Penguin Books, 2008.

———. *The Cash Nexus: Money and Power in the Modern World, 1700–2000.* New York: Basic Books, 2001.

———. *Colussus: The Price of America's Empire.* New York: Penguin Press, 2004.

———. *The Pity of War.* New York: Basic Books, 1999.

———. *The War of the World: Twentieth-Century Conflict and the Descent of the West.* New York: Penguin Books, 2006.

Ferrara, Peter J., ed. *Social Security: Prospects for Real Reform.* Washington, DC: Cato Institute, 1985.

Fetter, Frank. *Capital, Interest, and Rent: Essays in the Theory of Distribution.* Kansas City: Sheed, Andrews and McMeel, 1977.

Fisher, Antony. *Fisher's Concise History of Economic Bungling: A guide for Today's Statesmen.* Ottawa, IL: Caroline House Books, 1978.

Fisher, Ken. *The Wall Street Waltz: 90 Visual Perspectives.* Hoboken, NJ: John Wiley & Sons, 2008.

Flynn, John T. *As We Go Marching.* Garden City, NY: Doubleday, Doran, 1944.

———. *The Road Ahead.* New York: Devon-Adair, 1949.

———. *While You Slept.* New York: Devon-Adair, 1951.

Fox, Justin. *The Myth of the Rational Market: A History of Risk, Reward, and Delusion on Wall Street.* New York: Harper Collins, 2009.

Franklin, Benjamin. *The Completed Autobiography.* Edited by Mark Skousen. Washington, DC: Regnery, 2006.

French, Douglas E. *Early Speculative Bubbles and Increases in the Money Supply.* Auburn, AL: Ludwig von Mises Institute, 1992.

Freud, Sigmund, and William C. Bullitt. *Woodrow Wilson: A Psychological Study.* Boston: Houghton Mifflin, 1966.

Friedman, Milton, and Anna Jacobson Schwartz. *A Monetary History of the United States: 1867–1960.* Princeton, NJ: Princeton University Press, 1963.

Friedman, Milton, and Rose Friedman. *Free to Choose: A Personal Statement.* New York: Avon Books, 1980

———. *Tyranny of the Status Quo.* San Diego: Harcourt Brace Jovanovich, 1984.

Friedman, Milton, and Walter W. Heller. *Monetary vs. Fiscal Policy: A Dialogue.* New York: W. W. Norton, 1969.

Friedman, Milton. *Capitalism and Freedom.* Chicago: University of Chicago Press, 1962.

———. *Essays in Positive Economics.* Chicago: University of Chicago Press, 1953.

———. *Money Mischief: Episodes in Monetary History.* San Diego: Harcourt Brace, 1994.

Friedman, Thomas L. *The World Is Flat: A Brief History of the Twenty-First Century.* New York: Picador/Farrar, Straus, and Giroux, 2005.

Galbraith, John Kenneth. *The Great Crash 1929.* Boston: Houghton Mifflin, 1997.

Gamble, Richard M. *The War for Righteousness: Progressive Christianity, the Great War, and the Rise of the Messianic Nation.* Wilmington, DE: ISI Books, 2003.

Garrett, Garet, and Murray N. Rothbard. *The Great Depression and New Deal Monetary Policy.* San Francisco: Cato Institute, 1980

Garrett, Garet. *The Bubble That Broke the World.* Boston: Little, Brown, 1932.

———. *The People's Pottage.* Caldwell, ID: Caxton Printers, 1965.

Garrison, Roger. *Time and Money: The Macroeconomics of Capital Structure*. London: Routledge, 2001.

Gay, Peter. *The Science of Freedom*. Vol. 2 of *The Enlightenment: An Interpretation*. New York: W. W. Norton, 1969.

Gelinas, Nicole. *After the Fall: Saving Capitalism from Wall Street and Washington*. New York: Encounter Books, 2009.

Gilder, George. *The Spirit of Enterprise*. New York: Simon and Schuster, 1984

Gordon, David. *The Philosophical Origins of Austrian Economics*. Auburn, AL: Ludwig von Mises Institute, 1996.

Grant, James. *Money of the Mind: Borrowing and Lending in America from the Civil War to Michael Milken*. New York: Farrar Straus Giroux, 1992.

Gray, Alexander. *The Socialist Tradition: Moses to Lenin*. New York: Longmans, Green, 1946.

Greaves, Bettina B. *Free Market Economics: A Basic Reader*. The Foundation for Economic Education, 1975.

Greenspan, Alan. *The Age of Turbulence: Adventures in a New World*. New York: Penguin Books, 2008.

Gregg, Samuel. *The Commercial Society: Foundations and Challenges in a Global Age*. Lanham, MD: Lexington Books, 2007.

Grice-Hutchinson, Marjorie. *The School of Salamanca*. Oxford: Oxford University Press, 1952.

Groseclose, Elgin. *America's Money Machine: The Story of the Federal Reserve*. Westport, CT: Arlington House, 1966.

Gross, Daniel, ed. *Forbes Greatest Business Stories of All Time*. New York: John Wiley & Sons, 1996.

Haberler, Gottfried. *Prosperity and Depression: A Theoretical Analysis of Cyclical Movements*. Geneva: League of Nations, 1941.

Hagstrom, Robert G. *Investing: The Last Liberal Art*. New York: Texere, 2000.

Hahn, L. Albert. *Common Sense Economics*. New York: Abelard Schuman, 1956.

———. *The Economics of Illusion*. New York: Squier, 1949.

Hamilton, Alexander, James Madison, and John Jay. *The Federalist*. 1820. Reprint, Norwalk, CT: Easton Press, 1979.

Harries, Meirion, and Susie Harries. *The Last Days of Innocence: America at War, 1917–1918*. New York: Random House, 1997.

Harrod, R. F. *The Life of John Maynard Keynes*. New York: Harcourt, Brace, 1951.

Haskell, H. J. *The New Ideal in Old Rome: How Government in the Ancient World Tried to Deal with Modern Problems*. New York: Alfred A. Knopf, 1947.

Hayek, F. A., ed. *Collectivist Economic Planning*. 1935. Reprint, Auburn, AL: Ludwig von Mises Institute, 2009.

———. *The Constitution of Liberty*. Chicago: University of Chicago Press, 1960.

———. *The Counter-Revolution of Science: Studies on the Abuse of Reason*. London: Free Press, 1955.

———. *Individualism and Economic Order*. Chicago: University of Chicago Press, 1948.

———. *Monetary Theory and the Trade Cycle*. New York: Augustus M. Kelley, 1975.

———. *Prices and Production*. New York: Augustus M. Kelley, 1967.

———. *Profits, Interest, and Investment*. New York: Augustus M. Kelley, 1975.

———. *The Road to Serfdom*. Chicago: University of Chicago Press, 1994.

Hayes, Carlton J. H. *Modern Europe to 1870*. New York: Macmillan, 1953.

Hayward, Steven F. *The Age of Reagan: The Conservative Counterrevolution, 1980–1989.* New York: Crown Forum, 2009.

Hazlitt, Henry. *Economics in One Lesson.* New York: Three Rivers Press, 1979.

————. *From Bretton Woods to World Inflation: A Case Study of Causes and Consequences.* Chicago: Regnery Gateway, 1984.

Heilperin, Michael A. *Aspects of the Pathology of Money.* London: Michael Joseph, 1968.

————. *International Monetary Economics.* London: Longman, Green, 1939.

Heyne, Paul. *The Economic Way of Thinking.* 8th ed. Upper Saddle River, NJ: Prentice-Hall, 1997.

Higgs, Robert. *Crisis and Leviathan: Critical Episodes in the Growth of American Government.* New York: Oxford University Press, 1987.

Holcombe, Randall, ed. *15 Great Austrian Economists.* Auburn, AL: Ludwig von Mises Institute, 1999.

Homer, Sidney. *A History of Interest Rates.* New Brunswick, NJ: Rutgers University Press, 1963.

Hoover, Kenneth R. *Economics as Ideology: Keynes, Laski, Hayek, and the Creation of Contemporary Politics.* Lanham, MD: Rowman & Littlefield, 2003.

Hoppe, Hans-Hermann. *Economic Science and the Austrian Method.* Auburn, AL: Ludwig von Mises Institute, 1995.

Hülsmann, Jörg Guido. *Deflation and Liberty.* Auburn, AL: Ludwig von Mises Institute, 2008.

————. *The Ethics of Money Production.* Auburn, AL: Ludwig von Mises Institute, 2008.

————. *Mises: The Last Knight of Liberalism.* Auburn, AL: Ludwig von Mises Institute, 2007.

————, and Stephan Kinsella, eds. *Property, Freedom, and Society: Essays in Honor of Hans-Hermann Hoppe.* Auburn, AL: Ludwig von Mises Institute, 2009.

Humphrey, Thomas M. *Essays on Inflation.* 2nd ed. Richmond, VA: Federal Reserve Bank of Richmond, 1980.

Hutt, W. H. *The Keynesian Episode: A Reassessment.* Indianapolis: Liberty Press, 1979.

————. *Keynesianism—Retrospect and Prospect: A Critical Restatement of Basic Economic Principles.* Chicago: Henry Regnery, 1963.

————. *The Strike-Threat System.* New Rochelle, NY: Arlington House, 1973.

————. *The Theory of Collective Bargaining.* 1954. Reprint, Auburn, AL: Ludwig von Mises Institute, 2007.

————. *A Rehabilitation of Say's Law.* Auburn, AL: Ludwig von Mises Institute, 2007.

Hutton, Graham. *What Killed Prosperity: In Every State from Ancient Rome to the Present.* Philadelphia: Chilton, 1960.

Ingrassia, Paul. *Crash Course: The American Automobile Industry's Road from Glory to Disaster.* New York: Random House, 2010.

Jacobs, Jane. *Cities and the Wealth of Nations: Principles of Economic Life.* New York: Vintage Books, 1984.

————. *The Death and Life of Great American Cities.* New York: Random House, 1961.

————. *The Economy of Cities.* New York: Random House, 1969.

————. *The Nature of Economies.* New York: Vintage Books, 2000.

Jaeger, Werner. *Aristotle: Fundamentals of the History of His Development.* Translated by Richard Robinson. Oxford: Oxford University Press, 1962.

Jaki, Stanley L. *Means to Message: A Treatise on Truth.* Grand Rapids, MI: William B. Eerdmans, 1999.

———. *The Only Chaos and Other Essays.* Lanham, MD: University Press of America, 1990.

———. *The Origin of Science and the Science of Its Origin.* Edinburgh: Scottish Academic Press, 1978.

———. *The Relevance of Physics.* Edinburgh: Scottish Academic Press, 1992.

Johnson, Paul. *Enemies of Society.* New York: Atheneum Books, 1977.

———. *A History of the American People.* New York: Harper Perennial, 1999

———. *Modern Times: The World from the Twenties to the Eighties.* New York: Harper & Row, 1983.

Johnston, William M. *The Austrian Mind: An Intellectual and Social History, 1848–1938.* Berkeley: University of California Press, 1972.

Jouvenel, Bertrand de. *The Art of Conjecture.* Translated by Nikita Lary. New York: Basic Books, 1967.

Karmin, Craig. *Biography of the Dollar: How the Mighty Buck Conquered the World and Why It's under Siege.* New York: Crown Business, 2008.

Kasun, Jacqueline. *The War against Population: The Economics and Ideology of Population Control.* San Francisco: Ignatius Press, 1988.

Kates, Steven. *Say's Law and the Keynesian Revolution: How Macroeconomic Theory Lost Its Way.* Cheltenham, UK: Edward Elgar, 1998.

Kauder, Emil. *A History of Marginal Utility Theory.* Princeton, NJ: Princeton University Press, 1965.

Keegan, John. *The First World War.* New York: Alfred A. Knopf, 1999.

Kemmerer, Edwin Walter. *Gold and the Gold Standard: The Story of Gold Money, Past, Present, and Future.* New York: McGraw Hill, 1944.

Kengor, Paul. *The Crusader: Ronald Reagan and the Fall of Communism.* New York: Harper-Collins, 2006.

Kennedy, Paul. *The Rise and Fall of the Great Powers: Economic Change and Military Conflict from 1500 to 2000.* New York: Random House, 1987.

Keynes, John Maynard. *The Economic Consequences of the Peace.* New York: Harcourt, Brace, and Howe, 1920.

———. *The End of Laissez-Faire and the Economic Consequences of the Peace.* Amherst, NY: Prometheus Books, 2004.

———. *Essays in Persuasion.* New York: W. W. Norton, 1963.

———. *The General Theory of Employment, Interest, and Money.* New York: Harbinger, 1964.

———. *How to Pay for the War.* London: Macmillan, 1940.

———. *A Revision of the Treaty.* New York: Harcourt, Brace, 1922.

———. *A Tract on Monetary Reform.* Reprint, BN Publishing (online), 2008.

———. *A Treatise on Probability.* Reprint, BN Publishing (online), 2008.

Kindleberger, Charles P. *The World in Depression, 1929–1939.* Berkeley, CA: University of California Press, 1986.

Kindleberger, Charles P., and Robert Aliber. *Manias, Panics, and Crashes: A History of Financial Crises.* Hoboken, NJ: John Wiley & Sons, 2005.

Kirk, Russell. *Beyond the Dreams of Avarice: Essays of a Social Critic.* Chicago: Henry Regnery, 1956.

————. *The Conservative Mind: From Burke to Eliot.* 7th ed. Washington: Regnery, 1985.

————. *Edmund Burke: A Genius Reconsidered.* New Rochelle, NY: Arlington House, 1967.

————. *The Politics of Prudence.* Wilmington, DE: ISI Books, 1993.

————. *A Program for Conservatives.* Chicago: Henry Regnery, 1954.

————. *Prospects for Conservatives.* Washington, DC: Regnery Gateway, 1989.

————. *The Roots of American Order.* Lasalle, IL: Open Court, 1974.

Kirzner, Israel M. *The Economic Point of View: An Essay in the History of Economic Thought.* Kansas City: Sheed and Ward, 1976.

————. *Competition and Entrepreneurship.* Chicago: University of Chicago Press, 1973.

————. *Ludwig von Mises.* Wilmington, DE: ISI Books, 2001.

Kissinger, Henry A. *A World Restored: Europe after Napoleon, the Politics of Conservatism in a Revolutionary Age.* New York: Gosset & Dunlap, 1964.

————. *A World Restored: Metternich, Castlereagh, and the Problems of Peace 1812–22.* Boston: Houghton Mifflin, 1957.

Koehler, John. *Spies in the Vatican: The Soviet Union's Cold War against the Catholic Church.* New York: Pegasus Books, 2009.

Laffer, Arthur B., and Stephen Moore. *Return to Prosperity: How American Can Regain Its Superpower Status.* New York: Simon and Schuster, 2010.

Leaf, Jonathan. *The Politically Incorrect Guide to the Sixties.* Washington, DC: Regnery, 2009.

Levin, Mark R. *Liberty and Tyranny: A Conservative Manifesto.* New York: Threshold Editions, 2009.

Lewis, Hunter. *Where Keynes Went Wrong: And Why Governments Keep Creating Inflation, Bubbles, and Busts.* Mt. Jackson, VA: Axios Press, 2009.

Lewis, Michael ed. *Panic: The Story of Modern Financial Insanity.* New York: W. W. Norton, 2009.

Lewis, Nathan. *Gold: The Once and Future Money.* Hoboken, NJ: John Wiley & Sons, 2007.

Lukacs, John. *The Passing of the Modern Age.* New York: Harper & Row, 1970.

MacDonogh, Giles. *After the Reich: The Brutal History of the Allied Occupation.* New York: Basic Books, 2007.

Machlup, Fritz, ed. *Essays on Hayek.* Hillsdale, MI: Hillsdale College Press, 1976.

Mackay, Charles. *Extraordinary Popular Delusions and the Madness of the Crowds.* London: Noonday Press, 1932.

Mahoney, Daniel J. *Bertrand de Jouvenel.* Wilmington, DE: ISI Books, 2005.

Marron, Donald, ed. *30-Second Economics.* New York: Metro Books, 2010.

Marshall, Alfred. *Principles of Economics.* New York: Macmillan, 1961.

Mattingly, Harold. *Roman Imperial Civilization.* Garden City, NY: Doubleday Anchor Books, 1959.

McBriar, A. M. *Fabian Socialism and English Politics, 1884–1918.* Cambridge: Cambridge University Press, 1962.

McCraw, Thomas K. *Prophet of Innovation: Joseph Schumpeter and Creative Destruction.* Cambridge, MA: Belknap Press, 2007.

McElvaine, Robert S. *The Great Depression.* New York: Three Rivers Press, 1984.

McKeon, Richard, ed. *The Basic Works of Aristotle.* New York: Random House, 1941.

McLean, Edward B., ed. *Common Truths: New Perspectives on Natural Law.* Wilmington, DE: ISI Books, 2000.

Mee, Charles L., Jr. *The End of Order: Versailles 1919.* New York: E. P. Dutton, 1980

Meese, Henry, III, Matthew Spalding, and David Forte, eds. *The Heritage Guide to the Constitution.* Washington, DC: Regnery, 2005.

Meltzer, Allan H. *A History of the Federal Reserve.* Vol. 1. Chicago: University of Chicago Press, 2003.

Menger, Carl. *Investigations into the Method of the Social Sciences with Special Reference to Economics.* 1883. Reprinted with translation by Francis J. Nock, New York: New York University Press, 1985.

Menger, Carl. *Principles of Economics.* New York: New York University Press, 1976

Meyer, Hans. *The Philosophy of St. Thomas Aquinas.* Translated by Frederic Eckhoff. St. Louis: B. Herder, 1946.

Meyer, G. J. The Tudors: *The Complete Story of England's Most Notorious Dynasty.* New York: Delacorte Press, 2010.

Mill, John Stuart. *Principles of Political Economy.* 1848. Reprint, Fairfield, NJ: Augustus M. Kelley, 1987.

Minsky, Hyman P. *John Maynard Keynes.* New York: McGraw Hill, 2008.

Minton, Robert. *John Law: The Father of Paper Money.* New York: Association Press, 1975.

Mises, Ludwig von. *The Causes of the Economic Crises and Other Essays Before and After the Great Depression.* Edited by Percy L. Greaves Jr. Auburn, AL: Ludwig von Mises Institute, 2006.

———. *Economic Policy: Thoughts for Today and Tomorrow.* Chicago: Gateway Editions, 1979.

———. *Epistemological Problems of Economics.* Translated by George Reisman. New York: New York University Press, 1976.

———. *The Historical Setting of the Austrian School of Economics.* 1969. Reprint, Auburn, AL: Ludwig von Mises Institute, 2007.

———. *Human Action: A Treatise on Economics.* New Haven, CT: Yale University Press, 1949.

———. *Liberalism in the Classical Tradition.* Irvington-on-Hudson, NY: Foundation for Economic Education, 1985.

———. *Liberty and Property.* Auburn, AL: Ludwig von Mises Institute, 1988.

———. *Omnipotent Government: The Rise of the Total State and Total War.* 1944. Reprint, Grove City, PA: Libertarian Press, 1985.

———. *Profit and Loss.* Auburn, AL: Ludwig von Mises Institute, 2008.

———. *Socialism.* Translated by J. Kahane. New Haven: Yale University Press, 1951.

———. *Theory and History: An Interpretation of Social and Economic Evolution.* New Rochelle, NY: Arlington House, 1969.

———. *The Theory of Money and Credit.* 1935. Reprint, New York: Foundation for Economic Education, 1971.

———. *The Ultimate Foundation of Economic Science: An Essay on Method.* Princeton, NJ: D. Van Nostrand, 1962

Molnar, Thomas. *Utopia, the Perennial Heresy.* New York: Sheed and Ward, 1967.

Morley, Felix, ed. *The Necessary Conditions for a Free Society.* Princeton, NJ: D. Van Nostrand, 1963.

———. *For the Record.* South Bend, IN: Regnery Gateway, 1979.

Morris, Charles R. *The Two Trillion Dollar Meltdown: Easy Money, High Rollers, and the Great Credit Crash.* New York: Public Affairs, 2008.

Murphy, Robert P. *The Politically Incorrect Guide to the Great Depression and the New Deal.* Washington, DC: Regnery, 2009.

Murray, Charles. *Human Accomplishments: The Pursuit of Excellence in the Arts and Sciences, 800 B.C. to 1950.* New York: Harper Collins, 2003.

———. *Losing Ground: American Social Policy 1950–1980.* New York: Basic Books, 1984.

Neale, A. D. *The Antitrust Laws of the USA: A Study of Competition Enforced by Law.* 2nd ed. Cambridge: Cambridge University Press, 1970.

Nelson, Daniel Mark. *The Priority of Prudence: Virtue and Natural Law in Thomas Aquinas and the Implications for Modern Ethics.* University Park, PA: Pennsylvania State University Press, 1992.

Ostrogorsky, George. *History of the Byzantine State.* New Brunswick, NJ: Rutgers University Press, 1969.

Palyi, Melchior. *An Inflation Primer: Prices, Debt and the Declining Dollar.* Chicago: Henry Regnery, 1961.

———. *The Twilight of Gold, 1914–1936: Myths and Realities.* Chicago: Henry Regnery, 1972.

Patterson, Scott. *The Quants: How a New Breed of Math Whizzes Conquered Wall Street and Nearly Destroyed It.* New York: Crown Business, 2010.

Paul, Ron, and Lewis E. Lehrman. *The Case for Gold.* Washington, DC: Cato Institute, 1982.

Paul, Ron. *End the Fed.* New York: Grand Central, 2009.

Paulson, Henry, Jr. *On the Brink: Inside the Race to Stop the Collapse of the Global Financial System.* New York: Business Plus, 2010.

Peters, Harvey W. *America's Coming Bankruptcy.* New Rochelle, NY: Arlington House, 1975

Peters, Walter H. *The Life of Benedict XV.* Milwaukee: Bruce, 1959.

Phillips, C. A., T. F. McManus, and R. W. Nelson. *Banking and the Business Cycle: A Study of the Great Depression in the United States.* 1937. Reprint, Auburn, AL: Ludwig von Mises Institute, 2007.

Phillips, Kevin. *Bad Money: Reckless Finance, Failed Politics, and the Global Crisis of American Capitalism.* New York: Viking, 2008.

Pichon, Charles. *The Vatican and Its Role in World Affairs.* Translated by Jean Misrahi. New York: E. P. Dutton, 1950.

Pieper, Josef. *Guide to Thomas Aquinas.* Translated by Richard and Clara Winston. New York: Pantheon Books, 1962.

Pipes, Richard. *The Russian Revolution.* New York: Alfred Knopf, 1990.

Pirenne, Henri. Medieval Cities: Their Origins and the Revival of Trade. Translated by Frank D. Halsey. Princeton, NJ: Princeton University Press, 1925.

Plato. *The Republic.* Translated by Benjamin Jowett. Norwalk, CT: Easton Press, 1980.

———. *The Dialogues.* Translated by Benjamin Jowett. New York: Random House, 1937.

Powell, Jim. *Bully Boy: The Truth about Theodore Roosevelt's Legacy.* New York: Crown Forum, 2006.

———. *FDR's Folly: How Roosevelt and His New Deal Prolonged the Great Depression.* New York: Crown Forum, 2003.

———. *The Triumph of Liberty: A 2,000-Year History, Told through the Lives of Freedom's Greatest Champions.* New York: Free Press, 2000.

————. *Wilson's War: How Woodrow Wilson's Great Blunder Led to Hitler, Lenin, Stalin, and World War II.* New York: Crown Forum, 2005.

Quigley, Carroll. *Tragedy and Hope: A History of the World in Our Time.* New York: Macmillan, 1966

Rajan, Raghuram G. *Fault Lines: How Hidden Fractures Still Threaten the World Economy.* Princeton, NJ: Princeton University Press, 2010.

Reinhart, Carmen M., and Kenneth S. Rogoff. *This Time Is Different: Eight Centuries of Financial Folly.* Princeton, NJ: Princeton University Press, 2009.

Reisman, George. *Capitalism: A Treatise on Economics.* Ottawa, IL: Jameson Books, 1996.

Rickert, Heinrich. *Science and History: A Critique of Positivist Epistemology.* Edited by Arthur Goddard. Translated by George Reisman. Princeton, NJ: D. Van Nostrand, 1962.

Rist, Charles. *The Triumph of Gold.* Translated by Philip Cortney. New York: Philosophical Library, 1961.

Robbins, Lionel. *The Great Depression.* 1934. Reprint, Auburn, AL: Ludwig von Mises Institute, 2007.

————. *A History of Economic Thought: The LSE lectures.* Edited by Steven G. Medema and Warren J. Samuels. Princeton, NJ: Princeton University Press, 1998.

Roberts, Paul Craig. *The Supply-Side Revolution: An Insider's Account of Policymaking in Washington.* Cambridge, MA: Harvard University Press, 1984.

Rockwell, Llewellyn H., Jr., ed. *The Gold Standard: An Austrian Perspective.* Lexington, MA: Lexington Books, 1985.

Rockwell, Llewellyn H., Jr., Jeffrey A. Tucker, and Murray N. Rothbard. *Henry Hazlitt: A Giant of Liberty.* Auburn, AL: Ludwig von Mises Institute, 1994.

Röpke, Wilhelm. *Against the Tide.* Chicago: Henry Regnery, 1969

————. *Crises and Cycles.* 1936. Reprint, Auburn, AL: Ludwig von Mises Institute, 2007.

————. *Economics of the Free Society.* Chicago: Henry Regnery, 1963.

————. *A Humane Economy: The Social Framework of the Free Market.* Wilmington, DE: ISI Books, 1998.

————. *International Economic Disintegration.* London: William Hodge, 1942.

————. *International Order and Economic Integration.* Dordrecht, Holland: D. Reidel, 1959.

————. *The Moral Foundations of Civil Society.* 1948. Reprint, New Brunswick, NJ: Transaction, 1996.

————. *Welfare, Freedom, and Inflation.* Tuscaloosa: University of Alabama Press, 1964.

Rogge, Benjamin A. *Can Capitalism Survive?* Indianapolis: Liberty Fund, 1979.

Rommen, Heinrich A. *The State in Catholic Thought: A Treatise in Political Philosophy.* St. Louis: B. Herder, 1945.

Rostovtzeff, M. *The Social and Economic History of the Roman Empire.* Oxford: Clarendon Press, 1926.

Rothbard, Murray. *America's Great Depression.* New York: Richardson & Snyder, 1972.

————. *Making Economic Sense.* Auburn, AL: Ludwig von Mises Institute, 1995.

————. *Man, Economy, and State: A Treatise on Economic Principles.* Auburn, AL: Ludwig von Mises Institute, 2001.

————. *The Mystery of Banking.* New York: Richardson & Snyder, 1983.

Roubini, Nouriel, and Stephen Mihm. *Crisis Economics: A Crash Course in the Future of Finance.* New York: Penguin Press, 2010.

Rueff, Jacques. *The Age of Inflation.* Translated by A. H. Meeus and F. G. Clarke. Chicago: Henry Regnery, 1964.

————. *Balance of Payments.* Translated by Jean Clément. New York: Macmillan, 1967.

————. *The Monetary Sin of the West.* Translated by Roger Glémet. New York: Macmillan, 1972.

Rummel, R. J. *Death by Government.* New Brunswick, NJ: Transaction, 1994.

Sassone, Robert L. *Handbook on Population.* Santa Ana, CA: Life Quality, 1973.

Say, Jean-Baptiste. *A Treatise on Political Economy.* 1821. Reprint, Auburn, AL: Ludwig von Mises Institute, 2008.

Schama, Simon. *The Embarrassment of Riches: An Interpretation of Dutch Culture in the Golden Age.* New York: Alfred A. Knopf, 1987.

Scherman, Harry. *The Promises Men Live By.* New York: Random House, 1938.

Schoeck, Helmut, and James W. Wiggins, eds. *Scientism and Values.* Princeton, NJ: D. Van Nostrand, 1960.

Schumpeter, Joseph A. *Can Capitalism Survive?* New York: Harper Perennial, 1950.

————. *Capitalism, Socialism, and Democracy.* New York: Harper Books, 1942.

————. *Essays on Entrepreneurs, Innovations, Business Cycles, and the Evolution of Capitalism.* Edited by Richard V. Clemence. New Brunswick, NJ: Transaction Publishers, 2006.

————. *History of Economic Analysis.* New York: Oxford University Press, 1954.

————. *Imperialism and Social Classes.* Translated by Heinz Norden. New York: Augustus M. Kelley, 1951.

————. *The Theory of Economic Development.* New Brunswick, NJ: Transaction, 1983.

Schweikart, Larry, and Michael Allen. *A Patriot's History of the United States: From Columbus's Great Discovery to the War on Terror.* New York: Sentinel, 2004.

Schweizer, Peter. *Victory: The Reagan Administration's Secret Strategy That Hastened the Collapse of the Soviet Union.* New York: Atlantic Monthly Press, 1994.

Selgin, George A. *Praxeology and Understanding: An Analysis of the Controversy in Austrian Economics.* Auburn, AL: Ludwig von Mises Institute, 1990.

Sennholz, Hans F. *Age of Inflation.* Belmont, MA: Western Islands, 1979.

————. *Debts and Deficits.* Spring Mills, PA: Libertarian Press, 1987.

————. *Death and Taxes.* Cedar Falls, IA: Center for Futures Education, 1982.

Shafarevich, Igor. *The Socialist Phenomenon.* Translated by William Tjalsma. New York: Harper & Row, 1980.

Sheen, Fulton. *Philosophy of Religion.* New York: Appleton-Century-Crofts, 1948.

————. *Philosophy of Science.* Milwaukee: Bruce, 1934.

Shelton, Judy. *Money Meltdown: Restoring Order to the Global Currency System.* New York: Free Press, 1994.

Shlaes, Amity. *The Forgotten Man: A New History of the Great Depression.* New York: Harper Perennial, 2007.

Skidelsky, Robert, ed. *The End of the Keynesian Era.* London: Macmillan Press, 1977.

————. *John Maynard Keynes: Fighting for Freedom.* New York: Viking, 2001.

————. *John Maynard Keynes: Hopes Betrayed.* New York: Viking Penguin, 1986.

————. *John Maynard Keynes: The Economist as Savior.* New York: Penguin Press, 1992.

————. *Keynes: The Return of the Master.* New York: Public Affairs, 2009.

Skousen, Mark. *The Big Three in Economics: Adam Smith, Karl Marx, and John Maynard Keynes.* Armonk, NY: M. E. Sharpe, 2007.

————. *Economic Logic.* Washington, DC: Capital Press, 2008.

————. *The Making of Modern Economics: The Lives and Ideas of the Great Thinkers.* Armonk, NY: M. E. Sharpe, 2001.

————. *The Structure of Production.* New York: New York University Press, 1990.

————. *Vienna and Chicago: Friends or Foes? A Tale of Two Schools of Free-Market Economics.* Washington, DC: Capital Press, 2005.

Smart, William. *An Introduction to the Theory of Value.* 1920. Reprint, New York: Augustus M. Kelley, 1966.

Smith, Adam. *An Inquiry into the Nature and Causes of the Wealth of Nations.* 1776. Reprint, New Rochelle, NY: Arlington House, 1966.

Smith, Barry. *Austrian Philosophy: The Legacy of Franz Brentano.* Chicago: Open Court, 1994.

Sorkin, Andrew Ross. *Too Big to Fail: The Inside Story of How Wall Street and Washington Fought to Save the Financial System—and Themselves.* New York: Penguin Group, 2009.

Soros, George. *The Crash of 2008 and What It Means: The New Paradigm for Financial Markets.* New York: Public Affairs, 2008.

Sowell, Thomas. *Basic Economics: A Common Sense Guide to the Economy.* 3rd ed. New York: Basic Books, 2007.

————. *Economic Facts and Fallacies.* New York: Basic Books, 2008.

————. *The Housing Boom and Bust.* New York: Basic Books, 2009.

Sprague, O. M. W. *History of Crisis under the National Banking System.* 1910. Reprint, Fairfield, NJ: Augustus M. Kelley, 1977.

Standen, Anthony. *Science Is a Sacred Cow.* New York: E. P. Dutton, 1950.

Stanlis, Peter J. *Edmund Burke and the Natural Law.* Ann Arbor: University of Michigan Press, 1958.

Stark, Rodney. *Discovering God: The Origins of the Great Religions and the Evolution of Belief.* New York: Harper One, 2007.

Stark, Rodney. *The Victory of Reason: How Christianity Led to Freedom, Capitalism, and Western Success.* New York: Random House, 2005.

Steele, David Ramsay. *From Marx to Mises: Post-Capitalist Society and the Challenge of Economic Calculation.* Lasalle, IL: Open Court, 1992.

Stevenson, David. *Cataclysm: The First World War as Political Tragedy.* New York: Basic Books, 2004.

Stigler, George J. *Essays in the History of Economics.* Chicago: University of Chicago Press, 1965.

Stockhammer, Morris. *Thomas Aquinas Dictionary.* New York: Philosophical Library, 1965.

Stone, Brad Lowell. *Robert Nisbet.* Wilmington, DE: ISI Books, 2000.

Story, Joseph. *A Familiar Exposition of the Constitution of the United States.* 1840. Reprint, Chicago: Regnery Gateway, 1986.

Strigl, Richard von. *Capital and Production.* Auburn, AL: Ludwig von Mises Institute, 2000.

Stump, Eleonore. *Aquinas.* New York: Routledge, 2003.

Taleb, Nassim Nicholas. *Fooled by Randomness: The Hidden Role of Chance in Life and in Markets.* New York: Random House, 2005.

Tamedly, Elisabeth L. *Socialism and International Economic Order.* 1969. Reprint, Auburn AL: Ludwig von Mises Institute, 2007.

Tansill, Charles Callan. *America Goes to War.* Boston: Little, Brown, 1938.

Taylor, A. E. *Aristotle.* New York: Dover, 1955.

Taylor, A. J. P. *Bismarck: The Man and the Statesman.* New York: Alfred A. Knopf, 1961.

————*From Sarajevo to Potsdam*. New York: Harcourt, Brace & World, 1966.

Taylor, Thomas. *An Introduction to Austrian Economics*. Auburn, AL: Ludwig von Mises Institute, 1988.

Temin, Peter. *Lessons from the Great Depression*. Cambridge, MA: MIT Press, 1999.

Tett, Gillian. *Fool's Gold: How the Bold Dream of a Small Tribe at J. P. Morgan Was Corrupted by Wall Street Greed and Unleashed a Catastrophe*. New York: Free Press, 2009.

Thatcher, Margaret. *The Downing Street Years*. New York: Harper Collins, 1993.

Tocqueville, Alexis de. *Democracy in America*. 1835–1840. Translated by Henry Reeve. New Rochelle, NY: Arlington House, 1966.

Triana, Pablo. *Lecturing Birds on Flying: Can Mathematical Theories Destroy Financial Markets?* Hoboken, NJ: John Wiley & Sons, 2009.

Van Creveld, Martin. *The Rise and Decline of the State*. Cambridge: Cambridge University Press, 1999.

Van Overtveldt, James. *The Chicago School: How the University of Chicago Assembled the Thinkers Who Revolutionized Economics and Business*. Chicago: Agate, 2007.

Veryser, Harry. *Our Economic Crisis: Sources and Solutions*. Ft. Lauderdale, FL: Coral Ridge Ministries, 1992.

Vilar, Pierre. *A History of Gold and Money, 1450–1920*. Translated by Judith White. London: Humanities Press, 1976.

Voegelin, Eric. *The New Science of Politics: An Introduction*. Chicago: University of Chicago Press, 1987.

————. *Plato and Aristotle*. Vol. 3 of *Order and History*. Baton Rouge: Louisiana State University Press, 1957.

Vogt, Joseph. *The Decline of Rome*. London: Weidenfeld & Nicolson, 1993.

Walton, Gary M., and Hugh Rockoff. *History of the American Economy*. 6th ed. San Diego: Harcourt Brace Jovanovich, 1990.

Wanniski, Jude. *The Way the World Works*. Morristown, NJ: Polyconomics, 1989.

Warsh, David. *Knowledge and the Wealth of Nations: A Story of Economic Discovery*. New York: W. W. Norton, 2006.

Weatherford, Jack. *The History of Money*. New York: Crown, 1997.

Webster, Nesta H. *The French Revolution: A Study in Democracy*. 1919. Reprint, Hawthorne, CA: Christian Book Club of America, 1969.

White, Andrew Dickson. *Fiat Money Inflation in France*. New York: D. Appleton–Century, 1933.

Wieser, Friedrich von. *Natural Value*. 1893. Reprint, Fairfield, NJ: Augustus M. Kelley, 1989.

————. *Social Economics*. Translated by A. Ford Hinrichs. 1927. Reprint, New York: Augustus M. Kelley, 1967.

Willett, Thomas D., ed. *Political Business Cycles: The Political Economy of Money, Inflation, and Unemployment*. Durham, NC: Duke University Press, 1988.

Woods, Thomas E., Jr. *The Church Confronts Modernity: Catholic Intellectuals and the Progressive Era*. New York: Columbia University Press, 2004.

Xenophon. *Conversations of Socrates*. New York: Penguin Classics, 1990.

Yergin, Daniel, and Joseph Stanislaw. *The Commanding Heights: The Battle for the World Economy*. New York: Touchstone, 1998.

Zimmerman, Carle C. *Family and Civilization*. Wilmington, DE: ISI Books, 2008.

Zmirak, John. *Wilhelm Röpke*. Wilmington, DE: ISI Books, 2001.

Acknowledgments

As the Austrian School teaches with its description of the division of labor, every substantial work is really a cooperative effort involving hundreds of people extending over time and place. Through the years, literally hundreds of students, teachers, friends, and family contributed to this book by helping me hone the ideas and information presented here.

I have been privileged to know many of the figures referenced in this book. I am fortunate to have spent many hours with Russell Kirk, Peter Stanlis, Thomas Molnar, Leonard Read, Eric Voegelin, Roger Freeman, Gerhart Niemeyer, and Mark Skousen, and I was able to attend lectures by Ludwig von Mises, F. A. Hayek, Murray Rothbard, Milton Friedman, Erik von Kuehnelt-Leddihn, Stanley Jaki, Edmund Opitz, and Ben Rogge, among others. They have all been wonderful teachers.

I also want to thank my classroom instructors. My seventh-grade teacher at St. Veronica's School, Ed Schnaubelt, provided an understanding of the U.S. Constitution that has stayed with me for a lifetime. He was an outstanding teacher who showed a great love for his students. In so many ways, he was the beginning of this work. Ted Kopacki, who taught American history at De La Salle Collegiate High School, first ignited my interest in the events of the twentieth century and opened my mind to the importance of history. Professor Racz and Mrs. Gasprovich taught me from their direct experience much about the nature of communism and totalitarianism. And Dr. H. Theodore Hoffman, my mentor and longtime friend, introduced me to the Austrian School—and provided a wonderful example of what it means to be a gentleman.

In addition, I would like to thank my students and fellow faculty at St. Mary's High School, Star of the Sea High School, Northwood University, Hillsdale College, Walsh College of Accountancy and Business Administration, the University of Detroit Mercy, Ave Maria College, and Thomas More College of Liberal Arts for the hours of discussion that contributed to my education. All have helped bring this book into a sharper focus. In particular, I owe a debt to the late Stanislaw Budzinowski; Leonard Maliet; Desire Barath; Norbert Gossman; Hugh P. O'Neill, SJ; and Arthur McGovern, SJ, as well as current colleagues at the University of Detroit Mercy, especially Raphael Shen, SJ; Victoria Mantzopoulos; Roy Finkenbine; Charles Marske; and Donald Byrne, who has been my mentor for many years.

Many others deserve recognition as well:

Jay McNally provided invaluable advice as I wrote this book. He spent many hours reviewing the text, and as a veteran journalist he gave excellent suggestions for making complicated economic ideas understandable to the general public.

Young scholars David Betts, Deanna Kray, Jana Duggan, and Matthew Simpson did painstaking work in checking the endnotes in the manuscript.

Henry Saad of the Michigan Court of Appeals advised me on the fine points of the rule of law, while attorneys Albert Addis, Ralph Valitutti, Armand Velardo, and Daniel Wright II provided their expertise on various matters related to the law.

Gregory Todd of Walsh College alerted me to new works that proved helpful in my research. We also had many hours of discussion about the topics covered in the book, particularly the history.

Michael Curry, director of communications for Northwood University, made important stylistic suggestions and brought to my attention details that helped make the presentation more complete.

Jeffrey Nelson of the Intercollegiate Studies Institute (ISI) initially suggested that I write this book and graciously helped with the outline. His insights into the thinking of Edmund Burke also proved valuable.

Jamie Muter of Muter and Associates and Craig Fuller of Fuller Appraisal helped explain how Austrian marginal analysis applies to actual market conditions, and they also helped with statistical research.

Anthony Stokes, a former student in my MBA economics courses at the University of Detroit Mercy, made me aware of many of the problems investors face in the Detroit real estate market.

Steven Carpenter of Oakland Community College enthusiastically supported the writing of this book over the past five years.

Elizabeth Richards of Annandale, Virginia, offered brilliant insight into the nature and history of inflation from Roman times until today.

Paul Cwik of Mount Olive College helped put together the chapter on the Austrian trade cycle theory.

Greg Kaza of the Arkansas Policy Foundation has done important work on the Austrian School's influence through the twentieth century.

The Reverend Paul Ward provided many insights about the importance of Scholastic philosophy.

Annette Kirk, widow of Russell Kirk, now head of the Russell Kirk Center for Cultural Renewal, was very generous in allowing use of the Kirk library and offered helpful insights into Dr. Kirk's thinking.

Matthew Fisher of Rochester College and Northwood University provided valuable research and helped me refine the presentation of various Austrian ideas.

Joseph Weglarz, my colleague at the University of Detroit Mercy, was a source of constant encouragement. He generously lent me books from his private library, and his deep knowledge of the history of economic thought contributed substantially to the chapters on the development of economics.

Joshua Long of Ivy Tech Community College helped me with his insights on Federal Reserve monetary policy.

Forrest Nabors of the University of Alaska was enlightening in our discussions of the nature of the American Founding.

George J. Gardner of Walsh College was a wonderful resource on the history of the twentieth century.

Jane Ingraham and her daughter Laurie offered incisive insights into the operations of central banking.

Andrew Ball, for many years my capable assistant, provided me with a good deal of research and stylistic suggestions. He is now finishing his PhD in philosophy at the University of Alberta.

Austin Everett and Brother Jernej Sustar spent a good deal of time vetting chapters.

Jed Donahue of ISI Books patiently edited my work and gave me tremendous encouragement over the past three years. Without his editorial suggestions, this book would not have come into existence. He is an editorial genius.

Anthony Sacramone, managing editor of ISI Books, carefully copyedited the book and skillfully guided it to completion.

David Breuhan of Schwartz and Company, for many years my colleague at Walsh College, constantly brought me up to date on changing market conditions, offered insights into the steel tariff, and helped explain the role of interest groups in affecting public policy.

Joseph Salerno of Pace University provided crucial insights into the thought of Ludwig von Mises.

Thomas Lightbody introduced me to *The Freeman,* and Allen Clink first gave me *The Road to Serfdom.*

Robert E. Delaney of Baker College helped over the years with many suggestions on the presentation of economic ideas.

My wonderful brothers and sisters, Don, Paul, Ann, Betty, and Janet, and their spouses, Debra, Paul, Becky, Joe, and Mike, supported my work and provided encouragement all along the way.

My good friends Hubert and Dolores Bohle provided constant support and encouragement.

Others deserving thanks for their help and encouragement include Becky Riesterer, the librarian at Walsh College; Louis Palombit, my research assistant; Allan Mendell; Gregory Everett; Ed Weick; Joseph Drolshagen; Joseph Ficht; Gary Mallast; Joseph Katz; Don Freeze; Brian Addis; Glenn Clark; and my wonderful secretary, Donna Gormely, who helped in so many ways.

Finally, I would like to thank the following institutions for assisting my research: the Acton Institute, the Foundation for Economic Education, the Heritage Foundation (which stood ever ready as a source for statistics about the economy), Liberty Fund, the Ludwig von Mises Institute, the Russell Kirk Center for Cultural Renewal, and the University of Detroit Mercy Library.

Index

Acting Person, The (Wojtyla), 143
adjustable-rate mortgages, 25
age of classical liberalism: absence of
inflation during, 81–82; free trade
and international peace, 70–71; historical foundations, 63–64, 65; *La
Belle Époque,* 71; record of achievement, 63, 70; rise of the social
welfare state, 72–74; trade cycles
during, 70; underlying principles,
64, 65–70; World War I and the end
of, 74–78
Age of Inflation, 81
Ahamed, Liaquat, 238, 239
airline industry deregulation, 127
Aliber, Robert, 96, 246–47
Allen, Frederick Lewis, 92
Allen, Michael, 96
American Founders/Founding: age of
classical liberalism and, 65; free
trade and, 68; limited taxation and,
66; principle of subsidiarity and,
184; specie standard and, 69
America's Great Depression (Rothbard),
55–56, 91, 101, 219, 220
"anarcho-capitalism," 56
Anderson, Benjamin, 76, 94, 95–96, 177

Aquinas, Thomas: on the common
good, 189; on the family, 179;
on property rights, 168–69; on
prudence, 200–202; on purpose,
192; on reason, 202; on the rule of
law, 175; the School of Salamanca
and, 43
arbitrage, 161–62
Aristotle: on the categories of science,
12; on economics and science,
15–16; on the family, 179; on leisure
and work, 182; on property, 166,
169; on prudential judgment, 200;
on purpose in human action, 46
Asian banks, 30
assembly lines, 150
auctions, 40–41
Austrian School: approach to economic downturns, 249–52; the
Austrian multiplier, 249, 250–52;
on bank credit, 89; Böhm-Bawerk
and, 40–42; classical philosophy and, 199; commonalities
with Keynesians regarding the
trade cycle, 59; differences with
monetarism, 123; distinguishing
characteristics of, 35–36;

Austrian School (*cont.*)
  on the division of labor, 36, 148,
    155–57 (*see also* division of labor);
    economics conceived as a science
    of human action, 11, 16–19, 20, 36,
    46; emphasis on individual human
    action, 191 (*see also* human action);
    emphasis on the family, 179; Fet-
    ter and, 50–51; Hayek and, 48–50;
    Hazlitt and, 47–48; Hutt and, 51–52;
    importance of freely moving prices
    to, 177; importance of historical
    study to, 197–98; importance of
    savings to, 51, 181; on inflation, 88;
    Keynes-Hayek debate on the role of
    government intervention, 4–5, 101–
    2, 257–58; Carl Menger and, 37–40;
    Ludwig von Mises and, 44–46;
    modern popularizers, 56–57; prax-
    eology, 46, 191–92; predictions of
    the collapse of planned economies,
    59, 141–42, 143–44; prescience and
    effectiveness of, 5, 58–60, 253–55,
    258, 259; on production, 155–56; on
    property rights and liberty, 167–68;
    on rational self-interest, 187–88;
    recent contributors to, 57–58; Röpke
    and, 52–55; Rothbard and, 55–56;
    scarcity and, 195; Schumpeter and,
    43–44; spontaneous order concept,
    156–57; Strigl and, 55; theory of
    capital, 162–63; theory of interest
    as a time preference, 41, 138, 173;
    theory of the entrepreneur, 161–62,
    178; theory of the trade cycle, 225–
    26 (*see also* trade cycle); warnings of
    the housing bubble crisis of 2007–8,
    30–31, 59–60; Wieser and, 42–43
automotive industry: bankruptcies, 177;
    "Cash for Clunkers" program, 248,
    250; cyclical change and, 161; Ford
    Motor Company and the division
    of labor, 149–50; impact of the steel

tariffs of 2002, 211; merger mania
    in, 240; protectionism in the 1980s
    and, 140; structural change and, 159

Baker, James, 140
Banfield, Edward, 194
bank credit: expansion (*see* credit
    expansion); inflation following
    World War I and, 81; manipulation
    by central banks, 82; relationship to
    booms and bubbles, 89
bank credit inflation: in the 1920s,
    91–96; in the 1980s, 140; analysis
    and examples of, 88–91, 218–21;
    defined, 214; impact on interna-
    tional financial systems, 89
Banking and the Business Cycle (Phil-
    lips, McManus, and Nelson),
    83–84, 230, 234
Banking School, 70
banking system: impact of central
    banks on, 90; modern premise of,
    89–90
Bank of England, 218
bank portfolios, 222
bank reserve requirement, 83–84
banks: borrowing short and lending
    long, 239–40; credit contraction in
    economic downturns, 252; defla-
    tion and, 222; failures in the Great
    Depression, 239–40; in Hayek's
    analysis of the trade cycle, 48–49;
    in Mises's analysis of the trade
    cycle, 45; risky credit, 241; at the
    turning point in the trade cycle,
    244. *See also* central banks
Barone, Michael, 160
Barry, John, 76
Bastiat, Frédéric, 67–68, 106
Bear Stearns, 240
Bell, John Fred, 59
Belle Époque, La, 71
Belloc, Hilaire, 170

Benedict XV (pope), 75–76

Bernanke, Benjamin, 31, 124, 239, 253, 254

Bill of Rights, 184

Bismarck, Otto von, 72–73

Böhm-Bawerk, Eugen von: analysis of the division of labor, 163; economic insights of, 40–42; Mises and, 45; on roundabout production, 155–56; theory of capital, 162–63; theory of interest as a time preference, 41, 138, 173

Bolsheviks, 88

bonds, 219

boom-and-bust cycle. *See* trade cycle

booms: disequilibrium in, 229–34; end of, 243–45; inflationary psychology and euphoria, 234–36; lowering of interest rates at the beginning of, 226–29; malinvestments and misinvestments, 236–42. *See also* trade cycle

borrowing short and lending long, 239–40

bottom-up organizations, 157

"bracket creep," 121, 136

Brent, Paul, 245

Brentano, Franz, 143

Bresciani-Turroni, Costantino, 86–87, 207, 213

Bretton Woods agreements: achievements of, 221; criticisms and collapse of, 111–14; European economic revival and, 108–10; Hazlitt's critique of, 47, 111; inflation following the collapse of, 220–21; Nixon's scrapping of, 114, 116; overview of, 106–7; purpose of, 105; Rueff's critique of, 111–12; scholars on the achievements of, 107–8

Breuhan, David, 211

Buchanan, James, 132

builders: inventory loans and, 241

Buridan, Jean, 193

Burke, Edmund, 19, 202–3

Burner, Robert, 241

Bush, George W.: on the housing bubble crisis of 2007–8, 24; use of government spending as a fiscal stimulus, 247–48

business: burden of regulatory costs, 248–49; cost cutting in a downturn, 249–50; general effects of an economic downturn on, 252–53

business cycle: housing bubble crisis of 2007–8 and, 21; Keynes's positions on, 225; Mises's concept of, 45. *See also* trade cycle

business mergers, 240

busts: Austrian response to, 249–52; beginning of a recession, 246–47; credit contraction, 252; deflation, 253; the destruction of savings and capital, 252–53; Keynesian response to, 247–49; signs of, 245–46; the turning point in trade cycles, 243–45. *See also* trade cycle

"butterfly effect," 79–80

Byrne, Donald, 172

California government, 237–38

California Public Employees' Retirement System (CalPERS), 239

Cannon, Lou, 136

Cantillon effect, 88

Cantillon, Richard, 88

capital: Austrian theory of, 162–63; destruction of during economic downturns, 252–53; savings and capital formation, 181; Strigl's analysis of, 55

capital goods: boom of the 1920s, 96; increase in demand with artificially lowered interest rates, 229; interest rates and the value of capital goods, 50–51; Menger's concept of, 39;

capital goods (*cont.*)
  prices during the trade cycle, 233;
  in roundabout production, 41
capital goods industry: beginning of
  the boom-bust cycle in, 229
capital investment, 163
capitalism: Böhm-Bawerk's defense of,
  42
Capitalism and Freedom (Friedman), 123
capital structure: Hayek's analysis of, 49
capital theory, 39, 41
Carr, Sean, 241
cartel effect, 52
Carter, Jimmy, 126–28
cash crunch, 245
"Cash for Clunkers" program, 248, 250
caution, 202
central banks: during the age of classical liberalism, 82; bank credit
  inflation and, 90–91, 218–19; credit
  expansion at the beginning of the
  trade cycle, 226–27, 229; currency
  stabilization in the Bretton Woods
  system and, 107; in Hayek's analysis
  of the trade cycle, 48–49; impact
  on the modern banking system,
  90; inflation and, 81, 83–84, 90;
  involvement in the government
  budgetary process during World
  War I, 82; methods of injecting
  funds into the economic system,
  227; in Mises's analysis of the trade
  cycle, 45; quantitative easing of the
  money supply, 133; role in bubbles
  and busts, 224; at the turning point
  in the trade cycle, 244; validation
  process, 126. *See also* U.S. Federal
  Reserve
Central Intelligence Agency (CIA), 141
central planning. *See* planned
  economies
Chamberlain, John, 170–71, 176
chaos theory, 79–80

charity: private property and, 169
China: current financial relationship
  with the U.S., 112; population and
  economic expansion, 154
Christmas truce, 75–76
Chrysler bankruptcy, 177
church property: government seizure
  of, 170–71
circumspection, 202
Cities and the Wealth of Nations
  (Jacobs), 110
classical liberalism, 64, 65–70. *See also*
  age of classical liberalism
Clinton, Bill, 137–38, 243
commodity: in Menger's concept of
  economizing, 38; in Menger's concept of money, 39
common good, 186–89
communism: Austrian School's predictions of collapse, 59, 141–42,
  143–44; collapse of, 142–43; conditions after the collapse of, 165–66.
  See also planned economies
Community Reinvestment Act, 24
Congress of Vienna, 77
consol, 138
consumer goods: boom during the
  trade cycle, 242; Menger's concept
  of, 39; prices during the trade cycle,
  233; in roundabout production, 41
consumer spending: Keynesian stimulation of, 247–48
Continental Congress, 69
contracts, 66, 176–77
conventional changes, 158
Coolidge, Calvin, 243
cooperation, 147–48
Corn Laws, 68
corn production, 151–52
cost cutting, 249–50
cost-of-living adjustments (COLAs), 121
cost/price relationship: disequilibrium
  in, 233–34

cost-push inflation, 127
Cowen, Tyler, 30–31
Crain, Nicole V. and W. Mark, 248–49
Crash Proof (Schiff), 59–60
"creative destruction," 43
credit: consumer goods boom and spending on credit, 242; contraction of, 252; Mises's trade cycle theory and, 45; overexpansion as a cause of deflation, 222; risky, 241. *See also* bank credit; credit expansion
Credit Anstalt, 239
credit contraction, 252
credit expansion: deflation and, 222; malinvestments and misinvestments as a consequence of, 236–37; role in the Great Depression, 254; trade cycles and, 223–24; unemployment during the Great Depression and, 234; during World War I, 83
credit inflation, 206. *See also* bank credit inflation
criminal activity, 193–94
Crises and Cycles (Röpke), 54
Croesus, 205
Crowley, Roger, 217
Cuomo, Andrew, 25
currencies: classical liberalism and metallic-based currency, 65, 68–70; debasement and inflation, 205–6, 214–15; fiduciary currency, 218; Hayek's proposal for separating from the political process, 119; importance of a sound currency to prosperity, 171–74; key characteristics of a sound currency, 172–74; need for independence from federal policy, 174; problems with the flexible exchange-rate system, 124–25; stability during the age of classical liberalism, 81–82; value set by central banks, 82. *See also* currency stabilization

Currency School, 70
currency stabilization: instituted by the Bretton Woods agreements, 106–7; U.S. refusal to participate in, 99–100
cyclical economic change, 160–61

Dawson, Christopher, 66, 77
"death tax," 179–81
debasement, 205–6, 214–15, 217
debt monetization, 111, 113
Debts and Deficits (Sennholz), 136
Declaration of Independence, 65
deflation, 174, 221–23, 253
de Gaulle, Charles, 112
demand: elasticity of, 210–11
depression: of 1920–21, 251, 254–55. *See also* Great Depression
deregulation, 127
desirability: human action and, 193–95
Detroit, 169–70
Dietze, Gottfried, 66
Diocletian, 214–15
discounting, 50–51
discretionary expenditures, 28
disequilibrium: in the cost/price relationship, 233–34; between investment and savings, 231–33; between natural and market interest rates, 230–31; in the trade cycle, 229–30
Disraeli, Benjamin, 171
distribution of wealth: the division of labor and, 150–51; in the U.S. in 1929, 220
division of labor: the Austrian School on, 36, 148, 155–57; Böhm-Bawerk's analysis of, 163; cyclical change and, 160–61; distribution of wealth and, 150–51; the economy and, 163–64; Ford Motor Company example, 149–50; four factors of production, 161–63; frictional change and, 158–59;

division of labor (*cont.*)
    importance of the family to,
    179; influence of knowledge and
    technology on, 152–53; Menger's
    analysis of, 40; population and,
    153–54; principle of cooperation,
    147–48; seasonal change and, 158;
    Adam Smith's concept of, 149–52;
    structural change and, 159–60
docility, 201
Domitrovic, Brian, 108, 116, 118, 133,
    135
dot-com bubble, 23, 96, 235, 243
Dow Jones Industrial Average, 21–22,
    95, 238
dualism: methodological, 17, 46

Economic Consequences of the Peace,
    The (Keynes), 78
economic crises: depression of 1920–21,
    251, 254–55; in mortgage lending,
    24–25, 96; Panic of 1907, 241; sup-
    ply-side economics on the causes
    of, 133. *See also* Great Depression;
    housing bubble crisis of 2007–8;
    monetary crisis of 1971
economic freedom: classical liberalism
    and, 65, 67; the School of Sala-
    manca and, 44
Economic Harmonies (Bastiat), 67–68
economic modeling: as a factor in the
    housing bubble crisis of 2007–8,
    25–26; Stiglitz on, 26–27. *See also*
    mathematical economics
Economic Recovery and Tax Act of
    1981, 135–36
economics: commonalities among
    schools of, 58–59; conceived as a
    hard science, 10–15; conceived as
    a science of human action, 4, 11,
    15–20, 36, 46; current levels of
    government-economy codepen-
    dency, 185–86; cyclical economic

change, 160–61; division of labor
    and, 163–64 (*see also* division of
    labor); failures of the modern
    approach to, 17–18; frictional
    economic change, 158–59; human
    judgment of the good and, 199–203;
    importance and influence of ideas
    in, 33–34; influence on government,
    4; Keynes-Hayek debate on the role
    of government intervention, 4–5,
    101–2, 257–58; meaning of term, 16;
    proximate and ultimate goods, 194;
    rule of law and, 174–76; scarcity
    and, 195; seasonal economic change,
    158; structural economic change,
    159–60; value of questioned, 9–11
Economics in One Lesson (Hazlitt), 194
Economics of Inflation, The (Bresciani-
    Turroni), 207
Economic Way of Thinking, The
    (Heyne), 167
economizing, 38
effective tax rates, 85
elasticity of demand, 210–11
elastic products, 211
eminent domain laws, 175–76
England: currency debasement under
    the Tudors, 215; protections against
    the seizure of property, 170–71
entitlement programs, 27–29, 112–13,
    136
entrepreneurs/entrepreneurship:
    importance to prosperity, 178;
    Kirzner's theory of, 161–62
Erhard, Ludwig, 33, 54–55, 108–9
Erie Canal, 159–60
estate taxes, 179–81
Estrella, Arturo, 244
ethanol industry, 151–52
euphoria, 234–36
euro, 45
European Union, 29
exchange rates: flexible, 122–25

Fabian Society, 74
factor prices: at the beginning of a
  downturn, 245
family: division of labor and, 179;
  importance to prosperity, 179;
  threats from estate taxes, 179–81
Fannie Mae, 24
federal budget: mandatory and discretionary expenditures, 27–29. *See
  also* government debt
federal funds target rate, 23–24
Federal Housing Authority, 24
Federal Open Market Committee
  (FOMC), 224
Federal Reserve. *See* U.S. Federal
  Reserve
Federal Reserve Act, 84
Fetter, Frank A., 50–51
fiat inflation: analysis and examples
  of, 85–88, 217–18; defined, 82–83,
  213–14
fiat money: problem of public confidence, 125; U.S. progression to, 120
fiduciary currency, 218
financial engineering, 5, 10
financial institutions. *See* banks
first-order goods, 39, 155, 156
fiscal stimulus, 247–49
fixed assets: impact of inflation on, 213
flexible exchange rates, 122–25, 139
"flippers," 24
Florida land booms, 91–93
Ford, Henry, 150
Ford Motor Company, 149–50
Fordney-McCumber Tariff, 93, 97
foreign bond bubble, 93–95, 99
foreign exchange markets, 30
foreign investment: as an opening for
  credit expansion, 227–28
foreign markets: impact of inflation
  on, 211
foreign trade. *See* international free
  trade

foresight, 202
Foundation for Economic Education,
  57
fractional-reserve banking system,
  48–49
France: consequences of inflation
  accompanying the French Revolution, 212, 213; modern liberalism
  and the French Revolution, 64–65;
  Napoleon's reinstatement of a gold
  standard, 128; postwar economic
  recovery, 109
Freddie Mac, 24
free-market concept: the Austrian
  School and, 36; historical importance of, 33
free-market economy: the common
  good and, 187; conditions fostering
  prosperity (*see* prosperity); effect
  of cultural conditions on, 165–66;
  the importance of private property
  to, 166–71; resource allocation
  and, 157; spontaneous order and,
  156–57, 165
Free to Choose (PBS television series), 57
free trade. *See* international free trade
French Revolution, 64–65, 212, 213
frictional economic change, 158–59
frictional unemployment, 158
Friedman, Milton, 13–14, 57, 123–24,
  222
Full Employment Act of 1946, 23
future goods, 41

G5 nations, 140
Galbraith, John Kenneth, 92, 239
Garrison, Roger, 58
General Agreement on Trade and Tar-
  iffs (GATT), 106
General Motors bankruptcy, 177
*General Theory of Employment, Interest,
  and Money, The* (Keynes), 51, 101
German Historical School, 73

Germany: changes away from classical liberalism under Bismarck, 72–74; consequences of post–World War I inflation, 213; consequences of the Treaty of Versailles, 77–78; fiat inflation following World War I, 86–88; free-market concept and, 33; inflation during World War I, 85; post–World War II economic revival, 54–55, 108–9; reinstatement of a gold standard to halt inflation, 128; subsidization of Greece in 2010, 111; territorial expansion as an alternative to foreign trade, 105–6

Godek, Paul, 186

"gold commission," 137

gold standard: the Bretton Woods agreements, 107, 111–12, 113–14; classical liberalism and, 68–70; contemporary calls for the reestablishment of, 259; effect on inflationary expectations and interest rates, 138; Friedman's criticism of, 123; Reagan's failure to achieve, 137, 138–39, 259; reinstating to halt inflation, 128; stability of currencies during the age of classical liberalism and, 81–82

"good, the": human judgment of, 198–203

goods: proximate and ultimate, 194. *See also* capital goods; consumer goods

Gore, Thomas P., 215

government: eminent domain laws and, 175–76; influence of economic theory on, 4; malinvestments and misinvestments in the trade cycle, 237–38; in Menger's concept of money, 39; operation of currency should be independent of, 174; protections against the seizure of property, 170–71; rule of law and, 175–76

government debt: the housing bubble crisis of 2007–8 and, 27–29

government deficit: of 2004, 31; increase under Reagan, 136–37

government intervention: in the age of classical liberalism, 67; the Austrian School's skepticism of, 36; current levels of government-economy codependency and, 185–86; failure to lower unemployment during the Great Depression, 102–3; during and following World War I, 100–101; Hazlitt's critique of, 47–48; Keynes-Hayek debate on the role of, 4–5, 101–2, 257–58; as a legacy of World War I, 80–81; Mises's critique of, 46; Rothbard's writings on, 55–56; unequal impact of, 151–52

government regulation: costs to business, 248–49, 251

government revenue: relationship of taxation to, 134–35

government spending: cutting in an Austrian approach to economic downturns, 250–51; discretionary expenditures, 28; on entitlement programs, 27–29, 112–13, 136; as a fiscal stimulus, 247–48

Great Britain: economic growth during the age of classical liberalism, 66, 68; free trade and, 68; impact of World War I on, 76; limited taxation and, 66; post–World War II economic strategies, 110; rise of socialism in, 74; rule of law and respect for contracts, 66; trade cycles and, 70; yield on the consol under a gold standard, 138

Great Crash, The (Galbraith), 92

Great Depression: deflation and, 222, 253; disequilibrium in the cost/price relationship and, 233–34;

Friedman and Schwartz's analysis of, 123–24; protectionism as a contributing factor, 98; role of bank credit inflation in, 219–20; role of bank failures in, 239–40; role of credit expansion in, 254; role of stock market misinvestments in, 238; Rothbard's analysis of, 55–56; Smoot-Hawley Tariff and, 154; swindlers in, 239; unemployment during, 102–3

Great Society, 28

Greece, 29, 111

Greenspan, Alan, 25, 178, 224, 228, 235

Gresham's Law, 214

Harding, Warren, 251

harmony-of-interests doctrine, 67–68

Hauser, W. Kurt, 185–86

Hayek, Friedrich August: arguments against increased government intervention, 101–2; on Bismarck's welfare state in Germany, 73–74; criticism of planned economies, 142, 143; on the disequilibrium between investment and savings, 232, 233; on economic conditions in the 1970s, 34, 118–19; economic contributions of, 48–50; on economics conceived as a hard science, 10–11; on the end of booms, 243–44; on the flaws of socialism and planned societies, 156, 184; on the importance of contracts, 176; on the importance of rule of law, 175; Keynes-Hayek debate on the role of government intervention, 4–5, 101–2, 257–58; on laws and the common good, 187; notion of population and productivity, 54; on the prices of capital goods in the trade cycle, 233; on property rights and liberty, 167–68; review

of Keynes's *Treatise on Money*, 257; on separating currency from the political process, 119; suggested repeal of legal tender laws, 218; on the value of local institutions and decentralization, 183–84; view of the inflation-unemployment relationship, 119; warning of the 1929 crash, 255

Hayes, Carlton J. H., 64–65

Hayward, Steven, 137

Hazlitt, Henry, 47–48, 194

Heilbroner, Robert, 141–42

Helms, Jesse, 137

Henry VIII (king of England), 215

Henry VII (king of England), 215

Heyne, Paul, 167

Higgs, Robert, 100

higher-order goods, 39, 155, 156

Hildebrand, Dietrich von, 56

history: human action and, 197–98; prudential judgment and, 201

History of Economic Thought, A (Bell), 59

History of Money (Weathersford), 216

Hitler, Adolf, 86

Hoffer, Eric, 182–83

Hoffman, H. Theodore, 3

home equity loans, 242

Hoover, Herbert, 55–56, 97, 98, 101

household debt, 31

"Housing: Too Good to Be True" (Thornton), 60

housing and construction booms, 96

housing bubble crisis of 2007–8: the breakdown of economic modeling as a factor in, 25–27; consequences of, 2; creation of false prosperity as a factor in, 22–25; deflation during, 253; disequilibrium during, 229–30; failure of Bear Stearns and Lehman Brothers, 22, 240; fears of inflation following, 172;

housing bubble crisis of 2007–8 (*cont.*)
government debt as a factor in,
27–29; government intervention as
a cause of, 46; historical perspective on, 3; home equity loans and,
242; overview of factors causing,
21–22; role of bank credit inflation
in, 89; role of deflation in, 222–23;
role of euphoria in, 234–35; role of
false prosperity in, 22–25; role of
leverage in, 236; role of risky credit
in, 241; role of the Federal Reserve
in, 224; unheeded warning signs of,
29–31, 59–60
Hull, Cordell, 99, 106
human action: Austrian School's focus
on, 191; corollaries of, 196–98; desirability and, 193–95; economics conceived as the science of, 4, 11, 15–20,
36, 46; judgment of "the good,"
198–203; means to achieve the goal,
195–96; praxeology, 46, 191–92;
purpose and, 192–93; scarcity and,
195, 198; the School of Salamanca
and, 44; Schumpeter's emphasis on,
43, 44; three axioms of, 192
Human Action (Mises), 195–96
Humane Economy, A (Röpke), 207–8
human rights: private property and,
169–70
Husserl, Edmund, 143
Hutt, William H., 51–52
hyperinflation, 86–88

"I, Pencil" (Read), 57, 156–57
imputation, 39, 42
income: impact of 1970s inflation on,
121–22
income tax: "bracket creep," 121, 136;
supply-siders on, 133
individual rights: the "death tax" as an
infringement of, 180–81; during *La
Belle Époque*, 71

inflation: absence during the age of
classical liberalism, 81–82; Carter's
anti-inflation policies, 126–28;
causes of, 45; consequences of,
171–72, 210–13; cost-push inflation, 127; currency debasement and,
205–6, 214–15; decline under Reagan's economic recovery program,
136; description of the dynamics
in, 208–10; fears of following the
housing bubble crisis of 2007–8,
172; fiat inflation, 82–83, 85–88,
213–14, 217–18; following World
War I, 82–83, 85–96; general pattern
of, 206; Hayek on inflation in the
1970s, 34; historical repetition of the
inflationary pattern, 208; increase in
since the 1980s, 137, 138; Keynesian
economics on, 209; as a legacy of
World War I, 80; Mises on, 207, 208,
209; from the Nixon Shock, 116,
117–18, 121–22; points of injection
concept and, 88–89; problem of
inflationary expectations, 125–26;
reinstating a gold standard to halt,
128; relationship to unemployment
(*see* inflation-unemployment relationship); Röpke on, 207–8; specie
inflation, 216–17; transfer of wealth
and, 172–73, 213; types of, 213–21;
during World War I, 82, 83–85. *See
also* bank credit inflation
inflationary expectations, 125–26, 138,
209–10
inflationary psychology, 234–36
inflation-unemployment relationship:
Hayek's view of, 119; Keynesian
view of, 118; "misery index" of the
1970s, 118; the Phillips curve and,
22; in stagflation, 22–23
*Inquiry into the Nature and Causes of
the Wealth of Nations, An* (Smith),
149, 150, 151, 152, 187

insight, 201

insurance policies, 166

interest: as time preference, 41, 138, 173

"interest income," 41

interest rates: as indicator of a currency's soundness, 174; disequilibrium between natural and market rates, 230–31; effect of gold standard on, 138; as factor in the housing bubble crisis of 2007–8, 22–25; the Federal Reserve's mandate to manipulate, 22–23; in Hayek's analysis of capital structure, 49; lowering rates begins trade cycle, 226–29; natural rate of, 228–29; relationship to inflationary expectations, 138; under a sound currency, 173–74; at the turning point in trade cycle, 244; the value of capital goods and, 50–51

international financial systems, 89

international free trade: classical liberalism and, 65, 67–68; collapse following World War I, 80, 97–100; international peace and, 70–71; stabilization by the Bretton Woods agreements, 106; U.S. torpedoing of the London Conference, 99–100

international gold standard, 69

International Monetary Fund (IMF), 106–7

international reserve currency, 107, 111–14

inventory loans, 241

investment: disequilibrium between investment and savings, 231–33; in the stagflation era, 122

investors: natural rate of interest and, 228

Italy, 85

Jacobs, Jane, 19–20, 110

Japan: deflation of the 1990s, 174; post–World War II economic "miracle,"

110; territorial expansion as an alternative to foreign trade, 105–6

Jefferson, Thomas, 65

Jevons, William Stanley, 37–38

John Paul II (pope), 143

Johnson, Lyndon B., 28

Johnson, Paul, 82, 87, 109, 110

John XXIII (pope), 168

Kadlec, Charles, 139

Kahn, Alfred E., 127

Karl Marx and the Close of His System (Böhm-Bawerk), 42

Kelo v. City of New London, 175–76

Kennedy, John F., 248

Kennedy, Paul, 218

Keynes, John Maynard: at the Bretton Woods Conference, 107; on the disequilibrium between investment and savings, 232–33; on the end of booms, 244; on federal government manipulation of the money supply, 23; on inflation, 209; on the influence of economic ideas, 34; Keynes-Hayek debate on the role of government intervention, 4–5, 101–2, 257–58; on *La Belle Époque*, 71; positions on the business cycle, 225; on the possible effects of credit expansion, 59; on Say's Law of supply and demand, 51–52; skepticism about the use of mathematics in economics, 20, 35–36; support for Roosevelt's policy of national currency management, 100; on the Treaty of Versailles, 78

Keynes: The Return of the Master (Skidelsky), 107

Keynesian economics: American challenges to, 131–32; approach to economic downturns, 247–49; commonalities with the Austrian School regarding the trade cycle, 59;

Keynesian economics (*cont.*)
contemporary resurgence in, 258; economics conceived as a hard science, 19–20; failures of, 102–3, 258–59; Hazlitt's critique of, 48; Hutt's critique of, 51–52; on inflation, 209; influence of, 102, 103; Keynes-Hayek debate on the role of government intervention, 4–5, 101–2, 257–58; Nixon's devaluation of the dollar and, 118; opposition of supply-side economics to, 133; stagflation and, 118; substantial use of mathematics in, 36; view of the inflation-unemployment relationship, 118
Keynesianism—Retrospect and Prospect (Hutt), 52
Kindleberger, Charles, 95, 96, 246–47
Kirk, Russell, 148, 194
Kirzner, Israel, 57–58, 161–62, 188
Kissinger, Henry, 117
knowledge: Hayek's concept of economic knowledge, 49; human action and, 196–97; Mises on, 203; technology and, 152–53

labor theory of value, 42
Laffer, Arthur, 117–18, 132, 134
Laffer Curve, 134
laissez-faire, 67
land booms, 91–93
Lawrence, Andrew, 232
Lazear, Edward, 247
Lecturing Birds on Flying (Triana), 199
Lehman Brothers, 22, 240
leisure, 181–83
Lenin, Vladimir, 88
Leo XIII (pope), 170
leverage, 235–36, 246
Leys, Leonard de, 43
liberalism, 64
liberal Keynesians, 247–48

libertarianism, 57
liberty: property rights and, 167–68
limited taxation: classical liberalism and, 65, 66
loans: borrowing short and lending long, 239–40; deflation and, 222–23; on inventory, 241; risky credit, 241
local institutions, 183–84
London Conference of 1933, 99–100, 105–6
longitudinal processes, 156
Long-Term Capital Management, 17–18
Lords of Finance (Ahamed), 238
Lorenz, Edward, 79
Lucas, Robert E., 131–32
Ludwig von Mises Institute, 57, 60
Lukacs, John, 69

macroeconomics: focus of, 155; Röpke's criticism of, 16; use of mathematics in the teaching of, 36; value of questioned, 9–11
Madoff, Bernard, 239
Magna Carta, 170–71
malinvestments and misinvestments: in skyscrapers, 232; in the trade cycle, 226, 236–37; types of, 237–42
Malthus, Thomas, 153
mandatory expenditures, 27–29, 112–13
Manias, Panics, and Crashes (Kindleberger and Aliber), 246–47
marginal utility, 37–38, 198
Mariana, Juan de, 43
market interest rate, 230–31
market liquidity, 39
market power, 210–11
markets: inflationary expectations and, 209–10
Marshall, Alfred, 19
Marshall, John, 170
Marshall Plan, 110
Marx, Karl, 33

Marxism, 33, 34, 36, 42

mathematical economics: failures of, 17–18; Keynes's skepticism regarding, 20, 35–36; used in the teaching of macroeconomics, 36; value of questioned, 5, 10. *See also* economic modeling

Mattingly, Harold, 214

McCulloch v. Maryland, 170

McElvaine, Robert S., 219, 220

McManus, T. F., 83–84, 93, 230, 234

means to achieve the goal, 195–96

Meltdown (Woods), 24, 25

memory, 201

Menger, Carl: analysis of individual action, 191; analysis of production, 155; Brentano and, 143; on the "dogma of self-interest," 187; economic insights of, 37–40; on human action and scarcity, 195; influence of Burke on, 203; on knowledge and technology, 152–53; on means, 195; philosophers cited by, 199

mercantilism: description of, 149; goal of, 44; Adam Smith's critique of, 149–50, 151

mergers, 240

Merkel, Angela, 87

metallic-based currency: classical liberalism and, 65, 68–70

methodological dualism, 17, 46

Metternich, Prince Klemens Wenzel von, 77–78

Meyer, G. J., 215

microeconomics, 155

"misery index," 118

Mises, Ludwig von: on bank credit inflation, 218; on commonalities among schools of economics, 58–59; concept of the trade cycle, 2, 45; on the division of labor, 148; on the early spread of Austrian thinking, 35; economic contributions of, 44–46; on economics conceived as a hard science, 16–17; on entrepreneurship, 178; on factors influencing the purchasing power of the monetary unit, 122; Hazlitt and, 47; on human action and desirability, 193; on human action and uncertainty, 197; on human cooperation, 148; on the importance of historical study, 197, 198; on the "impossibility" of socialism, 141–42; on inflation, 207, 208, 209; on knowledge and experience, 203; on means and purpose, 195–96; on praxeology, 191–92; on purpose, 193; Röpke and, 53; Sennholz and, 57; sympathy to the idea of a Habsburg restoration, 56

Mishkin, Frederic S., 244

misinvestments. *See* malinvestments and misinvestments

modern liberalism, 64–65

Moley, Raymond, 99–100

monetarism: differences with the Austrian School, 123; flexible exchange rates, 122–25

monetary crisis of 1971: Nixon's response to, 114, 116–19; origins of, 113, 115, 116; warnings of, 115–16

Monetary History of the United States, A (Friedman and Schwartz), 123–25, 222

monetary policies: global impact of U.S. policies, 227–28

money: end of silver coinage in the U.S., 120–21; Fetter's analysis of money and the trade cycle, 51; fiat inflation, 82–83, 85–88, 213–14, 217–18; Menger's concept of, 39; Mises's analysis of the value of, 45. *See also* fiat money; new money

money supply: expansion in the U.S. in the early 1970s, 122;

money supply (*cont.*)
 expansion under the flexible-exchange-rate system, 124, 125; Federal Reserve policies and the housing bubble crisis of 2007–8, 22–24; the Federal Reserve's mandate to manipulate, 22–23; in Friedman and Schwartz's analysis of the Great Depression, 123–24; inflation and, 208–10; interest rates and, 173–74; Mises's trade cycle theory and, 45; quantitative easing, 133, 172–73, 208–10; in supply-side economics, 133
monopolies, 56
Moral Basis of a Backward Society, The (Banfield), 194
Morgenthau, Henry, 102
Morris, Charles R., 24
mortgage crises: bank credit inflation of the 1920s and, 96; housing bubble crisis of 2007–8, 24–25. *See also* housing bubble crisis of 2007–8
mortgage rates: at the beginning of a recession, 246
Mundell, Robert, 107–8, 132, 134

Napoleon Bonaparte, 128
NASDAQ, 23
National Bank Act, 84
National Industrial Recovery Act, 99
nationalization, 170
natural interest rate, 228–29, 230–31
Nelson, R. W., 83–84, 93, 230, 234
New Deal, 102–3
new money: the Cantillon effect, 88; creating to match higher prices, 126
New York City, 159–60
Nicomachean Ethics (Aristotle), 12, 200
Nixon, Richard, 114, 116–19
Nixon Shock: Carter's anti-inflation policies and, 126–28; economic measures of, 116; flexible exchange rates, 122–25; inflationary expectations, 125–26; inflation created by, 116, 117–18, 220–21; reactions to and consequences of, 116–19; stagflation, 120–22
normative economics, 13
Northwest Ordinance, 65

objective theory of value, 36
O'Connor, Sandra Day, 175
Ohlin, Bertil, 93
oil prices, 117, 211
open-market operations, 227
opportunity costs, 42, 198
Ordeal of Change, The (Hoffer), 182–83
Organization of Petroleum Exporting Countries (OPEC), 117
Orwell, George, 102
Ottoman Empire, 216–17
overpopulation, 54

Palyi, Melchior, 86, 105–6, 115, 233–34
Panic of 1819, The (Rothbard), 56
Panic of 1907, 241
St. Paul, 147
Paul, Ron, 57, 259
Paulson, Henry, 247–48
pension funds, 238–39
Phillips, C. A., 83–84, 93, 230, 234
Phillips curve, 22–23, 118
Physiocrats, 67
Pipes, Richard, 84
Pius XI (pope), 180–81, 184–85
planned economies: Austrian School's predictions of the collapse of, 36, 141–42, 143–44; collapse of, 142–43; consequences of the absence of freely moving prices, 177–78; Hayek's critique of, 48, 49–50; resource allocation and, 43, 46, 49; Wieser's defense of, 42–43. *See also* socialism
Plaza Accord, 140

Poincaré, Henri, 79
points of injection concept, 88–89
political liberalism, 64–65
population: division of labor and, 153–54
positive economics, 13–14
Powell, Jim, 68
practical science: economics conceived as, 4, 11, 15–20, 36, 46
praxeology, 46, 191–92
present goods, 41
price controls: in the Nixon Shock measures, 116; reactions to, 116–17, 118
prices: Böhm-Bawerk's analysis of, 40–41; deflation and, 222–23; disequilibrium in cost/price relationship, 233–34; importance of freely moving prices to prosperity, 177–78; Menger's subjective theory of value, 37–39; resource allocation and, 46, 49
Principles of Economics (Menger), 37, 152–53, 195
private property: importance to prosperity, 166–71. *See also* property rights
production: Austrian School analysis of, 155–56; concept of imputation, 42; four factors of, 161–63; population and, 153–54; roundabout process, 41, 155–56
production structure, 232
productivity: importance of contracts to, 176
"productivity dividend," 172–73
products: elastic, 211
Promises Men Live By, The (Scherman), 176
property rights: importance to prosperity, 166–71; rule of law and, 175–76
prosperity: the common good and, 186–89; effect of cultural conditions on, 165–66; entrepreneurship and, 178; family structure and, 179–80; the free movement of prices and, 177–78; importance of a sound currency to, 171–74; the importance of private property to, 166–71; leisure and, 181–83; role of false prosperity in the housing bubble crisis of 2007–8, 22–25; rule of law and, 174–76; sacredness of contracts and, 176–77; savings and capital formation, 181; spontaneous order and, 165; subsidiarity and, 183–86
protectionism: as a contributing factor in territorial expansion by Germany and Japan, 105–6; as a legacy of World War I, 80; Reagan's response to protectionist pressures, 139–40; in the U.S. following World War I, 97–99
proximate goods, 194
prudence, 200–203
"public choice" economics, 132
purchasing power: at beginning of trade cycle, 229; factors influencing, 122
purpose: human action and, 192–93

Quadragesimo Anno (Pius XI), 184–85
quantitative easing, 133, 172–73, 208–10
Quigley, Carroll, 97

ratings agencies, 26
"rational expectations": school of, 131–32
Read, Leonard E., 56–57, 156–57
Reagan, Ronald: 1980 presidential election, 128; collapse of communism and, 143; economic recovery program, 135–36; failure to achieve a gold standard, 137, 138–39; failure to slow entitlement spending, 136; increase in government deficit under, 136–37;

Reagan, Ronald (*cont.*)
    response to protectionist pressures,
        139–40; supply-side economics
        and, 129, 132, 135–37; tax increases
        under, 137
real estate: default on loans during the
        early 1930s, 96; impact of disequi-
        librium between natural and mar-
        ket interest rates, 231; malinvest-
        ment and misinvestment, 240–41
reason: prudential judgment and, 202
recessions: Austrian approach to, 4,
        5, 249–52; beginning of, 246–47;
        inversion of the yield curve as a sign
        of, 244–45; Keynesian response to,
        4, 5, 247–49
Reed, Larry, 57
regressivity principle, 150–51, 154
regulatory costs, 248–49, 251
Reinhart, Carmen, 201
Rerum Novarum (Leo XIII), 170
resource allocation: free markets and,
        157; Hayek on, 49; Mises on, 46;
        Wieser on, 43
Restoration of Property, The (Belloc), 170
retirement funds, 238–39
Rickenbacker, William F., 120–21, 122
Rise and Fall of the Great Powers, The
        (Kennedy), 218
risk management, 166
risky credit, 241
Road to Serfdom, The (Hayek), 48,
        101–2, 143, 258
Rockwell, Llewellyn, 56, 57
Rogoff, Kenneth, 201
Roman Empire, 206, 214–15
Roosevelt, Franklin Delano, 99–100
Roots of American Order, The (Kirk), 194
Roots of Capitalism, The (Chamber-
        lain), 170–71
Röpke, Wilhelm: criticism of commu-
        nism, 142; criticism of macroeco-
        nomics and economic forecasting,

16; emphasis on the role of human
        actors in the economy, 155; on free
        markets and resource allocation,
        157; the German postwar economic
        revival and, 108–9; on inflation,
        207–8; influence of World War I on,
        52–53; on population and produc-
        tion, 153–54; warnings about the
        growth of the U.S. welfare state,
        115–16; on World War I, 75
Rostovtzeff, Michael, 214–15
Rothbard, Murray: analysis of the Great
        Depression, 55, 91, 101; on bank
        credit inflation, 219, 220; on budget
        deficits and tax increases, 137;
        economic contributions of, 55–56;
        on means to achieve the goal, 196;
        on the "prehistory of the Austrian
        School," 199; reaction to the Nixon
        Shock measures, 116–17; suggested
        repeal of legal tender laws, 218
roundabout production, 41, 155–56
Rubin, Robert, 137
Rueff, Jacques, 81, 85, 109, 188–89, 227
rule of law: classical liberalism and,
        65, 66; importance to prosperity,
        174–76
Russia: fiat inflation following World
        War I, 87–88; inflation during
        World War I, 84, 85
Ryn, Claes, 10

Samuelson, Paul, 141
savers: natural rate of interest and, 228
savings: decrease in with a consumer
        goods boom, 242; destruction
        of during economic downturns,
        252–53; disequilibrium between
        investment and savings, 231–33;
        importance to prosperity, 181;
        importance to the Austrian School,
        51; natural rate of interest and,
        228–29; protected by a sound

currency, 173; in the stagflation era, 122; in Strigl's analysis of capital, 55
Say, Jean-Baptiste, 19, 133–34, 154
Say's Law, 51–52, 133–34, 154
scarcity, 38, 195, 198
Scherman, Harry, 176
Schiff, Peter, 59–60
Schmoller, Gustav von, 73
School of Salamanca, 43–44, 65
Schumpeter, Joseph, 14–15, 19, 43–44
Schwartz, Anna J., 123–24, 222
Schweikart, Larry, 96
science: categories of, 12; definitions of, 13; economics conceived as a hard science, 10–15; economics conceived as a practical science, 4, 11, 15–20, 36, 46; key characteristics of, 12–13
seasonal economic change, 158
self-interest: Austrian School's criticism of, 187–88; economic decision making and, 199; Rueff's criticism of, 188–89; Adam Smith on, 187
Sennholz, Hans F., 56, 57, 136, 180
Sheen, Fulton J., 13
Shelton, Judy, 108
shrewdness, 201–2
silver coinage: end of, 120–21
Skidelsky, Robert: on the Bretton Woods era, 107, 220, 221; on Keynes's response to national currency management, 100; on Keynes's views of disequilibrium between savings and investment, 232; on the New Deal's failure to lower unemployment, 102–3; on those using risk-management models, 26
Skousen, Mark, 58, 156
"skyscraper index," 232
small business: burden of regulatory costs, 248–49
Smith, Adam: on the distribution of wealth, 150, 151; on the division of labor, 149–50, 151, 152; on free trade, 67; on self-interest in economic activity, 187
Smoot-Hawley Tariff, 97–98, 154
socialism: Austrian School's predictions of the collapse of, 36, 141–42, 143–44; Böhm-Bawerk's criticism of, 42; fundamental beliefs, 72; in Great Britain, 74; Hayek's critique of, 49–50, 156; Mises's critique of, 46; resource allocation and, 43, 46, 49; rise of the social welfare state, 72–74; Wieser's defense of, 42–43. *See also* planned economies
Socialists of the Chair, 73
social responsibility: private property and, 169
Social Security, 28–29, 121
social welfare state, 72–74
Soviet Union, 141, 142–43
Spain: School of Salamanca, 43–44, 65; specie inflation and, 216
specie inflation, 216–17
spending: on credit, 242; as a fiscal stimulus, 247–48
spontaneous order, 50, 156–57, 165
stagflation: analysis of, 120–22; Carter's anti-inflation policies, 126–28; era of, 118; high unemployment and high inflation in, 22–23; supply-side economics on the causes of, 133
standard of living: impact of 1970s inflation on, 121
Stanlis, Peter, 203
steel tariffs, 211
Steil, Benn, 69–70
Stiglitz, Joseph, 26–27
stock market: credit inflation during the 1920s and, 95–96; fall at the beginning of a recession, 246; malinvestments and misinvestments in the trade cycle, 238–39
Story, Joseph, 69

Strigl, Richard von, 55
structural economic change, 159–60
Structure of Production, The (Skousen), 58, 156
student loans, 242
Suárez, Francisco, 66
subjective theory of value, 37–39
subsidiarity, 183–86
subsistence fund, 55
supply and demand, 51–52
supply-side economics: basic tenets of, 132–33; economic program to stimulate investment and production, 134; failure to achieve a gold standard, 137, 138–39, 259; failure to slow entitlement spending, 136, 259; goals of, 129; on the impact of inflation on the federal debt, 138; increasing government deficit under Reagan, 136–37; opposition to Keynesian economics, 133; Reagan and, 129, 132, 135–37; roots of, 132; Say and, 133–34; tax cuts and, 134–35
surplus: trade and, 38–39
swindlers, 239
Switzerland, 53

tariffs: Fordney-McCumber Tariff, 93, 97; General Agreement on Trade and Tariffs, 106; impact of the steel tariffs of 2002, 211; Smoot-Hawley Tariff, 97–98, 154; U.S. protectionism following World War I and, 97–99; the U.S. foreign bond bubble and, 93–94
taxation: classical liberalism and limited taxation, 65, 66; effect on the ownership of property, 170; relationship to government revenue, 134–35; in supply-side economics, 133
tax cuts: in the Austrian approach to economic downturns, 250–51; in a

Keynesian approach to downturns, 248; supply-side economics on, 134–35
tax increases: under Reagan, 137
tax rates: effective, 85; the Laffer Curve, 134
tax revenues: of the U.S. government, 185–86
Taylor, A. J. P., 66, 71, 73
"teaser rates," 25
technology: knowledge and, 152–53
Tenth Amendment, 184
Thatcher, Margaret, 143
Theory of Money and Credit, The (Mises), 45, 207
"Third Way," 54
This Time Is Different (Reinhart and Rogoff), 201
Thomas, Clarence, 175–76
Thornton, Mark, 60, 232
time preference: interest and, 41, 138, 173
top-down organizations, 157
trade: Menger's concept of, 38–39. *See also* international free trade
trade cycle: during the age of collaborative learning, 70; Austrian approach to the downturn, 249–52; Austrian School and, 2, 225–26; beginning of the recession, 246–47; credit contraction, 252; deflation, 253; the destruction of savings and capital in downturns, 252–53; disequilibrium, 229–34; Fetter's analysis of, 51; Hayek's analysis of, 48–49; inflationary psychology and euphoria, 234–36; Keynesian response to the downturn, 247–49; Keynes's positions on, 225; lowering interest rates at the beginning of, 226–29; malinvestments and misinvestments, 236–42; Mises's concept of, 2, 45; overview of, 226;

role of credit expansion in, 223–24; role of deflation in, 223; shared views of among schools of economics, 58–59; signs of the downturn, 245–46; the turning point in, 243–45. *See also* business cycle

trade unions: the cartel effect of, 52

transfer of wealth: bank credit inflation and, 218, 220; during times of inflation, 172–73, 213

Treatise on Money (Keynes), 257

Treatise on Political Economy (Say), 133

Treaty of Versailles, 77–78

Triana, Pablo, 199

Tucker, Jeffrey, 148

Tudor England, 215

tulip mania, 235

Tullock, Gordon, 132

Turgot, A. R. J., 67

Two Trillion Dollar Meltdown, The (Morris), 24

Ultimate Foundation of Economic Science, The (Mises), 46, 195–96

ultimate goods, 194

underdeveloped countries: population and economic expansion, 154

unemployment: frictional, 158; during the Great Depression, 102–3; Hutt's analysis of, 52; relationship to inflation, 22–23; wage distortion during the 1920s and, 234. *See also* inflation-unemployment relationship

unions: the cartel effect of, 52

United Arab Emirates, 232

United States: annual tax receipts, 185–86; anti-inflation policies under Carter, 126–28; bank credit inflation, 219–21; Bretton Woods agreements (*see* Bretton Woods agreements); Clinton's balancing of the budget, 137–38; conse-

quences of government-economy codependency and, 185–86; currency debasement, 206; current financial relationship with China, 112; debt monetization in, 113; depression of 1920–21, 251, 254–55; economic growth during the age of classical liberalism, 66, 68; extent of government intervention during World War I, 100; global impact of American monetary policies, 227–28; increase in money supply in the early 1970s, 122; inflation during World War I, 83–84; Marshall Plan, 110; monetary crisis of 1971 (*see* monetary crisis of 1971); Nixon Shock (*see* Nixon Shock); progression from a metallic-based currency to fiat money, 120; protectionism following World War I, 97–99; rule of law and respect for contracts, 66; specie standard and, 69; spending on entitlement programs and mandatory expenditures, 112–13; structural changes, 159–60; supply-side economics under Reagan, 129, 132, 135–37; torpedoing of the World Economic Conference, 99–100; trade cycles and, 70; use of government spending as a fiscal stimulus, 247–48

University of Chicago, 131, 132

University of Virginia, 132

U.S. Constitution: free trade and, 68; limited taxation and, 66; specie standard and, 69; tenets of classical liberalism and, 65

U.S. dollar: the Bretton Woods agreements and, 107, 111–14; devaluation by the Nixon Shock measures, 116, 117–18, 121

U.S. Federal Reserve: anti-inflation policies under Volcker, 127–28;

U.S. Federal Reserve (*cont.*)
  bank credit inflation and, 91–96,
  140; creation of, 82; debt monetization and, 113; expanded mandate
  of, 22–23; inflation during World
  War I and, 83–84; inflation following World War I and, 81; interest
  policies as a factor in the housing
  bubble crisis of 2007–8, 22–24, 25,
  31; open-market operations, 227;
  quantitative easing and, 172–73,
  208–9, 210; response to protectionist
  pressures under Reagan, 139, 140;
  role in the housing bubble crisis of
  2007–8, 224; supply-siders on, 133
"Use of Knowledge in Society, The"
  (Hayek), 49

validation process, 126
value: of capital, 39; labor theory of, 42;
  objective theory of, 36; paradox of,
  38; the School of Salamanca on, 44;
  subjective theory of, 37–39
Vitoria, Francisco de, 43
Volcker, Paul, 127, 128, 135

wages: distortion during the 1920s,
  234; impact of deflation on, 222
Wagner, Adolph, 73
Walras, Leon, 37–38, 44
Wanniski, Jude, 97, 134–35
Way the World Works, The (Wanniski),
  97
wealth. *See* distribution of wealth;
  transfer of wealth

wealth effect, 242, 245–46
Wealth of Nations, The (Smith), 67
Weathersford, Jack, 216
welfare recipients: impact of inflation
  on, 212
welfare state: Hazlitt's critique of, 47
West Germany. *See* Germany
Westley, Christopher, 205, 206, 214
White, Andrew Dickson, 212, 213
Wicksell, Knut, 228, 230
widow's mite parable, 38
Wieser, Friedrich von, 16, 42–43
Wilson, Woodrow, 76
Winter, George, 68
Withers, Hartley, 83
Woods, Thomas E., Jr., 24, 25, 254
workers: impact of inflation on, 212
World Economic Conference of 1933,
  99–100, 105–6
Worldly Philosophers, The (Heilbroner),
  141–42
World War I: collapse of free trade and
  global markets following, 97–100;
  economic consequences of, 80–81;
  the end of classical liberalism
  and, 74–78; extent of government
  intervention during, 100; historical legacy of, 79–80, 81; impact on
  Röpke, 52–53; inflation during, 82,
  83–85; inflation following, 82–83,
  85–96

yield curve, 239; inversion, 244–45

INTERCOLLEGIATE
STUDIES INSTITUTE
Educating for Liberty

ISI Books is the publishing imprint of the **Intercollegiate Studies Institute (ISI)**. Since its founding in 1953, ISI has been inspiring college students to discover, embrace, and advance the principles and virtues that make America free and prosperous.

Today ISI has more than 10,000 student members on some 1,500 campuses across the country. The Institute reaches these and thousands of other people through an integrated program of campus speakers, conferences, seminars, publications, student groups, and fellowships and scholarships, along with a rich repository of online resources.

ISI is a nonprofit, nonpartisan, tax-exempt educational organization. The Institute relies on the financial support of the general public—individuals, foundations, and corporations—and receives no funding or any other aid from any level of the government.

To learn more about ISI,
visit **www.isi.org** or call **(800) 526-7022**